# Sea Power and the Asia-Pac

With particular focus on the Asia-Pacific region, this book examines the rise and fall of sea powers.

In the Asia-Pacific region there has been significant expansion of sea-based economies together with burgeoning naval power. Many claim that these processes will transform the world's future economic and security relationships. The book addresses the question of the extent to which the notion of 'Asia rising' is reflected by and dependent on its developing sea power. A central theme is the Chinese challenge to long-term Western maritime ascendency and what might be the consequences of this.

In order to situate current and future developments this book includes chapters which analyse what sea power means and has meant, as well as its role, both historic and contemporary, in the rise and fall of great powers.

This book will be of much interest to students of naval power, Asian politics, strategic studies, war and conflict studies, IR and security studies.

**Patrick C. Bratton** is Assistant Professor of Political Science and Program Chair for Political Science and International Relations at the Hawaii Pacific University, Honolulu.

**Geoffrey Till** is the Director of the Corbett Centre for Maritime Policy Studies at King's College London. He is the author of a number of books, including, most recently: *The Development of British Naval Thinking* (Routledge 2006), *Globalization and the Defence in Asia* (co-ed. with Emrys Chew and Joshua Ho, Routledge 2008), and *Seapower: A Guide for the 21st Century* (second edition, Routledge 2009).

**Cass Series: Naval Policy and History**
Series Editor: Geoffrey Till
ISSN 1366-9478

This series consists primarily of original manuscripts by research scholars in the general area of naval policy and history, without national or chronological limitations. It will from time to time also include collections of important articles as well as reprints of classic works.

1  **Austro-Hungarian Naval Policy, 1904–1914**
   *Milan N. Vego*

2  **Far-Flung Lines**
   Studies in Imperial Defence in Honour of Donald Mackenzie Schurman
   *Edited by Keith Neilson and Greg Kennedy*

3  **Maritime Strategy and Continental Wars**
   *Rear Admiral Raja Menon*

4  **The Royal Navy and German Naval Disarmament 1942–1947**
   *Chris Madsen*

5  **Naval Strategy and Operations in Narrow Seas**
   *Milan N. Vego*

6  **The Pen and Ink Sailor**
   Charles Middleton and the King's Navy, 1778–1813
   *John E. Talbott*

7  **The Italian Navy and Fascist Expansionism, 1935–1940**
   *Robert Mallett*

8  **The Merchant Marine and International Affairs, 1850–1950**
   *Edited by Greg Kennedy*

9  **Naval Strategy in Northeast Asia**
   Geo-strategic Goals, Policies and Prospects
   *Duk-Ki Kim*

10 **Naval Policy and Strategy in the Mediterranean Sea**
   Past, Present and Future
   *Edited by John B. Hattendorf*

11 **Stalin's Ocean-going Fleet**
   Soviet Naval Strategy and Shipbuilding Programmes, 1935–1953
   *Jürgen Rohwer and Mikhail S. Monakov*

12 **Imperial Defence, 1868–1887**
   *Donald Mackenzie Schurman; Edited by John Beeler*

13 **Technology and Naval Combat in the Twentieth Century and Beyond**
*Edited by Phillips Payson O'Brien*

14 **The Royal Navy and Nuclear Weapons**
*Richard Moore*

15 **The Royal Navy and the Capital Ship in the Interwar Period**
An Operational Perspective
*Joseph Moretz*

16 **Chinese Grand Strategy and Maritime Power**
*Thomas M. Kane*

17 **Britain's Anti-submarine Capability, 1919–1939**
*George Franklin*

18 **Britain, France and the Naval Arms Trade in the Baltic, 1919–1939**
Grand Strategy and Failure
*Donald Stoker*

19 **Naval Mutinies of the Twentieth Century**
An International Perspective
*Edited by Christopher Bell and Bruce Elleman*

20 **The Road to Oran**
Anglo–French Naval Relations, September 1939–July 1940
*David Brown*

21 **The Secret War against Sweden**
US and British Submarine Deception and Political Control in the 1980s
*Ola Tunander*

22 **Royal Navy Strategy in the Far East, 1919–1939**
Planning for a War against Japan
*Andrew Field*

23 **Seapower**
A Guide for the Twenty-first Century
*Geoffrey Till*

24 **Britain's Economic Blockade of Germany, 1914–1919**
*Eric W. Osborne*

25 **A Life of Admiral of the Fleet Andrew Cunningham**
A Twentieth-Century Naval Leader
*Michael Simpson*

26 **Navies in Northern Waters, 1721–2000**
*Edited by Rolf Hobson and Tom Kristiansen*

27 **German Naval Strategy, 1856–1888**
Forerunners to Tirpitz
*David Olivier*

28 **British Naval Strategy East of Suez, 1900–2000**
Influences and Actions
*Edited by Greg Kennedy*

29 **The Rise and Fall of the Soviet Navy in the Baltic, 1921–1940**
*Gunnar Aselius*

30 **The Royal Navy, 1930–1990**
Innovation and Defence
*Edited by Richard Harding*

31 **The Royal Navy and Maritime Power in the Twentieth Century**
*Edited by Ian Speller*

32 **Dreadnought Gunnery and the Battle of Jutland**
The Question of Fire Control
*John Brooks*

33 **Greek Naval Strategy and Policy, 1910–1919**
*Zisis Fotakis*

34 **Naval Blockades and Seapower**
Strategies and Counter-Strategies, 1805–2005
*Edited by Bruce A. Elleman and Sarah C. M. Paine*

35 **The Pacific Campaign in World War II**
From Pearl Harbor to Guadalcanal
*William Bruce Johnson*

36 **Anti-submarine Warfare in World War I**
British Naval Aviation and the Defeat of the U-Boats
*John J. Abbatiello*

37 **The Royal Navy and Anti-Submarine Warfare, 1944–49**
*Malcolm Llewellyn-Jones*

38 **The Development of British Naval Thinking**
Essays in Memory of Bryan Ranft
*Edited by Geoffrey Till*

39 **Educating the Royal Navy**
18th and 19th Century Education for Officers
*H. W. Dickinson*

40 **Chinese Naval Strategy in the 21st Century**
The Turn to Mahan
*James R. Holmes and Toshi Yoshihara*

41 **Naval Coalition Warfare**
From the Napoleonic War to Operation Iraqi Freedom
*Edited by Bruce A. Elleman and S. C. M. Paine*

42 **Operational Warfare at Sea**
Theory and Practice
*Milan Vego*

43 **Naval Peacekeeping and Humanitarian Operations**
Stability from the Sea
*Edited by James J. Wirtz and Jeffrey A. Larsen*

44 **Indian Naval Strategy in the 21st Century**
*James R. Holmes, Andrew C. Winner and Toshi Yoshihara*

45 **Seapower**
A Guide for the Twenty-First Century (Second Edition)
*Geoffrey Till*

46 **Naval Power and Expeditionary Warfare**
Peripheral Campaigns and New Theatres of Naval Warfare
*Edited by Bruce Elleman and S. C. M. Paine*

47 **Sea Power and the Asia-Pacific**
The triumph of Neptune?
*Edited by Geoffrey Till and Patrick C. Bratton*

# Sea Power and the Asia-Pacific
The triumph of Neptune?

**Edited by Geoffrey Till and
Patrick C. Bratton**

LONDON AND NEW YORK

First published 2012
by Routledge
2 Park Square, Milton Park, Abingdon, Oxon OX14 4RN

Simultaneously published in the USA and Canada
by Routledge
711 Third Avenue, New York, NY 10017 (8th Floor)

*Routledge is an imprint of the Taylor & Francis Group, an informa business*

First issued in paperback 2013

© 2012 Selection and editorial matter, Geoffrey Till and Patrick C. Bratton, individual contributors; their contributions.

The right of the editors to be identified as the authors of the editorial material, and of the authors for their individual chapters, has been asserted in accordance with sections 77 and 78 of the Copyright, Designs and Patents Act 1988.

All rights reserved. No part of this book may be reprinted or reproduced or utilised in any form or by any electronic, mechanical, or other means, now known or hereafter invented, including photocopying and recording, or in any information storage or retrieval system, without permission in writing from the publishers.

*Trademark notice*: Product or corporate names may be trademarks or registered trademarks, and are used only for identification and explanation without intent to infringe.

*British Library Cataloguing in Publication Data*
A catalogue record for this book is available from the British Library

*Library of Congress Cataloging-in-Publication Data*
Sea power and the Asia-Pacific: the triumph of Neptune/edited by Geoffrey Till and Patrick C. Bratton.
   p. cm. – (Cass series–naval policy and history, ISSN 1366–9478; 47)
   1. Sea Power–Pacific Area. 2. Seapower–Pacific Area–History.
   3. Pacific Area–History, Naval. 4. Pacific Area–Strategic Aspects.
   5. Navies–Pacific Area. 6. Navies–Asia. I. Till, Geoffrey. II. Bratton, Patrick C.
   VA620.S43 2011
   359′.03091823–dc22
                                                                    2011013748

ISBN: 978-0-415-60934-0 (hbk)
ISBN: 978-0-415-72386-2 (pbk)
ISBN: 978-0-203-80250-2 (ebk)

Typeset in Baskerville
by Wearset Ltd, Boldon, Tyne and Wear

# Contents

|  |  |
|---|---|
| *List of contributors* | ix |
| *Preface* | xiv |
| *List of abbreviations* | xvi |

| | | |
|---|---|---|
| 1 | **Introduction: sea power and the rise and fall of empires**<br>GEOFFREY TILL | 1 |

**PART I**
**The navies of the Asia-Pacific**  17

| | | |
|---|---|---|
| 2 | **The United States as a Pacific power**<br>PATRICK C. BRATTON | 19 |
| 3 | **Maritime power and the Asia-Pacific: US naval perspectives**<br>KEVIN R. JOHNSON | 46 |
| 4 | **China: its maritime traditions and navy today**<br>CARL OTIS SCHUSTER | 56 |
| 5 | **The evolution of the People's Liberation Army Navy: the twin missions of area-denial and peacetime operations**<br>MICHAEL MCDEVITT AND FREDERIC VELLUCCI JR. | 75 |
| 6 | **Japan's maritime past, present and future**<br>ALESSIO PATALANO | 93 |
| 7 | **India's growing naval power: Indian Ocean in focus**<br>HARSH PANT | 111 |
| 8 | **Singapore and sea power**<br>JOSHUA HO | 130 |

## Contents

9  The sea power and navy of the Republic of Korea  144
   SEONG-YONG PARK

10 Australia's maritime past, present and future  166
   ANDREW FORBES

## PART II
## Transitions  191

11 British sea power and imperial defence in the Far East:
   sharing the seas with America  195
   GREG KENNEDY

12 The British Pacific Fleet and the decline of empire?
   Adaptations to change  214
   JON ROBB-WEBB

13 Conclusions: transitions and futures  237
   PATRICK C. BRATTON AND GEOFFREY TILL

   Index  269

# Contributors

**Patrick C. Bratton** is Assistant Professor of Political Science at Hawaii Pacific University. He was born in Honolulu, Hawaii, and lived much of his life in Alaska. He graduated with a BA in History from the University of Alaska, Fairbanks. He then went on to complete graduate studies at the University of Wales, Aberystwyth (United Kingdom), the Université de Rennes 2 (France), and received his PhD from The Catholic University of America. His research focuses on foreign policy, strategic and security studies, particularly in South Asia. He has published articles in leading security journals such as: *Journal of Strategic Studies, Naval War College Review, Strategic Analysis, Contemporary Security Policy,* and *Comparative Strategy.*

**Andrew Forbes** is a Visiting Senior Fellow at the Australian National Centre for Ocean Resources and Security, University of Wollongong; a Research Fellow at the Centre for Foreign Policy Studies, Dalhousie University; an Associate of the Corbett Centre for Maritime Policy; and a Member of the International Institute for Strategic Studies, London. He is the Australian representative to the CSCAP study group on maritime security and to the International SLOC Group.

**Joshua Ho** is a Senior Fellow at the S. Rajaratnam School of International Studies, Singapore and works in the Maritime Security Programme. Joshua is a serving Naval Officer with 24 years of service and currently holds the rank of Lieutenant Colonel. He has served in various shipboard and staff appointments including the Command of a missile gun boat and stints in the Naval Operations, Plans, and Personnel Departments and the Future Systems Directorate, MINDEF. He has also held concurrent appointments of Honorary Aide de Camp to the President, Secretary to the Naval Staff Meeting, and Secretary to the Policy and Strategy Meeting, MINDEF. He has edited or co-edited five volumes: *Best of Times, Worst of Times: Maritime Security in the Asia-Pacific, The Evolving Maritime Balance of Power in the Asia-Pacific: Maritime Doctrines and Nuclear Weapons at Sea* and *Globalization and Defence in the Asia-Pacific: Arms Across Asia, Realising Safe and Secure Seas for All* and *Southeast Asia*

x   Contributors

and the Rise of Chinese and Indian Naval Power: Between Rising Naval Powers. He has also published in local and overseas journals, including *Asian Survey, Australian Army Journal, Australian Journal of Maritime and Ocean Affairs, Contemporary Southeast Asia, Defence Studies, Journal of the Australian Naval Institute, Maritime Affairs, Korean Journal of Defense Analyses, Marine Policy, Military Technology, Ocean Development and International Law, Pointer,* and *Security Challenges* as well as contributed to numerous book chapters.

**Kevin R. Johnson** is a career naval officer, who served at sea around the world including the Command of the nuclear powered submarine USS *OLYMPIA* (SSN 717). In January 2004, Captain Johnson reported to the staff of Commander, US Pacific Fleet in Hawaii as the Deputy Chief of Staff for Fleet Training. Following staff realignment, he moved to the N5 Directorate as Head of the International Plans and Policy and eventually as the Deputy Director for Plans and Policy where he oversaw Pacific Fleet's military planning efforts in the Western Pacific and Indian Oceans. Following retirement from the United States Navy in 2010, Captain Johnson continues to exercise his expertise in Asia-Pacific military affairs as a consultant.

**Greg Kennedy** is a member of the Defence Studies Department, King's College London, based at the Joint Services Command and Staff College in Shrivenham. He taught at the Royal Military College of Canada, is an adjunct assistant professor of that university. He received his PhD from the University of Alberta in 1998. He is the author of *Anglo-American Strategic Relations and the Far East, 1933–1939* (Frank Cass 2002) and has published internationally on strategic foreign policy issues, maritime defence, disarmament, diplomacy and intelligence. Other books include co-editing with Keith Neilson, *Far Flung Lines: Studies in Imperial Defence in Honour of Donald Mackenzie Schurman,* and sole editor of *The Merchant Marine in International Affairs, 1850–1950,* both in the Frank Cass series on Naval History and Policy; co-edited with Keith Neilson, *Incidents and International Relations: People, Personalities and Power* (Praeger 2002).

**Michael McDevitt** is a Vice President and Director of CNA Strategic Studies, a division of CNA (Center for Naval Analyses) – a not-for-profit federally funded research centre in Washington, DC. CNA Strategic Studies conducts research and analyses that focus on strategy, political-military issues and regional security studies. It has particularly strong East Asian, Middle East, and Iranian security research teams, as well as recognised expertise in leadership analyses, international engagement and partner capacity building. During his navy career Rear Admiral McDevitt held four at-sea commands; including an aircraft carrier battlegroup. He received a BA in US History from the University of

Southern California and a Masters degree in American Diplomatic History from Georgetown University. He is also a graduate of the National War College in Washington, DC. He spent a year as a CNO Strategic Studies Group Fellow at the Naval War College. He was the Director of the East Asia Policy office for the Secretary of Defense during the first Bush Administration. He also served for two years as the Director for Strategy, War Plans and Policy (J-5) for US CINCPAC. Rear Admiral McDevitt concluded his 34-year active duty career as the Commandant of the National War College in Washington DC. In addition management and leadership responsibilities as the founder of *CNA Strategic Studies* McDevitt has been an active participant in conferences and workshops regarding security issues in East Asia, and has had a number of papers published in edited volumes on this subject.

**Harsh V. Pant** teaches at King's College London in the Department of Defence Studies. He is also an Associate with the King's Centre for Science and Security Studies and an Affiliate with the King's India Institute. His current research is focused on Asian security issues. His most recent books include *Contemporary Debates in Indian Foreign and Security Policy* (Palgrave Macmillan), *Indian Foreign Policy in a Unipolar World* (Routledge) and *The China Syndrome* (HarperCollins).

**Seong-yong Park** is an Adjunct Assistant Professor at the Department of Political Science and Diplomacy in Chonbuk National University, Republic of Korea and also a Research Manager at the Chonbuk Unification Education Centre of the Ministry of Unification in Jeonju. His doctoral work was on 'The Development of the Republic of Korea Navy in a Changing National Defence and Northeast Asian Security Environment' in which he earned a PhD from the University of Salford, United Kingdom.

**Alessio Patalano** is Lecturer in War Studies at the Department of War Studies, King's College London, and specialises in East Asian security and Japanese naval history and strategy. Dr Patalano is the Director of the Asian Security and Warfare Research Group (ASWRG) and Research Associate at the King's China Institute. Since 2006, he is Visiting Lecturer in naval strategy and East Asian security at the Italian Naval War College (ISMM), Venice. In Japan, Dr Patalano has been a Visiting Scholar at Aoyama Gakuin University and at the National Graduate Institute for Policy Studies (GRIPS), both in Tokyo, and is currently Adjunct Fellow at the Institute of Contemporary Asian Studies, Temple University Japan. Dr Patalano's articles have appeared in academic and professional journals in English, Japanese and Italian. His first book, *First Line of Defence: Imperial Traditions, Military Identity and Japan's Post-war Naval Power* is forthcoming in 2011 by Stanford University Press.

xii  *Contributors*

**Jon Robb-Webb** joined the Department of Defence Studies, King's College London in September 2000 as a Lecturer. He previously taught at the Joint Services Command and Staff College during the academic year 1998/99, which included an appointment at RAF Henlow teaching and lecturing to the RAF Junior Division. Prior to this Jon taught on the BA and MA War Studies programmes at King's College London. Jon obtained a first degree in Politics and International Relations and a Post Graduate Certificate of Education from the University of East Anglia. He taught in a variety of state schools before taking the MA in War Studies at KCL. He has worked for the Royal Navy's Defence Studies and lectured to both the Ministry of Defence and the Royal United Services Institution. From May 1996 until January 1999 he was editor of the *War Studies Journal*. Jon Robb-Webb is currently publishing his PhD on the British Pacific Fleet and post-Second World War naval policy. In addition he has published on the naval war in the Mediterranean and Allied Grand Strategy.

**Carl Otis Schuster** currently serves as the Director of Cubic Applications Virtual Analysis Center in Honolulu. United States Navy Captain (ret.) Schuster teaches courses at the Hawaii Pacific University, Honolulu in Twentieth Century Naval Warfare, Intelligence Studies and Chinese National Security and Military Doctrine.

**Geoffrey Till** is Emeritus Professor of Maritime Studies at King's College London, Director of the Corbett Centre for Maritime Policy Studies, and Visiting Senior Research Fellow at the Defence Studies Department at the UK Joint Services Command and Staff College. In 2007 he was a Senior Research Fellow at the S. Rajaratnam School of International Studies, Singapore and in 2008 the inaugural Sir Howard Kippenberger Visiting Chair in Strategic Studies at the Victoria University of Wellington. In November 2009 he returned to the S. Rajaratnam School as Visiting Professor. In addition to many articles and chapters on various aspects of maritime strategy and policy defence, he is the author of a number of books. His most recent are a major study *Seapower: A Guide for the 21st Century* second edition (Routledge 2009), *The Development of British Naval Thinking* (Routledge 2006) and an edited volume with Emrys Chew and Joshua Ho, *Globalization and the Defence in Asia* (Routledge, 2008).

**Frederic Vellucci Jr.** is a Research Analyst in the China Studies division at CNA. He holds an MA in Asian Studies from the Elliott School of International Affairs at George Washington University, and a BA in History and Chinese from the University at Buffalo. Prior to joining CNA, he worked as an analyst focusing on East Asian contemporary affairs for a number of organisations in Washington, DC, including the National Bureau of Asian Research and Intellibridge Corporation. He studied

Mandarin Chinese at the Beijing University of Technology, Capital Normal University, and at the Hopkins-Nanjing Center. He is currently pursuing a JD at the George Washington University Law School. His research at CNA in Washington has focused on US–China relations, Chinese naval strategy, and military modernisation. Additional research interests include the nature of China's expanding international activities and the evolution of US military alliances in Asia.

# Preface

The role of sea power in the rise and fall of nations and sometimes of empires is the theme of this book. The following chapters will explore this question with particular reference to the Asia-Pacific region, since this is now emerging as so manifestly maritime an area. How is the importance of sea power being seen in the region, how is it being developed and with what likely commercial and strategic consequence? The leitmotiv below these questions perhaps, is the broader issue of the modern day validity of the ideas of Mahan and other maritime strategists in the developing conditions of the twenty-first century. In brief, do such views continue to convince today? The following chapters will explore this claim more deeply by considering maritime development in some of the leading countries of the Asia-Pacific region. What emerges from these reviews is the dynamism of maritime power, a phenomenon that rises and falls, in ways that affect the relative power of nations and which can transform the strategic environment. The book will accordingly conclude with a section that looks at the concept and nature of maritime transition.

We would like to thank all our contributors for their timely delivery of chapters from around the world which address these issues. Their cooperation made possible our task of expanding and turning the results of a successful and of course enjoyable conference held at the Hawaii Pacific University in the summer of 2009 into a book that we hope will contribute to a developing debate about the importance of sea power in the Asia-Pacific region. Doing this electronically between two peripatetic editors, one based most of the time in Hawaii and the other, most of the time, in the United Kingdom has been quite a challenge and the discipline and good order of our contributors has helped a great deal.

The conference itself was only possible with the hard work and help of support teams both at Hawaii Pacific University and in the Corbett Centre for Maritime Policy Studies of the King's College Defence Studies Department at the UK Staff College. The work of Sarah Somers, Lynda Hobbs and Lyn Reynolds in doing so much to organise a conference in a wonderful place they could not attend was particularly appreciated. At HPU the contributions of Professors Carlos Juarez and Russell Hart, as well as the graduate students in the Diplomacy and Military Studies programme were critical to the successful organisation of the conference. We owe special thanks to Kevin O'Reilly for his patience in indexing the volume for us. We are grateful for the participation of many local experts like Denny Roy of the East–West Center, General (ret.) David Bramlett, and Captain (United States Navy) Jan Schwartzenberg. Finally, we would also like to thank the administrative staff in the College of Humanities and Social Sciences who supported the project, particularly: Dean Dr. Stephen Combs, Associate Dean Bill Potter, and administrative assistants Joan Ishaque and Jean Zee.

Patrick would like to thank his darling wife Gwenaelle and his wonderful son Vincent for all their support and patience with this project. Grateful to his wife Cherry for putting up with yet another trip to Hawaii, Geoff likewise thanks her for unremitting support and counsel.

# Abbreviations

| | |
|---|---|
| AAT | Australian Antarctic Territory |
| ACV | Air cushion vehicle |
| ADF | Australian Defence Force |
| AFZ | Australian Fishing Zone |
| AIP | Air-independent-propulsion |
| AIS | Automatic identification system |
| ANZUS | Australia, New Zealand, United States Security Treaty |
| AO | Fleet oiler |
| AOR | Replinishment oiler |
| APCSS | Asia-Pacific Center for Security Studies |
| ASC | Australian Submarine Corporation |
| ASCM | Anti-ship cruise missile |
| ASEAN | Association of Southeast Asian Nations |
| ASSeT | Accompanying Sea Security Teams |
| ASW | Anti-submarine warfare |
| ATV | Advanced technology vehicle |
| AWACS | Airborne warning and control system |
| BAD | British Admiralty Delegation |
| BPF | British Pacific Fleet |
| C4I | Command, control, communications, computer and intelligence |
| CARAT | Cooperation afloat readiness and training |
| CENTO | Central Treaty Organization |
| CINC/COMINCH | Commander-in-Chief |
| CINCBPF | Commander-in-Chief British Pacific Fleet |
| CINCPAC | Commander-in-Chief Pacific |
| CINCPOA | Commander-in-Chief Pacific Ocean Area |
| CINCSWPA | Commander-in-Chief South West Pacific Area |
| CMC | Central Military Commission |
| CNF | Commonwealth Naval Forces |
| CNO | Chief of naval operations |
| CODOD | Combined cruise diesel and dash diesel |
| CODOG | Combined diesel or gas |
| COE | Center for Excellence in Disaster Management and Humanitarian Assistance |

| | |
|---|---|
| CSBA | Center for Strategic and Budgetary Assessment |
| CSI | Container Security Initiative |
| DDG | Guided missile destroyer |
| DDGH | Destroyer guided missile with helicopter |
| DDH | Helicopter-carrying destroyer |
| DE | Destroyer escort |
| DFZ | Declared Fishing Zone |
| DGPS | Differential global positioning system |
| DMS | Defence Maritime Services |
| DPRK | Democratic People's Republic of Korea |
| EARL | East Asia Response Private Limited |
| ECDIS | Electronic chart display and information system |
| EEZ | Exclusive Economic Zone |
| ENC | Electronic navigation chart |
| ERZ | Exclusive Resources Zone |
| FF | Fast frigate |
| FFG | Guided missile frigate |
| FFH | Fast frigate helicopter |
| FFX | Future frigate experimental |
| GDP | Gross domestic product |
| HARTS | Harbour craft transponder system |
| ICJ | International Court of Justice |
| IJN | Imperial Japanese Navy |
| IMF | International Monetary Fund |
| IMSCB | Indonesian Maritime Security Coordinating Board |
| IONS | Indian Ocean Naval Symposium |
| ISPS | International Ship and Port Facility |
| ISR | Intelligence, surveillance and reconnaissance |
| JMSDF | Japan Maritime Self Defense Force |
| KDX | Korean destroyer experimental |
| LCH | Landing craft heavy |
| LHA | Landing helicopter assault |
| LHD | Landing helicopter dock |
| LO | Liaison officer |
| LPA | Landing platform amphibious |
| LPD | Landing platform dock |
| LPH | Landing platform helicopter |
| LPX | Landing platform experimental |
| LSA | Landing ship assault |
| LSD | Landing ship dock |
| LST | Tank landing ship |
| MCM | Mine countermeasure |
| MMEA | Malaysian Maritime Enforcement Agency |
| MPA | Maritime and Port Authority |
| MSTF | Maritime Security Task Force |
| NATO | North Atlantic Treaty Organization |
| NATS | Naval Air Transport Service |

| | |
|---|---|
| NCAGS | Naval Cooperation and Guidance of Shipping |
| NCS | Naval Control of Shipping |
| NDPO | National Defence Programme Outline |
| NEO | Non-combatant evacuation |
| OSRL | Oil Spill Response Limited |
| PAJ | Petroleum Association of Japan |
| PCC | Pohang class corvette |
| PCG | Police Coast Guard |
| PLA | People's Liberation Army |
| PLAN | People's Liberation Army Navy |
| PLANAF | People's Liberation Army Air Force |
| POCC | Port operations control centre |
| PRC | People's Republic of China |
| PSI | Proliferation Security Initiative |
| QDR | Quadrennial Defense Review |
| RAAF | Royal Australian Air Force |
| RAF | Royal Air Force |
| RAN | Royal Australian Navy |
| RIMPAC | Rim of the Pacific |
| RMN | Royal Malaysian Navy |
| RN | Royal Navy |
| ROK | Republic of Korea |
| ROKN | Republic of Korea Navy |
| RSN | Republic of Singapore Navy |
| SAM | Surface-to-air missile |
| SEATO | South-East Asian Treaty Organization |
| SLBM | Submarine launched ballistic missile |
| SLOC | Sea lines of communication |
| SOLAS | Safety of Life at Sea |
| SOSRC | Singapore Oil Spill Response Centre |
| SSGN | Ship submersible guided missile nuclear |
| SSK | Ship submersible conventional |
| SSN | Ship submersible nuclear |
| STOBAR | Short take off but arrested recovery |
| SUA Convention | Convention for the Suppression of Unlawful Acts against the Safety of Maritime Navigation |
| TEU | 20-foot equivalent unit |
| TNI-AL | Indonesian Navy |
| TSS | Traffic separation system |
| UNCLOS | United Nations Convention on the Law of the Sea |
| USN | United States Navy |
| VLS | Vertical launch system |
| VTIS | Vessel Traffic Information System |
| VTS | Vessel Traffic Services |

# 1 Introduction

## Sea power and the rise and fall of empires

*Geoffrey Till*

In the summer of 1747, the Emperor Quianlong had a Jesuit architect, Father Giuseppe Cartiglione, build him a summer palace to house his collection of European curiosities. It became known as the Calm Sea Palace. Maritime themes predominated. In the Garden of Perfect Clarity, stone dolphins sported in cascades of water. Everywhere, the European baroque style fitted happily with Chinese motifs and building techniques.

Everything about the place and, indeed, its process of construction showed that even the famous Middle Kingdom for all its often discussed self-absorption, was well aware of the cultural, intellectual, scientific and commercial benefits of this eighteenth-century version of globalisation. One of the results of this was the extraordinary collection of eighteenth- and nineteenth-century European (and mainly British) gilt clocks still to be found on display in the Forbidden City. British clock-makers like James Cox even came to live in Guangzhou 1760–1 in order to teach their trade to the locals. In the nineteenth century, as a result, the Chinese made their own 'European' clocks.

These linkages echoed the close interaction of the Chinese and European porcelain trade that had started some 200 years earlier. The Chinese were first into the business of making porcelain. From the late sixteenth century, the Europeans wanted it, but for the next 150 years could not make it themselves. Accordingly they sent extensive orders, along with exact specifications of colour, subject and shape to Jingdezhen in China for local manufacture. This resulted in a trade of mass production measured in millions of pieces every year. But this was a two-way trade. The Europeans imported Chinese designs too and copied them; in turn European ideas affected the Chinese porcelain industry too.

This trading relationship also blossomed into tea and silks but it depended absolutely on the passage of hundreds of merchantman sailing between Western Europe and China, Japan and other parts of the Far East. It was a thoroughly maritime enterprise.

Had he known about the palace and more about the porcelain trade Alfred Thayer Mahan would probably have cited it as evidence of his major thesis that sea power was central to human development and to the rise and fall of empires and nations. As he said: 'Control of the sea by maritime commerce and naval supremacy means predominant influence in the world ... [and] is the chief among the merely material elements in the power and prosperity of nations'.[1]

## Defining sea power

Sea power was and is not simply about what it takes to use the sea (although that is obviously a prerequisite). It is also the capacity to influence the behaviour of other people or things by what one does at or from the sea. This approach defines sea power in terms of its consequences, its outputs not the inputs, the ends not the means.

It is, moreover, about the sea-based capacity of states to shape events both at sea and on land. As that other great master of maritime thought, Sir Julian Corbett, never tired of saying, the real point of sea power is not so much what happens at sea, but how that influences the outcome of events on land:

> Since men live upon the land and not upon the sea, great issues between nations at war have always been decided – except in the rarest cases – either by what your army can do against your enemy's territory and national life, or else by fear of what the fleet makes it possible for your army to do.[2]

Sea power is clearly a larger concept than land power or airpower, neither of which encompasses the geo-economic dimensions of human activity to the extent that sea power does. As a Bangladeshi author has interestingly remarked:

> Unlike the army and the air force, whose size and firepower have to be related to that of potential adversaries, the size of the navy is determined by the quantum of maritime assets and interests that you have to safeguard.[3]

There are two main components to sea power, its military, naval dimension and the other, maritime, commercial aspects of sea-faring. Considerations of naval power dominated Mahan's writings. What he emphasised were the advantages of navies with great warships and effective weaponry, with better tactics and more advanced technology, and above all perhaps with first-rate commanders able to wield their fleets with ruthless efficiency. The Portuguese broke into the Indian Ocean because they had all these advantages and so prevailed against the much larger navies they encountered there. If there was a revolution in maritime affairs at this time, it was the combination of the maritime nail and naval artillery of the Portuguese men of war. Local vessels, held together by coconut fibre could not stand the shock of heavy artillery. Their practice was to ram and board – fighting, infantry style, at close quarters. At the battle of 1502 off the Malabar Coast a small Portuguese fleet under Vicente Sodre faced a huge local armada in which several hundred Red Sea dhows joined forces with the fleet of the King of Calcutta; the Portuguese simply stood off and battered their adversaries to pieces from a distance.

Such fighting and geo-strategic advantages were not, however, the exclusive property or the invention of the Portuguese or of anyone else. After all, many of the navigational advances made towards the end of the European middle ages derived from contact with the Islamic world, even down to the use of the word 'Admiral' which in Arabic once meant the 'Prince at Sea'. Across the other side of the world, the Koreans deployed the first armoured warship and, of course, China of the Song dynasty (from AD 1000–500) boasted 'the world's most powerful and technologically sophisticated navy'.[4]

But what *was* distinctive about the European approach to sea power in the sixteenth to the twentieth century was that they had discovered and were able to exploit the huge advantage to be derived from the close association between the military and mercantile aspects of sea power. A recent school of thought has taken this argument a little further and sought to explore the association of this all round maritime supremacy with systems of beliefs and of styles of government. The argument goes like this:

The world's nations can be divided into two categories, 'maritime' states and 'territorial' ones. The latter concerned with the defence of their land borders against external attack and internal insurrection, tended to be dominated by warrior elites, with centralised forms of government and financed by enforced levies. 'Maritime' states on the other hand were either islands, big and small, or protected from attack by the physical conformation of their borders. Seafaring and trade produce merchants. Merchants accumulate wealth and political power in order to defend and develop it. Their much more sophisticated financial institutions facilitated long-term borrowing of the sort that could sustain the fleet. Often they will prevail in government, and enforce their ideas on others. 'The essence of the merchant ethic', says Peter Padfield, 'was freedom'.[5] These are the ideas that encouraged trade in the first place: freedom of information and therefore of opinion, open and responsive government, fair taxation, social enterprise – all the liberal values so familiar today. In the seventeenth century, the English marvelled at the freedoms of the Dutch. Thus Sir William Temple, the English Ambassador reported that 'strange freedom that all men took in boats and inns and all other common places, of talking openly whatever they thought upon all public affairs both of their own state, and their neighbours'.[6] A century later the Frenchman, Montesquieu said much the same thing about England calling it 'the freest country in the world'. That freedom was both a product of commercial enterprise and something that facilitated it. Because of the wealth and the resources it generated these freedoms were at the heart of maritime power. Nicholas Rodger makes the essential point: navies need consensus because they require the maximum involvement of seafarers, ship owners, urban merchants, financiers and investors. Autocracies manage armies well enough, because that is much more a matter of simply mobilising manpower and the equipment it needs.[7]

It would be easy to fall into the trap of concluding that these values were Western values, but they are not. They are *trading* values and have been espoused by other peoples at various times. The China of the 500-year-long Song dynasty was one example of this. Despite overland threats from the North and West, naval power was important to the regime, and it had a distinctly mercantile approach. Protecting the merchant fleet against some particularly powerful and well-armed pirates was a high priority. This resulted in the construction of a chain of naval bases along the coast, the development of a convoying system and encouragement of new and sophisticated means of boarding and close engagement, since it was much better to seize or destroy pirate ships than merely to drive them away.[8]

Arguably, the connections between maritime power, liberalism, trade and prosperity are as true now as such authors claim they were then, although the economic success of the guided democracy of Singapore and, so far, of China's state capitalism, may suggest the need for some modifications of this view. For all that, as trade-efficient economies, democracies are used to the free exchange of information which is at the heart of successful trade and it seems no coincidence that they are also the leaders of the information revolution.

But for many these were, and maybe remain, unsettling thoughts. Some regimes, discerning the risks and the challenges inevitably associated with maritime power, have deliberately pulled up the drawbridge against its apparent advantages and opportunities. One Chinese emperor did that quite consciously. After nearly 500 years of deeply impressive and rounded maritime endeavour, the construction of all sea-going ships and foreign travel were banned because China's rulers did not know where it would all end.[9] A little later, in 1639, the Japanese under the Tokugawa shogunate followed suit, turned their back upon the sea and based their system on domestic peace and agricultural taxes. Japan's culture flourished, but the Japanese fell further and further behind global developments until their self-imposed isolation was rudely shattered by the United States Navy in 1853.

The Russians, too, have always been ambivalent about the sea. Peter the Great developed and built a navy specifically to attract trade and Western ideas and even moved his capital to St Petersburg in order to accommodate all this. His navy was full of foreigners; he personally learned about ship-building in Amsterdam and Deptford. He did everything he could to turn Russia into a trading nation. For many of his subjects and his successors this was all too much. Despite its periodic brilliance (especially at the end of the eighteenth century under the great Admiral Ushakov), the navy was seen by conservatives as basically un-Russian and a source of ideas dangerous to the existing system, which of course it was. When Stalin shot most of his admirals in the late 1930s he was in one sense conforming to an ancient Russian tradition of eliminating possible sources of insurrection; but paradoxically the admirals he spared were exactly those who said that the Soviet navy needed to modernise and follow the general lines of development set by the British, American and Japanese navies.

In this, Stalin was tacitly acknowledging the difficulty of insulating his regime from the pervasive influences of modern maritime power. The Japanese and Chinese had already discovered this. According to K. M. Pannikar, the Indians' neglect of the sea (after an earlier period of maritime endeavour) led in their case to three centuries of dominance by the Portuguese, Dutch and British.[10]

## Sea power: a virtuous circle

Sea power can also be represented as a tight and inseparable system in which naval power protects the maritime assets that are the ultimate source of its strength and effectiveness. The likes of Mahan would claim that a virtuous circle was at work for from maritime trade, the Europeans were able to derive maritime resources that could be diverted to naval purposes when the need arose. Partly this was matter of having ports, merchant hulls and seamen that could be used to support the navy directly. Partly naval strength rested on the ability to build, and even more important, maintain and supply, warships that came through governments having access to the sophisticated financial infrastructures[11] that maritime trade encouraged.

All this underpinned naval strength in a whole variety of ways:

- Mercantile finance could be used to fund naval effort. This meant it was much easier for the maritime powers (that is naval powers with a strong mercantile element) to build a navy than it was for the merely naval powers. At the end of the seventeenth century, the French (at this time much less maritime than the British) showed that with a real effort they could out-build the British and produce a bigger and indeed very fine fleet – but they could not maintain it. The British simply outlasted them. Maritime powers could devote huge resources to building and maintaining a fleet but at less real cost, and they often had enough left over to support the wider war effort and, in Britain's case to subsidise allies as well.
- Mercantile finance from the profits of trade also funded access to a mass of industrial and technological developments. The Royal Navy of the eighteenth century and all of its supporting dockyard and

manufacturing infrastructure for example was the world's biggest industrial enterprise by far.¹²
- This could be translated into specific military advantage. The British industrial lead in coke-smelting techniques and steam machinery for example meant it was much easier for the Royal Navy than the French to copper-bottom its ships – making them more nimble and faster than old ships would otherwise have been.

All this made for an approach to war that was uniquely cost-effective and does much to explain why the maritime powers predominated over the merely naval ones and in most cases in the last few centuries over the continental ones too.

The interconnections were perfectly summarised by the French Minister of Marine in 1901, J. I. de Lanessan,

> If we wish to become a great commercial democracy, which will necessitate a great development of our mercantile marine and important progress in our Colonial empire, we must possess a fleet of such strength that no other power can dominate to our detriment the European waters on which our harbours are situated, or the oceans where our merchant ships circulate.¹³

The failure of de Lanessan's project to develop France into a great maritime power, however, demonstrates that this virtuous circle was not a closed system – it could be influenced decisively from outside. In this case the overland threat from Germany essentially broke the circle up. Much the same thing happened to Oman and China when their land borders were threatened by neighbours.

The conclusion that seems to emerge from this is that sea power has two aspects to it which are closely related, naval power on the one hand and, on the other, the commercial maritime power that derives from seaborne trade, the fishing industry, ship-building and so forth. Sea power is much more intimately connected with the socio-economic forces of human development than is either land power or air power. Maritime strategy, in turn, may be seen as a much broader, more flexible and ultimately more effective source of national power, prosperity and success than its land or air equivalents – provided of course that statesmen wield it intelligently.¹⁴ The British of the era of the Napoleonic wars understood this point very well. For them 'maritime power' meant a potent mix of a small relatively agile army, and extensive naval and economic power which in turn made possible a wide ranging grand strategy based on economic pressure exercised through sea power. As Liddell Hart put it, there were two aspects to this maritime strategy, 'one financial which embraced the subsidising and military provisioning of allies; the other military, which embraced seaborne expeditions against the enemy's vulnerable extremities'. In the Napoleonic wars 'whatever was said and hoped by Englishmen who day-dreamed of quick victories, the method pursued in the end was financial attrition'. Even with the cost of the war spiralling from £29 million per annum in 1804 to over £70 million in 1813, 'Britain was able to sustain a level of expenditure that far outstripped that of every other country in Europe'.[15]

What made this possible was the simple fact that the British Empire was founded on sea power, and that sea power was founded on trade. The Royal Navy maintained the international stability in which trade could flourish; it protected the trade routes and the merchant ships that plied them; its command of the sea made possible the movement and supply of land-forces who protected the colonies and Britain's commercial interests from overland attack and internal disorder. The Royal Navy was disposed and deployed accordingly around the world to protect the imperial system – a system that depended on safe and rapid communications of all sorts.[16] Trade and the Royal Navy, in short, held the empire together and made Britain the wealthiest and most powerful of all nations.[17]

All of this would seem to suggest that Mahan's prognostications were, in essence, right and that perhaps four characteristics of the sea explain what, to him, were the manifest strategic, cultural and economic advantages of sea power, and which remain so today.

In brief, they were:

- The sea is a resource for protein in the shape of fish, minerals of various sorts, oil and gas – which explain why nations contest its ownership. Although this is a global phenomenon this maritime competitiveness is particularly prevalent in the Asia-Pacific region where jurisdiction over parts of the North East Pacific and the East and South China Seas is now the subject of bitter dispute.
- The sea is a medium of transportation and exchange. The world trading system is manifestly sea-based. This explains why countries closely linked to the sea benefit economically. It also explains why the sea routes, and especially the choke points are so important strategically. It was the advent of steampower, above all else, that knitted the British Empire together.[18] The defence of trade, and the *conditions* for trade was consequently the Royal Navy's top priority.
- The sea is a medium for information and the spread of ideas. Maritime trade and the exchange of ideas and information appear inseparable. To a large extent this maritime equivalent of the World Wide Web has been taken over by the real thing, of course. But even today the world's reliance on the many undersea fibre-optic cables means that the sea retains some of its importance as a medium of information. Moreover the sea itself is a great storehouse of scientific knowledge that is as yet largely untapped, a great quarry of 'unknown unknowns'.

- The sea is a medium for dominion over other countries, peoples and markets. Thus as Corbett said only sea power explained how it was 'that a small country [like Britain] with a weak army should have been able to gather to herself the most desirable regions of the earth, and to gather them at the expense of the greatest military powers'.[19] Naval power provided command of the sea which in turn allowed and supported fast, effective, maritime interventions ashore wherever British interest required it. The British intervention against Ethiopia in 1867 was a classic, if brutal example of the kind.[20]

And all this provided what Niall Ferguson has called 'world dominion on the cheap'. The British devoted rather less than 2.5 per cent of their GNP to defence, maintained only 215,000 soldiers but a navy of 100,000. Before the First World War, they built 27 dreadnoughts, the Death Stars of their time, for £49 million, less than the annual interest charge on the national debt.[21]

## Sea power: qualifications and limitations

If all this can fairly be said to encapsulate the views of Mahan and other navalists of his persuasion, then balance requires us to look, at least briefly, at the reasons why others are sceptical of such claims, before embarking on a review of maritime developments in the Asia-Pacific region.

The apparently persuasive Mahanian narrative rests quite heavily on the success of the European version of maritime power over the past 400 years or so. But to what extent does that example actually sustain Mahan's view?

Portuguese success, for example, was arguably less inevitable and pre-ordained than often claimed. It was helped by the fact that many key African and Asian states and polities looked inwards rather than out to sea but nonetheless the Portuguese stumbled into an Indian ocean dense with mercantile activity. Globalisation – or at least global connectedness – was not a European project. Moreover disease, unfamiliar topography, climates the Europeans found hostile, the limitations of distance and inter-European disputes and rivalries all limited what their navies could do.[22] There were perhaps only 7,000 Portuguese between Sofala and Macao in the 1540s. Even so, naval power helped, and better sources of market information ensured, that they came, stayed and prospered. The real take-over only came with the onset of European industrialisation, a sophisticated system of credit that could finance distant enterprise and the more developed concept and achievement of command of the sea, based on naval power of the machine age. Even then, trade was the objective not the establishment of empire. Where they could the British were content to trade with advantage as in South America and China (with its treaty ports) without having to assume the burdens of empire.

All this should not be taken to mean that the maritime powers always prevail, for manifestly, they do not. Being maritime, brings vulnerabilities as well as opportunities. Sophisticated maritime powers depend on a complex network of shipping that imports raw materials, food and uncompleted goods, and exports finished and manufactured products. This can be a delicate system, and a dangerous source of vulnerability especially when the distracting effect of continental threats, or governmental neglect, or the appearance of a stronger maritime adversary produces a navy insufficient to protect the wider maritime system on which it ultimately depends. Concerns about these centrifugal tendencies were widely felt even by the British at the apparent height of their imperial power. Thus Rudyard Kipling's elegy to empire at the time of Queen Victoria's Diamond Jubilee of 1987:

> Far-called, our navies melt away;
> On dunes and headlands sinks the fire;
> Lo, all our pomp of yesterday
> Is one with Nineveh and Tyre![23]

As the fate of the Netherlands in the late seventeenth century and Japan, more dramatically in the mid-twentieth century show, not just the interests but the very survival of the maritime power may be at stake if their inescapable vulnerabilities are successfully exploited by others.

Many argued at the time of the Cold War, that the North Atlantic Treaty Organization (NATO) had such dangerous vulnerabilities too. As its name suggests, it was an alliance as much separated by the ocean as it was joined by it. Its strategic coherence and economic survival depended on sea-based transportation which sometimes seemed dangerously exposed to the burgeoning Soviet Navy and land-based air-forces. Accordingly much of NATO's naval resources were directed at the defence of those unavoidable maritime vulnerabilities. This combined with the often remarked superiority of the offence at sea meant that much of NATO's maritime effort was devoted to ensuring that NATO did not lose a possible war with the Soviet Union, rather than providing a means by which NATO could win it.

In short, the demanding but essentially protective function that sea powers usually have, limits their capacity to impose their will on others, and may make them dangerously vulnerable to external pressure both at sea and from overland. The great British geographer, Halford Mackinder and his followers saw this as a grave, historic and developing weakness.

Such geo-politicians pointed out that many long-lasting empires had moreover been based on land power not sea power. Mahan and others had made too much of the Columbian era, which was in fact the exception to the rule. The Mongols for example created a massive empire lasting some 500 years that was about as far from the sea as it is geographically possible to get. The great Eurasian empire of Genghiz Khan and his successors stretched from Europe to the Pacific and took in South Asia and much of the Middle East as well. But this was an empire based on horsepower not sea power, although in places the Mongols did approach the sea. Moreover, the Mongol Empire turned into a great force of 'global connectedness' if not globalisation. Genghiz (1206–27) with speed, surprise and the ability to operate across incredible distances conquered more peoples and territory in 25 years than Rome had managed in 400, and it was at the time the most densely populated areas of the world's surface. Genghiz galvanised the Silk Route and established what was in effect a free trade zone stretching from Korea to the Balkans, introduced a universal alphabet, the first international postal system and a body of law and regulation that encouraged trade to flourish, German miners to work in China and Chinese doctors to practice in Persia.[24] Tamerlane carried this still further dominating the great overland trunk road of Eurasian commerce.[25] The rise of Muscovy over Gogol's 'golden green ocean of the steppes' echoed all this in some respects. This was a Eurasian Sparta that exploited the trade routes of the interior of the Mackinder's 'world island' but which rested in practice on social and political oppression.[26]

Further, the geo-politicians argued that the 'world political potential of sea power had been in full retreat long before the first submarine had plunged below the surface and the first plane had taken to the air'.[27] This was because land communications were improving. Transcontinental railways were facilitating the concentration of industrial capacity as a route to power rather than the acquisition of colonies. Clearly, the German economic rise of the late nineteenth century did not depend on sea power.[28]

In some cases, these arguably non-maritime empires were able to develop ever better means of exploiting the vulnerabilities of the maritime powers. Their continental riches enabled them to develop significant naval forces (like the German U-boats of the First and Second World Wars) that had no protective function to distract them and which could be wholly devoted to offensive campaigns of sea denial against the maritime powers that, by definition, depended on their capacity to use the sea. Soviet Russia and Nazi Germany were countries that did not conform to the Mahanian stereotype of navies based on mercantile strength and their arguably associated liberal values. And yet, despite that, the German Navy's campaign of sea denial based on a first-rate if small surface fleet and, even more, on its submarine arm caused the Western allies major difficulties during the First and Second World Wars. Nor could those same allies afford to disregard the challenge posed from the late 1960s by the Soviet Navy.

The navy of imperial Japan did not fit all aspects of the Mahanian narrative, either. For one reason or another, merchant classes in Japan only achieved political prominence in the period after the Second World War. Before then, information exchange was limited and governmental power was unchecked constitutionally. Instead of reflecting the liberal, trading values identified by Peter Padfield, the Imperial Japanese Navy was imbued with the samurai spirit of medieval times.[29] As far as the imperial Germany of 1914 was concerned the business and industrial class *were* politically important, but this certainly wasn't an example of the liberal sea-based democracy of the British or American sort.[30] In both cases sea power served different kinds of states and pursued different kinds of purposes. Neither navy, for example, was concerned about the need to protect trade. Moreover, the contemporary rise of Chinese sea power, and perhaps the recovery of Russian sea power too, is associated with a regime of authoritarian rather than liberal capitalism.[31]

Most empires were not, finally, either 'sea powers' or 'land powers'; they tended to be both, in varying degree. The Ottoman Empire for example exploited the position of Constantinople to dominate maritime communications and trade in the Black Sea, the Aegean and the Mediterranean and developed the kind of navy that went with it. But at the same time, it had a large standing army centred on the janissaries, a tightly disciplined force of infantry. It was the same with the Mughal Empire in India. Enriched by extensive sea-based trade with the Middle East and benefiting from the size and sophistication of its own internal market, Mughal India was a still a prosperous and sophisticated empire with a mighty army when the first Europeans arrived to perch uneasily on its flanks in their factories.

Imperial China likewise rested on a mix of both land power and sea power, the balance between the two shifting from one dynasty to another. The Chinese had extensive sea-based trading links with the rest of Asia and the Indian Ocean and a sophisticated economy linked by a network of internal waterways.[32] From the Tang to the Song dynasties sea-based trade was more important than the Silk Road to Central Asia and beyond. In 1403–24, Emperor Yung-Lo engaged in ambitious naval adventures, being determined to take over Vietnam. At the same time, there occurred the famous voyages into and across the Indian Ocean of Zheng He.[33] His successor, however, concerned about the effects of all this on the nature of Chinese society and the political system, famously turned his back on the sea and focussed instead on attempting to deal with the Mongol tide lapping at the Great Wall.[34] Maritime trade was restricted to internal waterways and coastal waters though maritime raiding, smuggling and piracy remained rife. If this was sea power, it was arguably of a different kind from the version dominating the Mahanian narrative.

China's turn from the sea under the later Ming and through the early Qing dynasties did not lead to national decline moreover, and the Chinese empire founded on its continental strength and an artful combination of hard and soft power[35] was arguably at its apogee in the second half of the eighteenth century. China retained most of its links with the outside world, but the sheer size of its internal market (bigger than the whole of Europe's) meant that in relative terms China's international trade was quite small.[36] China's view of the fundamental unimportance of maritime trade was expressed by Emperor Quianlong to Lord Macartney in 1793:

> Our dynasty's majestic virtue has penetrated into every country under heaven, and kings of nations have offered their costly tribute by land and sea. As your Ambassador can see for himself, we possess all things. I set no value on objects strange or ingenious, and have no use for your country's manufactures.[37]

But under the later Qing this world gradually fell apart. The dynasty failed to recognise the challenge of the sea-borne West. The Opium Wars and the 1884 destruction of China's new if wooden fleet by the French in a dispute over Vietnam[38] revealed some of the consequences for China of a systemic neglect of sea power even in a strategic and cultural system preoccupied with other things. When the lessons of this were hammered home by the Taiping rebellion and the naval defeat at the hands of the upstart Japanese in 1894–5 led to a search for a new and more effective way of constructing China, and their discovery of Mahan.[39]

China's turning away from the sea did however allow a sudden explosion of Japanese maritime endeavour for a century from 1540, but here too the Japanese in their turn maintained only carefully controlled links with the outside world and later became much more introspective.[40] The Japanese took the maritime failures of the Qing dynasty to heart and subsequently embarked on a course of determined navalism that became one of the great challenges to Western maritime power in the Pacific in the twentieth century.

The existence of these mixed empires of land and sea-power (as nearly all of them were) raises another set of issues and questions. Which of the two kinds of national power were the most important? Did land-power in the shape of both concentrated commercial and industrial power plus the existence of strong ground forces provide the conditions for the construction of naval forces, or was it generally the other way about, as Mahan argued? Paul Kennedy has tended to argue for the former, pointing out the extent to which Britain's industrial decline, relative to its rivals, undermined the basis for its naval supremacy.[41]

## Transitions

In consequence of its relative economic decline, Britain passed the baton to the United States as the leading maritime power through the Second World War, arguably sometime between the North African and Normandy landings, in one of the clearest examples of a peaceful great power transition. The United States emerged from that conflict with what, according to many observers, everyone but Americans recognised was soon to become an unofficial empire. By 1955, the US economy dominated the world system, it had around 450 military bases in 36 countries and its navy stood supreme.

Britain and its empire in the shape of Canada, Australia, New Zealand and South Africa, propped up by the United States eventually merged into what some have called the Anglosphere. 'The Anglo-American alliance', says John Darwin, 'was a remarkable example of cooperation between a declining imperial power [which expected to recover] and its most obvious successor'.[42] Not surprisingly, then, this was a 'liberal empire' and one that bore many similarities with its British predecessor:

> The world system today as managed by the United States preserves most of the chief features key features of the British system that existed before World War II: a liberal, maritime, international order that promotes the free flow of capital and goods and the development of liberal economic and political institutions and values.[43]

Two points need to be made about this. The first is the emphasis on the word 'liberal', the notion that certain characteristics of government facilitate economic growth and development and so should be actively encouraged. These include such things as secure property and contract rights, personal liberty, stable, responsive incorrupt government and so on.[44]

Second, Mead's emphasis on the word 'maritime' is significant because the British Empire was plainly not based on demographic advantage, nor on the *size* of its commercial activity, which at its peak in the 1870s amounted to no more than 9 per cent of the world's GNP.[45] It was the consequence of entrepreneurial skill, industrial and technological prowess, a general capacity to win wars (though often losing the first round) and perhaps above all on naval strength. Mahan wrote of the 'overwhelming power, destined to be used as selfishly, as aggressively, though not as cruelly, and much more successfully than any that had preceded it. This was the power of the sea'.[46] This was and continues to be a 'maritime order', based on sea power, both naval and commercial – and one that has indeed shaped the world.

The fact that in so many ways the rising powers of India and China seem to be recovering the maritime aspects of their pasts and also to be following the Western trajectory towards full involvement in, and part ownership of, a globalised sea-based trading system, and that the development of their naval power seems increasingly central to their concerns, suggests that for all his terrible simplicities, and despite all the qualifications and limitations to the central argument discussed earlier, Mahan might have been right after all.

## Notes

1 Cited in William E. Livezey, *Mahan on Sea Power* (Norman, OK: University of Oklahoma Press, 1981), pp. 28–2.
2 Sir Julian Corbett, *Some Principles of Maritime Strategy* (London: Longmans, Green, reprinted with Introduction by Eric Grove (Annapolis, MD: Naval Institute Press, 1988 [1911]), p. 67.

3 Alam, Cdre Mohd Khurshed, 'Maritime Strategy of Bangladesh in the New Millennium' *Bangladesh Institute of International Studies Journal*, Vol. 20, No. 3, 1999.
4 Paul C. Forage, 'The Foundations of Chinese Naval Supremacy in the Twelfth Century' in Jack Sweetman (ed.) *New Interpretations in Naval History 10th Symposium* (Annapolis, MD: Naval Institute Press, 1991), p. 6.
5 P. Padfield, *Maritime Dominion and the Triumph of the Free World* (London: John Murray, 2009), p. 3.
6 Cited in P. Padfield, *Maritime Supremacy and the Opening of the Western Mind* (Woodstock and New York: Overlook press, 1999), p. 69.
7 N. A. M. Rodger, *The Safeguard of the Sea: A Naval History of Britain. Vol. 1 660–1649* (London: Harper Collins, 1997), pp. 432–3.
8 Forage (1991), op. cit., pp. 8–9.
9 See the conclusion of J. K. Fairbank, cited in Kishore Mahbubani, *The New Asian Hemisphere: The Irresistible Shift of Global Power to the East* (New York, Public Affairs, 2008), p. 268. China, Fairbank claimed, was not a natural trader.
10 K. M. Pannikar, *Asia and Western Dominance: A Survey of the Vasco da Gama Epoch of Asian History* (London: George Allen and Unwin, 1959).
11 Typically it was the maritime Dutch who invented the world's first lottery loan system, the world's first central bank and the joint-stock company. The maritime British followed suit, later developing modern insurance. Niall Ferguson, *The Ascent of Money* (London: Penguin Books, 2008), pp. 35, 128–33, 186.
12 N. A. M. Rodger, *The Wooden World: An Anatomy of the Georgian Navy* (London: Collins, 1986), p. 29.
13 J. I. de Lanessan, *La Programme Maritime de 1900–1906* (Paris, 1903).
14 This essential point is made with much insight in Martin Robson, *Britain, Portugal and South America in the Napoleonic Wars: Alliances and Diplomacy in Economic Maritime Conflict* (London: I. B. Tauris, 2011), pp. 1–5, 13, 19–20ff.
15 Ibid.; B. H. Liddell Hart, 'Economic Pressures or Continental Victories', *Journal of the Royal United Services Institute*, No. 76 (1931), pp. 495–500, and *The British Way in Warfare* (London: Faber & Faber, 1932), p. 7; D. A. Baugh, 'Great Britain's "Blue-Water" Policy, 1689–1815', *International History Review*, Vol. 10 (1988), p. 56; C. Esdaile, *The Wars of Napoleon* (London: Longman, 1995), p. 156.
16 Paul Kennedy, *The Rise and Fall of British Naval Mastery*, third edition (London: Fontana Press, 1991), pp. 169–71; James Morris, *Pax Britannica* (London: Faber & Faber, 1968), p. 99.
17 James Morris, *Pax Britannica*, p. 99; see also James L. Stokesbury, *Navy and Empire* (New York: William Morrow and Co Inc, 1983).
18 Niall Ferguson, *Empire: How Britain made the Modern World* (London: Penguin, 2004), p. 166.
19 Corbett, op. cit., p. 49.
20 Ferguson, *Empire*, op. cit., pp. 176–7. Such operations were known at the time, with devastating candour, as 'butcher and bolt'.
21 Ibid., p. 247. It may have been cheap – but at the time it didn't feel it to the British at least. Jon Tetsuro Sumida, *In Defence of Naval Supremacy: Finance, Technology, and British Naval Policy* (Boston: Unwin Hyman, 1989), pp. 3–36. For a similar, less academic, more political view 50 years on, see James Callaghan, *Time and Chance* (London: Collins, 1987), pp. 119, 211. The same kind of declinist angst is arguably present in the United States of the early twenty-first century. Niall Ferguson, *Colossus: The Rise and Fall of the American Empire* (New York: Penguin Books, 2005).
22 John Darwin, *After Tamerlane: The Rise and Fall of Global Empires 1400–2000* (London: Penguin, 2008), pp. 13–15.
23 Rudyard Kipling, *Recessional*, 1897.

*Introduction* 15

24 Jack Weatherford, *Genghiz Khan and the Making of the Modern World* (New York: Three Rivers, 2004), Introduction.
25 Darwin, *After Tamerlane*, op. cit., pp. 6, 35–6.
26 Darwin, *After Tamerlane*, op. cit., p. 72.
27 R. Strausz-Hupe, *Geopolitics: The Struggle for Space and Power* (New York: Putnam, 1942), p. 26.
28 Padfield, *Dominion*, op. cit., p. 74.
29 Padfield, *Dominion*, op. cit., pp. 68–71.
30 Padfield, *Dominion*, op. cit., pp. 122–6.
31 Timothy Garton Ash, 'We Friends of Liberal International Order Face a New Global Disorder', *Guardian*, 11 September 2008.
32 Darwin, *After Tamerlane*, op. cit., p. 41; Charles Horner, *Rising China and its Postmodern Fate: Memories of Empire in a New Global Context* (Athens: University of Georgia Press, 2009), pp. 39–40.
33 Martin Stuart-Fox, *A Short History of China and Southeast Asia: Tribute, Trade and Influence* (Crow's Nest, NSW: Allen and Unwin, 2003), pp. 82–9.
34 Horner, *Rising China*, op. cit., pp. 43–52. Some historians indeed believe the Zheng He voyages to have been a military mission with the strategic aim of outflanking the Mongols.
35 Horner, *Rising China*, op. cit., pp. 63–4.
36 Darwin, *After Tamerlane*, op. cit., pp. 105, 130; Stuart-Fox, *A Short History* op. cit., pp. 47–51.
37 Quoted in Stuart-Fox, *A Short History*, op. cit., p. 116.
38 Darwin, *After Tamerlane*, op. cit., p. 275.
39 Horner, *Rising China*, op. cit., pp. 74–7.
40 Darwin, *After Tamerlane*, op. cit., p. 134.
41 This issue is discussed later, in Chapter 13.
42 Darwin, *After Tamerlane*, op. cit., p. 470.
43 Walter Russell Mead, *God and Gold: Britain, America and the Making of the Modern World* (London: Atlantic Books, 2007), p. xiv.
44 Ferguson, *Colossus*, op. cit., p. 179.
45 Mead, *God and Gold*, op. cit., p. 351.
46 Mead, *God and Gold*, op. cit., p. 86.

# Part I
# The navies of the Asia-Pacific

# 2 The United States as a Pacific power

*Patrick C. Bratton*

At the close of the first decade of the twenty-first century, the United States is still the dominant power in the Asia-Pacific region. US power rests on a combination of hard and soft power assets ranging from the most powerful military in the world, a network of alliances with many key states in the region, a generally strong economy, to an attractive cultural and educational model. Over the past 60 years it has built a dense, US-focused network of alliances, partnerships and institutions with an emphasis on both economic and security cooperation.

However, there are also concerns about US decline, which is one of the major questions of this volume. Will the United States be able to continue its dominant position in the Pacific or have to deal with a "graceful decline" as the British did in the 1930s through the 1950s? The rise of China and India, drawn out wars in the Middle East and South Asia on the one hand and the economic crisis since 2008 on the other have all been used by pundits as indicators of the decline of Pax Americana in the Asia-Pacific.[1]

This chapter shall examine the basis for US power in the Asia-Pacific, looking at its historical background and then its contemporary aspects. While this is a volume about maritime power, this chapter shall not focus on the United States Navy because that is the subject for the following chapter. However, particular attention will be given to the relationship between maritime power, American-led institutions and alliances in Asia and democratization. Last, some of the challenges to US power will be addressed, the rise of China, disengagement, geography, sea denial and managing its alliance network.

## US influence in the Asia-Pacific region

In terms of geography, size and quality of economic and military assets and also its position of leadership in a dense network of alliances and institutions, the United States is clearly the leading power of the Asia-Pacific region and has been for at least 60 years. The US has been well positioned to utilize all aspects of sea power in the Asia-Pacific, using the sea for resources, as a medium of transportation and exchange, a medium for the spread of ideas and to exert influence in the region.[2] This has been possible because American power covers virtually the entire spectrum from hard to soft power and it has also used this power to build a dense network or system of institutions (both formal and informal) that sets up rules, norms and "buy in" from most of the powers in the region.[3]

Geography has helped the United States play a role as an "extra-regional balancer" for the region. Because it does not share a land border with any of the major powers in the region, it is able to make alliances with many regional powers without having the baggage of territorial disputes that have caused crises between many Asian states.[4] This allows the United States to play a role as a broker between powers to manage rivalries and reduce tensions. For example, prepositioned US forces in Japan perform a dual task of coupling both countries and strengthening their alliance, and also ostensibly reassure neighboring countries by making Japanese rearmament unnecessary. Smaller countries have looked to the United States for reassurance against larger and possibly aggressive neighbors and to "keep the peace" in the region by managing conflicts.[5]

In terms of hard power, the United States has maintained the largest fleet and the most sophisticated ground and air forces in the region since at least World War II. These forces, in particular its unmatched naval forces, serve as a security guarantor in the region.[6] In recent years much of these forces have shifted from territorial defense to power projection.[7] In addition, it maintains alliances with many of the leading powers or with smaller countries in critical geographic positions. The United States benefits from unique power projection capabilities because these alliances give the United States a network of overseas military bases. The ability of the United States to project power and wage a decade-long war in such a distant part of Asia as Afghanistan is a case in point.

In terms of soft power, the United States maintains the largest diplomatic establishment, a dense network of official (track one), semi-official (track two) and private diplomatic and educational networks. Moreover it has the largest single economy that is dependent on foreign imports and foreign servicing of debt.[8] Given that most of Asia's successful economies achieved much of their growth by exporting goods to the West, in particular the United States, the "rise of Asia" has been tied to the US economy. Before the 2008 global financial crisis, the US trade balance with the Asia-Pacific in 2007 was $404,000 million ($717,000 million in imports from Asia, and $313,000 million in exports to Asia); in contrast, the trade balance with Europe/Eurasia was $121,000 million and with the Americas/Western Hemisphere $166,000 million. After the crisis in 2009, the US trade balance with the Asia-Pacific was $310,000 million ($596,000 million in imports from Asia and $295,000 million in exports to Asia) in contrast to Europe/Eurasia ($72,000 million) and the Americas/Western Hemisphere ($66,000 million).[9] The economies of the United States and

Asia are so interconnected that from 2008 to 2010 trade with Europe dropped by half, trade with the Western Hemisphere dropped by two-thirds, while trade with Asia declined only by about one-quarter.

While more difficult to measure in terms of concrete effects, American culture and best practices in business and educational systems have also spread across the Pacific and serve as a major attraction for visitors and students. US universities have consistently occupied about 80–90 percent of the top ten or 20 world's best universities according to most measures.[10] The largest percentage of these students comes from Asia (62 percent from Asia as compared to 13 percent from Europe in 2008) and four of the five largest groups of students come from countries in the Asia-Pacific (India, China, South Korea and Japan).[11] Beyond traditional universities, many US-based private institutions like think-tanks have assisted in building up a network of track-two diplomacy in the region since the early 1990s.[12]

The US government has heavily invested in sponsoring these types of exchanges through a combination of military and diplomatic means. The State Department sponsors a wide variety of programs like the international visitors program, leadership training programs and exchanges through institutions like the East–West Center.[13] One way is through traditional means like naval port calls, expansion of joint exercises, and anti-piracy cooperation, but also more innovative ways like the Proliferation Security Initiative (PSI).[14] In the past 20 years the United States has also increased cooperation through institutions such as the Asia-Pacific Center for Security Studies (APCSS), and the Center for Excellence in Disaster Management and Humanitarian Assistance (COE) bringing in a wide cross section of leaders from both inside and outside government. Ideally the links that are facilitated by the United States will both lead to regional cooperation and give the United States a personal connection with the next generation of leaders in the participating countries.

Last, given its history as a maritime trading state, the United States is a liberal democracy that values both a free political and economic system.[15] While at times it does not always seem like an advantage, it does mean that its leadership and policies get periodically renewed. Unpopular leaders or policies can be replaced by elections, which allow new ones to come in. This can give the United States remarkable staying power in the long-run even if at times it causes difficulties in terms of taking quick action.[16] As Wallace Thies writes,

> In democracies, ambitious strivers with new ideas are always appearing on the scene ... In this way, democracies learn, adapt, and change. Not everyone may agree that the correct lessons have been learned, but democracies do learn from past mistakes.[17]

Much of this argument also applies to the relations between the United States and its democratic allies in Asia. How real and substantive the differences in US foreign policy between different administrations is a matter of debate, but the perception of change can make real change possible.[18]

This synergy of both hard and soft power components has played a vital role in the United States to maintain "good order at sea" in the Asia-Pacific.[19] The United States working with its partners and allies has made a large commitment to maintaining security and stability of the maritime realm in the region for extraction and management of resources, safe transportation of good and resources, and the exchange of information. The ability of the United States to do this in many respects lies with the history of its commercial and military involvement in Asia since the early nineteenth century.

## History

### Commercial and religious roots, 1780s–1898

American power in the Pacific has been multi-dimensional almost from its very beginnings. It started mostly in the form of merchants and then Christian missionaries. As compared to other great powers, one could make a strong case that US sea power and interest in the Pacific was originally driven by the private sector. American merchants were trading with China, Korea and the East Indies even before independence from Great Britain.[20] In the nineteenth century American interests in the Pacific were mostly commercial and cultural. They focused on trading, whaling and missionary activities.

American naval efforts in the Pacific were episodic during this period, mostly used to support and protect commercial interests.[21] However, in times of crisis naval squadrons would be sent for military actions, in particular expeditions to "open" Asian kingdoms to trade, or for reprisals for incidents and attacks on American commerce or citizens.[22] In rapid succession the American Republic began to make treaties with most major kingdoms in Asia.[23] In addition to American commercial interests, there also came cultural ones, in particular American missionaries and also American educational models (particularly for westernizing states like Meiji Japan). In the early nineteenth century, American missionaries joined the merchants in the Pacific to make converts throughout Asia and Oceania.[24] As several observers increasingly have noted through the nineteenth century, there becomes a tacit and at times not so tacit alliance between the missionaries and the merchants/industrialists in order to expand American influence.[25]

### The dilemmas of imperial defense, 1898–1945

The transformation of the United States into a great power in the late nineteenth century led to a similar transformation in US maritime power.

In the 1890s–1900s, the United States surpassed the United Kingdom in key measures of power like iron/steel production, per capita level of industrialization, world share of manufacturing output, and industrial output and size of the economy.[26] Up until the 1890s, US economic growth mostly came from its domestic market rather than foreign trade. However, with the end of westward expansion the United States faced a question of whether to get more involved in great power affairs in Asia.[27] Last, in terms of leadership, the presidencies of both Theodore Roosevelt and Woodrow Wilson sought a more active role for the United States in international affairs at the start of the twentieth century.[28]

This coincided with a radical shift in US naval power from a cruiser force – that concentrated on protecting US commerce and raiding that of the enemy in wartime – to a fleet of battleships that would seek to establish sea control through decisive battle with another battle fleet.[29] The shift from the 1880s to the early twentieth century is striking. The US went from a small cruiser fleet to the third-largest fleet of battleships in the world by 1913. US victory over Spain and the annexation of territories in the Pacific in 1898 – the Philippines, Guam and Hawaii – seemed to vindicate the importance of a battle fleet to win control of the sea.

US possessions in the Pacific introduced two new issues into American thinking about the Asia-Pacific. First, a battle fleet of steam powered ships would also need coaling stations and secure bases in the Pacific to operate effectively.[30] Once the United States had overseas bases, it could play a more active role in the Pacific, in particular promoting the Open Door policy in China. The fact that large numbers of American troops in 1900 were deployed to pacify the Philippines allowed the United States to make a sizeable contribution to the international expedition to put down the Boxers.[31]

Second, just as overseas bases gave the United States positions from which to project power, they also complicated US defense policy by requiring defense of the possessions. The navy and army were tasked with defending these possessions from exterior threats and also maintaining US rule over potentially hostile populations.[32] As the European powers with Asian empires became more pre-occupied with the World Wars in Europe, it was Japan that emerged as the major threat.[33]

However, while the United States recognized Japan as a threat, it was another matter to be in a position to make effective plans or deploy military resources to deal with it. There was a disconnect between a passive US diplomatic strategy and war plans that called for an offensive war that would strike into Japanese home waters.[34] American defenses in the Pacific were hampered by a combination of lack of cooperation between the war and navy departments, lack of resources, lack of realistic planning about how to deal with threats, a domestic public that was at times strongly isolationist and lack of direction from Washington. In the words of Brian Linn, "for almost four decades the central question in the Pacific was unchanged: how to defend distant, militarily weak possessions against a strong and aggressive regional power."[35]

Yet for all the pre-war difficulties the United States had in working out its Pacific strategy, it handled the war with Japan remarkably well. Maritime power was decisive in this theater for the United States and its allies. The United States adapted to fighting in a wide variety of regions from the sub-Arctic of the Aleutian campaign to the tropical climate of New Guinea. While it is easy to argue that the result was a foregone conclusion given the material disparities between the two nations, it must be said that the United States gave more attention to the entire spectrum of maritime operations in the Pacific: submarine warfare against shipping, amphibious operations, carrier air strikes and naval gunfire support against land targets, protecting sea lanes, working well with the allies and forcing inter-service cooperation.[36] One could make a strong case that these advantages the United States had over Japan were due to its tradition as a maritime nation that had to deal with overseas territories and protecting trade during wartime.[37]

Most importantly, the war in the Pacific transformed the role of the United States in the Pacific from primarily protecting its possessions to becoming the dominant power. The United States became the dominant power in several island countries and territories across the Pacific, Southeast Asia and Northeast Asia. The US victory in the Pacific laid the framework for its alliance structure in the Cold War, with the United States having to plan for the future of a rebuilt Japan, and the newly independent nations of Asia that by the end of the 1940s stretched from Korea through Indonesia to Pakistan.

## *Cold War: hot wars and alliances, 1945–90*

With the conclusion of World War II, the United States found itself engaged in traditional commitments in Asia.[38] US military forces remained strong in Asia throughout most of the Cold War, US maritime dominance of the region being a particular feature of this.[39] In addition, the United States fashioned a strong alliance and institutional system co-opting past adversaries and securing new partners.

US strategy in the Pacific was based upon a dual-track of making security agreements with key allies and also assisting Asian states with economic development. This strategy had some similarities to the US plans in Europe of securing allies through a combination of a security alliance – North Atlantic Treaty Organization (NATO) – and economic recovery – the Marshall Plan. Again the United States saw the threat of communism as multi-dimensional, not primarily a military threat (in particular before 1950) and so it required a multi-spectrum response. What was needed was not only a traditional security guarantee from attack, but also assistance to develop stable economic and political systems.[40]

Regionally the United States fashioned the "San Francisco System" which consisted of bilateral security alliances between the United States and Japan (1951 and then 1960), South Korea (1953), the Philippines (1951), Taiwan (1955 until 1980) and Thailand (1954 as part of the Manila Pact/South East Asian Treaty Organization (SEATO) and then 1962 Communiqué).[41] In addition, the United States and Pakistan signed a Mutual Defense Agreement that was not part of the San Francisco System in 1954. However, unlike the Euro-Atlantic system one that stressed multilateral institutions like NATO, the Western European Union and the European Economic Community, the San Francisco System was a "hub and spokes" system where countries like Japan and South Korea had closer relations with the United States thousands of miles away than with each other.[42]

Additionally, there were important differences between the two regions in terms of economics and domestic politics. In Europe, the United States was largely rehabilitating developed economies that had been devastated by war. In Asia, with the exception of Japan, none of the countries in Asia were industrialized or developed. So the United States emphasized programs to build up export-driven economies and opened the US market in favorable arrangements to facilitate that growth.[43] This also resulted in orientating the economies of Asia towards the United States and away from China and the subsidizing of US bases.[44]

This bilateral system served a dual purpose of dealing with external threats from the Soviet Union and other communist states and also gave the United States more influence over its allies to control their behaviour.[45] Allied behavior sparked two fears. First, there was a fear of entrapment, or an irresponsible ally "chain-ganging the United States" into an unwanted war was arguably more real in Asia than Europe.[46] The United States worried at various times in the early Cold War about South Korea or Taiwan taking risky aggressive actions against their communist neighbors.

The second difficulty was that the instability of these regimes could bring the United States into conflicts that were not always critical to US security interests. Most of these allies were non-democratic regimes, which were at times unstable and unpopular. The United States often faced a difficult choice of either tying aid and assistance to force political reforms and risk losing the client state, or ignoring authoritarian rule or rampant corruption and giving aid to "securitize" the state from external or internal threats.[47] In the case of South Vietnam, as the government failed to deal with the insurgency, the United States had to step in and take on the burden of the conflict at great cost to itself domestically and internationally.

### *Post-Cold War: globalization, non-traditional security and the rise of Asia*

US concerns since the Cold War have focused on expanding trade and globalization, managing the growth of Asian powers like China and India, managing regional conflicts, combating terrorism and helping states deal with non-traditional security issues and concerns. In the immediate post-Cold War years, US foreign policy was often categorized by drift without the driving goal of containment. There were concerns in the region that the United States would retreat from Asia and reduce its deployed presence. Yet, US alliances and the majority of forward deployed forces remained in the 1990s and expanded post-9/11. In addition to these formal defense relationships, the United States has greatly expanded its set of informal relations in the region with countries that have traditionally been reluctant to enter into formal alliances, in particular Singapore and India.[48] In response to conflicts in Afghanistan and the Persian Gulf, the Indian Ocean and South Asia has become increasingly important to US interests.[49]

In terms of soft power, both the Clinton and Bush Administrations stressed expansion of trade in the region, and expanded and deepened Asian economic institutions.[50] One of the main objectives of US foreign policy in the region was to spread globalization, both in terms of free trade and also free political systems. These efforts helped the deepening of economic ties and institutions that was mentioned before.[51] Yet, along with the benefits of globalization, one could argue that there came a rise in non-traditional security threats and issues that often represent the "dark side of globalization": trafficking in drugs, arms and people, violation of intellectual property rights, money laundering, climate change, piracy, pandemic diseases and transnational terrorism.[52] These "new security issues" have challenged the traditional US security network in the region.

During the Cold War, the United States had the luxury of planning around a single threat of communism and correspondingly its alliance system focused on either external state threats or internal insurgencies. In contrast, in the 1990s and 2000s, the United States and its allies found themselves dealing with a multitude of issues and even questions about the continued validity of the San Francisco System. Just as pundits argued that NATO had no purpose with the demise of the Soviet Union, there were concerns about the future of US alliances in Asia, in particular with Japan and South Korea. However, the United States has attempted to keep its alliances relevant, hedging against China, managing North Korean threats, and increasing focus on transnational and non-traditional security issues: terrorism, proliferation, climate change, pandemic diseases, natural disasters, organized crime, piracy, security of sea lines of communication (SLOC) etc. are increasingly seen as just or perhaps even more relevant than traditional security issues like interstate war and proliferation. In the 2009 unclassified PACOM strategy, in a list of key challenges, at least half are explicitly non-traditional security issues.[53]

US forces and those of allied nations in the Pacific deal more frequently with deploying military assets like carrier groups for tsunami relief rather than conducting force projection with bombing strikes.[54] Generally, the

United States has been able to shift or modify its Cold War arrangement of the San Francisco Alliance System and its PACOM-centered Asian foreign policy to focus on transnational issues and new actors.[55] The United States also became more concerned with the activities of terrorism groups, particularly in Southeast and South Asia. Disaster management has been such a priority that the United States formed COE in 1994 to assist with civil–military cooperation during disaster relief. In recent years, the United States has become more involved in planning for and coordinating policies dealing with pandemic diseases that have concerned the region.

## Challenges and vulnerabilities to US influence in the Asia-Pacific

### The rise of China

Perhaps the greatest challenge to US influence in the Pacific is the rise of China. Countless observers have commented on the "rise of Asia" for at least the past 30 years or more. During this same period, many have worried about "American declinism." Coincidentally, these concerns have focused on the eclipse of the United States by an Asia-Pacific country. In the 1980s, this was widely thought to be Japan, and since the late 1990s to be China, though India has drawn attention as well.[56] As mentioned earlier, one of the great strengths of US power in the Pacific is the maintenance of its modified San Francisco System of alliances, partnerships, institutions and networks. What has made this successful was the United States' ability to convince powers that it was in their own interest to join its institutional system and help maintain it rather than seek to challenge or overthrow it. While the United States was able to do this with Japan, the open question is whether it can do this with China. One can make a strong case that China too thinks of itself as a "hub" country, with spokes reaching out to neighbors, who are expected to be deferential to China's wishes. Perhaps the most important Asian foreign policy issue facing the United States is to help create a situation in which two such hub states (People's Republic of China, PRC and United States) can co-exist.[57]

This question has mostly focused on China and has emphasized a US effort to give a mixture of inducements and at times resistance to Chinese actions to help it become a "responsible stakeholder" in the international system.[58] The George W. Bush and Obama Administrations have tried further integrating China and India into the existing institutional system with initiatives like US–China Strategic Economic Dialogue, the G-2, the 2005 US–India Nuclear Deal, and rebalancing International Monetary Fund (IMF) voting weights. However, critics of this engagement policy have become more heated in the aftermath of the 2008 global financial crisis. In the last couple of years, China has taken a more assertive stance against the United States or Western international order: at times harassing US naval vessels, taking an oppositional stand at the Copenhagen Climate Summit, and attempting to use its economic weight to force concessions out of other countries.[59] While fears that we are seeing a Chinese overthrow of the US-led international system are perhaps overblown at this time, these tensions underscore the difficulties the United States will continue to have in making space for these rising countries. However, Chinese actions in recent years could actually strengthen the San Francisco System by threatening its neighbors and provoking balancing behavior against China. Some have observed this behavior as these countries reassess their defense budgets and strengthen their alliances or relationships with the United States.[60]

Related to some of the following concerns about US power, it must be noted that American efforts to "make room for Asia" have at times come at the expense of other American interests and conflict with American allies in other regions. This has been particularly evident in plans to reform or rebalance international institutions. Several commentators have remarked that institutions like the UN Security Council and the IMF reflect a 1944–5 balance of power dominated by the United States and its European allies that no longer reflects the realities of the contemporary world. Not surprisingly, European powers resist ideas to include more Asian powers on the Security Council or to give more voting power to Asian countries in the IMF and little progress has been made.[61]

## *Decline versus disengagement?*

Related to the rise of Asia is the question of American decline. The United States still remains one of the three largest economies in the world, along with the EU and China, even though the share of US economic power in the world has continued to shrink since at least the 1970s.[62] It remains the country with the third-largest population in the world in the 2000s, while in contrast Britain ranked seventh in terms of population among the great powers in its period of relative decline (1890–1914).[63] Similarly, the British share of global economic output in 1913 was 8 percent, while the United States in 1998 remained quite high at 22 percent.[64] Also, while Britain attempted to retain "splendid isolation" until grudgingly making alliances with France and Japan in the early 1900s, the United States has always based a significant portion of its power on alliances and co-opting potential rivals.

Moreover, talk of US decline at time obscures more than it reveals. One can make a strong case that rather than conceptualizing this as the "decline of the United States" it could be conceptualized more as the "rise of the rest." The dominant position the United States held in the world economy in the 1940s and 1950s had much to do with the devastation of the economies of Europe and Asia because of World War II. The talk about "the rise of Japan and Germany" in the 1970s and 1980s was more about their recovery of previous positions in the world economy rather than a massive US decline. Fareed Zakaria has made a similar point about the contemporary rise of not only Asia but countries like Brazil rather than a US decline.[65] Moreover, research since the 2008 crisis indicates that since most Asian economies are dependent upon exports to the United States and EU, and not on intra-regional consumption, Asia will have difficulties "continuing its rise" without an economically prosperous West.[66] Also, as several observers have commented on recently, it is premature to talk of a world now dominated by China and India. In many cases, Chinese economic influence and military modernization and Indian military or institutional capabilities have been somewhat oversold and these two states still have many constraints on their abilities to rise to superpower status and influence.[67]

Though talk of US decline is perhaps premature, one could be legitimately concerned about US disengagement or retrenchment. As Frank Klingberg presciently observed 60 years ago, the United States tends to oscillate between periods of activism abroad and periods of retrenchment.[68] Given the combined constraints of the 2008 economic crisis and long, unpopular and costly wars in both Iraq and Afghanistan, there are concerns about a US retreat as the United States extricates itself from these conflicts.[69] One fear has been the inadvertent effects of the United States readjusting its network of security arrangements. In the 1970s, as the United States withdrew from Southeast Asia, a couple of major changes modified US involvement in the Asia-Pacific. First, the Nixon Administration opened relations with the PRC and the Carter Administration continued American realignment with the ending of the Mutual Defense Pact with Taiwan and shifting recognition to the PRC. Second, as part of the Nixon Doctrine and also followed by the Carter Administration, the United States wanted to rebalance its alliances with its Asian allies asking them to contribute more to their own security. South Korea and Taiwan started their own nuclear weapons programs in response to these actions and fears of US abandonment of the region. It was only with some difficulty that the United States managed to halt these programs.[70]

If in the next couple of years, the United States continues its withdrawal from Iraq and particular Afghanistan, what will the regional effects be? Pakistani officials have long worried about the United States being an unreliable ally. Even with an alliance dating back to 1954, the United States suspended military aid during the 1965 war with India, and tensions and suspicions in the 1970s were only partially addressed when the United States needed Pakistan again for fighting the Soviets in Afghanistan.[71] In the 1990s, once the Soviets left, the United States again dropped Pakistan and started putting economic pressure on it because of its nuclear weapons program.[72] The need to invade Afghanistan resuscitated the alliance, but suspicions about the United States (exacerbated by drone attacks and other raids on Pakistani soil) have only increased. Many in the region wonder what will happen after the United States disengages: Increased Pakistani and Indian competition to stabilize Afghanistan? An expansion of Chinese influence? Increased ties between China and Pakistan (as happened when the United States largely abandoned Pakistan following the Soviet retreat from Afghanistan in 1989)? How credible will US efforts to improve relations with India be if the United States leaves India and Pakistan "holding the bag" in Afghanistan? These questions cause uneasiness in the region.[73]

## Geography and the tyranny of choice

When discussing US influence in Asia, one must remember that the United States is a global power, not just an Asia-Pacific one. Since the start of the twentieth century, the United States has had to split its attention and its resources to pursue opportunities and to deal with threats in multiple regions. However, even for a superpower like the United States, it is impossible to give equal attention to all the regions of significant interest globally, let alone all the subregions of Asia. A recurrent accusation is that the United States is too fixated on one or two crises in the short term and lets the other critical issues in other areas drift since they seemed less immediate.[74] At times US policies in one region in response to a particular set of circumstances can work at cross purposes to US interests in another region or subregion. Originally this was seen as a division between the "Atlanticists" who called for attending to the military balance in Europe or strengthening or expanding NATO, and in contrast the "Asia-Firsters" who stressed shoring up allies against insurgents or major powers in Asia (in particular China) and the dynamic economic growth of the region.[75]

Militarily this dilemma drove war plans in the interwar years. Naval interpretations of Mahanian theory at the time argued that it was folly to divide the fleet, so it was a question of having a battle fleet in one sea and a cruiser fleet in the other. Until the end of World War I, the US fleet of battleships remained in the Atlantic to deal with a potential German naval threat.[76] Then it shifted battle fleet/force to the Pacific and the Atlantic was left with a smaller cruiser force.[77] It was only in 1940, on the eve of war, that the United States was able to start building a two-ocean navy for fighting war simultaneously in the Atlantic and the Pacific.[78] There was also a paradox in the desire to keep the fleet from being tied to the defense of exposed bases in the Pacific, and the necessity of forward naval bases in order to successfully gain command of the sea over Japan.[79] These difficulties were never adequately solved by various renditions of the Orange and then Rainbow war plans, and were still unanswered when the Japanese struck Pearl Harbor in December 1941.[80]

However, this limited choice between historical/cultural ties to Europe versus economic trade with a rising Asia is too simplistic for today's reality. Instead it has focused on a debate over whether dealing with China and

North Korea in Asia or instability in the Middle East/South Asia is more vital for US strategic interests. This was seen in the compromise made in the 1997 Quadrennial Defense Review that called for US forces to be able to fight two simultaneous major theater wars, generally thought to be a war in the Middle East and also a conflict in Asia.[81] However, President Obama's Secretary of Defense Robert Gates publicly questioned the commitment of the United States to maintain this two-region capability and the 2010 QDR (Quadrennial Defense Review) is seen as moving away from this concept.[82] In contrast, many Asia watchers have worried that the United States in the past ten years has become too committed to the Middle East and is letting China push the United States out of Asia.[83] This problem will only become more acute in the future as the possibility of cuts in the defense budget seems more likely and the military becomes smaller.[84]

The US decision to invade Iraq in 2003 while reconstructing Afghanistan illustrates the consequences of having to choose. Many observers have noted that the war in Iraq drained significant military and reconstruction resources away from Afghanistan in the crucial period right after the fall of the Taliban government (2002–3). The absence of these resources seems to have played a direct cause in the difficulty the United States has had with state building and fighting the Taliban there for the past several years.[85]

However, this is actually more complicated that even a simple choice between Middle East and Asia, it is also a question of where in Asia should the United States concentrate.[86] From the start of the twentieth century through the mid-1950s, Northeast Asia in terms of China, Japan, the two Koreas and Taiwan were the most important for US strategic considerations. Then in the mid–late 1950s through the 1970s, this shifted to Southeast Asia and propping up allied regimes. In the 1990s, the synergistic effect of the rise of India, the linkage between Pakistan and militant/terrorist groups, and the overt nuclearization of India and Pakistan in 1998 has finally caused the United States to take South Asia and the Indian Ocean seriously as well.[87] This increasing focus on South and Central Asia has caused the United States to reduce its military forces deployed in South Korea and to give Seoul the lead role in dealing with any potential conflict with North Korea. Moreover, US forces remaining in South Korea have moved their focus from territorial defense of Korea to power projection for a wider variety of contingencies.[88]

The difficulty for the United States is determining which types of issues and threats are the most important for US interests. Essentially the threats that one sees as most pressing or dangerous leads one to see certain subregions as more important than others. For example, if the major American concerns in Asia are the rise of China and instability on the Korean Peninsula, then attention needs to be paid to Northeast Asia and conventional forces. However, if terrorism is the driving goal for US policy, then the

United States would seemingly need to concentrate on South and Southeast Asia and work with local governments to eliminate terrorist groups and shore up the stability of weak states like Pakistan, the Philippines, Thailand and Indonesia.

Moreover, policy that makes sense in one region or context can work at cross purposes in another.[89] For example, US security and economic policies towards Japan in the 1980s and 1990s at times seemed to run in opposite directions: on the one hand, strengthening the security alliance with Japan, and on the other hand, enacting trade policies that indicated Japan was the principal economic threat to the United States.[90] These types of mixed messages have only continued in the past ten years. The efforts by the United States to improve relations with India – both for commercial and strategic reasons – have been suspected of running counter to US efforts to deal with nuclear proliferation, as many critics of the 2005 Indo-US Nuclear Deal have pointed out.[91] It must be noted that even close allies like South Korea – who has an acute problem dealing with waste from its own nuclear reactors – have not been allowed terms similar to those for India and have been vocal in calling attention to this double standard.[92]

US involvement with Pakistan has been even more complicated. When the United States has needed Pakistan for access to Afghanistan both in 1979–89, and again from 2001 to the present, ostensibly this has worked against US counter-proliferation policy by accepting or condoning the Pakistani nuclear weapons program. Private groups associated with this program, like the AQ Khan network, have assisted nuclear weapons programs in places like North Korea, Myanmar, Iran and Libya.[93] In short, one could argue that compromises the United States made to fight in Afghanistan have worked against US counter-proliferation goals in other parts of Asia. Moreover, in attempting to have good relations with both India and Pakistan, the United States was forced to take positions that tended to frustrate both sides, such as the US stance during the 2001–2 Crisis or selling advanced weaponry like F-16 fighters to Pakistan (that are more useful in a war with India than fighting the Taliban).[94]

## *Sea denial*

Related to this issue of geographic overstretch are concerns about sea denial. While it is true that US military spending dwarfs that of other states, and one would have to combine the next 16 or 18 major powers' defense budgets to match those of the United States, many worry about the continued ability of the United States to project power in all the locations and circumstances it desires.[95]

Generally this focuses on "the ability to prevent an enemy from using the sea to do them harm."[96] So rather than try to match the United States symmetrically and contest US sea control, other states would use weapons and tactics to keep the United States from controlling the sea at least in key areas like off their coasts, in the littorals and perhaps at crucial choke points like narrow straits using weapon systems like submarines, mines and anti-ship missiles.[97] The United States has given special attention to the rise in Chinese People's Liberation Army Navy (PLAN) capabilities that seem aimed at sea denial or "anti-access" against the United States Navy.[98] Naturally this seems to focus on denying the United States sea control in the vicinity of the Taiwan Strait.[99] In addition to the conventional fears of submarines and anti-ship missiles, there are American concerns of the growth in Chinese cyberwarfare and anti-satellite technology that would be used in any Taiwan scenarios.[100] Also there are fears about the rise in PLAN submarine capabilities to conduct anti-shipping operations against Taiwan and other island states, perhaps even Japan.[101] Despite some debate about how effective Chinese military modernization has been, it is perhaps the major conventional security concern in the Asia-Pacific for US planners.[102]

In addition to concerns about Chinese military modernization, there are concerns about other potential asymmetric challenges to US power given the degree of weapons proliferation to other powers and even non-state actors.[103] These threats include the ability of Iranian forces to close the straits of Hormuz, of pirate or even terrorists attacks to impede traffic through the Malacca Straits, or of terrorist attacks against US vessels like the USS *Cole* incident.[104] However, although this is a persistent fear among American naval planners, it must be remembered that this is ultimately a defensive strategy on the part of a weaker power, instead of a strategy that will contest US sea control over the region.

### *Maintaining alliances: democratization and threat perception*

A recurring issue for the United States is how the domestic politics of allies affects US alliances and goals and how threat perceptions can differ between the United States and its regional allies. For most of the Cold War, the United States worked with non-democratic regimes in Asia. Since the 1980s, many of these countries have transitioned to democracies. At times this shift has in the short term strained alliance relations with the United States, but one could make a strong case that alliances between democracies are stronger in the long term and better at renewing themselves.[105] Another issue that is a challenge for the United States is to manage the differences in perceptions among these allies.

Regarding the first point, traditionally the United States worked with authoritarian leaders and/or the military/security forces of Asian countries.[106] Japan and at times the Philippines were the exceptions to this, but even there the United States enjoyed cozy relations with the ruling Liberal-Democratic Party in Japan (which dominated government until 1994 for a short period and then again until 2009) and President Marcos of the Philippines. The necessities of dealing with the communist threat and the uncertainties of opposition parties (that were thought to be either communist sympathizers or anti-US) made these relationships attractive for generations of American leaders. Even with more stable allies, there have been lingering resentments about US encroachments on allied sovereignty and complicity with military and authoritarian regimes. In particular, US military ties with the military in Indonesia, Thailand and Pakistan have proved to be a mixed blessing, in particular when those militaries are involved in human rights abuses, coups, or sponsoring violent militants.[107]

US alliances with states like South Korea, Pakistan, the Philippines, Japan, Taiwan and even New Zealand have been strained by a wide variety of domestic forces including: democratization, civil–military relations and domestic politics.[108] In recent democratizing states – like South Korea, the Philippines and Taiwan – there remained a connection in many people's minds between the United States and old oppressive regimes because of American support for the military and security forces. Moreover, there were also the usual tensions and frictions that resulted from having large US bases in the Philippines, Japan and South Korea.[109]

For example, many Koreans partially blame the US military forces in Korea for allowing the Korean government and military to take brutal actions like the Gwangju massacre.[110] The election of politicians like Kim Dae-jung and Roh Moo Hun in South Korea in the late 1990s and early 2000s made the United States worry that South Korean initiatives like the Sunshine Policy would work at cross-purposes with US efforts to put pressure on Pyongyang.[111] Similar, but even more dangerous has been the rise in anti-Americanism in Pakistan due to the perceived American support of the Pakistani military and violations of Pakistani sovereignty, in particular drone strikes and cross border raids.[112]

Although Taiwan is no longer a formal US ally, its democratization complicated cross-strait relations and US efforts to engage China. In particular, during the late 1990s and early 2000s when Taiwan was governed by presidents who had "pro-independence" tendencies – like Lee Teng'hui and Chen Shui-bien – many commentators worried about a "Taiwan problem" rather than a "China problem," that Taiwanese domestic politics would cause Taiwan to take risky actions that would initiate another Straits Crisis.[113]

Even in established democracies there have been tensions especially about perceived violations of sovereignty. At times there were protests about US intelligence facilities in Australia.[114] Similarly, domestic politics that focused on anti-nuclear sentiments were one of the main reasons for the unraveling of the US–New Zealand part of the Australia, New Zealand, United States Security Treaty (ANZUS) in the 1980s.[115] Similarly, concerns in the Philippines about sovereignty, nationalist sentiment, influenced by the history of US backing of rulers like Marcos, led to the end of American use of Clark Air and Subic Naval bases in 1991.[116] Many pundits worried about a crisis in the US–Japan alliance with clumsy efforts of the Hatoyamo governments in 2008–9 to close the US base in Okinawa in part because of continued frictions between local residents and US forces there.[117]

This is not to say that domestic politics and democracy will be the end of the San Francisco System. In fact, one can make the opposite argument. Alliances of democracies tend to be stronger than those of non-democracies, or one democracy with non-democracies. This allows members "to act in concert *despite* disagreements among its members."[118] Democracy allows the alliance to endure and repair itself after the crisis because the leaders or policies that caused the tensions are replaced with others. For example, the elections of Lee Myung-bak in South Korea and Ma Ying Jeou in Taiwan, respectively, served to improve relations with the United States, and in the case of President Ma also relaxed tensions across the strait. Similarly, the replacement of Hatoyama as prime minister helped end the US–Japan "alliance crisis of 2009–10." US alliances with countries like Japan, South Korea and the Philippines has survived multiple successions of governments and arguably come out stronger as something supported not only by an authoritarian leader, or a dominate political party, but something supported by the majority of the mainstream political spectrum.

Beyond domestic politics, another area of concern in managing alliances has been the divergence of perceptions between the United States and its allies. This has surfaced in two particular areas: (*a*) allies having different threat perceptions of external powers and (*b*) two or more US allies or partners having security rivalries or strained relations with each other. For an example that illustrates both fears, the United States and South Korea's threat perceptions in relation to China, North Korea and Japan have diverged rather publically.[119] A similar case could also be made between the United States and Pakistan also concerning China and India, where the United States wants to balance its relationship between both Pakistan and India, while Pakistan sees China as its closest ally and India as an existential threat.[120]

Second, the United States often engages states in alliances or partnerships that are each other's security rivals, or at least have strained relations because of historical legacies. The United States was forced to play a delicate balancing act by its efforts to both maintain its alliance with Pakistan and improve relations with India.[121] Similarly, though the United States has effective security cooperation with both Japan and South Korea, getting these two allies to work closer together has proven quite difficult.[122]

## Conclusion

The greatest strength of American sea power and influence in the Asia-Pacific is that it has been multidimensional, combining naval, commercial, institutional and informational/cultural elements, from almost its very beginnings. This stands in contrast with other powers in the region that have concentrated only on naval power (imperial Japan and the Soviet Pacific Fleet) and proved to have very short periods of influence in the region. Moreover, the United States has pursued its sea power in conjunction with many allies and partners, which made them invest in a US-dominated system and see that supporting the system is more beneficial than challenging it.

American sea power developed originally from commercial interests, but quickly became supplemented by both cultural and naval aspects. It has also continually stressed building up a network of alliances and partnerships in the region to facilitate stability and pursue its interests. While originally the rise in the US projection of power was more an offshoot of internal economic growth in the nineteenth century, since the twentieth century US economic and military power is largely dependent on American maritime control or at least influence in key regions like the Asia-Pacific. American democracy – and now the mostly democratic nature of its alliance network – has allowed it to refresh itself and help its alliance system and security policies adapt over time to deal with new issues and threats.

Some of the main US problems have resulted from the fact that the United States is a global power and not only an Asia-Pacific one. At various times in the past and present, the United States has faced difficult decisions on where it has to concentrate: in the Asia-Pacific, in Europe, or in the Middle East? Policies and choices in one region of Asia can have negative repercussions on others. The societies and perceptions of many US allies in Asia are changing and this will change the US relationship with those states. At times these differences and domestic politics can makes relations quite strained. Last, given the sheer size and varieties of issues in the Asia-Pacific, the United States has had difficulty in managing issues that can range from instability and terrorism in Pakistan to piracy and pandemic diseases in Southeast Asia to North Korean nuclear and missiles tests.

## Notes

1 For a recent critical review see David Bell, "Political Columnists Think America is in Decline, Big Surprise," *New Republic*, October 7, 2010.
2 Geoffrey Till, *Seapower: A Guide for the Twenty First-Century*, second edition (London: Routledge, 2009), pp. 20–32, 6–23.
3 For the classic argument on "hegemonic stability theory" see Robert Keohane, *After Hegemony: Cooperation and Discord in the World Political Economy* (Princeton: Princeton University Press, 1984), pp. 31–41. For an optimistic view of Washington's ability to continue this system in future in Asia, see William Tow and Amitav Acharya, "Obstinate or Obsolete? The US Alliance Structure in the Asia-Pacific," *International Relations Working Paper* 2007 (4) Australian National University.

4 Most recently the dispute between China and Japan over the Diaoyutai/Senkaku islands has attracted considerable attention, see "Getting Their Goat: Trouble over some Caprine Islands," *The Economist*, September 16, 2010, Tania Branigan and Justin McCurry, "Japan Release Chinese Fishing Boat Captain," *Guardian*, September 24, 2010; and "Japan, US Affirm Cooperation on Disputed Senkahu Islands," *Japan Times*, October 12, 2010. However, there are a wide range of both maritime boundary and border disputes between most dyads in the Asia-Pacific, Japan–Korea (Liancourt Rocks), North and South Korea (Northern Limit Line), China and many ASEAN (Association of Southeast Asian Nations) members in the South China Sea/Spratlys, China and Vietnam (Paracels), China and India (border, in particular Aksai Chin and Arunachal Pradesh), and many others.
5 Thomas Christensen, "China, The US–Japan Alliance, and the Security Dilemma," in John Ikenberry and Michael Mastanduno (eds.) *International Relations Theory and the Asia-Pacific* (New York: Columbia University Press, 2003), pp. 26–7, 31–5; and Mastanduno, "Preserving the Unipolar Moment: Realist Theories and US Grand Strategy after the Cold War," *International Security*, 21 (4) Spring 1997: 60–73. More generally, see Richard Betts, "Wealth, Power and Instability: East Asia and the United States after the Cold War," *International Security* 18 (3) 1993–4: 34–77; Robert Art, "Geopolitics Updated: The Strategy of Selective Engagement," *International Security*, 23 (3) Winter 1998–9: 79–113; and Avery Goldstein, "Balance-of-Power Politics: Consequences for Asian Security Order," in Muthiah Alagappa (ed.) *Asian Security Order: Instrumental and Normative Features* (Stanford: Stanford University Press, 2003), pp. 171–209.
6 A classic example is how the dispatch of two carrier groups off Taiwan brought the 1995–6 Taiwan Straits Crisis to a quick halt, see Wallace Thies and Patrick C. Bratton, "When Governments Collide in the Taiwan Strait," *Journal of Strategic Studies*, 27 (4) December 2004: 556–84.
7 Bruce Vaughn, "US Strategic and Defense Relationships in the Asia-Pacific Region," *CRS Report*, January 22, 2007: 12–14. Online, available at: www.fas.org/sgp/crs/row/RL33821.pdf.
8 Although the actual share of the regional economy has decreased.
9 All trade information from the US International Trade Commission, *US Trade by Geographic Regions*, online, available at: www.dataweb.usitc/gov/scripts/Regions.asp.
10 For example, the *Times Higher Education* World University Ranking, online, available at: www.timeshighereducation.co.uk/world-university-rankings/2010–2011/top-200.html; the *US News and World Report* ranking, online, available at: www.usnews.com/articles/education/worlds-best-universities/2010/09/21/worlds-best-universities-top-400-.html; the Chinese Academic Ranking of World Universities, online, available at: www.arwu.org/ARWU2010.jsp, and QS, online, available at: www.topuniversities.com/university-rankings/world-university-rankings/home.
11 Karin Fischer, "Number of Foreign Students in US Hits New High Last Year," *Chronicle of Higher Education*, November 16, 2009, online, available at: http://chronicle.com/article/Number-of-Foreign-Students-in/49142/. India and China topped the list as the two countries with the most students with about 100,000 students each, South Korea came in third with about 75,000, and Japan fifth with 30,000. These four countries accounted for almost half of the total of 670,000 international students. Online, available at: http://chronicle.com/article/Top-Countries-of-Origin-of-/49158/.
12 Jurgen Ruland, "The Contribution of Track Two Dialogue towards Crisis Prevention," *ASIEN*, 85, October 2002: 84–96.

13 For the International Visitors Program, see US Department of State website, online, available at: http://exchanges.state.gov/ivlp/ivlp.html for the East–West Center journalism exchange program see their website, online, available at: www.eastwestcenter.org/journalists.
14 US Department of State, "Proliferation Security Initiative," Bureau of International Security and Nonproliferation, online, available at: www.state.gov/t/isn/c10390.htm; and Eben Kaplan, "The Proliferation Security Initiative," *Council on Foreign Relations Backgrounder*, October 19, 2006, online, available at: www.cfr.org/publication/11057/proliferation_security_initiative.html.
15 Till, *Seapower*, 36–7.
16 Samuel Huntington, *The Common Defense: Strategic Programs in National Politics* (New York: Columbia University Press, 1961), pp. 446–7.
17 Wallace Thies, *Why NATO Endures* (New York: Cambridge, 2009), 297.
18 Rightly or wrongly the George W. Bush Administration was unpopular with the population in many allied nations. The election of Barak Obama in 2008 offered a perceived chance for the United States and its allies "to reset" relations. For example, Pew Research Center, "Confidence in Obama Lifts US Image around the World," July 23, 2009, online, available at: http://pewglobal.org/2009/07/23/confidence-in-obama-lifts-us-image-around-the-world/; and "World Warming to US Under Obama, BBC Poll Suggests," *BBC*, April 19, 2010, online, available at: http://news.bbc.co.uk/2/hi/in_depth/8626041.stm.
19 For more on this concept, see Till, *Seapower*, 33–7 and chapter 11, "Maintaining Good Order at Sea," 286–321.
20 Kim Young-Sik, "The Ginseng 'Trade War'," *Association for Asian Research*, July 9, 2003, online, available at: www.asianresearch.org/articles/1438.html.
21 The Pacific and East India naval squadrons were set up in the 1830s, but army interest in the Pacific before the Spanish–American War was almost negligible. See Brian Linn, *Guardians of Empire: The US Army and the Pacific, 1902–1940* (Chapel Hill: University of Chapel Hill Press, 1997), pp. 5–8.
22 Including the Sumatran Expeditions (1830s), the Second Opium War (1856–60), the Formosan Expeditions (1861 and 1874), Korea (1881) and the China Relief Expedition against the Boxers (1900). However, there were exceptions to the limited American naval presence in the Pacific, like during the Mexican War when a large portion of the United States Navy was sent to the Pacific to supplement the Pacific Squadron in the California campaign.
23 Siam (Treaty of Amity and Commerce, 1833); China (Treaty of Wanghia, 1844), Japan (Convention of Kanagawa 1854, then Harris Treaty of 1858); and Korea (Chemulpo Treaty of 1882). However, it must be noted that in the cases of Japan and Korea, these were not necessarily purely commercial ventures and were not always easy either. Japan under the Tokugawa Shogunate and Korea under the Joseon dynasty were strongly isolationist and had resisted Western encroachments. Commodore Perry's skilful use of gunboat diplomacy in 1853 and 1854 succeeded where many other attempts, in particular by the Russian Empire, had failed. In contrast the initial effort to "open" Korea failed with destruction of the USS *General Sherman* in 1866. It would be almost two decades before the United States would have a treaty with the Korean government. See also, James Gould, "American Imperialism in Southeast Asia before 1898," *Journal of Southeast Asian Studies*, 3 (2) 1972: 306–14.
24 Some of the more important legacies of this today are the large Christian populations in South Korea and the Philippines and also the large number of American style, Christian universities were founded in places like Japan and South Korea; and also many of the first generation of American Asia experts were from missionary families and grew up in Asia.

25 The example par excellence of this activity was Charles Denby, the American Minister to China in the 1880s; see Charles Campbell, "American Business Interests and the Open Door in China," *Far Eastern Quarterly*, 1 (1) November 1941: 43–58. The United States was not unique in this respect, this was similar to what Great Britain and France did, essentially using the protection of Christians and missionaries to expand commercial and military interests.
26 Paul Kennedy, *The Rise and Fall of the Great Powers*, 199–202, 242–9; David Singer and Melvin Small, "The Composition and Status of the International System: 1815–1940," *World Politics*, 18 (2) January 1966: 260–3; and Mearsheimer, *The Tragedy of Great Power Politics*, 220.
27 In 1913, 8 percent of GNP from foreign trade in comparison to 26 percent for United Kingdom; see Kennedy, *The Rise and Fall of the Great Powers*, 244.
28 For example, Roosevelt's "corollary" to the Monroe Doctrine, his sailing of the Great White Fleet around the world, and his helping to broker the peace agreement for the Russo-Japanese War in Portsmouth, New Hampshire. For Wilson, there is his expedition into Mexico, entry in World War I and his Fourteen Points during the Versailles Peace Talks, see Henry Kissinger's chapter "The Hinge: Theodore Roosevelt or Woodrow Wilson," in *Diplomacy* (New York: Simon and Schuster, 1994), pp. 29–55.
29 George Baer, *One Hundred Years of Sea Power: The US Navy 1890–1990* (Stanford: Stanford University Press, 1994), pp. 9–15.
30 Baer, *One Hundred Years of Sea Power*, 25–6.
31 This continued into the interwar years with Yuantze Patrol along China's river systems. Kennedy, *The Rise and Fall of the Great Powers*, 246–7.
32 See Brian Linn, *Guardians of Empire*, in particular chapters 4 and 6.
33 Baer, *One Hundred Years of Sea Power*, 42–6; and Brian Linn, *Guardians of Empire*, 84–9.
34 Baer, *One Hundred Years of Sea Power*, 127–8; and 148–53.
35 Brian Linn, *Guardians of Empire*, xii.
36 David Evans and Mark Peattie, *Kaigun: Strategy, Tactics, and Technology in the Imperial Japanese Navy, 1887–1941* (Annapolis: Naval Institute Press, 1997), pp. 492–503.
37 Evans and Peattie, *Kaigun*, 110.
38 John Lewis Gaddis, *We Now Know*, 55–62. Further complicating this were the difficulties American European allies were having in re-establishing their rule over Asian colonies after losing them to the Japanese. The United States was initially caught between supporting independence movements and aiding their European allies who were needed for dealing with the Soviet Union in Europe.
39 In particular in the early 1950s in response to the Korean War and the massive Truman conventional forces build-up, in the 1960s because of the Vietnam War, and again in the 1980s as the navy took greater notice of the Soviet Pacific Fleet as part of the "maritime strategy." Baer, *One Hundred Years of Sea Power*, 320–31, 384–93; and 423–8.
40 Militant ideologies like communism were seen to spread during periods of political and economic chaos, like during the 1930s. The combination of economic assistance, trade and a security guarantee were as critical to allow its allies the chance to rebuild their economies and not damage their economies with large military expenditures. The very existence of the alliance was seen to be more important than any actual deployment of military forces to the allied country. See Thies, *Why NATO Endures*, 91–9.
41 Kent E. Calder, "Securing Security Through Prosperity: The San Francisco System in Comparative Perspective," *Pacific Review*, 17 (1) 2004: 135–57, in particular 138–9; and Victor Cha, "Power Play," 161.

42 There were attempts at creating multilateral organizations during the "pactomania" of the Eisenhower Administration in the 1950s: the ANZUS alliance with Australia and New Zealand (1952), South East Asian Treaty Organization (SEATO, 1954), and Central Treaty Organization (CENTO, 1955). However, these multilateral alliances (with the exception of ANZUS) never proved completely satisfactory, and were dissolved in the 1970s in the aftermath of the Vietnam War. Though it only included three members, In the 1980s the US–New Zealand part of ANZUS was suspended following a row over port calls by US vessels with nuclear weapons. While the US–Australia and Australia–New Zealand parts of the alliance still function well, the re-establishing of close cooperation between the United States and New Zealand militaries has been slow. See Wallace Thies and James Harris, "An Alliance Unravels: The United States and ANZUS," *Naval War College Review*, 46 (Summer 1993): 98–126.

43 Calder, "Securing Security through Prosperity," 227; T. J. Pempel, "The Developmental Regime in a Changing World Economy," in Meredith Woo-Cummings (ed.) *The Developmental State* (Ithaca: Cornell University Press, 1999), pp. 153–6 and 173–8; and Drezner, "Bad Debts," 11–12.

44 Kent E. Calder, "Securing Security Through Prosperity: The San Francisco System in Comparative Perspective," *Pacific Review*, 17 (1) 2004: 143–5.

45 Cha, "Powerplay," 163–4.

46 For the concepts, see Thomas Christensen and Jack Snyder, "Chain Gangs and Passed Bucks: Predicting Alliance Patterns in Multipolarity," *International Organization*, 44 (2) Spring 1990: 137–68. For US fears in Europe, see Marc Trantenberg, *A Constructed Peace*, 84–91; Thies, *Friendly Rivals: Bargaining and Burden-Shifting in NATO* (Armonk: ME Sharpe, 2003), 30–64, 250–8 and Thies, *Why NATO Endures*, 99–119.

47 For an excellent discussion of the dilemmas of securitization vs. reform see Douglas McDonald, *Adventures in Chaos: American Intervention for Reform in the Third World* (Cambridge: Harvard University Press, 1992).

48 For Singapore this has included the Memorandum of Understanding, US access to the Changhi Naval Base, and later a Strategic Framework Agreement (2005); for India it is under the New Framework for the US–India Defense Relationship (2005).

49 Robert McMahon, *The Cold War on the Periphery: The United States, India, and Pakistan* (New York: Columbia, 1994), pp. 337–47.

50 These initiatives include the North American Free Trade Association (NAFTA), the Asia-Pacific Economic Cooperation Forum (APEC), the focus on "BEMs" Big, Emerging Markets (China, India, Indonesia, South Korea, Mexico, Brazil, Argentina, Poland, Turkey and South Africa); and Free Trade Agreements with Singapore, Australia and – waiting for ratification – South Korea. See Office of the United States Trade Representative, "Free Trade Agreements," online, available at: www.ustr.gov/trade-agreements/free-trade-agreements. For more on "BEMs" see Jeffrey Garten, "The Big Emerging Markets," *Columbia Journal of World Business*, 31 (2) Summer 1996: 6–31.

51 For an in-depth look on international institutions in Asia, see Nick Bisley, *Building Asia's Security*, Adelphi Paper 408 (London: IISS, 2009).

52 Moisés Naím, "The Five Wars of Globalization," *Foreign Policy* (January/February 2003): 28–36.

53 US PACOM, "Strategy: Partnership, Readiness, Presence," April 2009, 4, online, available at: www.pacom.mil/web/pacom_resources/pdf/pacom%20strategy%2002APR09.pdf.

54 For example, see US Department of Defense, "US Forces Aid Tsunami Relief Efforts in Southeast Asia," online, available at: www.defense.gov/home/features/tsunami/index.html.

55 Tow and Acharya, "Obstinate or Obsolete?," 6–12.
56 Paul Kennedy, *Rise and Fall of the Great Powers*; and Kishore Mahbubani, *The New Asian Hemisphere: The Irresistible Shift of Global Power to the East* (New York: Public Affairs, 2008).
57 My thanks to Wallace Thies on this point.
58 For variety of views see, Gerald Segal, "East Asia and the 'Constrainment' of China," *International Security*, 20 (4) Spring 1996; Alastair Iain Johnston, "Is China a Status Quo Power?" *International Security*, 27 (4) Spring 2003: 5–56; and Zheng Bijian, "China's 'Peaceful Rise' to Great Power Status," *Foreign Affairs* (September/October, 2005): 18–24.
59 For naval harassment, see Peter Ford, "US–Chinese Naval Standoff the Latest in a String of Clashes," *Christian Science Monitor*, March 10, 2009; and Capt. Raul Pedrozo, "Close Encounters at Sea: The USNS *Impeccable* Incident," *Naval War College Review*, 62 (3) Summer 2009: 101–11. For Copenhagen, see Mark Lynas, "How Do I Know China Wrecked the Copenhagen Deal? I Was In the Room," *Guardian*, December 22, 2009. For economic coercion, see Daniel Drezner, "Bad Debts: Assessing China's Financial Influence in Great Power Politics," *International Security*," 34 (2) Fall 2009: 7–49; and Keith Bradsher, "China Said to Widen Its Embargo of Minerals," *New York Times*, October 19, 2010. For a pessimistic look at Chinese learning about the costs and benefits of the use of force see, Thies and Bratton, "When Governments Collide in the Taiwan Strait."
60 For various perspectives, see Evan Medeiros, "The New Security Drama in East Asia: The Responses of US Allies and Security Partners to China's Rise," *Naval War College Review*, 62 (4) Autumn 2009: 37–52; Edward Wong, "China's Disputes in Asia Buttress Influence of US," *New York Times*, September 22, 2010, online, available at: www.nytimes.com/2010/09/23/world/asia/23china.html?_r=2&hp; and Rahul Singh, "ASEAN Invites India, US to Keep China in Check," *Hindustan Times*, September 22, 2010, online, available at: www.hindustantimes.com/ASEAN-invites-India-US-to-keep-China-in-check/H1-Article1-603510.aspx.
61 Dan Drezner, "The New New World Order," *Foreign Affairs* (March/April 2007): 36–46; and Lesley Wroughton, "Analysis: Power Struggle Threatens to Paralyse IMF," *Reuters*, August 26, 2010, online, available at: www.reuters.com/article/idUSTR67P3D320100826.
62 Aaron Friedberg, "The Strategic Implications of Relative Economic Decline," *Political Science Quarterly*, 104 (3) Autumn 1989, 402–3; and Paul Kennedy, *Rise and Fall of the Great Powers*, 432–7.
63 Kennedy, *Rise and Fall of the Great Powers*, 199.
64 Niall Ferguson, *Empire: The Rise and Demise of the British World Order and the Lessons for Global Power* (New York: Basic Books, 2002), p. 314.
65 Fareed Zakaria, *The Post-American World* (New York: W. W. Norton, 2008). About 20 years ago Samuel Huntington made a similar point, "The US – Decline or Renewal," *Foreign Affairs*, 67 (Winter 1988/89): 76–96.
66 See Soyoung Kim, Jong-Wha Lee and Cyn-Young Park, "The Ties that Bind Asia, Europe, and the United States," *Asian Development Bank Economics Working Paper Series*, no. 192 (February 2010), online, available at: www.adb.org/Documents/Working-Papers/2010/Economics-WP192.pdf.
67 For China see Drezner, "Bad Debts," 7–49; and Minzin Pei, "Think Again: Asia's Rise," *Foreign Policy*, June 22, 2009. For India, see Baldev Raj Nayar and T. V. Paul, *India in the World Order: Searching for Major-Power Status* (New York: Cambridge University Press, 2003) in particular chapter 3 "The Constraints on India: International and Domestic," 65–114; and Stephen Cohen and Sunil Dasputa, *Arming Without Aiming: India's Military Modernization* (Washington, DC: Brookings, 2010).

42  P. C. Bratton

68 Many decades ago, Frank Klingberg's research revealed that the United States since its inception has gone through periods of extroversion and introversion in foreign affairs, rotating between periods of extroversion for about 27 years and introversion for about 22 years. If one takes his framework and forecast past its early 1950s publication date, it works remarkably well. Recovering from introversion in the 1920s and 1930s, because of World War II and the height of the Cold War in the 1940s–1960s US foreign policy was marked by activism from about 1940 or 1941until about 1967–8 with the US decision to exit the Vietnam War, then through the 1970s and into the 1980s it was relatively introverted. Then with the end of the Cold War and the successful military actions in Panama and the Gulf, the United States entered into another period of activism that culminated in the costly intervention in Afghanistan and Iraq from about 1990–2007. With the public tired of long wars in both countries and also the pain of the 2008 global financial crisis according to Klingberg the United States should be introverted until about 2030 or so. See Frank Klingberg, "The Historical Alternation of Moods in American Foreign Policy," *World Politics*, 4 (2) January 1952: 239–73.

69 At times domestic politics and fatigue of external activities can cause delays or even reverses, like the difficulties of ratification of the Korea–US Free Trade Agreement (KORUS), Kim Young-jin, "2 US Senators Urge KORUS FTA Ratification before G-20," *Korea Times*, May 11, 2010, online, available at: www.koreatimes.co.kr/www/news/nation/2010/06/116_65722.html.

70 See the chapters by Jonathan Pollack and Mitchell Reis, "South Korea: The Tyranny of Geography and the Vexations of History," 254–92; and Derek Mitchell, "Taiwan's Hsin Chu Program: Deterrence, Abandonment, and Honor," 293–314, in Kurt Campbell, Robert Einhorn and Mitchell Reiss (eds.) *Nuclear Tipping Point: Why States Reconsider Their Nuclear Choices* (Washington, DC: Brookings, 2004). See Daniel Drezner, "The Trouble with Carrots: Transaction Costs, Conflict Expectations, and Economic Inducements," *Security Studies*, 9 (1) 1999: 188–218; and Bruce Cummings, *Korea's Place in the Sun: A Modern History* (New York: W. W. Norton, 2005), pp. 363–6.

71 Dennis Kux, *Disenchanted Allies: The United States and Pakistan, 1947–2000* (Washington, DC: Wilson Center, 2001), pp. 158–68.

72 Kux, *Disenchanted Allies*, 360–6.

73 Shanthie Mariet D'Souza, "Obama's Afghan Strategy: Surge or Retreat?" *IDSA Comment*, December 14, 2009, online, available at: www.idsa.in/idsacomments/ObamasAfghanStrategy_smdsouza_141209.

74 For a typical example of criticisms of Obama "forgetting about Asia," see Joshua Kurlantzick, "How Obama Lost His Asian Friends," *Newsweek*, July 6, 2010, online, available at: www.newsweek.com/2010/07/06/how-obama-lost-his-asian-friends.html.

75 Richard Betts, *Soldiers, Statesmen and Cold War Crises* (New York: Columbia University Press, 1991), pp. 81–4.

76 The Navy had set up a separate Pacific Fleet in 1907, however, it was based on cruisers not capital ships so the Pacific fleet did not get any permanently assigned capital ships until 1919. Baer, *One Hundred Years of Sea Power*, 45–8.

77 Baer, *One Hundred Years of Sea Power*, 90–3.

78 Baer, *One Hundred Years of Sea Power*, 130–5.

79 Linn, *Guardians of Empire*, 89; and Spector, *Eagle Against the Sun*, 19.

80 Baer, *One Hundred Years of Sea Power*, 120–8.

81 US Department of Defense, *Quadrennial Defense Review 1997*, Sections III and IV, online, available at: at www.fas.org/man/docs/qdr/index.html.

82 US Department of Defense, Office of the Assistant Secretary of Defense (Public Affairs), "Press Conference with Secretary Gates and Adm. Mullen," June 18,

2009, online, available at: www.defenselink.mil/transcipt.aspx?transcriptid=4435. See also Erin Fitzgerald and Anthony Cordesman, "The 2010 Quadrennial Defense Review: A+, F or Dead on Arrival," *CSIS Working Paper* (August 27, 2010); and Kathleen Hicks and Samuel Branne, "Force Planning in the 2010 QDR," *Joint Forces Quarterly*, 59 (4) 2010: 136–42.

83 Michael Green has made this point as well, "Asia in the Debate on American Grand Strategy," *Naval War College Review*, 62 (1) Winter 2009: 4. For an example of a Chinese writer elaborating that US preoccupation in the Middle East is beneficial to China, see Li Shuisheng, "US Arrogance Replace by Strategic Contraction: Trends of US Military Strategy As Drawn from the Quadrennial Defense Review Report," Academy of Military Science, February 12, 2010, available on Steven Clemmon's website, *Washington Note*. Online, available at: www.thewasihngtonnote.com/archives/2010/02/if_you_could_se/. See also Joshua Kurlantzick, "How Obama Lost His Asian Friends," *Newsweek*, July 6, 2010, online, available at: www.newsweek.com/2010/07/06/how-obama-lost-his-asian-friends.html.

84 Ronald O'Rourke, "Programs vs. Resources: Some Options for the Navy," *Naval War College Review*, 63 (4) Autumn 2010: 25–37.

85 Seth Jones, *In the Graveyard of Empires: America's War in Afghanistan* (New York: W. W. Norton, 2010), in particular 124–9.

86 In the 1920s and 1930s – the United States could never decide until late in the 1930s – where in the Pacific was the priority for defense? The distant possessions in the West? Or the more defensible possessions in the Eastern Pacific based upon Hawaii? Even if it was decided that the Philippines should be defended, the navy and army disagreed over which areas in the Philippines should be defended and how they should be. Spector, *Eagle Against the Sun: The American War Against Japan* (New York: Vintage Books, 1985), pp. 54–5; Baer, *One Hundred Years of Sea Power*, 92–3, 120–8, 155–6; and Linn, *Guardians of Empire*, 249.

87 Roy Kamphausen, "US national defense strategy and implications for the Asia-Pacific," paper for the 2005 Pacific Symposium, National Defense University, Washington, DC, June 9, 2005; James Holmes and Toshi Yoshihara, "China and the United States in the Indian Ocean: An Emerging Strategic Triangle?" *Naval War College Review*, 61 (3) Summer 2008: 41–60; and Robert Kagan, *Monsoon: The Indian Ocean and the Future of American Power* (New York: Random House, 2010).

88 Jung Park, *Looking Back and Looking Forward*, 16–17.

89 Robert Jervis, "Complexity and the Analysis of Political and Social Life," *Political Science Quarterly*, 112 (Winter 1997–8): 589.

90 Mastanduno, "Preserving the Unipolar Moment," 83–5.

91 George Perkovich, "Faulty Promises: The US–India Nuclear Deal," *Policy Outlook*, Carnegie Endowment for International Peace, September 2005, online, available at: www.carnegieendowment.org/files/po21/perkovich.pdf.

92 Choe Sang-Hun, "US Wary of South Korea's Plan to Reuse Nuclear Fuel," *New York Times*, June 13, 2010, online, available at: www.nytimes.com/2010/07/14/world/asia/14seoul.html?_r=2&ref=world.

93 For more details, see Gordan Corera, *Shopping for Bombs: Nuclear Proliferation, Global Insecurity, and the Rise and Fall of the A. Q. Khan Network* (Carlton North: Scribe, 2006).

94 Patrick C. Bratton, "Signals and Orchestration: India's Use of Compellence during the 2001–02 Crisis," *Strategic Analysis*, 34 (4) July 2010: 603–4.

95 Robert Rubel, "Talking About Sea Control," *Naval War College Review*, 63 (4) Autumn 2010: 38–47.

96 Till, *Seapower*, 153–4.

97 Till, *Seapower*, 206–7 and 238–40.

98 Bernard Cole, "Beijing's Strategy of Sea Denial," Jamestown Foundation, *China Brief*, 6 (23) May 2007, online, available at: www.jamestown.org/single/?no_cache=1&tx_ttnews%5Btt_news%5D=4001; Marshall Hoyler, "China's 'Antiaccess' Ballistic Missiles and US Active Defense," *Naval War College Review*, 63 (4) Autumn 2010: 84–105; and Andrew Erickson and David Yang, "Using Land to Control the Sea? Chinese Analysts Consider the Antiship Ballistic Missile," *Naval War College Review*, 62 (4) Autumn 2009: 53–86. For background on Chinese naval modernization see, Bernard Cole, *The Great Wall at Sea: China's Navy in the Twenty-First Century* (Annapolis: Naval Institute Press, 2010); and David Shambaugh, *Modernizing China's Military: Progress, Problems, and Prospects* (Berkeley: University of California Press, 2004).

99 Ronald O'Rourke, "China Naval Modernization: Implications for US Navy Capabilities – Background and Issues for Congress," *CRS Report* (August 26, 2010): 3–6.

100 Rourke, "Chinese Naval Modernization," 4; Ashley Tellis, China's Military Space Strategy," *Survival*, 49 (3) September 2007: 41–72; and Gumeet Kanwal, "China's Emerging Cyber War Doctrine," *Journal of Defense Studies*, 3 (3) 2009, online, available at: www.idsa.in/system/files/jds_3_3_gkanwal_0.pdf.

101 Michael O'Hanlon, "Why China Cannot Conquer Taiwan," *International Security*, 25 (2) Fall 2000: 51–86; Shambaugh, *Modernizing China's Military*, 320–2; and Ralph Cosa, Brad Glosserman, Michael McDevitt, Nirav Patel, James Przystup and Brad Roberts, "The United States and the Asia-Pacific Region: Security Strategy for the Obama Administration," *CNAS Report* (February 2009) 23, online, available at: www.cnas.org/files/documents/publications/CossaPatel_US_Asia-Pacific_February2009.pdf.

102 The feeling the author gets from his PACFLT students is the fear of a replay of the Russo-Japanese War. Where China plays the role of Japan as the weaker power who concentrates its resources in a key sector to establish dominance over an overstretched United States who fills in for Russia. For a useful counter-example, see Bernard Loo, "Chinese Military Power: Much Less than Meets the Eye," *RSIS Commentaries*, 111 (September 2010), online, available at: www.rsis.edu.sg/publications/Perspective/RSIS1112010.pdf.

103 Maj. General (Ret.) Khalid Abdullah Al Bu-Ainnain, "Proliferation Assessment of Cruise Missiles in the Middle East," *INEGMA Special Report* (3) December 2009, online, available at: www.inegma.com/download/Gen.%20Khalid%20Paper%20Cruise%20Missiles.pdf.

104 Caitlin Talmadge, "Closing Time: Assessing the Iranian Threat to the Strait of Hormuz," *International Security*, 33 (1) Summer 2008: 82–117; and Wayne Ma, "Singapore Terrorist Warning: A Singapore Navy Advisory Says Oil Tankers Could Be Targeted," *Wall Street Journal*, March 4, 2010, online, available at: http://online.wsj.com/article/SB10001424052748704187204575100951022980916.html.

105 Thies, *Why NATO Endures*, 296–302.

106 Syngman Rhee and General Park Chung Hee in South Korea, Generalissimo Chaing Kai-shek in Taiwan, Marshal Sarit in Thailand, General Phoumi Nosovan in Laos, Suharto in Indonesia, Generals Ayub Khan and Zia-ul-Huq in Pakistan, all stand out as prominent examples.

107 For Indonesia, see Abraham Denmark, Rizal Sukma and Christine Parthemore, "Crafting a Strategic Vision: A New Era of US-Indonesia Relations," *CNAS Report* (June 2010); Thailand, Emma Chanlett-Avery, "Political Turmoil in Thailand and US Interests," *CRS Report*, May 26, 2009, online, available at: www.fas.org/sgp/crs/row/R40605.pdf; and Pakistan, Fair and Chalk, *Securing Pakistan* and Husain Haqqani, *Pakistan: Between Mosque and Military* (Washington, DC: USIP, 2005).

108 Calder, "US Foreign Policy in Northeast Asia," 232–3.
109 In particular see the work by Sheila Smith, *Shifting Terrain: The Domestic Politics of the US Military Presence in Asia* (Honolulu: East–West Center, 2006), online, available at: www.eastwestcenter.org/index.php?id=82&pub_ID=1979&class_call=view&mode=view.
110 Cummings, *Korea's Place in the Sun: A Modern History*, 382–91; Kim Hakjoon, "A Brief History of the US–ROK Alliance and Anti-Americanism in South Korea," *Shorenstein APARC Research*, 31 (1) May 2010: 25–37; Victor Cha, "South Korea: Anchored or Adrift?," *Strategic Asia 2003–2004: Fragility and Crisis* (National Bureau of Asian Research: Seattle, 2003), pp. 109–31; and Tow and Acharya, "Obstinate or Obsolete?" 20–1.
111 Kent E. Calder, "Securing Security Through Prosperity,"151–2.
112 Christine Fair and Peter Chalk, *Fortifying Pakistan: The Role of US International Security Assistance* (Washington, DC: USIP, 2005), pp. 71–2; and David Kilcullen and Andrew Exum, "Death from Above, Outrage Down Below," *CNAS Commentary*, May 17, 2009, online, available at: http://cnas.org/node/945.
113 Chas. Freeman, "Preventing War in the Taiwan Strait: Restraining Taiwan – and Beijing," *Foreign Affairs* (July/August 1998): 6–11; and also Yoshihide Soeya, "Democratization in Northeast Asia and Trilateral Cooperation," in Tae-Hyo Kim and Brad Glosserman, *The Future of US–Korea–Japan Relations: Balancing Values and Interests* (Washington, DC: CSIS, 2004), pp. 86–9.
114 In particular the facilities of Nurrunger and Pine Gap, see Des Ball, *A Suitable Piece of Real Estate: American Installations in Australia* (Sydney: Hale & Iremonger, 1980).
115 Wallace Thies and James Harris, "An Alliance Unravels: The United States and ANZUS," 98–126.
116 Sheila Smith, *Shifting Terrain*, 9.
117 Sheila Smith, "Political Tremors in Tokyo," *Council on Foreign Relations First Take*, June 2, 2010, online, available at: www.cfr.org/pulication/22289/political_tremors_in_tokyo.html.
118 Thies, *Why NATO Endures*, 296.
119 Given the deep economic interdependence between South Korea and China that happened since the end of the Cold War, a strong reduction in anti-North Korea fears in the South and continued historical and nationalist tensions between South Korea and Japan, managing relations between these two allies at times while dealing with regional threats is not always easy, see Samuel Kim, *The Two Koreas and the Great Powers* (New York: Cambridge, 2006), in particular the chapter, "China and the Two Koreas," 42–101; Hyeong Jung Park, *Looking Back and Looking Forward: North Korea, Northeast Asia and the ROK–US Alliance* (Washington, DC: Brookings: 2007), online, available at: www.brookings.edu/~/media/Files/rc/papers/2007/12_north_korea_park/12_north_korea_park.pdf; Tae-Hyo Kim, "Limits and Possibilities of ROK–US–Japan Security Cooperation," 4–6, and also Michael McDevitt, "The Current State and Future Prospects for Trilateral Security Cooperation," in Ralph A. Cossa, Tae-Hyo Kim and Brad Glosserman (eds.) *The Future of US–Korea–Japan Relations* (Washington, DC: CSIS).
120 Stephen Cohen, *The Idea of Pakistan* (Brookings: Washington, 2004), pp. 120–4; and Peter Lavoy, "Pakistan's Foreign Relations," in Devin Hagerty (ed.) *South Asia in World Politics* (Lanham: Rowman & Littlefield, 2005), pp. 56–8.
121 Cohen and Dasgupta, *Arming Without Aiming*, 171–6, 180–3.
122 Kim, "Limits and Possibilities of ROK–US–Japan Security Cooperation," 4–13.

# 3 Maritime power and the Asia-Pacific

US naval perspectives

*Kevin R. Johnson*

## Introduction

Global prosperity is contingent on the free flow of ideas, goods and services. The United States has been an advocate for the freedom of the seas and secure sea lines of communication (SLOC) since its foundation. For more than 60 years, the United States along with allies, partners and friends have secured the global commons for the benefit of all. The SLOC in the Asia-Pacific have long been, and for the foreseeable future, will continue to be, of critical strategic importance to the United States. The Asia-Pacific region is vital to the security and stability of a globalized economy, and the economic health of the region is dependent on the free flow of goods and material on the SLOC. Challenges to the security of these SLOC include the transshipment of arms and weapons technology, maritime boundary disputes, transnational criminal activity, and the widespread availability of anti-access technologies and capabilities. To meet these challenges, the United States Navy has embarked on a campaign to promote maritime partnerships within the Asia-Pacific region and around the world.

The United States was built on the fundamental principle of the freedoms and rights of individuals. Over a century ago, Rear Admiral Alfred Thayer Mahan wrote that these freedoms extended beyond the borders of our country, out onto the high seas and common waterways that encircle our world.[1] These ideals were clearly in mind when Congress, under the authority of the new constitution, passed the Naval Act of 1794 that established the foundations of a permanent navy. The need for a navy had surfaced almost a decade before when US merchantmen were harassed while transiting to and from the Mediterranean Sea. Raiding parties, collectively known as the "Barbary pirates," from the North African Berber states of Morocco, Algiers, Tunis and Tripoli, carried out this harassment. This was not a problem when America was part of the British Empire and merchantmen were protected by the Royal Navy, however this protection ceased after the American Revolutionary War and merchantmen flying the American Flag were now easy targets for the corsairs of the Barbary States to seize vessels and hold their cargo and crew as a means to compel the US government to pay an annual tribute. The US government did pay this tribute for several years; at times the amount of tribute paid each year amounted to almost 20 percent of the United States' entire annual revenue.[2] This harassment wasn't limited to so called "lawless" regimes; during the French Revolution, the Royal Navy interfered with US merchantmen conducting trade with France while at the same time the French interfered in trade between America and Great Britain. These events ultimately compelled the US Congress to approve the Naval Act and thus the United States Navy was born out of the need to use sea power to protect maritime commerce.

This foundation of the United States Navy on establishing and maintaining freedom of navigation and commerce as well as asserting the rights of the United States as a sovereign nation remain basic strategic tenets that shape the United States Navy's activities not only in the Asia-Pacific region, but also around the globe. This policy was paramount in some of the initial forays by the United States Navy into the Pacific when, in 1820, Captain John Henley of the USS *Congress* was directed to proceed to Canton, China "on important service for the protection of commerce of the United States in the Indian and China Seas,"[3] as well as Commodore Matthew Perry's efforts to open Japan to maritime commerce.

This chapter provides the perspective of the United States Navy on its role in exercising maritime power to assure the security of the maritime domain in the Asia-Pacific region.

## US strategic view in assuring freedom of the seas

For the United States, freedom of the seas and secure SLOC remain basic strategic interests that shape our activities around the globe. This has been in our national character since we inherited the concept from the British when, under Oliver Cromwell, the British Commonwealth government enacted the Convoy Act of 1650 to establish a naval requirement for the protection of shipping.[4] John Adams, the second president of the United States, expressed this concept in a letter to Richard Rush, "Neither nature nor art has partitioned the sea into empires. The ocean and its treasures are the common property of all men."[5] Woodrow Wilson re-iterated the United States' fundamental position on freedom of navigation in his "Fourteen Points" speech delivered to Congress on January 8, 1918 in which his second point stated: "Absolute freedom of navigation upon the seas, outside territorial waters, alike in peace and in war, except as the seas may be closed in whole or in part by international action for the enforcement of international covenants."[6] Our history is full of examples where we have sacrificed for those freedoms in order to ensure maritime security for the benefit of all nations.[7] To operationalize the concept, the United States established the Freedom of Navigation program in 1979 as a means to challenge excessive maritime claims. This program, administered jointly by the Department of State and Department of Defense and executed by the United States Navy, challenges claims made by coastal states that are inconsistent with international law, as reflected in the United Nations Convention on Law of the Sea, which, if unchallenged, would impose restrictions on the freedom of navigation of ships and aircraft of the United States as well as other nations.[8]

Today, off the Horn of Africa, the United States Navy is working with a multinational task force, Combined Task Force (CTF) 150/151, to combat piracy off Somalia and the Gulf of Aden. This is an area of intense interest for the international community as this area is a strategic link between the Indian Ocean and the Mediterranean Sea. Some 3.3 million barrels of oil pass through this region each day, an amount that comprises 7 percent of all oil moved at sea by tankers.[9] Nowhere are competing maritime territorial claims and their potential impact on freedom of navigation more pronounced than in the South China Sea. The South China Sea is the second most used sea-lane in the world, with 50 percent of total annual merchant fleet tonnage passing through the Strait of Malacca, the Sunda Strait and the Lombok Strait.[10] Several countries have competing and overlapping claims with the People's Republic of China (PRC) claiming almost the entire body as their own.[11] Though the PRC has stated that they will respect the freedom of passage of ships and aircraft in accordance with the demands of international law, this offers small comfort and is somewhat a "Sword of Damocles" hanging over those nations that border the South China Sea as well as those countries that depend on the free flow of commerce that transit its sea lanes. Reiterating that freedom of navigation is a fundamental US policy, Secretary of State Clinton, at the Association of Southeast Asian Nations (ASEAN) Regional Forum in Vietnam, declared that a peaceful resolution of territorial disputes over the South China Sea is in the "national interest" of the United States. She also lobbied for a multilateral solution to the question.[12]

The right of access and freedom of the seas will continue to be of national interest to the United States and is reflected in several strategic documents. The development of a formal naval strategy for the United States Navy began with Rear Admiral Mahan. His premise that control of the sea provided the means to control trade and resources, not only in time of war to ensure dominance over an opponent, but also during the peace where command of the sea was necessary to dominate maritime trade which in turn was the foundation for building and maintaining national power. His strategic point of view came at a time in American history when the United States had completed its "manifest destiny" and began to look well beyond its borders and view itself as a rising global power. The fundamental ideal of maintaining a navy for the protection of commerce was reflected in varying degrees in several United States Navy policy and strategy papers written during the twentieth century. US Naval

Policy (1922), described the fundamental naval policy of the United States as, "the Navy of the United States should be maintained in sufficient strength to support its policies and its commerce, and to guard its continental and overseas possessions."[13] Elmo Zumwalt, the chief of naval operations (CNO) from 1970 to 1974 commissioned several studies including Project Sixty and "US Strategy for the Pacific/Indian Ocean Area in the 1970s" which concluded that sea control, to assure a sealift capability, was a critical mission for the navy.[14] The *Strategic Concepts for the US Navy* published as Naval Warfare Publication 1 in 1976 reiterated the need for free and open maritime trade as a requirement to maintain US economic superiority; and was one of the first that codified the existing role the navy plays in protecting SLOC.[15] There were clear operational reasons for codifying this concept. This was the midst of the Cold War and the United States' strategy was to maintain a capability to carry the fight forward from the United States to combat zones overseas, therefore maintaining the SLOC open between the United States and Europe and Asia was absolutely essential for the United States to prevail in a conflict with the Soviet Union. In the 1990s, the United States Navy's Strategy, *Forward from the Sea*, provided the maritime service's role in advancing the US National Military Strategy to assure forward presence. The United States Navy's forward presence in the Asia-Pacific region was necessary to nurture stability in the region, and this stability contributed to the Asia-Pacific being the fastest growing economic market in the world at the time.[16] Today, our National Defense Strategy reiterates how the United States has worked diligently to ensure secure SLOC worldwide and that,

> For more than sixty years, the United States has done its part in protecting the global commons with our allies and partners for the benefit of all. Global prosperity is contingent on the free flow of ideas, goods, and services.[17]

The US Pacific Command's Strategy describes freedom of the seas or freedom of movement as a basic and elemental tenet for seafaring nations and those nations reliant on the sea for trade. It is an enduring strategic imperative that drives our actions to counter threats to lines of communication and commerce.[18] Finally, the United States Navy CNO's *Cooperative Strategy for Twenty First Century Seapower*, highlights that despite our best intentions, we cannot protect the freedom of the seas and monitor SLOC alone. In the future greater numbers of vessels will engage in transoceanic trade. Maritime nations can and should work together to ensure safe navigation, stewardship of the environment, and security for ships and their crews at sea.[19]

These strategic ideals are reflected in the Pacific Fleet commander's vision of a credibly led, combat and surge ready fleet, prepared in peace or war to advance regional security and prosperity through cooperation with common purpose navies in the Asia-Pacific region. This vision further refines the mission and priorities that are used by the Pacific Fleet to carry out their day to day operations around the Asia-Pacific rim.

## Strategic context of the Asia-Pacific for the United States Navy

The importance of the Asia-Pacific region in global affairs cannot be overstated. The region is a collection of dense and diverse populations that include a number of sizable militaries. It is an economic powerhouse that is fostering an intense competition for resources and much of these resources move throughout the region by the sea.

The Asia-Pacific region encompasses the largest maritime area of operations for the United States Navy; this represents a significant challenge that is characterized as the "Tyranny of Distance." It typically takes a ship 19 days to transit from the West Coast of the United States to its on station area in the Western Pacific. To illustrate the huge extent of this area, consider the Indonesian archipelago, itself only a small portion of this vast area of responsibility. If overlaid on the continental United States, the archipelago would stretch from Miami, Florida on one end to Seattle, Washington on the other. According to the list of the 50 busiest commercial shipping ports reported by the American Association of Port Authorities, the Pacific is home for 56 percent of the world's largest commercial ports including the top five: Singapore, Shanghai, Hong Kong, Shenzhen and Busan.[20] So it is not surprising that the region is a nexus of maritime world trade. Include in this mix a number of strategic choke points along with vast archipelagic nations and the result is a complex environment for maritime stakeholders to deal with.

Relationships in this region are also complex. Historical rivalries, long term memories from World War II, rising nations and a host of impoverished countries and potential failed states with untapped natural resources have led to intense competition for influence both from within and outside the region. It is not a region that favors multinational security arrangements, for a variety of reasons, a Eurocentric view of a collective of nations working together on common security issues has failed to gain a solid foothold in the region – though recent events involving the ASEAN and the ASEAN Defense Ministers Meeting (ADMM) would imply that this view may be changing.

The United States has long standing interests in the region and these are reflected partly in the treaty relationships the United States has maintained with Australia, Japan, South Korea, the Philippines and Thailand that have endured for several decades.

## Security challenges for the United States Navy

The Asia-Pacific region is vital to the economic prosperity of the United States and the economic success of the region depends on the free flow of maritime commerce on the SLOC. The security of the SLOC is an important mission of the United States Pacific Fleet. The demand for raw materials and finished goods that travel by sea, and converge in the maritime choke points in Southeast Asia will continue to increase. The well-being, not only of the United States, but also that of the global economy depends on the collective ability of maritime nations to ensure the free flow of goods, undisturbed, through these SLOC. Ensuring maritime security in the Asia-Pacific region is important to global economic stability, but there are challenges that impede the achievement of this goal.

The proliferation and shipment of weapons of mass destruction and other arms for purposes of disrupting legitimate commerce and freely elected governments is of international concern. Pariah states such as North Korea and Burma continue their quest for nuclear and missile technologies as a means to ensure the survival of their repressive regimes. The recent ballistic missile test launches by North Korea, essentially comprising a common threat, has had the unintentional effect (from the North Korean perspective) of facilitating closer cooperation between the United States, Japan and South Korea in the area of ballistic missile defense.

There are several areas within the Asia-Pacific region where maritime boundary disputes, involving excessive baseline claims or access to resources could erupt into conflict between two or more nations at any time. The Spratly Islands, all or portions of which are claimed by as many as six nations, continue to be a focal point for tension in the South China Sea despite the ASEAN countries and the PRC signing a Declaration of Conduct to ensure peaceful settlement of issues involving the Spratlys. The PRC, Taiwan and Japan have an ongoing dispute over the Senkaku Islands in the East China Sea and even Japan and South Korea have exchanged diplomatic broadsides over a rocky outcrop called Tak Do/Takeshima in the East Sea/Sea of Japan; the geographic names depend on whether you take the Korean or Japanese point of view. The lack of a defined maritime boundary between the exclusive economic zones (EEZs) and extended continental shelves of China and Japan is a source of potential conflict as both sides vie to exploit petroleum and natural gas resources from the sea floor of the East China Sea.

Add to this mix, the plethora of unscrupulous characters that use the maritime domain to take advantage of seams between borders to carry out transnational criminal activities such as human trafficking, piracy and terrorism; some of which supports ongoing insurgencies and civil unrest in the Philippines and Southern Thailand.

For many years the United States Navy and the Pacific Fleet has looked to the Western Pacific and Asia as the single point of operational focus, however, with the terrorist attacks of 2001 in the United States, that focus has been bifurcated and the United States Navy now works closely with their brethren in the US Coast Guard to ensure maritime homeland defense for Hawaii and the West Coast of the United States.

Finally, there are the "traditional" challenges faced by modern navies of anti-access technologies due to the relatively low cost and abundance of sea mines as well as the expanding market and availability of modern quiet diesel-electric submarines. Maintaining an anti-submarine warfare capability requires a huge investment in material as well as training. It is still very much an art that requires intensive training to maintain the level of proficiency needed to detect and interdict modern quiet submarines. With the encroachment of training areas and legal challenges to the training use of sonar, the United States Navy has had to develop innovative and non-invasive means to conduct training and maintain this proficiency.

## Meeting the challenges through maritime partnerships

To meet many of these challenges, the United States Navy maintains a continuous naval presence in the region. This presence is the result of rotating naval forces from the West Coast of the United States through the region on extended deployments and by maintaining a fleet of forward deployed naval forces home ported in Japan. The Pacific is the only region in the world in which the United States maintains a forward deployed naval force of this type. The "tyranny of distance" is a major reason for making this arrangement necessary as well as cost effective. It would require three times the number of ships stationed along the West Coast of the United States to meet the same presence requirements as that provided by the 18 ships home ported in Japan. This presence is necessary to secure the national interests of the United States, but at the same time these interests are shared with other like minded countries in the region. Hence the current navy strategy stresses the importance of maritime partnerships in achieving maritime security and regional stability.

Today, the Pacific Fleet is meeting the chief of naval operation's strategic objective by participating in over 120 joint and combined exercises and conducting 350 port visits in the Asia-Pacific region each year. The Seventh Fleet commander, home ported with the forward deployed naval forces in Yokosuka, Japan; holds operational level staff talks with nine different countries, pursuing improved interoperability and cooperation. This is complemented by the Pacific Fleet commander's travels throughout the region and his personal engagement with naval leaders. In a typical six-month period he will travel to the Philippines, Vietnam, New Zealand, Japan, Singapore and Kiribati and this pace and diversity will be duplicated with other countries over succeeding semi-annual periods. The Pacific Fleet is continuing to expand many of the traditional bi-lateral engagements that have been conducted in the past to achieve a more multilateral focus throughout the region. The Navy has increased the number of multilateral exercises and engagements beyond the 20-member Western Pacific Naval Symposium (WPNS)[21] and the biennial Rim of the Pacific Exercise.[22] Pacific Partnership, the ongoing humanitarian and civic assistance deployments in the region include medical and engineering teams from multiple countries. The Malabar exercise led by India has periodically included multiple nations, and the Pacific Reach submarine rescue exercise maintains a multinational roster.[23] There are opportunities to expand relationships with Japan and Korea to foster tri-lateral cooperation and to expand participation in the Cobra Gold and CARAT[24] exercises in Southeast Asia.

Following the successful response by naval forces to provide humanitarian assistance and disaster relief for the 2004 South Asian tsunami, and the follow on deployment of USNS *Mercy* to the region in 2006, the United States Navy has added humanitarian civic assistance as a core navy mission. In the Asia-Pacific, this mission is known as Pacific Partnership. The first Pacific Partnership deployment by USS *Peleliu* was conducted in 2007 and is representative of what current and future missions look like – a large deck military platform or hospital ship, manned by an international team of medical and engineering professionals along with unique skill sets provided by non-governmental organizations (NGOs) to provide sustained support in humanitarian and civic assistance throughout the Asia-Pacific region.

In this manner; through bilateral and multilateral engagements, humanitarian assistance programs and continuous forward presence; the United States Navy is meeting the challenge to assure maritime security in the Asia-Pacific region.

## Conclusion

Freedom of the seas and secure SLOC have been strategic interests of the United States since our founding as a nation. Early in our history we actively defended our rights, freedoms and sovereignty on the seas from greater naval powers. It is recognized that it is neither desirable, nor feasible, to serve as the guardian of these principles on our own. Around the Asia-Pacific Rim, the United States Pacific Fleet works in conjunction with allies, friends and partners to serve the "wide common" that Mahan wrote about 120 years ago. As long as ships travel the seas carrying commerce, the United States Navy will continue to be one of the key players in protecting the maritime highways within the Asia-Pacific and around the world. The security of the SLOC and the ability to travel freely on the high seas will remain of strategic importance to the United Sates for the foreseeable future.

## Notes

1 Mahan, A. T. (1890) *The Influence of Seapower Upon History, 1660–1783*, Boston: Little, Brown and Company, p. 557
2 In his paper on *Hamilton and the Federalist Financial Revolution, 1789–1795* (online, available at: www.alexanderhamiltonexhibition.org/about/Sylla%20-%20Federals%20Revolution.pdf) Richard Sylla reports US federal revenues of

$6.1 million. Gerald Gawalt in *America and the Barbary Pirates: An International Battle against an Unconventional Foe* (online, available at: http://memory.loc.gov/ammem/collections/jefferson_papers/mtjprece.html) reports that the US government paid "nearly a million dollars in cash, naval stores, and a frigate to ransom 115 sailors from the Dey of Algiers."

3 *Gold Braid and Foreign Relations, Diplomatic Activities of US Naval Officers 1798–1883*, by David F. Long, United States Naval Institute, 1988, p. 208.

4 *Doctrine and Fleet Tactics in the Royal Navy*, Dr. James J. Tritten, from the "Newport Papers" Newport Paper 9, Naval War College, Newport Rhode Island, December 1995.

5 Adams, John, *The Works of John Adams*, Letter to Richard Rush dated April 5, 1815.

6 "Fourteen Points Speech," *Wikisource, The Free Library*, online, available at: http://en.wikisource.org/w/index.php?title=Fourteen_Points_Speech&oldid=2074915.

7 Quasi-war with France, 1798–1800, occurred in response to France seizing American merchantmen trading with Great Britain. The Barbary Wars (1801–1805, 1815), ended the practice of paying tribute to the Barbary States of North Africa to ensure free passage for merchant vessels in the Mediterranean Sea. The War of 1812 (1812–1815), between the United States and Great Britain was in part caused by Great Britain's imposing sanctions against the United States trading with France and the practice by the Royal Navy at the time of impressing merchant seaman (who were US citizens) for service in the Royal Navy. "Impressing" was the practice of stopping ships at sea and taking sailors off or abducting sailors ashore to man warships. In 1917, the United States entered the fight against Germany in World War I as a direct result of the German practice of unrestricted submarine warfare against neutral shipping. Up to that point, the general feeling in the United States was to avoid war and maintain our neutrality. Unprovoked attacks on US shipping pushed the United States to war. More recently, the United States conducted Operation Earnest Will (1987–1988) in which the United States reflagged and escorted Kuwaiti oil tankers to protect them from indiscriminate attack during the Iran-Iraq war.

8 James K. Greene, *Freedom of Navigation: New Strategy for the Navy's FON Program*, Naval War College Paper, February 1992.

9 World Oil Transit Chokepoints, Energy Information Administration, online, available at: www.eia.doe.gov/cabs/World_Oil_Transit_Chokepoints/Full.html.

10 US Energy Information Administration website, online, available at: www.eia.doe.gov/cabs/South_China_Sea/Shipping.html.

11 Communication from the Permanent Mission of the PRC to the United Nations to the Secretary General dated May 7, 2009.

12 *Washington Post*, "Clinton Wades into South China Sea Territorial Dispute," July 23, 2010.

13 National Archives and Record Administration (NARA), Washington, DC and College Park, MD, Record Group 80, Proceedings and Hearings of the General Board, January 17, 1925, "Naval Policy."

14 John B. Hattendorf, *The Evolution of the US Navy's Maritime Strategy, 1977–1986*, Newport Paper 19 (Newport, RI: Naval War College Press, 2004).

15 John B. Hattendorf, ed., *US Naval Strategy in the 1970s: Selected Documents*, Newport Paper 30 (Newport, RI: Naval War College Press, 2007).

16 "Asia's Emerging Economies," *The Economist*, November 16, 1991, p. 16.

17 National Defense Strategy, June 2008, p. 16.

18 United States Pacific Command, USPACOM Strategy, November 2008, p. 7.

19 *A Cooperative Strategy for Twenty First Century Seapower*, October 2007.

20 American Association of Port Authorities World Port Rankings 2008. Rankings based on container traffic measured in 20-foot equivalent units (TEUs).

21 The WPNS was established in 1988 as outgrowth of the CNO's International Sea Power Symposium to provide a forum for discussion of maritime issues, both global and regional, and in the process, generate a flow of information and opinion between naval professionals leading to common understanding. WPNS Member Nations are Australia, Brunei, Canada, Chile, China, Indonesia, Malaysia, New Zealand, Papua New Guinea, Philippines, Singapore, Korea, Thailand, United States, Japan, Tonga, Cambodia, Vietnam, Russia and France. Bangladesh, India, Mexico and Peru are observer nations. Besides the biennial symposium and annual working groups, WPNS sponsors multilateral seminars and exercises that are open to all member and observer navies.
22 In 2008 RIMPAC had participants from the United States Navy, US Coast Guard, Japan, Australia, Canada, Chile, Korea, the Netherlands, Peru, the United Kingdom and Singapore. The goal of the exercise is to demonstrate the United States Navy's commitment to working with our global partners in protecting the maritime freedom as a basis for global prosperity and to ensure stability throughout the Pacific.
23 Pacific Reach practices the ability to mobilize assets worldwide in the unlikely event a submarine becomes disabled and is not able to return to the surface on its own. Goals include enhancing submarine rescue capability, fostering mutual trust among participating countries, demonstrating capability and interoperability among participating submarine and submarine rescue vehicles, and developing submarine rescue techniques. Participants include the United States, Japan, Australia and Singapore. Observing nations included Canada, China, Chile, France, India, Indonesia, Thailand and the United Kingdom.
24 CARAT is an acronym for 'cooperation afloat readiness and training' and is a series of bilateral confidence building naval exercises between the United States Navy and Thailand, Malaysia, Singapore, Indonesia, Brunei and the Philippines.

# 4 China

## Its maritime traditions and navy today

*Carl Otis Schuster*

Although it is not widely known or appreciated, China has a long maritime tradition, dating back to at least 250 BC when Chinese goods were first delivered by ship to Hellenistic Egypt. In fact, by then, China's merchant ships had been transporting China's products to South and Southeast Asia for nearly a century. Chinese goods were of such quality that they were sought after by the leading empires of the ancient world. Moreover, China's Imperial Navy protected that trade throughout the South China Sea for over 700 years. However, China's cycle of inward looking leadership and domestic troubles have limited its maritime operations to sporadic forays during periods of visionary leadership and economic expansion. Most Western views of China's maritime past have been shaped by its 300-year cycle of domestic focus that began with the late Ming period and ended only recently under the Communist Party's post-Mao leadership. Additionally, many Western observers denigrate China's maritime experiences, noting that it has not fought many open ocean naval battles and has had only one great admiral, Admiral Zheng He. One could argue that his voyage was one of diplomacy and trade; that he fought no major naval engagements and therefore was not a great admiral in the Western sense. Yet, to accept that view is to ignore China's historical military focus on deterring war and limiting imperial ambitions. Imperial China had no desire for global conquest. In fact, its ambitions were limited to protecting its frontiers and domestic stability; and it employed its military forces appropriately.

China today is enjoying a naval resurgence at a time when Western navies are in decline. The once unrivaled British Royal Navy is down to less than 25 major warships and a handful of submarines[1] and even its successor on the world's oceans, the United States Navy has dropped below 300 warships for the first time since before World War I.[2] Meanwhile, China's fleet is growing at the pace of 1–2 submarines and major surface combatants a year. Beijing has even announced its interest in acquiring aircraft carriers.[3] Chinese naval officers have added Mahan to their required reading list in addition to the traditional Chinese military classics such as Sun Tzu. Chinese leaders speak openly of developing the capability to control the waters out to the "First Island Chain," which encompasses the waters from the Aleutian Island chain down past the Kuriles and Ryukyus to the South China Sea's disputed Spratly Islands archipelago by 2015,[4] and the waters as far off as Guam by 2030. China's leaders view these goals as part of a defensive strategy intended to prevent the United States or any other major power from interfering with Chinese trade or striking mainland China from the sea.[5] The People's Liberation Army Navy (PLAN) has a key role in China's strategic requirement to win a "local war under informatized conditions." That requirement has driven the navy to develop offensive capabilities to conduct limited sea control operations in order to enforce sovereignty and territorial claims in the East and South China Seas.

## Moving beyond coastal defense

PLAN today is a far cry from its post-revolution roots as a coastal defense force under Chairman Mao. Mao's PLAN was the world's largest numerically, with more naval units than any other fleet. However, the overwhelming majority of its force consisted of short-range patrol boats incapable of operating effectively beyond China's immediate littoral. Its few oceangoing warships were early 1950s-era Soviet cast-offs or Chinese-built copies with obsolete gun systems, sensors and anti-submarine warfare weapons. Its more than 1,000-missile-armed patrol boats were capable of inflicting severe damage on a World War II-era amphibious landing force but would have been hopelessly outclassed and easily destroyed by any intense and concentrated series of air strikes. Its submarines were not any better. Its license-built versions of the Soviet Romeo-class were noisy, short-ranged and severely deficient in sensor and weapons capability. The evolutionary improvements of the Ming-class in the 1970s did little to change that reality. However, the China of the Mao era was very inward looking. It had no major international partners, conducted little if any international trade and its national security doctrine was founded in "People's War," based on an enemy invading and trying to occupy Chinese territory.

That situation and mindset no longer suits China's economic, political or national security needs. Deng Xiaoping's reforms did not take hold until the mid-1980s but within one decade of Mao's 1976 death, Deng had transformed China's economy from an island of stagnation to burgeoning dragon feeding its first products into global markets.[6] Since then, China has become a major ocean trading nation, making freedom of the seas a fundamental national interest. It is now the world's second-largest economy, second-largest exporter and third-largest trader[7] with a vast appetite for both raw materials and export markets, over 90 percent of which is transported over the world's oceans.[8] For example, China is the world's second-largest oil importer with over 60 percent of its petroleum products coming from the Persian Gulf.[9] More importantly, oil imports will rise dramatically in the years ahead as China's rapidly growing hunger for automobiles escalates[10] and although China has invested heavily in alternative fuel research and Central Asia to reduce its dependence on oil imports, especially maritime-transported petroleum, that reliance will continue to expand well into the next decade. China is also the single largest importer of copper, iron ore, manganese and a vast array of commodities, including gold and silver. Also, a growing number of Chinese academics and commentators have noted China's dependence on overseas trade and stated China needs sea power.[11] At present, the United States dominates the world's sea lanes and even though it has shown no interest in constricting or interfering with Chinese maritime trade, Beijing cannot take America's benign attitude for granted, particularly as long as Taiwan remains a potential flash point in US–China relations. Building a fleet to protect its trade and developing the expertise and infrastructure for open ocean operations is one potential solution to those concerns.

However, China faced a difficult challenge in starting its fleet building program. The chaos of the Cultural Revolution had severely disrupted its scientific community and industrial development. Modern warships and naval operations require high technology communications equipment and sensors as well as long-range air defense and anti-surface ship weapons systems. China lacked the industrial and technological base to provide those capabilities to its ships. Also, its ship building capacity was limited and employed largely obsolescent construction designs and techniques. Thus, China's first modern naval warships had to be acquired from foreign sources and it initiated a two-tiered program to fill that need. It also necessitated a patient, incremental and evolutionary, rather than revolutionary approach to its naval modernization program.

China's growing export income enabled it to initiate that effort by the late 1980s, allowing it to pursue radars and close-in weapons from Britain and France, respectively. The PLAN also acquired two Soviet-built Kilo-class diesel-powered submarines, which were two generations ahead of the submarines then in Chinese-service. The naval program hit a snag, as did China's other military modernization efforts, in 1989 when Western nations responded to the Tiananmen Square incident, where PLA (People's Liberation Army) security crushed a pro-democracy demonstration, by embargoing weapons and military technology sales to Beijing. That led China to seek its weapons and sensor systems elsewhere and Beijing found a ready supplier in the cash-strapped Soviet Union.

## Moving towards a blue-water navy

The early Soviet Union purchases favored the PLA Air Force since America's success in Desert Storm demonstrated the effectiveness of modern fourth generation aircraft. With tensions over Taiwan rising as the 1990s progressed, Beijing gave priority to acquiring air defense systems and new fighter aircraft. The PLAN made do by applying new weapons systems and sensors to existing hull designs while its engineers studied the Western systems they had acquired and information about other systems and technologies available in the public domain and via dual-use digital equipment purchases. The resulting Jianghu III- thru V-class guided missile frigates and Luda I- thru III-class guided-missile destroyers incorporated improved electronic and propulsion systems, but the changes were incremental. The frigates had only limited ocean endurance (ten days).[12] The Kilos, two Luhu-class DDGs (guided missile destroyers) and a handful of Ludas constituted the PLAN's only oceangoing warships and the navy had only two blue-water logistics units to support them.

President Yeltsin's 1998 visit to China opened the door to expanded defense cooperation with the Russian Republic. It was a renewed but mutually beneficial partnership. Russia's military industrial capacity was greater and more advanced than China's but Russia lacked the financial resources to sustain it, much less advance it. China had the cash but its military and maritime industrial and technological base was 20 years behind Russia's and 30 behind that of the West. Again, the PLA Air Force initially was the primary benefactor, receiving the Su-27 Flanker, but the PLAN also benefitted. It purchased four Sovremenny-class DDGs sitting on the ways in Russia's Sevreneja Shipyard. Although they were equipped with 1980s technology weapons and sensor systems, they were the PLAN's first truly modern oceangoing warships.[13]

The first unit was delivered in 1999 and its SA-N-7 surface-to-air missile (SAM) system gave the PLAN its first "beyond-close in" air defense system. More importantly, the Sovremenny's SS-N-22 Sunburn supersonic wave-hopping anti-ship cruise missile (ASCM) marked a generational improvement over the older, less capable subsonic ASCMs carried by China's indigenous designs. Access to the technology, particularly the combat systems and command, control and communications systems proved a boon to Chinese naval commanders and ship designers. Many naval analysts saw the ship's arrival as an alarming development but China limited the purchase to the four units. It became readily apparent, these destroyers were viewed as a stop gap, intended to provide an immediate technological and operational jump, both to fill an operational need and for commanders and crews to gain experience with modern systems and blue-water operations.

In retrospect, the indigenous contemporary helo-capable Luhai-class is a better indicator of PLAN thinking in surface ship design and capabilities. Its combined diesel or gas (CODOG) turbine propulsion provides economical cruise and rapid acceleration qualities on a small engineering crew base. Although it lacks the Sovremenny's area air defense capability, its embarked helicopter gives it a greater anti-submarine warfare, surface surveillance and over-the-horizon search and targeting capability. However, it too has proven to be an interim design, probably used to test and develop the procedures and tactics of employing helicopters and other new technologies in naval operations.

By 2004, China had settled on its basic surface warship requirements and designs. The mainstay of the Chinese destroyer force is the Type 051C (Luhai II) and Type 052C (Lu Yang II) class DDGs. Equipped with the HQ-9 or license-built improved version of the Russian S-300 (SA-N-6) SAMs, phase array radars and digital combat systems, they represent China's first naval units with a long-range area air defense capability. The Type 052Cs show some stealth characteristics; that is, its hull and superstructure have been shaped to reduce radar cross-section. Their phase array radars are similar to the American AN/SPY-1 radars on the Aegis-class cruisers and Arleigh Burke-class DDGs. Phased array radars are inherently more reliable and capable than mechanical-antenna radar systems and their digital combat systems can handle and engage a much larger number of targets. They also expanded the ships' command and control capabilities. The S-300s "track-via-missile" guidance system is also similar to that of its American Aegis counterpart, making it more effective against maneuvering targets than traditional SAMs. The ships' vertical launch system (VLS) accelerates its reaction time over rail launch systems. The ships' engineering plants reportedly also feature diminished noise and infrared signatures, making them more difficult to track and engage.[14] Their C-802 ASCMs are not as capable as the SS-N-22 but the 052Cs are still a more formidable unit. They have a greater range, faster reaction times, better sensor systems and their embarked helicopters provide an over-the-horizon surveillance capability as well as expanding the ships' range of missions. China is building roughly two units at a time and commissioning at least one every 14–18 months. At that rate, the PLAN will have about ten units of each class in service by 2020.

They will be complemented by the Type 054A (Jiangwai)-class guided missile frigates, which first entered service in 2008. Like the 052Cs, they incorporate some stealth features, reduced radar cross section, propulsion system silencing and diminished infrared signatures. While its HQ-16 (SA-N-12) SAM system lacks the range of the HQ-9s carried by the destroyers, it has the same multiple engagement, track-via-missile and rapid reaction capabilities, making it a very effective medium range air defense system. They use a combined cruise diesel and dash diesel (CODOD) propulsion system. The Type 054As are being built at a rate of two a year: eight are already in service as of August 2010 and if the building rate continues apace, China will have 20 in service by 2015, making the 054A China's most numerous oceangoing combatant.

The submarine force also benefitted from the renewed Sino-Russian defense partnership. The PLAN received ten improved Kilo-class submarines between 1998 and 2010.[15] The newer submarines represented a significant advance over the earlier versions. They were both quieter and faster, and were equipped with better passive and active sonar systems.[16] Their digital combat systems and state-of-the art electronics suites used less space, required less power and offered vastly improved detection, tracking and engagement capabilities. The hull coatings have also been improved, further reducing its also small sonar-cross section and noise levels. Other changes reportedly have also cut its magnetic signature, increasing the difficulty involved in detecting and tracking these already stealthy submarines. They reportedly also are equipped with wake-homing torpedoes.[17]

More importantly, the new Kilos enabled Chinese officials to study Russian advancements in submarine design. That exposure and acquisition of Western diesel engines and computer systems led directly to the indigenous Yuan-class submarines now under construction in China.[18] Some defense analysts speculate that the Yuan-class is equipped with an air-independent-propulsion (AIP) system that significantly extends their capacity to operate underway, from 3–4 days to as many as 15 days. If true, then the Yuan-class represents a major improvement in Chinese conventional submarine capabilities. Only a handful of these submarines are in service and there is little reporting on the construction rate but it probably consists of one unit every 1–2 years. The bulk of China's submarine force consists of obsolete Song- and Ming-class units that represent only incremental improvements over the 1950s-era Romeos built during the Maoist period. However, most of these will be decommissioned in the coming years as more Yuan-class units enter service.

The most significant improvement in PLAN naval capabilities arose at the turn of the century with the construction of the nuclear-powered Chin-class attack submarines. Apparently based on the Russian Victor-III class SSN (ship submersible nuclear), these submarines are significantly quieter, safer, faster and far more capable than the earlier Han-class units built in the 1970s to 1980s. They extend the PLAN's operational reach into the farthest ocean areas and will pose a major challenge to any naval task force operating in an open ocean area. The same technology has been incorporated in the Jin-class nuclear-powered ballistic missile submarine (submarine launched ballistic missile, SLBM) that recently entered service. It isn't clear how many of these expensive units China plans to build but they have drawn significant interest and concern about China's submarine force.

Logistics ship construction has not kept pace with warships construction. The two ship Dayun-class ocean-going fleet support ships and Fuqinq-class fleet oilers were built in the 1990s but construction of the more capable Fuchi-class replenishment ship didn't begin until 2002, shortly after the PLAN conducted its first "around-the-world" cruise. The PLAN now has two units in service but it isn't clear how many are under construction. So far, the PLAN is rotating its Fuchi- and Fuqinq-class auxiliaries to support its long-range deployments. More will be needed if the PLAN intends to expand its current deployment levels.

Finally, there is the matter of naval power projection, which consists of three elements – sea-based air power, sea-based missile power and amphibious warfare capabilities. At present, China has no aircraft carriers, no sea-based land attack cruise missiles and its amphibious warfare units are limited in range and lift capability, probably because they were intended to support the retaking of coastal islands and possibly a war with Taiwan. However, that may be changing as China's overseas presence and interests continue to expand. It has commissioned one ocean-going Type 071 Yuzhao-class LPD (landing platform dock) that can carry up to four landing craft or air cushion vehicles (ACVs), 2–4 helicopters and a battalion of naval infantry.[19] It has been accompanied by the construction of ten Yuting-class tank landing ships (LSTs). Both classes are ocean-going units capable of sustained operations in the open ocean, with proper logistics support. Their immediate mission probably is to support any South China Sea amphibious operations but they could also constitute an amphibious readiness group deployed to support any maritime contingency, ranging from humanitarian assistance missions to a non-combatant evacuation (NEO). More ominously, the current force could also conduct a brigade-sized amphibious assault against a lightly to moderately defended coastal objective.

With respect to the other two elements of naval power projection, sea-based missile and air power, China's current capacity lies in its ballistic missile submarines, which appear to intended as a regional deterrent force. The missiles' range is sufficient to reach China's most likely strategic competitors, India, Russia and the United States, and China's "minimum nuclear deterrent strategy" suggests the SLBM force will be limited in size, probably 5–8 units carrying a total of 80–128 missiles. There has been little Chinese discussion about indigenous land-attack cruise missile development but they do have one under development, the reputed 2,500 km range HN-3 which reportedly can be launched from a standard 533 mm submarine torpedo tube.[20] It probably will enter service before 2020 and will give the PLAN its first deep power projection capability if the navy develops the intelligence and targeting capabilities to employ the missiles effectively.

The final and most visible and expensive component of naval power projection is the aircraft carrier. Aircraft carriers have been subject of much debate in China over the last 20 years. Until recently, Chinese defense commentators have viewed aircraft carriers as an expensive tool of imperialism or an unnecessary and obsolete naval weapons system whose utility is open to question.[21] As mentioned above, that view has changed over the last decade. For example, Reuters reported in March 2007 that an "unnamed Chinese lieutenant general" had stated China was going to build its own aircraft carrier, provided research and development went smoothly.[22] General Huang Xeuping told journalists in December 2008 that China was considering aircraft carrier construction.[23] Many Western commentators believe the first Chinese aircraft carrier is already under construction and will start sea trials in 2015.[24] China has acquired Su-27s and has been in negotiations with Russia for the purchase of up to 50 carrier-capable Su-33 fighters.[25] China has also initiated a four-year carrier aviator training program involving approximately 50 pilots.[26] Nonetheless, there is little information to confirm China is about to commission its first aircraft carrier. Moreover, Communist Party leaders remain concerned about spending and some Chinese commentators remain skeptical about the carrier's utility in modern naval operations.[27]

The PLAN's aviation component presently consists of two elements, the small but modern and growing sea-based helicopter force; and the older but longer ranged shore-based fixed wing regiments.[28] The helicopters are indigenous derivatives of the French Super Frelon and Dauphin helicopters, both of which are modern and very capable. Both can carry C-802 anti-ship missiles, support anti-submarine warfare and surface surveillance and targeting missions. They are also very good transport helicopters that can be used for at sea re-supply missions. The shore-based fixed wing force is undergoing modernization. The fighter regiments are transitioning away from the obsolescent F-7 to newer indigenous F-8 Finback fighters and JH-11 long-range fighter interceptors (Chinese version of the Russian Su-30).[29] Despite the increased combat capabilities introduced by these new fighters, they lack the range to support a task force operating more than a few hundred miles from a shore base.

The PLAN Air Force's (PLANAF) long-range surveillance and strike elements are woefully obsolete. The strike regiments continue to use the late 1940s-era B-6 (license version of the Soviet Tu-16). These planes are slow, have a large radar cross-section and their electronics, both sensor and countermeasures, are over 40 years behind the times. They would not fare well in any engagement against a modern naval task force, particularly one supported by airborne warning and control system (AWACS) aircraft and enjoying local fighter support such as that provided by an aircraft carrier. The PLANAF's two reconnaissance regiments' Y-8 aircraft have the range and sensor systems to be relatively effective reconnaissance and surface surveillance platforms and the same can be said of the H-5 seaplanes used for anti-submarine warfare. However, the latter's sensor and weapons are obsolescent and probably would not prove effective against a modern nuclear-powered submarine manned by a well-led and highly trained crew. All of the current shore-based support aircraft will be replaced by more modern designs by decade's end.

The PLAN's naval infantry has remained static in size at 10,000 men but it is being modernized. The North and South Sea Fleets, those closest to likely combat areas, each have one naval infantry brigade.[30] One equipped with weapons and landing craft of 1950s-era design, they are now receiving ACVs, new armored amphibious tracked vehicles and mobile artillery. The force's capacity to assault a beach has improved significantly over the last 20 years, but its capabilities remain limited to taking lightly defended offshore islands or other objectives close to Chinese territory (such as the Spratly Islands). However, the force's size fits its doctrinal mission, in the case of an assault, of seizing a beach and holding it for subsequent landing of follow-on army units that will exploit the landing. The PLAN's naval infantry have the capacity to conduct amphibious raids and, if close to China or in a benign environment, conduct a noncombatant evacuation operation.

Although constructing naval units is an expensive undertaking, it is a minor challenge compared to building the core of trained and experienced seaman; logistics support systems and capability, and naval infrastructure to support large-scale, long-distance naval operations. One reason for the PLAN's initially slow pace of expansion can be found in its lack of experience in blue-water naval operations and modern naval technology. Fleet training has undergone significant reforms over the last decade as tactical and technological skills have come to replace party ideology as the dominant feature of military training. The last six years have seen a major expansion in the use of computer simulations for education and training. Also, the navy has deployed mobile training teams to help crews install, maintain and use computer systems and networks on their ships. The PLA also began to emphasize higher education, particularly among the officers, as part of the modernization effort.[31] Deng Xiaoping had emphasized the need for a highly educated military force familiar with advanced technology and military theories and doctrine.[32] By 2003, that had expanded to include a push to have non-commissioned officers acquire junior-college education to meet the need for the PLA to "leap frog" development of the modernization drive.[33] Thousands of military personnel have been enrolled in civilian universities and PLA delegates to the 2005 Party Congress reported that the majority of PLA officers now had a college or higher degree.[34] Chinese commentators and leaders studied the lessons learned from the two Persian Gulf Wars and probably are studying the lessons of the Afghanistan conflict. Naval officers noted the advantages and complexity of applying naval forces in such situations far from home.

## Naval diplomacy and open ocean operations

Indeed, the PLAN has approached open ocean operations very cautiously. The first show-the-flag visits began in 1980 and consisted primarily of auxiliaries or 1–2 ship deployments to regional countries. The first port visit to United States took place in 1989 when the training ship *Zhen He* visited Hawaii. However, these were little more than training cruises involving little naval activity other than navigation. The first operational deployment began in April 1998 and was very limited in scope; 2–3 ships operating in the South China Sea, and duration, under two weeks.[35] A year later, three ships, two combatants and an auxiliary, visited Hawaii and by 2000, PLAN ships had conducted port visits in South Africa and Pakistan. These missions had two purposes, to show China's growing naval capabilities but also to gain experience in conducting long-range deployments. In 2002, the PLAN launched its then-most ambitious naval operation, a 132-day around the world cruise that took two of its ships, the Luhu-class DDG Qingdao and the replenishment ship *Taicang* to visit ten ports in ten cities (Singapore, Egypt, Turkey, Ukraine, Greece, Portugal, Brazil, Ecuador, Peru and French Polynesia).[36] However, as with the earlier deployments, this was little more than a training cruise.

Fleet exercises and deployments became increasingly complex as the twenty-first century's first decade advanced. The new classes of warship enjoyed far more capable weapons, sensors and command and control systems. Exercises began to explore new systems, tactics and procedures as ship-borne helicopter operations and early forms of networkcentric operations, called informatized operations in Chinese writings, were explored. The PLAN was gaining in importance as China's shipbuilding capacity and trade expanded. However the PLAN remained cautious, despite the new doctrine and technological advances in its equipment and ships.

Meanwhile, China was expanding its participation in United Nations missions, sending five military observers to the UN Truce Supervision Organization in the Middle East in 1990.[37] It made its first deployment of peacekeepers in 1992, when it deployed 800 PLA engineering troops to the UN Transitional Administration in Cambodia.[38] Beijing subsequently agreed in principle to participate in the UN Standby Arrangements System and in 2002, deployed 15 civilian policemen to the UN Transitional Authority in East Timor. Since then, China has deployed peacekeeping troops to Lebanon, Liberia, the Democratic Republic of the Congo and Sudan. Although none of these deployments involved naval forces, China's growing involvement in and importance to the United Nations was a driving factor in the PLAN's expanded maritime operations of recent years and its first major naval deployment.

In fact, many Chinese naval commentators pushed for China's involvement in the international community's western Indian Ocean anti-piracy operations, arguing it would give the PLAN vital experience in supporting long-range naval deployments and working with other navies, as well as demonstrate China's commitment to the international community's mutual interest in peace and stability at sea.[39] Beijing had voted in favor of UN Security Council Resolution 1897 that called on all states with the capacity to combat piracy off Somalia to do so. Therefore, conducting the mission would enhance China's position in the UN and contribute to the protection of Chinese shipping and trade, much of which passed through those waters.

However, Chinese officials remain sensitive to international perceptions of their naval buildup and operations, conducting an active diplomatic and strategic communications effort to allay concerns about its naval buildup.[40] The first anti-piracy deployment was preceded by public discussion, carried on in professional journals and via interviews on state radio, starting in August 2008. Most of the commentary favored deployment but at least one naval officer opposed doing so, saying it would be expensive and difficult to support, expose the ships and crews to terrorist threats and prove futile in the end.[41] Military and party leaders were weighing the international and domestic implications to their first naval deployment directed at protecting Chinese shipping since 1949. The decision probably was made before November's end since China deployed a three-ship squadron to the Indian Ocean just before Christmas in 2008.[42] The first squadron's operations received extensive publicity in China's English- and Chinese-language press.

The deployment continues to this day and Beijing is discovering that long-term operations far from home impose a maintenance and logistical strain on the ships and crews involved. Some Chinese naval officials have already stated China needs overseas bases.[43] However, China's official position remains that it is not seeking permanent overseas bases. It should also be noted that all public statements in favor of bases have stated the requirement in terms of gaining approval from regional countries and those participating in the anti-piracy mission. In addition to their anti-piracy operations, the deployed units have been conducting port visits throughout the region and benefits from access agreements China has negotiated with Yemen and is pursuing basing arrangements with Djibouti, the country that already hosts contingents from all the other international naval contingents conducting anti-piracy operations.

The PLAN's East Africa and Persian Gulf port visits illustrate China's appreciation of the diplomatic aspects of a navy's mission. The groups have conducted port visits to Manila, Singapore, Bangladesh and Sri Lanka en route to their anti-piracy operating area. That aspect of the Indian Ocean deployment has expanded over the last year. Two of the units conducted a port visit in the Persian Gulf, visiting Abu Dhabi and entered the Mediterranean to port visits in Egypt, Greece and Italy. Also, Beijing's recently commissioned hospital ship *Peace Ark* departed China on 31 August to conduct its "Harmonious Mission 2010" deployment. As of December 2010, the ship had made stops at Chittagong – Bangladesh, Djibouti, Mombasa – Kenya, Aden – Yemen, Dar el-Salaam – Tanzania, and the Seychelles. It received an enthusiastic welcome, as did all the Chinese port visits, but more importantly, the hospital ship's clinical and other medical services provided a much needed assistance to local populations, earning Beijing significant goodwill in a region of growing economic and strategic importance to the People's Republic of China (PRC).

These deployments have also played a significant domestic political role in that the attendant publicity has done much to bolster national pride. Virtually every domestic Chinese-language media outlet has carried pictures and reports of the escort group's accomplishments and how it marks both China's growing naval capabilities and its expanding and positive role on the global stage. The South Sea Fleet's political commissar, Huang

Jiangxi, told China's national radio that the PLAN's Indian Ocean force has escorted 1,643 Chinese and foreign ships since the first group and that such operations are now considered normal.[44] He also noted the South Sea Fleet's importance in protecting China's interest in the South China Sea where other countries' interests collide with China's. One example of that, which he did not mention in his interview but was noted in the Chinese media when it happened, came on 9 March 2009 when five Chinese naval units harassed the USNS *Impeccable*, which was conducting oceanographic surveillance operations in international waters east of Hainan Island. Chinese officials claimed the American vessel's research activities were illegal.[45]

Beijing's position under the United Nations Convention on the Law of the Sea (UNCLOS) is that the Convention's 200-nm Economic Exclusion Zone (EEZ) constitutes territorial waters and China's 1992 law proclaims the waters of the South China Sea and surroundings its claimed islands as national territory.[46] Therefore, in China's view, the *Impeccable's* activities in China's claimed territorial waters were illegal. The incident received widespread cover in both the US and Chinese press. The Chinese public's reaction was strongly nationalistic. A Sina.com survey of online users conducted on 12 March 2009 indicated 62.5 percent of the respondents felt their navy ought to chase the US ships away and 32 percent felt the navy should have opened fire on them. Only 3.1 percent felt action should be limited to diplomatic protest. In the public's eye, the PLAN is becoming China's first line of defense and its most visible mark of China's status as a global power. It should also be noted that defending national sovereignty and territorial integrity is one of the PLA's primary missions under China's National Security Strategy.[47]

The South China Sea incident is not the only indicator that China's naval operations will be limited to anti-piracy operations, trade protection and "show-the-flag" activities. More recently, the PLA has initiated a more aggressive naval exercise program within the "First Island Chain." In mid-March 2010, six Chinese warships and two auxiliaries steamed through the Miyako Strait to conduct an exercise in the Bashi Channel south of Taiwan. The ships' exercises included "live-fire" and simulated opposed forces operations with units from the South Sea Fleet. J-8 fighters, a KJ-200 AWACS aircraft and anti-submarine warfare (ASW) aircraft provided air support before the flotilla returned to base in early April. However, that deployment was followed almost immediately by a larger ten-ship squadron from the East Sea Fleet on 10 April 2010. Again passing through the Miyako Strait, this squadron conducted ASW exercises east of Taiwan. Coming on the heels of the first deployment and while the Vietnamese reportedly were harassing Chinese fishing vessels in the Spratly Islands area, this second deployment received extensive television, radio and news coverage in China, Japan and Vietnam. The Vietnamese vessels reportedly withdrew, providing a clear demonstration of a fleet's deterrent effect on another country's actions.

China's growing naval operations, particularly the increasing distances and complexity of its fleet exercises and deployments, highlight Beijing's expanding naval capabilities. However, it is not the rapid sort of buildup that marked Germany's challenge to British naval power in the early years of the twentieth century. China is doing more than just building warships and submarines. As stated above, it has also expanded its naval training programs. Each of its fleets has extensive training programs, including simulations centers for conducting a range of training activities from those designed to increase individual officer and crew proficiency to simulators that test and train staffs and combat center teams in realistic combat-related scenarios intended to hone team and commander tactical skills. Naval aviators have undergone ship's command training. It is apparent China is patiently investing in the human capital required to man and operate a much larger ocean-going fleet that will become a significant ocean-going fleet strength and capability sometime late in this or the next decade. Meanwhile, Beijing's leaders have become more confident in their fleet's capacity and are more willing to employ it as an instrument of national security. These recent exercises and the ongoing anti-piracy operations are a testament to that fact.

The PLAN's continued expansion, including the acquisition of an aircraft carrier, the refurbishment of the former Ukrainian hybrid aircraft carrier *Varyag* is underway, and PLAN's pace of submarine construction have raised concerns among China's neighbors and in Washington, DC. Moreover, there is a striking and, in some eyes, ominous similarity between the "second island chain" that Beijing's national strategy delineates as the area the PLAN must dominate, and the boundaries of Japan's planned outer defensive perimeter of World War II. Additionally, few missed the significance of the aforementioned naval operations east of Taiwan, in the South China Sea in and near the disputed Spratly Islands. Naval exercises are becoming more common and more realistic. Vietnam, among others, is expanding its naval forces, particularly its submarine arm in response. Nonetheless, China's navy still lacks the logistics capability and sea-borne aviation force required to conduct a major force deployment far from its shores. However, it is approaching the ability to challenge hostile forces within the South China Sea and west of the Ryukyus and should achieve that goal by 2015.

## The future

What will China's fleet consist of by that time? Fleets can be built fairly rapidly but as the fleet enlarges, so too do its maintenance, operating and personnel costs. Wages are already on the rise and will continue as the PLAN has to compete with private industry for the pool of technologically adept personnel required to man and operate a modern fleet. Quality of life issues will also become a factor as tomorrow's naval recruits will be drawn from more affluent and comfortable backgrounds than those of the previous decade. They and their families increasingly will judge the naval service as a career from a lifestyle perspective, comparing against what they might enjoy on the outside. That means the personnel portion of the budget will begin to grow more rapidly by the decade's end if the PLAN wants to recruit and retain these personnel. Sending more ships to sea means burning more fuel and consuming more supplies and other logistical materials. Also, the ships that are new today will require more maintenance as they age and the number of units in the yards and dry dock will grow in consonance with the size of the fleet and its operating schedule. Finally, the crews recruited to the service at the buildup's beginning will start to retire in the 2020s, adding a pension cost to the national budget. All of these costs and those of expanding the shore infrastructure to support the fleet will come at the expense of shipbuilding and ultimately shape the force's size.

Given all these factors, China's navy of 2025 probably will consist of about 400 major ships with 2–3 operational and one training aircraft carrier, 30 DDGs, about 50 guided missile frigates; 4–5 nuclear-powered ballistic missile submarines, 20 nuclear-powered and 40 conventional attack submarines. The submarines and surface ships will carry long-range land attack cruise missiles and the PLAN will have a large, highly developed fleet command, control, communications, computer and intelligence (C4I) support system. The fleet's logistics force will include 15 major fleet support ships and another 40–50 smaller logistics ships. It probably will have sufficient amphibious lift to land three brigades of naval infantry when mobilized for an assault close to China and a single brigade out to the second island chain. That will also provide the capacity to put one reinforced battalion at sea and one on alert for emergency deployment. Naval aviation assets will consist of three carrier air wings, three shore-based strike regiments, nine maritime surveillance/ASW regiments and four sea-based helicopter elements. The fleet will also have a significant unmanned aerial vehicle force, some shore-based and some sea-based.

## Conclusion

The big question then remains, how China will employ its fleet. History may provide some insights. Although China has a long history of maritime operations, the bulk of its historical naval experiences are riparian. Yet three patterns stand out in its open ocean naval operations. First and foremost, the fortunes of China's navies have always followed and reflected that of its maritime commerce. That is, its navy has never preceded its merchant ships nor forced open any markets to trade. Second, there is no record of China ever establishing a permanent naval base or presence outside Chinese territory. It has always deployed its fleets as a self-contained entity, its supplies and logistical components accompanying the deploying squadrons and returning home with them.[48] Third; however, when it has had a strong fleet, it has not been reluctant to employ it against China's enemies in the South China or Yellow Seas. Finally and perhaps, most importantly, the navy's fortunes have always ebbed and flowed in consonance with China's overseas trade and trade policies, prospering in periods when oceanic trade was well established and encouraged, suffering decline and diminishment during periods of retrenchment or prohibition against overseas commerce.

Nonetheless, few nations enjoy China's nearly 3,000 years of maritime and naval history and tradition. China conducted its first naval operation in 1043 BC when King Wu of Zhou ferried his army across the Yellow River to attack his enemy's capital and its first recorded naval engagement also occurred on the Yangzi River in 549 BC.[49] The first operation probably involved modified merchant craft but China's diverse kingdoms were building naval warships by the seventh century BC.[50] None appear to have been oceangoing warships but rather were purpose built galleys that either transported troops or served as fighting platforms intended to attack city walls or protect those platform ships and the transports. The Chinese state of Wu was the first to build oceangoing ships, putting its fleet to sea in the fifth century BC.

Chinese mariners were the first to use a magnetic compass and the first to use rudders and sails to control their ships.[51] Chinese shipping reached as far as West Africa during the tenth century but the Soon dynasty was the first to establish a permanent fleet in 1132 and China remained a major naval power for the next 300 years. The Yuan dynasty conducted major amphibious operations, twice attempting to invade Japan, only to see its fleets destroyed by typhoons, and landing armies on the Annamese (modern Vietnam) and Java (modern Indonesia) coasts.[52] The Ming dynasty's fleets and ships were vastly larger than any in Western Europe,[53] and were equipped with cannon and Greek fire.[54] Admiral Zhang He's voyages and fleet marked Imperial China as the world's most powerful maritime and economic power and yet, within 50 years, China closed its doors to world trade. Coming just as Europe was launching its global exploration and imperial expansion, that decision ultimately led to China's economic and military decline, leaving it vulnerable to foreign aggression from the sea. Unaccustomed to invasion threats from the sea, the Manchu dynasty ignored the pernicious effects of European intrusion into its affairs until it was too late.

Today the Chinese refer to the period from the 1830s to the end of World War II as the "Century of Humiliation" and that historical experience has been one of the driving factors behind China's national security doctrine over the last 60 years. Recent economic progress and expanding commercial trade has reawakened China's interest in maritime affairs. As in the earlier imperial dynasties, the PLAN arose out of the need to protect Chinese maritime trade and facilitate its diplomatic position on the global stage. Therefore, its operations should be viewed in that context.

Historically, China has always taken a strong view of developments along its frontier and within its traditional sphere of influence, which incorporates the Korean Peninsula, Southeast Asia, Burma and the South China Sea; a historical pattern that has given rise to American and regional concerns about China's naval program. In fact, China's national defense focus on the first and second island chains in many ways reflects a combined appreciation of its recent and long-standing historical experience and thinking. Its development of an anti-carrier ballistic missile demonstrates a perceived need to deny those waters to any hostile maritime power(s) that may contest or challenge Beijing's interests there (e.g. the United States).[55] Within that region, particularly in areas contiguous to Chinese territorial waters, Beijing increasingly will use the PLAN to assert its maritime claims. This will manifest itself primarily in the South China Sea where the People's Republic will use its naval power to pressure both regional and outside maritime players to recognize its maritime and territorial claims. However, it may also come into play if one of Burma's maritime claim disputes with its neighbors escalates into a crisis.

However, China's naval actions will be more circumspect in the more distant waters. Its naval operations outside the first and second island chains will fall more into the category of presence and trade protection. In addition to the need to "show-the-flag" in the growing number of countries with which China enjoys friendly relations and strong interests, China's expanding commercial activities around the world have transplanted thousands of Chinese citizens into countries farther and farther afield from their homeland. The quest for raw materials has placed many of them in regions and areas of limited stability. Also, China's expanding diplomatic presence in developing countries outside East Asia, which includes an equivalent to the American Peace Corps in Africa,[56] precludes Beijing from taking a disinterested and purely rhetorical view of developments in those countries. For example, Deputy Foreign Minister Zhai Jun has already stated China's readiness for a wider role in East Africa's regional security.[57] Although the bulk of that assistance will consist of financial and development aid, it will also lead to more Chinese working in that noticeably unstable region. More importantly, there is a growing resentment against the Chinese presence in many of these countries. Although not yet a physical security problem, by 2020, China may face an expatriate safety and security problem in those countries.

Kenya's early 2008 post-election unrest generated concern over the safety of China's citizens in that country. Should a similar future outbreak result in a large Chinese death toll, Chinese leaders will face domestic pressure to station an "in area" naval force, or deployment of one. Foreign Ministry and many party leaders will resist those calls, and try to restrict China's overseas military presence to those acting in support of UN-mandated missions. However, one day a crisis will come where that security policy proves deficient in protecting Chinese lives or interest. That decision won't come quickly or soon, but China's historical aversion to placing military forces far from home eventually will give way to domestic pressures to have the capacity to protect its citizens and support its international partners. Historical traditions and lessons probably will drive the navy to develop some type of self-contained offshore sea-based logistics structure rather than face the expense, force protection and political price of building and maintains an overseas naval basing structure.

## Notes

1 International Institute for Strategic Studies, *The Military Balance 2010*, London, 2010, p. 169.
2 Ibid., pp. 33–34.
3 Huang Xueping, Defense Ministry Spokesman, 23 December 2009 Press conference on China's deploying a squadron to the Gulf of Aden to fight piracy.
4 International Institute for Strategic Studies, Strategic Comments, May 2010.
5 Cooper, Cortez, *The PLA Navy's "New Historic Missions,"* RAND Corporation, Santa Monica, 2009, p. 2.
6 Marti, Michael, *China and the Legacy of Deng Xiaoping*, Brassey's, Washington DC, 2002, pp. 15–16.
7 World Bank, *China's New Trade Issues in the Post-WTO Accession Era*, p. 5.
8 Cole, Bernard, D., *The Great Wall at Sea: China's Navy Enters the 21st Century*, Annapolis, US Naval Institute, 2001, p. 63.
9 *Asia Times*, "China Secures Myanmar Energy Route, 2 April 2009, p. 1.
10 Shirouzou, Narihiko, "China's Auto Sales Run Hot," *Wall Street Journal China Real Time Report*, New York, 23 October 2010, online, available at: http://online.wsj.com/article/SB10001424052702303871104575567193323098232.html?mod=WSJ_hps_sections_business.
11 *Xinhua* [Chinese language edition translated by Anthony Miccarrelli], "Beijing Professor: Modern China Needs Sea Power," 10 December 2007.
12 Wertheim, Eric, *Combat Fleets of the World*, fifteenth edition, US Naval Institute, 2007, pp. 119–121.
13 Ibid., p. 115.
14 Ibid., p. 114.
15 Ibid., pp. 112–113.
16 Ibid.
17 Ibid., p. 113.
18 Ibid., p. 111.
19 *Sino Defense*, online, available at: www.sinodefence.com/navy/amphibious/type071.asp.
20 Wertheim, loc cit, p. 108.
21 Pillsbury, Michael, *China Debates the Future Security Environment*, Washington DC, National Defense University, 2000, pp. 83–84, 293.
22 *Reuters*, "China Says Aircraft Carrier Possible by 2010," 7 March 2007.
23 *Agence France Presse via Defense News*, 23 December 2008.
24 Willard, Robert, Admiral United States Navy (CDR US Pacific Command), in response to journalist questions in New Delhi on 5 December 2009, stated "Beijing is determined to have one [aircraft carrier] by 2015." Asahi Shimbun reported on 29 August 2009 that China had begun construction of a 60,000-ton "Ski Ramp" carrier that would be completed by 2015.

25 O'Rourke, Ronald, *China Naval Modernization: Implications for US Navy Capabilities – Background and Issues for Congress*, Congressional Research Office, 26 August 2010, p. 19.
26 Ibid., also, jczs.sina.com reported on 14 April 2005 that the Ganghzou Navy Academy had graduated nine naval aviators with professional degrees in warship command as part of a preparation effort for the day when China's first aircraft carriers entered service.
27 Zhong, Jin, "China: Modern Concept Beyond Aircraft Carrier," *Modern Navy*, July 2010 (translated by the Department of Defense).
28 Wertheim, loc cit, p. 107.
29 Ibid.
30 *Military Balance*, loc cit, pp. 402–403.
31 *PLA Daily*, "PLA Nanjing Military Region Coastal Defense Brigade Officers Interested in Postgraduate Courses," 5 May 2005. The *PLA Daily* also ran a series of articles on the popularity of online training classes and the growing number of naval officers gaining advanced engineering degrees.
32 Marti, Michael, loc cit, pp. 80, 82.
33 Shi Tinghzhi and Yu Dabo, "NCO Cadets with Junior College Education Start on the Job Study," *PLA Daily*, 10 July 2003. The PLAN had a similar program underway that year.
34 Huang Guozhou, "PLA Delegates to Congress Comment on Military Modernization," *PLA Daily*, 25 May 2005.
35 Shambaugh, David, *Modernizing China's Military*, Los Angeles, University of California Press, 2004, p. 101.
36 Virtual Information Center, PLAN World Cruise 2002, Honolulu Hawaii, 23 September 2002, p. 1.
37 He, Yin, *China's Changing Policy on UN Peacekeeping Operations*, Stockholm, Institute for Security and Development Policy, July 2007, p. 25.
38 Ibid.
39 Jin Yinan, Major General, PLA, in a radio interview over Chinese state radio on 4 December 2008.
40 Medeiros, Evan, "The Responses of US Allies and Security Partners to China's Rise," *Naval War College Review*, Autumn 2009, Newport, Naval War College, pp. 39, 40.
41 Unidentified Naval Officer, "Dispatching Our Navy to Patrol Somali Waters Will Not Be Easy," *Huanqiu*, 10 December 2008.
42 *China Views*, 26 December 2010, p. 1. The article noted China's past reluctance to join in such multi-national naval operations but that the deployment demonstrated "China's goodwill toward fellow nations and its resolve to make the world a safer place."
43 Yin Zhuo, "Overseas Bases Needed." Yin Zhuo stated on state radio on 29 December 2009 that the bases were needed to support anti-piracy operations. He also said, "I believe regional countries and countries taking part in the anti-piracy patrols would understand if China established a relatively permanent coastal supply base."
44 Chin Xin and Tao Hongxiang Interview on Chinese National Radio, 6 March 2010.
45 Ma Zhaoxu, China's Foreign Ministry Spokesman, quoted in *Reuters*, "China Says US Naval Ship Broke the Law," 10 March 2009.
46 Huang Xeupeing, Defense Ministry Spokesman Statement dated 12 March 2009, "US Ship is Operating Illegally in China's Economic Exclusion Zone (EEZ)."
47 Cole, loc cit, *Great Wall at Sea*, p. 9.
48 Levathes, Louise, *When China Ruled the Seas: The Treasure Fleet of the Dragon Throne 1405–1433*, Oxford, Oxford University Press, 1994, p. 54.

49 Graff, David and Higham, Robin, *A Military History of China*, Cambridge, Westview Press, 2000, pp. 82–83.
50 Ibid.
51 Cole, loc cit., p. 2
52 Levathes, *When China Ruled the Seas*.
53 Cole, loc cit, p. 3.
54 Peers, C. J., *Soldiers of the Dragon: Chinese Armies 1500 BC–AD 1840*, London, Osprey Publishing, 2006, pp. 140–141.
55 Reed, Charlie and Slavin, Erik, "Admiral: China Progressing on Anti-Carrier Missile System," *Stars and Stripes*, 29 December 2010, p. 1. Report on Admiral Willard's 28 December interview with Asahi Shimbum.
56 Alden, Chris, *China in Africa*, New York, Zed Books, 2007, p. 27.
57 *Agence France Presse*, "Zhai Jun Says China Ready for Regional Security Role," 27 January 2010. Assistant Foreign Minister Zhai Jun was quoted by Radio Rwanda as saying, "China is ready to play a constructive role in promoting sustainable stability and security in the Great Lakes Region [of East Africa]." This most likely refers to providing volunteers and aid workers as well as material and other forms of development assistance to the impoverished region which suffers heavily from poverty and inter-tribal violence that has the potential to escalate into a conflict involving all four nations that share the region (Rwanda, Uganda, Kenya and the Democratic Republic of the Congo).

# 5 The evolution of the People's Liberation Army Navy

## The twin missions of area-denial and peacetime operations

*Michael McDevitt and Frederic Vellucci Jr.*[1]

## Introduction

Building and sustaining a navy capable of conducting a "modern war under high-tech informationalized conditions,"[2] as the Chinese put it, is a very expensive proposition. The fact that Beijing has made the decision to allocate scarce resources for this objective suggests that the Chinese leadership, which has traditionally not been schooled in "things maritime," believes that the strategic interests of the state can be secured only with a robust naval force. This is a historic departure from the strategic traditions of China. Throughout China's long history, its strategic orientation could be categorized as continental and hence its strategic tradition – its way of thinking about and framing strategic security related issues – has largely focused on land war. A PLAN (People's Liberation Army Navy) senior captain writing in 2004 in the journal *Chinese Military Science* characterized this land-based geostrategic perspective "from beginning to end" as emphasizing "land power at the expense of sea power."[3] While this was historically accurate and probably was a widely held perspective among many PLA (People's Liberation Army) naval officers when written, the truth is that by 2004 the leadership of the PLA had long since recognized China's growing dependence on the sea and its historic vulnerability along its seaward approaches.

China's strategic situation began to change with the collapse of the Soviet Union. The risk of cross-border aggression from Beijing's northern neighbor moderated. The threat of invasion – the primary worry of Chinese or indeed most Eurasian strategists for many centuries – has all but disappeared. In the mean time, China's economic growth over the past 20 years has become heavily dependent on trade, most of which is carried in containers loaded on ships. As a result, the security of the maritime domain is a growing preoccupation for China.[4] As China's global interests have evolved so too has its conception of what sort of navy it needs.

This chapter argues that PLAN development is proceeding on two separate but related tracks, or vectors. The first vector is its primary wartime mission, the defense of China proper and its sovereign territory which, from Beijing's perspective, includes Taiwan. In this mission the PLAN is a major player, but not the only one in what would be a joint campaign (the PLA Air Force and Second Artillery also play major roles) to defeat an approaching naval force bent on attacking China or intervening on behalf of Taiwan. Doctrinally the PLA considers this contingency as "offshore active defense."[5] It is more popularly known in the west by the US-coined term "anti-access and area-denial."

The second vector revolves around a variety of missions that the PLAN should perform during peacetime. The most recent PLA Defense White Paper characterized this mission set as "Military Operations Other Than War" (MOOTW).[6] This is something new for the PLAN, and is a direct result of China's expanding global economic interests which have created global political interests. It is unlikely that when Liu Huaqing developed his "island chain" approach to maritime strategy he foresaw the tremendous growth in China's global trade and quest for natural resources (especially energy).[7] Nor is it likely that he foresaw the People's Republic of China's (PRC) growing international role in UN peacekeeping. The idea that thousands of PRC citizens would be working or traveling abroad didn't seem likely to any student of China 20 years ago. The fact that those citizens might need protection from terrorists or criminals seemed equally implausible.

This combination of China's expanding overseas interests and corresponding need for security has created a "demand signal" for a PLAN that can support UN-sanctioned missions, protect PRC interests abroad with a show of force, possibly respond to situations where PRC citizens are in jeopardy or require evacuation,[8] protect sea lines of communication, respond to natural disasters and demonstrate PRC resolve in support of embattled friends in Africa and along the South Asia littoral. As this chapter will discuss, these are issues that Beijing and the PLAN have been seriously thinking about. As China's global interests have expanded over the last decade the PLAN, unique among the PRC's military services, is now deeply involved in integrating distant, prolonged peacetime operations as part of its core mission set.

These new missions (for the PLAN) also require a different mix of naval capabilities than the wartime offshore active defense. During wartime the surface ship component of the PLAN is much less significant than its submarine force and land-based naval aviation arm. However, during peacetime missions the surface force has pride of place. The PLAN is learning how best to deploy and sustain surface combatants, amphibious ships and support ships on distant stations for long periods of time. They are learning quickly, as the deployments of PLAN surface ship task groups to the Gulf of Aden and Northern Arabian Sea on anti-piracy patrols has demonstrated. These deployments are a real world "battle-laboratory" for the PLAN, providing it an opportunity to observe the day-to-day operations of most of the world's great navies and absorb best practices for its own use.

## Rationalizing a two-vector navy

Several separate but interrelated factors animated China's leadership to actively support the development of the PLAN: (*a*) what the PLA calls the "main strategic direction," which essentially means the direction from which threats to China and its interests originate; (*b*) the need to deter Taiwan's independence and, if necessary, to deter or defeat an approaching United States Navy relief force if the PRC elects to attack Taiwan; (*c*) the historically novel situation for China in which international seaborne trade is what drives the economic growth of China; including the fact that China's economic development is increasingly dependent on oil and natural gas that is delivered by ships, and finally, (*d*) China's global economic interests have translated into global political interests that can often best be reinforced by a navy capable of operating globally on a sustained basis – at least as far as MOOTW missions are concerned.

The most important of these animating factors is the need to protect the nation and defend China's sovereignty. China's experience with European and Japanese colonialism in the nineteenth and early twentieth centuries clearly demonstrated the need for an effective maritime defense concept to counter Beijing's strategic vulnerabilities to enemy attacks from the sea. Thanks to adroit Chinese diplomacy, its land frontiers are stable and with the exception of India, it has resolved all of the territorial disputes it has had with its neighbors. However, from Beijing's perspective looking eastward, offshore the situation is more strategically problematic. China's maritime approaches are replete with unresolved sovereignty issues and genuine vulnerabilities. This has been true since the nineteenth century. Vulnerability to attack from the sea has been a problem for Beijing since at least 1842, when the Treaty of Nanking ended the First Opium War. This three-year conflict with Great Britain exposed imperial China's military weakness to attacks from the sea and ushered in the so-called century of humiliation by triggering a sequence of military and diplomatic humiliations perpetrated by Westerners and the Japanese that came primarily *from the sea*.

Today, China has the resources and political coherence necessary to address this problem. This is important since the vast majority of China's outstanding sovereignty claims and unresolved strategic issues are *maritime* in nature. For example:

- Taiwan is an island. It is the combination of Taiwan's air defense and the threat of intervention by the US military (primarily the United States Navy) that effectively keeps the Taiwan Strait a moat rather than a highway open to the PLA.
- Perhaps of almost equal strategic significance to Beijing is the geostrategic reality that China's economic center of gravity is on its eastern seaboard, which is extremely vulnerable to attack from the sea – a military task the United States is uniquely suited to execute.

- Territorial disputes with Japan over islands and seabed resources in the East China Sea remain unresolved. Anytime sovereignty is an issue one cannot overlook the possibility that Asian nations might resort to the use of force. Both Japan and China have emphasized their claims by the periodic deployment of naval and coast guard vessels to the region. The September 2010 incident between a Chinese fishing boat and two Japanese coast guard ships is only the most recent illustration of these disputes' continuing volatility.[9]
- Unsettled territorial disputes, and their concomitant resource issues, remain with respect to the Spratly Islands and the South China Sea – another maritime problem that has been the cause of a number of recent incidents.[10]
- China's entire national strategy of reform and opening depends largely upon maritime trade and commerce. China's economy is driven by the combination of exports and imports. This trade travels mainly by sea.
- Finally, there is the issue of energy. It has become commonplace to observe that the PRC will increasingly depend upon foreign sources of oil and natural gas, most of which come by sea.

Although neither Washington nor Beijing officially acknowledges it, Beijing's primary military competitor is the United States, which is the world's foremost naval power that maintains – as it has for the past 50 years – a significant naval presence on China's "doorstep."[11] Should China elect to use force to resolve either reunification with Taiwan or any of its outstanding maritime claims, the United States is the one military power that could deny China success. With its air and naval presence in the region, the United States has the potential to stymie any attempt to use the growing capability of the PLA to settle these issues by *force majeure*. The United States is also closely allied with China's historical antagonist Japan, which also has an excellent navy and a formidable maritime tradition.

The importance of unresolved maritime issues to China's leadership was highlighted by the December 2004 Chinese Defense White Paper, which swept aside assumptions regarding land-force preeminence when it stated that the PLAN, the PLA Air Force and the ballistic missile force – the Second Artillery – are to receive priority in funding. Further, it explicitly lays out its ambitions for the PLAN, Air Force and Second Artillery:

> While continuing to attach importance to the building of the Army, the PLA gives priority to the building of the Navy, Air Force and Second Artillery force to seek balanced development of the combat force structure, *in order to strengthen the capabilities for winning both command of the sea and command of the air, and conducting strategic counter strikes* [emphasis added].[12]

The evolution of the PLA Navy  79

The point is that the development of the PLAN has been based on sound strategic rationale, and while Beijing has not made this case in any comprehensive official fashion the body of work by serious naval analysts, along with combination of Chinese Defense White Papers, credible Chinese language articles, and the US Department of Defense Annual Reports to Congress on the development of the PLA provide a sound basis for understanding PLAN developments.[13]

**The wartime vector – anti access/area-denial**

As the strategic case for navy building began to emerge some 25 years ago, the Party and its Central Military Commission (CMC) had to make decisions regarding what sort of navy to build. The choices were relatively straightforward. One was to copy the model of the Imperial Japanese Navy (IJN), which had a balance of all the capabilities necessary for what today would be called a "blue-water" navy.

Besides being counter-cultural to a land force-dominated PLA, an IJN-like navy would have been very expensive and very difficult to make credible in terms of capability, training and technology. Attempting to create such a navy would also have presented a clear challenge to the stabilizing presence that the United States and its allies had created in the Western Pacific and along the East Asian littoral, because the wartime mission of such a navy would clearly revolve around defeating a foreign navy in a battle for sea control of the Western Pacific. That would have signaled to China's neighbors that Beijing was interested in projecting credible combat power anywhere along the East Asian littoral.

China's relationship with Russia provided the second, more obvious template for the PLA – adapt the defensive Soviet-style sea-denial model. Not only would this approach avoid the financial, technical and political costs associated with building a balanced blue-water force, but it also comported with the geostrategic circumstances facing China which are very similar to what the Soviets faced in terms of threats from the sea. The template is straightforward: create a very reliable open ocean surveillance system to detect approaching naval forces, and then use that information to dispatch submarines and land-based aircraft to attack the approaching navy before it can get within range of the mainland.

It is not a coincidence that PLA's concept of offshore defense seems to be based on how the Soviets thought about maritime strategy.[14] The Soviets developed a defensive maritime strategy with thresholds established at various distances from the Soviet Union's coasts. These thresholds were de facto "lines-in-the-water." The difference between the Soviets and China is that the PLA has elected to define distance-related thresholds in terms of "island chains."[15]

The Soviet template considered the waters closest to the mainland, out to approximately 200 nm, an area that Soviet naval forces and land-based air forces must be able to "control." Beyond this threshold, moving further to sea (to a range of about 1,200 nm) the Soviets' strategy was to "deny or contest" those waters to the United States Navy. In other words, the military requirement is sea control close in and sea denial as the distances from the mainland increase.

For China the 200-nm sea control zone results in a requirement for the PLAN to "control" the Yellow Sea, much of the East China Sea, the Taiwan Strait, the Tonkin Gulf and at a minimum, the northern portion of the South China Sea. This sea control area also closely approximates the PRC's exclusive economic zone (EEZ) and also generally follows the contour of the so-called "first island chain" that stretches southeast from Japan, through the Ryukyu's, Taiwan, and the Pratas and Paracel islands in the northern portion of the South China Sea. Not surprisingly, this sea control zone is where most of the recent maritime incidents between the United States and China have taken place, including the 2001 EP-3 incident, the 2009 USNS *Impeccable* incident and China's 2010 protests over the participation of the *George Washington* CSG in military exercises in the Yellow Sea.

If the entire South China Sea is included within the first island chain threshold the "sea control" zone runs beyond 200 nm in that one area. While this deviation makes it even harder to actually execute the mission of sea control because of the increase in water space, including the entirety of Beijing's territorial claims in the South China Sea in the sea control zone makes sense. Plotting 200-nm EEZ radius circles around each of the various islands and features it claims makes it easy for the PLA to conclude that the South China Sea belongs within the sea control area. It also creates a "requirement" to improve the military potential of disputed islands as bases or outposts in the South China Sea. For example, the airfield on Woody Island in the Paracel Group is an important contributor to the ability to execute a sea control mission in the South China Sea.

Beyond the first island chain threshold the open ocean expanse extends to what the PLA terms the "second island chain." This second threshold approximates the Soviet 1,200-nm "line in the water." Except in China's case the line is probably closer to 1,300 nm because this is the range the Chinese ascribe to Tomahawk cruise missiles.[16] This vast area between 200–1,300 nm essentially encompasses the Philippine Sea. This is the area in which use of the seas would be "contested." The PLA ambition is to win the contest for sea control and deny it to US naval forces.

This discussion is not as arcane as it might seem. These thresholds establish requirements for specific PLAN capabilities and as such are a "driver" of what capabilities the PLA will seek in its weapons and platforms. By establishing specific distances and areas where certain "military effects" are desired it becomes simpler to then define precise operational characteristics for specific weapons systems, and to determine how many ships, submarines and aircraft are required to accomplish the intended missions. These thresholds also help organize thinking in the creation of what could be termed a layered defense.

By integrating surveillance, land-based aircraft, submarine and cruise missiles with the PLA's most sophisticated arm, its ballistic missile force, Beijing is creating a genuinely joint (multi-service) area-denial (AD) capability in which the navy plays an important but not the leading role.[17] Of course, A2 (Pentagonese for anti-access) and AD are US coined terms, first introduced into official Defense Department lexicon in the 2001 Quadrennial Defense Review.[18] Both are now commonly used to characterize attempts to prevent the US military from intervening should China elect to attack Taiwan. The basic idea is to keep approaching United States Navy aircraft carrier strike groups from getting within tactical aircraft operating ranges. Or, as Commander of the US Pacific Command, Admiral Robert Willard recently testified, "to challenge US freedom of action in the region."[19]

In Pentagon terminology A2 is often used synonymously with AD. They are normally referred to together, as in anti-access/area-denial, or A2/AD. A very recent report by the influential research organization, the Center for Strategic and Budgetary Assessment (CSBA), differentiates among the two by equating A2 as the attempt to deny access to large fixed bases, such as Kadena Air Force base in Okinawa, so US Air Force fighters cannot become involved in a cross strait conflict.[20] CSBA's parsing now defines AD as those capabilities intended to defeat mobile maritime forces.

It goes without saying that these are US and not Chinese terms. While they are useful characterizations because they describe the operational objective (or military effect) the PLA is trying to accomplish if operations are successfully executed, they are not used by the PLA – it refers to "active defense" instead. A good discussion of the strategic concepts that form the basis for understanding active defense is found in the PLA's *Science of Military Strategy*. It says, "active defense is the essential feature of China's military strategy and is the keystone of the theory of China's strategic guidance." The PLA argues that "active defense" is actually a "strategic counterattack" because if an enemy "offends our national interests, it means the enemy has already fired the first shot." It is the mission of the PLA "to do all we can to dominate the enemy by striking first." It goes on to instruct "we should try our best to fight against the enemy as far away as possible, to lead the war to the enemy's operational base ... and to actively strike all the effective strength forming the enemy's war system."[21]

It is important to recognize that while the focus of this chapter is the PLAN, China's approach to A2 should in fact be considered a joint military operation – in that it involves more than one service. It involves the PLAN, PLA Air Force and the Second Artillery. Even though most of the fighting would take place off China's littoral at sea or on neighboring islands with US bases, many of the most important capabilities that the PLA would employ are in the other PLA services and not the PLAN.

It is also important to recognize that from China's perspective an A2 campaign is inherently defensive; it is a responsive operational concept designed to react to the problems posed by US forces close to or closing in on the Chinese mainland. While it is has been developed with a Taiwan contingency in mind, the concept itself has broader applicability than simply a Taiwan conflict scenario.

This is a central point, A2 capabilities are important to China beyond a Taiwan contingency. The operational concept and attendant military capabilities resident in A2 are relevant to the defense of the Chinese mainland from attack from the sea; a vulnerability that has plagued China since the Opium War era. Thus, even if the prospect of conflict over Taiwan evaporates at some point in the future, the PLA capabilities associated with A2 will almost certainly not disappear.

This approach to wartime maritime strategy also fits well with the political message that Beijing has been sending the world: China's rise will be peaceful and non-threatening. Fielding an obviously defense-oriented operational concept is tangible evidence that China is not going to become an expeditionary or power-projection threat. Of course, as China's access-denial capabilities get better, the security situation for US allies in Northeast Asia becomes worse; because China has the potential to deny maritime reinforcement should those allies be under attack. The PLAN submarine force in particular is a capability-based threat to Japan's maritime lifelines that Japan cannot, and probably will not, ignore.

For the rest of Asia, an access-denial strategy fits well with China's broader strategic objectives of not creating powerful enemies in the region, because the naval portion of access denial is not the sort of capabilities one associates with power projection. Specifically, submarines are the central PLAN contribution to access-denial and the PLAN's focus on commissioning many more diesel than nuclear submarines also helps reinforce the positive diplomatic message of a "peaceful development." They fit within the template of East Asian naval developments that have South Korea, Singapore and Malaysia joining Japan, Taiwan and Australia as nations with conventionally powered submarines whose mission is primarily defensive.

## New demand signals: new strategic missions and objectives

The combination of China's expanding global interests and equities, plus pressure from the United States to become a responsible stakeholder, have created a new "demand signal" for Chinese maritime capabilities that went beyond what is needed for area-denial. Today the PLAN needs forces that can support UN sanctioned missions, protect Chinese interests abroad with shows of force, and in the future protect or evacuate its citizens in jeopardy, protect sea lines of communication, respond to natural disasters and demonstrate national resolve in support of embattled friends in Africa and along the South Asia littoral. These are missions that an A2 naval force is not well equipped to execute. The PLA, especially the PLAN, has been forced by circumstances to evolve.

## The leadership response to new demands

On December 24, 2004, recently-promoted CMC Chairman Hu Jintao announced a new set of strategic missions and objectives for the Chinese armed forces.[22] This speech marks a major turning point in Chinese thinking about the role of the PLA with major implications for the PLAN. These *New Historic Missions* are:

- The PLA should guarantee the rule of the Party.
- The PLA should safeguard national economic development and territorial sovereignty. Ensuring China's sovereignty, territorial integrity and domestic security during its "strategic opportunity period."[23] This includes responsibility for dealing with Taiwanese and ethnic separatist issues, non-traditional security issues, territorial land and maritime disputes and domestic social security problems.[24]
- Safeguarding China's expanding national interests. This mission calls on the armed forces to broaden their view of security to account for China's growing national interests. This refers to resource security, sea lane of communication (SLOC) security, and maritime rights and interests. It also calls on the PLA to consider the security of China's overseas investments and presence.
- Helping to ensure world peace. To accomplish this goal the *New Historic Missions* call upon the armed forces to both increase participation in international security activities (such as peacekeeping, search and rescue, and anti-terror operations) as well as to improve its military capabilities to "deal with crises, safeguard peace, contain war, and win a war."[25]

The first mission, defending the rule of the Chinese Communist Party, had always been a PLA mission. The second mission also was not new – the PLA had always been tasked with defending sovereignty and territorial integrity and had long been tasked with defending economic development. What the *New Historic Missions* changed was the degree to which these two tasks were linked together. This underlined the extent to which Chinese leaders saw national economic development and national security as being linked together.

The third and fourth missions were new and very significant. For the first time, the PLA (and therefore the PLAN) was being assigned responsibilities well beyond China and its immediate periphery. This was official recognition that China's national interests now extended beyond its borders and that the PLA's missions were to be based on those expanding interests, not just geography. It was also an official announcement that

Chinese leaders saw China as a global actor with a role to play in support of global stability through peacekeeping and other missions.

Furthermore, the announcement of *New Historic Missions* appears to have had implications for the modernization of the PLAN. Since the *New Historic Missions* speech, there has been an ongoing discussion about developing a new operational concept, termed *yuanhai* in Chinese, translated as "distant seas," which would extend PLAN operations beyond regional seas.[26] This term appears to be used alongside the "offshore active defense" which is still used to frame doctrinal development and potential operations in regional waters near China.[27] The PLAN is now conducting anti-piracy operations off the Horn of Africa – its first ever out-of-area operation – as part of an international effort. While Chinese military, civilian analysts and policymakers are apparently still fleshing out the concept of "distant seas," it is clear that trade and economic expansion overseas are creating new political interests and security concerns which are putting pressure on Chinese leaders to look at maritime issues in new ways.

## The impact of globalization on Chinese maritime thinking

While this debate goes on, in his *New Historic Missions* speech, Hu Jintao clearly identified expanding national interests beyond China's borders as a mission for the PLA. He stated that globalization was tying China to the rest of the world and that "China needed the world and that the world needed China."[28] This phrase is also included in the 2006 Defense White Paper.[29] Furthermore, Hu said that the oceans were a key medium of "international contact" that connected China with its new and expanding overseas interests.[30] Essentially, this was an open ended declaration that any economic interest of China's anywhere in the world that is in any way connected to the sea is a potential maritime interest. As two professors from the PLA's Dalian Naval Academy noted:

> In the past, the military's *Historic Missions* emphasized the need to respond to external security threats, [and] protect the country's territorial land, seas, and airspace, and the scope of military vision was restricted geographically and physically to three-dimensional space. [Now however,] the military's *New Historic Missions* have been expanded to include not only defense of the nation's survival interests but also defense of the nation's [economic] development interests. This means not only protecting the security of territorial land, sea, and airspace; it also means protecting maritime security, space security, and electromagnetic security as well as other aspects of national security. These new requirements reflect major changes to [China's] security situation, and have affected a major expansion of the military's missions, tasks, and strategic field of vision.[31]

The evidence seems clear that China's maritime interests have steadily expanded from predominantly territorial and sovereignty interests, to economic interests connected with the EEZ, to global maritime interests. China's thinking about the role and uses of military force is changing, and this change is reflected in ongoing discussions of expanding China's naval operations. In large measure these discussions have revolved around the *peacetime* uses of the navy, the PLA has embraced the concept by borrowing the US military acronym – MOOTW, which means military operations other than war, or more simply peacetime operations.[32]

Specifically, the *New Historic Missions* have caused the PLA to focus on developing new capabilities to fight terrorism, and conduct peacekeeping and humanitarian assistance operations. As a result of this new thinking, the PLAN now places a higher priority on non-traditional security and MOOTW. China's 2008 Defense White Paper for the first time described MOOTW as an important role of national military forces, and noted that the PLA is developing MOOTW capabilities.[33] The authoritative Academy of Military Science volume, the *Science of Naval Training*, outlines five main types of MOOTW that the PLAN is training for:

- Actions conducted domestically during peacetime; this includes emergency natural disaster relief as well as closely coordinated actions with the People's Armed Police Coast Guard units in support of law enforcement organizations to combat smuggling, arrest drug dealers, etc.;
- Demonstrations of armed force and military deterrence;
- Actions focused on preserving national and social stability, participating in maritime security cooperation including peacekeeping and counter-terrorism;
- Military diplomacy;
- At-sea search and rescue actions including those conducted independently, in cooperation with other services and branches, civilian forces, or international forces.[34]

The notion of military diplomacy is particularly important. As PLAN Political Commissar Hu Yanlin noted in 2006:

> The purpose of naval diplomacy has evolved from isolated ship visits to ship visits coordinated with larger political and diplomatic activities. In terms of content, these activities have evolved from working against traditional security threats to working against an expanding number of non-traditional security threats including piracy and multinational criminal organizations.[35]

## Implications for the future

As the *New Historic Missions* speech has made clear, China's leaders are now thinking about a much wider range of interests than are covered within the concept of "offshore active defense" which after all is essentially a wartime defensive concept, and is not particularly relevant for operations beyond the second island chain during either peace or war. On the other hand the notion of a navy capable of operating on "distant seas," would, according to a 2007 *Military Science* article have the capability to:

> Protect strategic SLOC and preserve freedom of movement on the high seas. Distant seas capabilities include: maritime patrols, surface and subsurface operational capabilities, island and reef offensive/defensive operational capabilities, seaboard assault capabilities, at-sea operations command, and comprehensive support capabilities.[36]

The article went on to state that the interests that are to be defended under the concept of "distant seas" include energy assets in the Persian Gulf, Africa and Latin America; SLOC between China and the Middle East; more than 1,800 Chinese fishing vessels operating on the distant seas and off the waters of 40 different nations; ocean resources in international waters; and the security of overseas Chinese.[37]

It is unclear if the PLA will try to integrate the two concepts (offshore active defense and distant seas), the "vectors" of this chapter's title, into a comprehensive maritime strategy for the navy or elect to keep them as separate concepts – one which is "joint" and intended mainly to defend China from attack and is mainly relevant during a time of war, and the other – distant seas – which has broader applicability across the potential spectrum of conflict, and is more Navy-centric than joint.

Some Chinese security analysts argue that the PLAN will continue to focus on building an offshore defense but will develop capabilities for occasional long distance missions as contingencies arise. However, other military analysts have written articles that suggest that the ability to conduct long-distance operations will become a more routine mission in the future and that the distant seas operations concept will replace that of offshore defense. An article by Professor Tang Fuquan of the PLA Dalian Vessel Academy notes that while the "offshore defense" concept remained useful throughout the 1980s and 1990s, since the new century Hu Jintao has been emphasizing that the PLAN must continue increasing its operational capabilities within the offshore sea area (but) it must also gradually begin to transition to distant seas defense and develop "distant sea mobility operations capabilities."[38] The leadership of China has come to recognize that offshore active defense is essential but not sufficient when it comes to sea-lanes and interests around the world.

In response to these new international developments, the CMC has adjusted China's national military strategy – the *Military Strategic Guidelines* – twice in the past eight years.[39] These adjustments have highlighted the value of naval power to China. An analysis of China's response during this period reveals that the PLAN's status has been made a "strategic service" and given priority for modernization, and directed to expand its operational focus to include: (*a*) Continuing to improve its offshore active defense capabilities; (*b*) Introducing expanding roles and missions for protecting China's increasingly important maritime and overseas economic interests; (*c*) Emphasizing MOOTW which include fighting terrorism, and conducting peacekeeping and humanitarian assistance operations.

The PLAN is likely to continue developing the capabilities required for conducting MOOTW and responding to non-traditional security threats. This is both a legitimate policy response to rising non-traditional security challenges in the post-11 September world as well as a policy choice by Beijing to help sensitize regional powers to a rising PLAN.

## Conclusion: offshore active defense (access denial) is not enough

The revision of the *Historic Missions* is a clear indicator that a naval strategy built only around the concept of protecting the maritime approaches to China is not sufficient. As a wartime strategic concept it makes sense, but during peacetime the navy is also expected to support the interests of the state. The PLAN is now actively thinking through how to integrate distant, prolonged operations as part of its core mission set (such as its current anti-piracy patrols in the Gulf of Aden). As PLAN Political Department Deputy Director Rear Admiral Yao Wenhuai has argued, developing new distant seas capabilities is vital for protecting China's national security and development: "As modern PLAN weapons increase in range and precision and the naval battlefield expands from the offshore to the distant seas, the development of distant seas mobile capabilities will become increasingly important for protecting national security and development."[40] More recently, Senior Colonel Chen Zhou, who has played an important role in the drafting of China's Defense White Papers, has also weighed in on the need to take greater steps towards protecting its overseas interests. Arguing that China should be able to project power, especially naval power, in pursuit of peacetime missions in support of China's legitimate overseas interests, Chen notes,

> We should expand the sphere of maritime activity, strive to demonstrate our presence in some critical strategic regions, use diplomatic and economic means to establish strategic supporting points, and make use of berthing points to which we legally get access from relevant countries in relevant sea areas.[41]

Chen makes it clear that he is not talking about a permanent global network of bases, but he does lend credence to the "string of pearls" argument that has caused concern in India, by making the case that China should consider the development of some kind of support facilities in more than one region that could be used to support a routine, though not necessarily permanent, presence for the Chinese Navy in the future. (Something the United States Navy has called "a place not a base.")[42]

While the views of Chen Zhou are not official policy, his role as an author of China's Defense White Papers suggests that his views are influential. There is no question that the anti-piracy patrols have highlighted the requirement for a place where PLAN ships can call where they can reliably receive fuel, fresh food and water. A place where sailors can go on liberty without risk and a place near an airport where spare parts and personnel can routinely be received.

The PLAN is learning how to deploy and sustain surface combatants, amphibious ships and support ships to distant stations for long periods of time. In this regard the anti-piracy patrols provide an ideal "battle laboratory" for the PLAN, it can observe best practices of all the major navies in the world.

While continuing to maintain a defensive strategy to protect China and its possessions, the PLAN will also deploy surface warships whose primary utility will be to provide peacetime presence, sea lane monitoring and crisis response. This "second-iteration navy" will not only be useful to China in furthering its own interests but will also demonstrate that China too can be a responsible stakeholder in a military sense.

Because the PLAN is embarked on a new operational vector that is very different from offshore active defense access, it will in important ways require different sorts of capabilities, such as more logistics support ships, amphibious helicopter capable ships, more destroyers with better endurance and air defenses (this usually means bigger because increased range demands more storage capacity). Such missions have almost certainly created the basic rationale behind the PLAN's apparent decision to build a modest aircraft carrier force.[43] They understand the importance of air cover for distant operations that could involve combat, and have also observed the value of helicopters in many of these missions. Looking into the future it is not hard to imagine how the emphasis on "distant seas" operations could result in a PLAN that becomes a more balanced force in terms of its range of capabilities and begins to resemble the US or French navies.

Thus, the decision to use the PLAN in a wider variety of "peacetime" MOOTW will almost certainly result in bigger and more capable Chinese warships that will become much more visible globally. The upshot is they are likely to raise more concerns about China's rise and its intentions in the countries of Southeast Asia and along the Indian Ocean littoral because they will be visible manifestations of Chinese power projection. Ironically, because a global PLAN will be more visible, it may be the peacetime uses of its navy rather its wartime "off-shore active defense" force that causes more nations to become concerned about the negative implications that China's military modernization could have on their own security.

It is worth keeping in mind that the two vectors discussed in this chapter do not mean or imply the development of "two Chinese navies." This construct was used simply to make the point that the missions and attendant hardware capabilities of the PLAN in wartime and peacetime are different, but not mutually exclusive. Until the past few years the focus has been on the wartime missions. Now that China's leadership has decided to expand the mission set associated with naval operations, it is inevitable that additional capability will be added so the PLAN can accomplish the new missions. In so doing they have been provided the impetuous necessary for the PLAN to become better-rounded (balanced), and will over time be better able to support Chinese national interests, wherever in the world they might be.

## Notes

1 This chapter represents the opinions of the authors alone, and should not be construed as representing the views of either CNA (Center for Naval Analyses) or the Department of the Navy.
2 For more information on this PLA concept and current Chinese efforts to prepare for military combat under these conditions, see: Dave Finkelstein, "China's National Military Strategy: An Overview of the Military Strategic Guidelines," pp. 103–106, in Roy Kamphausen and Andrew Scobell, eds., *Right-Sizing the People's Liberation Army: Exploring the Contours of China's Military*, US Army Strategic Studies Institute Press, September 2007.
3 Senior Captain Xu Qi, "Maritime Geostrategy and the Development of the Chinese Navy in the Early Twenty-First Century," 2004 *China Military Science*, translated and published by Andrew Erickson and Lyle Goldstein in the *Naval War College Review*, Autumn, 2006, vol. 59, no. 4, pp. 51–63.
4 Peng Guangqian and Yao Youzhi, eds., *The Science of Military Strategy*, Beijing: Military Science Publishing House, Academy of Military Science of the People's Liberation Army, 2005, pp. 3–13. These pages contain a very interesting and fulsome discussion of China's history of strategic thought.
5 Jiang Shenggong, "Offshore Defense Strategy [*Jinhai Fangyu Zhanlue*]," in Shi Yunsheng, ed., *The PLA Navy Encyclopedia*, Beijing: Maritime Press, 1998, vol. 2, p. 1154.
6 Information Office of the State Council of the People's Republic of China, *China's National Defense in 2008*, January 2009, p. 12.
7 Liu Huaqing, *Memoirs of Liu Huaqing*, Beijing: People's Liberation Army Press, 2004.
8 There is no official indication that this is a mission that has been assigned to the navy. While ongoing debates suggest this is an important driver of *military* modernization, for the time being it appears that the PLA would rely on its air force for evacuation operations. This is sensible given that the PLAN only maintains a presence in the Gulf of Aden region *at this time*.
9 Martin Fackler and Ian Johnson, "Arrest in Disputed Seas Riles China and Japan," *New York Times*, September 19, 2010, p. A1.
10 Mark Landler, "Offering to Aid Talks, US Challenges China on Disputed Islands," *New York Times*, July 23, 2010, p. A4.
11 The US Seventh Fleet is permanently stationed in East Asia. The flagship and the *George Washington* carrier strike group call Yokosuka, Japan their home port. In addition an amphibious task group is located in Sasebo, Japan.

12 PRC Defense White Paper, December 2004, Information Office of the State Council of the PRC, December 2004, Beijing. Online, available at: http://english.people.com.cn/whitepaper/defense2004.
13 CNA's Project Asia convened the first in-depth conference on the PLAN ten years ago. One of the presentations, by this author, addressed the reality that Chinese A2 strategies, which were just beginning to receive attention, seemed to be based on Soviet era concepts of sea denial, see Michael McDevitt, *The PLA Navy: Past, Present and Future Prospects*, A Conference Report, CNA Corporation, Alexandria Virginia, May 2000. For an overall discussion of PLAN strategy see Bernard D. Cole, *The Great Wall at Sea: China's Navy Enters the Twenty-First Century*, second edition, Annapolis, MD: US Naval Institute Press, 2010. For an official unclassified view see Office of Naval Intelligence, *The People's Liberation Army Navy, A Modern Navy with Chinese Characteristics*, Suitland, MD: Office of Naval Intelligence, August 2009. Fortunately we have available the now declassified National Intelligence Estimate NIE 11–15–82D *Soviet Naval Strategy and Programs Through the 1990s*, March 1983 which provides a factual template of the approach China is following. The NIE is found in John B. Hattendorf Jr., *The Evolution of the US Navy's Maritime Strategy, 1977–1986*, Naval War College Newport Paper 19, Center for Naval Warfare Studies, 2004. Senior Captain Xu Qi, "Maritime Geostrategy and the Development of the Chinese Navy in the Early Twenty-First Century," 2004, *China Military Science*, translated and published by Andrew Erickson and Lyle Goldstein in the *Naval War College Review*, Autumn 2006, vol. 59, no. 4, pp. 51–63. Over the course of 2009, the issue of ASBM's and China's A2 strategy has received considerable attention. See for example; Michael S. Chase, Andrew S. Erickson and Christopher Yeaw, "Chinese Theater and Strategic Missile Force Modernization and its Implications for the United States," *Journal of Strategic Studies*, February 2009, pp. 67–114; Andrew S. Erickson and David D. Yang," On the Verge of a Game-Changer," *US Naval Institute Proceedings*, May 2009, pp. 26–32; Andrew Erickson, "Facing A New Missile Threat From China, How The US Should Respond To China's Development Of Anti-Ship Ballistic Missile Systems," *CBSNews.com*, May 28, 2009; Andrew S. Erickson and David D. Yang, "Using the Land to Control the Sea? Chinese Analysts Consider the Antiship Ballistic Missile," *Naval War College Review*, Autumn 2009, vol. 62, no. 4, pp. 53–86. Important Chinese language articles on PLAN development include: Ge Dongsheng, ed., *Guojia Anquan Zhanlue Lun* [Theory of National Security Strategy], Beijing: Military Science Publishing, 2006; Lu Rude, "*Zai Da Zhanlue zhong gei Zhongguo Haiquan Dingwei* [Defining Sea Power in China's Grand Strategy]," *Renmin Haijun* June 6, 2007; Yao Wenhuai, "*Jianshe qiangda haijun, weihu woguo haiyang zhanlue liyi* [Build a Powerful Navy, Defend China's Maritime Strategic Interests]," *Guofang*, no. 7, 2007; Zhang Wei, *Guojia Haishang Anquan* [National Maritime Security]," Beijing: Haichao Chubanshe, 2008.
14 Cole, *The Great Wall at Sea: China's Navy Enters the Twenty-First Century*, pp. 163–164. Dr Cole makes the important point that PLAN Commander Liu Huaqing in the mid-1980s had been a student at the Voroshilov Naval Academy when Sergi Gorshcov, later leader of the Soviet Navy, was an instructor. See also an excellent discussion of Soviet influence in You Ji, "The Evolution of China's Maritime Combat Doctrines and Models: 1949–2001," Institute of Defense and Strategic Studies (IDSS), Singapore, Working paper 22, May 2002. pp. 2–8.
15 Senior Captain Xu Qi, in Erickson and Goldstein, *Naval War College Review*, p. 57.
16 Li Xinqi, Tan Shoulin, Li Hongxia (Second Artillery Engineering College, Xian, China), "Precaution Model and Simulation Actualization on Threat of Maneuver Target Group on the Sea," August 1, 2005, in author's possession.

17 Ronald O'Rourke, *China Naval Modernization: Implications for US Navy Capabilities – Background and Issues for Congress*, CRS Report for Congress, updated December 23, 2009. CRS website, Order Code RL 33153: 8. This is the single best open-source compilation of information on the PLAN available to scholars and research specialists. Another invaluable source is the DOD Annual Report to Congress, "Military Power of the Peoples Republic of China 2009," March 25, 2009, online, available at: www.defense.gov?pubs/pdf's/China_military_power_report-2009.pdf.
18 *The Report of the 2001 Quadrennial Defense Review*, September 30, 2001, Department of Defense, no longer available on DOD website, copy in author's possession, p. 25. The report speaks about A2 and AD as they relate to one of America's fundamental strategic concepts – *deterring forward*. Specifically, it goes on to say, "deterrence in the future will continue to depend heavily upon the capability resident in forward stationed and forward deployed combat and expeditionary forces."
19 Statement of Admiral Robert Willard, United States Navy, Commander US Pacific Command before the House Armed Services Committee on US Pacific Command Posture, March 23, 2010, p. 12, in author's possession.
20 Jan Van Tol Mark, Gunzinger, Andrew F. Krepinevich and James Thomas, *Air Sea Battle: A Point of Departure Operational Concept*, Center for Budgetary and Strategic Assessment, May 2010, footnote 1, p. 1. Online, available at: www.csbaonline.org/4Publications/PubLibrary/R.20100518.Air_Sea_Battle__A_/R.20100518.Air_Sea_Battle__A_.pdf.
21 Peng Guangqian and Yao Youzhi, eds, *The Science of Military Strategy*, Beijing: Military Science Publishing House, Academy of Military Science of the People's Liberation Army, 2005, pp. 459–461.
22 Hu Jintao, "Understand the New Historic Missions of our Military in the New Period of the New Century," National Defense Education website of Jiangxi Province, online, available at: http://gfjy.jiangxi.gov.cn/yl.asp?did+11349.htm. For additional information on the Chinese Armed Force's New Historic Missions, see Daniel Hartnett's unpublished paper, "Towards a Globally Focused Chinese Military: The Historic Missions of the Chinese Armed Forces," Summer 2008.
23 The phrase "strategic opportunity period" is a standard term that refers to a period when various international and domestic factors create a positive environment for a nation's economic and social development. Jiang Zemin first used this term during his report to the Sixteenth Party Congress (November 8, 2002) in reference to the first 20 years of the twenty-first century.
24 Sun Kejia, Liu Feng, Liu Yang, Lin Peisong, eds., *Faithfully Implementing Our Military's Historic Missions in the New Period of the New Century*, Beijing: Ocean Tide Press, 2006, pp. 102–126.
25 Wang Zhaohai, "Honestly Undertake the Historic Missions of Our Armed Forces in the New Period of the New Century," *Seeking Truth*, no. 23, 2005, p. 25.
26 The term *yuanhai* can also be translated as "open seas" or "distant oceans." Some English sources translate the term as "blue water." However, current usage of the term indicates that the Chinese are not using the term to describe what the United States Navy would consider a blue-water navy. We have chosen "distant seas" as it is the most commonly used translation.
27 The 2008 Defense White Paper states that China continues to develop its ability to conduct "offshore" operations while gradually building its ability to conduct operations in distant seas. *China's National Defense in 2008*, Beijing: Information Office of the State Council, 2009.
28 Hu Jintao, "New Historic Missions."

29 Ibid.; and *China' National Defense in 2006*.
30 Hu Jintao, "New Historic Missions."
31 Fang Yonggang and Xu Mingshan, "Focusing on Implementing the Military's Historic Missions and Strengthening Navy Grassroots Development," p. 84.
32 Zhang Yongyi, ed., *The Science of Naval Training*, Beijing: Academy of Military Science Press, 2006, p. 250.
33 Information Office of the State Council, *China's National Defense in 2008*, online, available at: www.china.org.cn/government/central_government/2009-01/20/content_17155577.htm.
34 Ibid.
35 Yongyi, *The Science of Naval Training*, p. 250.
36 Lu Xue, "Views on Improving the Armed Forces' Ability to Execute the Historic Missions," *Zhongguo Junshi Kexue*, no 5, 2007, p. 107.
37 Ibid.
38 Tang Fuquan and Wu Yi, "A Discussion of China's Maritime Defense Strategy," *Zhongguo Junshi Kexue*, no. 5, 2007.
39 See Daniel Hartnett's unpublished paper, "Towards a Globally Focused Chinese Military: The Historic Missions of the Chinese Armed Forces," Summer 2008.
40 Yao Wenhuai, "Build a Powerful Navy, Defend China's Maritime Strategic Interests," *Guofang*, no. 7, 2007, pp. 1–2. RAdm Yao was Deputy Director of the PLAN's Political Department at the time the article was published.
41 Chen Zhou, "On Development of China's Defensive National Defense Policy under New Situation," *Zhongguo Junshi Kexue*, no. 6, 2009, pp. 63–71.
42 Ibid., See also "Jiefangjun Bao Article on Building PLA Strategic Power Projection Capability," *Jiefangjun Bao* OSC Translation, August 26, 2010, CPP20100826702001.
43 Li, Nan and Christopher Weuve, "China's Aircraft Carrier Ambitions: An Update," *Naval War College Review*, Winter 2010, p. 15. Online, available at: www.usnwc.edu/publications/Naval-War-College-Review/2010–Winter.aspx.

# 6 Japan's maritime past, present and future[1]

*Alessio Patalano*

## Introduction

In the growing literature on the emergence of contemporary East Asia, China is often portrayed as a case in point of how sea power influences the ways in which a nation-state redefines its international status and influence. Prospects of a former Soviet aircraft carrier flying Chinese colors sometime in the future or of a new generation of diesel submarines patrolling Asian waters are evidence enough of a "red star" rising over the Pacific, one ready to challenge American prominence on the great commons. Yet, whereas China's maritime empowerment is still in the making, Japan's is not. Japan possesses today one of the world's most technologically advanced fleets, with a surface force more than twice the size of the Royal Navy's and a submarine component twice that of the French Navy. This force is complemented in its constabulary functions by a large and capable coast guard. Crucially, Japan's contemporary naval power is not the result of a rearmament following post-Cold War changes in the international system, as it is the case of other Asian state actors. It is the product of a post-war economic system and longstanding geographic features that made (and continue to make) the pursuit of a degree of sea power not a matter of choice but a strategic imperative.

This chapter examines the evolution of Japan's maritime experience. It argues that the country's insular geography and scarcity in primary resources represented key factors that shaped the role sea power played in Japan's ascendancy to the international stage. The chapter explains how Japan's present outlook as a maritime nation, one relying on maritime trade and access to the sea for the supply of raw materials for its survival, is not a natural consequence of its geography. Rather, it is the result of a learning experience. Seafaring habits were developed early in Japanese history but it was only in the nineteenth century that a true national awareness vis-à-vis maritime affairs consolidated. The chapter details how, at the turn of the century, Japan's rise in the business of naval warfare was marked by its leaders' attempt to use the sea as a barrier against foreign interference. The strategic ramifications of the difference between an awesome naval shield and a force designed to protect critical economic vulnerabilities were realized only too late, and Japan paid the highest price for it. Learning from the past, Japan's post-war naval rearmament was pursued as a means to protect the country's vital maritime interests, eventually making the navy a central component of the country's national security.

## A "local affair": sea power in pre-modern Japan

In pre-modern Japan, sea power was not a matter of state. It was an economic and political resource at the service of local seafaring communities that inhabited the archipelago's southwest coasts, the Inland Sea and the Ryukyu Islands. Militarily, regional sea lords used nautical expertise and privately owned naval platforms for political gains in a country dominated by factions competing for power. Sea power granted these coastal areas a degree of autonomy in exchange for support to military campaigns that included naval operations.

Geography contributed to the early development of Japanese sea power in two ways. First, the stretch of water that separated the main islands of Japan from the eastern edges of the Eurasian continent proved to be wide enough to isolate them until the beginning of the nineteenth century (only the Mongol expeditions of 1274 and 1281 posed a serious threat to the archipelago). Strong currents, the westbound North Pacific stream known by Japanese inhabitants as *kuroshio* and the cold sub-arctic southbound *oyashio* stream, acted as a natural shield discouraging ambitions of conquest, whilst their average speeds of 2–3 knots even very close to the shores made oceanic navigation a hazardous affair. In this respect, the renowned 1830s woodblock print *The Great wave off Kanagawa* by artist Hokusai captured in a most iconic fashion the perilous nature of the waters surrounding Japan. Such a separation from the continent allowed the Japanese to choose the degree of engagement with their immediate neighborhood, favoring the development of a strong national character. Until the seventh century BC, separation did not entail complete isolation and regular economic, cultural and political exchanges with neighboring communities in Korea and China were maintained. Indeed, by the sixth century BC, the Yellow and East China Seas and the Sea of Japan represented core highways for a two-way trade of commodities and luxury goods as well as knowledge transfers in the field of literature, writing system, religion and technology from China through the Korean peninsula.

Second, the waters surrounding Japan constituted an ideal environment for fishing and soon became a crucial source of food for the population of the archipelago. Communities tended to concentrate in coastal areas and developed seafaring habits, especially along the Inland Sea, a protected warm-water channel ideally located to favor domestic sea communication and transport.[2] Recent archaeological studies confirmed that fishing and navigation techniques were an integrated part of the Japanese socio-economic system since the late Jōmon period (fifth to sixth centuries BC).[3] By the time a series of laws banning oceanic navigation were endorsed in the seventeenth century, the sea had entered Japan's daily life and customs, and maritime commercial enterprises were endeavors familiar to the Japanese both at the domestic and trans-regional levels. Recent scholarship emphasized how, between the fourteenth and fifteenth centuries, cities like Hyōgo, Onomichi, Tsuruga and Hakata, the Ryukyu Islands, were all flourishing commercial hubs of a wider maritime network. In this period, the port city of Sakai, located at the estuary of the Yamato River in the Bay of Osaka, stood out as an East Asian Venice, a semi-independent city state ruled by a group of oligarchs selected among representatives of the main commercial families. Building on Fernand Braudel's intellectual tradition, before the seventeenth century, Japan's maritime communities were key elements of an East Asian Mediterranean-like network stretching from the archipelago, through the Ryukyus and China to the western end of the South China Sea.[4]

The relative autonomy enjoyed by these maritime cities was a distinctive sign of a fragmented political system, one that did not favor the emergence of a "national concern" vis-à-vis Japan's maritime frontiers and as a result, no national standing fleet existed. In the fourteenth and sixteenth centuries, the main threat to maritime enterprises was represented by organized bands of pirates known as *wakō*, operating between Japan and coastal areas of Korea and China.[5] Until the unification of the country completed by Tokugawa Yeyasu in 1603, naval engagements occurred rarely and the majority took place in Japanese waters as part of domestic inter-clan rivalries and power struggles. The most significant of such engagements was the Battle of Dannoura, fought in April 1185 in the Strait of Shimonoseki, off the southern tip of Honshu. For half a day, the 840 ships of the Minamoto clan and the 500 units of the Taira were locked in a decisive fight to assert political influence over the Imperial court at the end of a five-year-long conflict also known as the Gempei War (1180–1185). Though the fleet led by Taira no Munemori was considered to be better manned, experienced in sea battles and more knowledgeable of the local tides, "neither fleet could boast of any definitive organization. Victory rested not on Taira's naval tactics, "ships were small, clumsy, oar-propelled junks, ... probably mainly fishing or ferry boats commissioned for the purpose."[6] Rather, it was achieved by the superior hand-to-hand combat capabilities of the Minamoto forces and the ability of their archers.

Similar political circumstances surrounded subsequent naval actions of the pre-modern period. The most significant difference was that by the sixteenth century feudal lords controlling maritime domains fielded fleets employing distinctive naval tactics. This was the case of the Murakami *suigun*, or sea lords, a feudal family pre-eminently based on the islands of Noshima, Kuroshima and Innoshima that "ruled the waves" of the Inland Sea. Reportedly, the naval forces of the lords of Murakami were organized in squadrons that attacked their opponents in single columns, with the leading ship firing bows and harquebuses, followed by units launching incendiary grenades as the enemy came at closer range. The central and rear parts of the battle line included troopships tasked to move in and offload boarding parties.[7] Seamanship and tactics enabled the Murakami *suigun* to contribute to the military campaigns of the late sixteenth century, though they were eventually defeated by the naval forces of the most powerful lord of the time, Oda Nobunaga, in a culminating fleet engagement on the Kizu River in 1578. With larger material resources at Oda's disposal, the bulk of his forces was centered on the *tekkōsen*, a warship covered with iron plates and equipped with three cannons – a rare feature on Japanese naval vessels of the time – specifically developed to counter the Murakami's tactics. In this and other naval battles that occurred in the turbulent Sengoku period (fifteenth to seventeenth centuries), a politically fragmented Japan became a battleground in which naval power was a function of land campaigns and naval bombardments, blockades and amphibious assaults were the tools to wider theatre gains.

In medieval Japan, the only notable exceptions to coastal and riverine actions were the 1592 and 1597 ruinous campaigns against Korea conducted by Oda's successor, Hideyoshi Toyotomi. Once Oda had established himself as a dominant military figure, Hideyoshi chose a path of continuity and sought to pursue his predecessor's ambition to expand Japanese power and influence on the continent.[8] To that end, he mobilized Japanese naval forces though he retained their overall command, imposing tactical choices that limited the actions of Japan's more experienced naval commanders like Kuki Yoshitaka, Katō Yoshiaki and Tōdō Takatora. In both campaigns, naval forces suffered from two core problems: they did not operated in a concerted fashion and, they had to give priority to the transport of troops to follow Hideyoshi's plan to win the land campaign. Sea control remained a secondary task and this offered an advantage to the Korean navy. This was a force of seasoned professionals under the command of Admiral Yi Sun-Sin, an experienced commander who had developed its skills fighting Japanese pirates. Carefully orchestrated tactical maneuvers, superior naval artillery and the deployment of "turtle-ships," or *Kobukson*, a sort of primitive dreadnought featuring iron plating covered with spikes to prevent boarding actions, sealed the destiny of Hideyoshi's campaigns.[9]

The Korean expeditions weakened Hideyoshi and paved the way for a new phase of political struggle that concluded in the unification of Japan under the shogunate of the Tokugawa family. In 1600, Tokugaka Yeyasu brought stability to the archipelago and progressively, a series of self-isolating policies to deal with the growing economic competition of Dutch, Portuguese, Spanish and English merchants reaching East Asian shores.[10] In 1635, all feudal lords were prohibited the construction of ocean-going vessels, with the shogunate navy consisting only of one large warship and a few small vessels. Japan entered a 265-year period of self-isolation, or *sakoku*. Maritime affairs returned to be the primary occupation of the regional feudalities in Southwest Japan. There, warlords of the Kyushu's areas of Nagasaki, Kagoshima and Fukuoka, were allowed to keep trade connections with mainland China, the Ryukyus and Korea, as well as small foreign trading posts such as the Dutch presence on the island of Dejima in Nagasaki. For these domains, sea power continued to be a tool of local statecraft and maritime trade and seafaring habits remained at the heart of the economic systems.[11]

## The "shield of the empire": sea power in modern Japan

By the first half of the nineteenth century, growing interest in Europe and the United States for overseas economic expansion, combined with technological innovations that favored oceanic sailing, were reversing the long-lasting role attributed to the waters of the archipelago. From natural shield of the nation's independence, the sea was becoming a gateway for foreign interference. A first systematic analysis of Japan's evolving naval problem appeared as early as 1791, at the hand of a geographer and scientist from the region of Sendai (northeast of Honshu), Hayashi Shihei. In his treatise, he warned against foreign pressure and urged the Tokugawa government to acquire naval power as an essential means to protect the nation's maritime frontiers and sovereignty.[12] In 1853, Hayashi's concerns materialized in the form of the American flotilla of "black ships" under the command of Commodore Matthew Perry that dropped anchor in Uraga harbor, near Edo (present Tokyo), with the intent of establishing commercial relations with Japan. On 31 March 1854, the signing of the Convention of Kanagawa with the United States marked the formal "return" of the archipelago into the international system and drew the seclusion period to a close.

The re-opening of Japan to the world prompted a period of political turmoil and social transformation that ended with the demise of the Tokugawa regime and the creation of a modern state. In this phase of Japanese history, also known as "Meiji restoration," Japan engaged in a substantial process of military modernization, abolishing the feudal system with the samurai class at its centre, replacing it with a national army and navy. The samurai ethos, based on a life at the service of a feudal lord, was to be passed on to the *esprit de corps* of the armed forces as loyalty to the emperor. Accordingly the defence of national interests took priority over local agendas. In the naval realm, it is no coincidence that seafaring dominions from Kyūshu took the lead in the construction of a vision for a national force. In particular, a handful of samurai oligarchs associated with the most advanced of these feudalities, Satsuma (present Kagoshima), well acquainted with the technological developments of the West, joined other reformers who contributed to the end of the Tokugawa rule, and subsequently maneuvered to promote naval expansion within the newly established political system.[13]

The opening years of the 1860s witnessed events that had fully exposed the weaknesses of Japanese naval defenses. In 1861, Russia sought to take control of a small port on the island of Tsushima, an operation frustrated only by the intervention of two British units, and in August 1863, a squadron of British frigates led by HMS *Euryalus* bombarded the port of Kagoshima which annihilated the naval forces mustered by Satsuma. After the last Tokugawa loyalists were defeated, Meiji authorities focused on the administrative process to build, train and sustain a national navy. The Ministry of the Navy was established in 1872, controlling a modest fleet of 14 warships and three transports. Yet, the creation of a modern national organization was only half of the problem. The navy's top brass knew that, whilst naval power had now entered the grammar of Japan's statecraft, the force held a position of junior service vis-à-vis the army. As such, in the following decades, naval leaders from Satsuma like Kawamura Sumiyoshi, Saigō Tsugumichi and Yamamoto Gombei, or Gonnohyōe, worked hard to create a wider national awareness about its functions and purposefulness.[14] From 1881 to 1906, members of the "Satsuma faction" continuously headed the Navy Ministry, providing continuity in leadership, imprinting a regional flavor to a national institution and molding the country's emergence in the business of naval warfare.[15]

Even though those who governed the service at its inception were pre-eminently samurais with limited or no professional naval background, they were all determined to succeed in transforming Japan into a naval power capable of safeguarding its sovereignty and interests. Initially, the navy was tasked with coastal defense and domestic security. In the early Meiji period, this latter function was also the most crucial. The fleet was in fact deployed to bombard towns and transport troops in support of the army's effort to suppress domestic rebellions, notably those led by members of the Saga clan (1874) and by Saigō Takamori (1877).[16] Throughout the 1880s, the navy's missions started extending beyond Japan's domestic waters, especially as the threat perception of China and Russia grew within political and military circles. New missions were matched by increased funding. In July 1889, a standing fleet of six capital ships was established and in July 1894, on the verge of the conflict with China, the Combined Fleet, composed by the standing and western fleets came to life. The Combined Fleet gauged Japan's ambition to empower itself with the means to defend national shores and influence North-eastern Asian security to that effect. No longer just a coastal force, the navy was set on course to be the nation's forward defensive shield.

Between the end of the nineteenth and the first two decades of the twentieth centuries, Japanese naval power was put to test, proving that it could protect the vital maritime space surrounding Japan, and in so doing, enhance its international standing. The direct involvement in three wars and one international crisis made the navy's function apparent. The First Sino-Japanese (1894–1895) and the Russo-Japanese Wars (1904–1905) were the first two major tests of fire for the Imperial Japanese Navy (IJN). These conflicts shared a common core strategic objective. Political and military leaders wanted to prevent Japan's major regional rivals, China and Russia, from gaining control over the Korean peninsula and southern Manchuria, especially the Liaotung Peninsula, and to use them as staging platforms to threaten the security of the archipelago.[17] In both wars, the IJN developed a similar tactical approach, one in which achieving command of the sea in the early stages of the conflict was essential to guarantee continued logistical and operational support to the army's effort on land. Operationally, the annihilation of the enemy's main battle force, the Beiyang Fleet (in the war with China) and the Russian Pacific Fleet (in the case of the war with Russia) gained utmost priority. Tactically, in the preparations for the two naval campaigns, the IJN plans had to take into account a slight numerical disadvantage, and efforts were made to offset this inferiority by maximizing the homogeneity of the units within the fleet, their speed and firepower. Concurrently, the development of tactics for night engagements and the use of torpedoes received great attention. These characteristics, coupled with intense, dedicated training, gave the IJN an edge that the service fully demonstrated in the two decisive battles of the wars, the Battle of the Yalu (17 September 1894), and the Battle of Tsushima (27 May 1905). In both engagements, the Japanese battle line managed to cross in front of that of its opponent, concentrating devastating firepower against parts of the adversary's fleet and achieving complete victory. In the Battle of Tsushima, the IJN "Trafalgared" the Russian Baltic Fleet and for that reason, the event entered popular imagination in Japan as an iconic moment summarizing the success of the country's modernization. Internationally, it marked the first time a major European power was defeated by a non-European nation, and sealed Japan's entrance in the Olympus of the world's leading powers.

At the beginning of the twentieth century, sea power proved its value as a passport for Japan's status as a significant player in international affairs on two other occasions. A Japanese expeditionary force of approximately 20,000 soldiers and marines supported by 18 warships defined the country's military participation during the 1900 Boxer rebellion, the single largest foreign contribution to the crisis. Later on in World War I, the navy was at the forefront of Japan's alliance commitments to Britain. After an initial participation in the siege of the German naval base in Qingdao in the opening phases of the war, the core of the IJN's involvement took place between April 1917 and the end of the conflict. Following requests from authorities in London, the IJN formed three special squadrons for sea lane defense duties in the Mediterranean Sea and around Australian and New Zealand. In the European theatre, the Mediterranean squadron vitally contributed to escort regional traffic at a time when Germany had engaged in unrestricted submarine warfare. It completed more than 300 sorties, escorting 790 ships, and conducted 24 effective attacks against German units claiming at least 13 sunk or damaged submarines.[18] By the time the squadron returned to Japanese waters, the navy had gained a very different experience. For the first time, it had been deployed far from regional theatres where it had not been tasked to defend the maritime perimeter of the nation's territories. Rather, it was entrusted to escort convoys and protect sea lanes, a task the flotilla completed without engaging in ship-to-ship actions. In the Mediterranean Sea, the defensive shield of the empire had become a naval arm of country's wartime diplomacy.

In the interwar period, debates on the role of Japan's naval power shifted back to the question of the defense of the nation's frontiers, now expanded to form a colonial empire stretching from the archipelago's northern periphery to Korea, Taiwan, the Pescadores and former German possessions in the Marianas and Marshall Islands. With an extended imperial perimeter to defend, the IJN could not count on sufficient financial means to meet the challenge presented by what it had considered since 1907 its principal "hypothetical" rival in the Pacific, the United States Navy (USN). International naval armament limitations and domestic economic austerity, worsened by the unchanged rivalry with the imperial army over resource allocations, affected the naval strategy and policy. A "hypothetical" enemy was essential to justify requests for funds. In turn, this process favored a debate in which the annihilation of a numerically superior adversary was the primary objective and strategic options focused on tactical and technological problems to perfect speed, armor protection and firepower.[19] By the mid-1930s, studies analyzing a war with the United States channeled these views into an "interception-attrition" strategy. This aimed at reducing the strength of the American fleet before luring it into a duel in which a line of battleships headed by the gargantuan battleship *Yamato* would entrust Japan with the keys to the supremacy of the Pacific.[20] The IJN was to seize the initiative, securing a defensive perimeter for the empire and provoking a reaction from the USN. Long-range submarines were to ambush American units crossing the Pacific, whilst repeated night torpedo actions conducted by heavy cruisers and destroyers were to prepare the ground for aircraft carriers and battleships.[21] In the Japanese naval debate, all considerations became functions of such scenarios to the detriment of strategic flexibility and ability to fully explore the tactical potential of new technologies like radar.[22]

In the months preceding the war, the idea of a raid to sink the American battle fleet whilst at anchor in Pearl Harbor represented the pinnacle of an approach seeking a way to force the United States into a condition of relative inferiority to Japan. Against this intellectual demarche, two factors received little attention. First, Japan's war machine and industrial might depended on imported raw materials, and throughout the 1930s, domestic demand drove a substantial increase in imports, consumer and capital goods first, and capital goods, raw materials and food later.[23] Second, the first "world" conflict had changed nature of war, and a confrontation with the United States in the Pacific was more likely to be a total all-out effort than a limited contest similar to those Japan had fought against China and Russia. Both factors had crucial repercussions at the strategic level. A protracted war meant that the navy had to identify areas that would guarantee supplies of oil, rubber and other raw materials and defend the sea lanes transporting them in order to sustain a protracted war effort. In the interwar period, the IJN had developed the notion of an expansion of the empire towards the resource-rich areas of Southeast Asia, also known as southern advance (*nanshin-ron*). Yet, this represented more the navy's attempt to set forth an alternative strategy to the army's "northern advance" (*hokushin-ron*) on the Asian continent. The establishment of a secure imperial defensive line on the high seas following the destruction of the USN was deemed to be sufficient to allow safe movements within the empire's internal lines of maritime communication.

Throughout the war, years of rigid choices critically affected the service's performance. As the war progressed and the USN engaged in a ruthless offensive campaign against Japanese merchantmen, inherent doctrinal deficiencies in anti-submarine warfare (ASW), combined with the failure to reassign sufficient naval assets to convoy escort duties, or to shift the focus of the IJN's submarine effort from ambushing front-line units to the harassment of American sea-based logistics doomed Japan's war at sea.[24] In an attentive analysis of Japanese combat performance in the conflict, Paul Dull concluded that from Guadalcanal to Cape St. George and until October 1943, the IJN fought admirably, achieving more victories in ship-to-ship engagements than its foe. Intensive training, refined tactics, effective flashless powder, outstanding optical equipment, lethally swift long-range torpedoes were the core reasons that made the Japanese "superb night fighters." By the end of 1943, however, the quality of the IJN had deteriorated to the point of no return, whilst the American military machine was reaching levels of production that Japan was in no condition to match.[25] The IJN had emerged from the tumultuous years of the Meiji restoration as a professional, modern, national force. It had succeeded in creating a national maritime tradition and wider awareness vis-à-vis naval matters. It had not managed to overcome differences with the army and inform national strategy with the wider political and diplomatic advantages of naval power beyond a few limited occasions. Hence, Japan entered the Pacific War with a potent naval force capable of tactical superiority, but not with a maritime strategy to safeguard primary resources, and at sea, the nation's fate was decided.

## The "trident of a maritime state": sea power in post-war Japan

In August 1952, shortly after Japan regained its independence, preliminary research on the future requirements of Japanese naval defense was conducted under governmental supervision by a consultative body, the Systems Investigative Committee (SIC). The SIC considered it appropriate to focus on the wartime problem of securing the continued flow of vital primary resources to the archipelago as a starting point for its proceedings. It did so as a way of bringing together Japan's new constitutional limitations on the use of force, as they were enshrined in the 1947 constitution, whilst assessing the contemporary relevance of a problem that had brought the entire country to a state of utter devastation. The SIC's report concluded that sea lanes' defense was to be considered one of the core objectives of national security, whilst maritime convoying and ASW were to constitute the guiding principles of the navy's procurement policy. A second set of priorities identified in the document concerned the acquisition of the necessary capabilities to prevent foreign aggressions against Japanese territory.[26] The opinion expressed in the report was shared by a large number of influential former IJN officers, who played a key role in the re-establishment of the post-war naval service and initial post-war defense politics, notably Nomura Kichisaburo, Hoshina Zenshiro and Yamanashi Katsutoshin. A similar study conducted in 1956, under the aegis of the newly formed Defence Agency, reinforced this vision adapting it to Cold War dynamics, pointing out that the susceptibility of the Japanese archipelago and maritime arteries to eventual Soviet hostile military actions, underlined the need to reconstitute and maintain a modern fleet.[27]

Assessments of this kind notwithstanding, until the second half of the 1960s, naval rearmament plans did not hold a key place in the Japanese government's agenda, especially in light of Japan's limited financial and industrial potential. This did not diminish the significance of these initiatives as they represented the first post-war attempt in which the security dimension of Japan's economic dependence on the sea was factored into a basic national "maritime" strategy.[28] In the short-term, naval policy was a less pressing issue compared to the strengthening of ground and air forces, and the new naval service, the Japan Maritime Self Defense Force (JMSDF), was tasked with coastal defense from foreign invasions, ASW in home waters and short-range strategic lift in support of the army.[29]

In the 1970s, a shift in the political perception of core priorities for national security occurred and an intense debate took place over what were the best means to protect them. At the outset of the Cold War, one of the key political figure of the time, Prime Minister Yoshida Shigeru (1946–1947, 1948–1954), had prioritized economic rehabilitation and sought for Japan a low profile in military matters.[30] This formula, later known as the Yoshida doctrine was essential to Japanese economic recovery in the 1950s and fast expansion in the 1960s. Yet, economic results had not change geography and they could be achieved only by virtue of secure access to trade and maritime transportation. University of Kyōto Professor Kōsaka Masataka, advisor to Prime Minister Ōhira Masayoshi (1978–1980), was the first to adopt in the 1960s and 1970s the terms "maritime state," or *kaiyō kokka*, and "trading state," or *tsūshō kokka*, to explain the distinctive features of Japan's successful industrial recovery.[31] The archipelago had chosen an export-oriented development, which increased "both the vulnerability and the influence of Japan" worldwide. In turn, this economic system created a crucial dependence on shipping, and, he argued, if raw materials were to be less easily accessible "Japan would suffer."[32]

The 1973 oil crisis showed the dramatic implications of Kōsaka's analysis, shaking "Japan's economic and social systems at their very foundations," and Japan's defense policymakers took to heart the question of "maintaining the safety of maritime transportation."[33] Provided the increasing size and potential of the Soviet fleet in the Pacific, policymakers concerns were matched by the JMSDF's strategic priorities which included sea lanes' defense among its core missions (albeit within home waters) since 1966.[34] In 1976, when the National Defence Programme Outline (NDPO), the document that defined the guidelines for Japan's Cold War Defence Policy, was officially adopted an expanding consensus existed on the role of naval defense in national security. Consistently, the document called for a balanced fleet, one that could adapt to peacetime surveillance as well as deterring aggressions while preserving the flow of goods from and to the archipelago. In this respect, the new defense policy effectively placed the navy at the heart of Japanese national security, directly linking its existence with the country's vital maritime interests.

The JMSDF's fleet target goal was set at as approximately 60 major surface vessels to conduct ASW operations, and some 220 aircraft to patrol Japan's maritime space.[35] The service's efforts were mainly directed at countering the Soviet naval build-up in East Asia which was estimated to include a powerful submarine fleet of 125 boats, almost half of them nuclear-powered, ideally suited to conduct raiding activities to harass Japanese shipping.[36] The 1978 Guidelines for US–Japan Defence Cooperation further emphasized this point, stressing cooperation on matters of sea lanes' defense. By supporting the USN in patrolling the western Pacific, the JMSDF became the emblem of Japan's commitment to contain the Soviet Union, and in doing so, it could implement in the Sea of Japan and the East China Sea its naval strategy. In 1981, Prime Minister Suzuki Zenko's (1980–1982) pledge to commit Japan to the protection of its sea lanes out to 1,000 nm crystallized the navy's cardinal double role in national security for the remainder of the Cold War. The service stood as front-line guarantor of the nation's economic interests; concurrently, it was a central player in the alliance management requirements.

At the beginning of the 1990s, the JMSDF's capabilities matched the nation's security requirements. It fielded a large, professional, modern fleet composed of four flotillas, each including one helicopter-carrying destroyer (DDH), seven destroyers and eight helicopters (three carried by the DDH and the remaining five deployed on an equal number of destroyers), to perform ASW operations.[37] The fleet could operate far from coastal shores with the thee Towada class of fast combat support ships (AOE), but it remained unbalanced in that it had deficiencies in fleet air defense and long-range strategic lift. In 1995, the adoption of a new NDPO to address the changes in the international system following the end of bipolar confrontation introduced new elements in the Japanese debate and offered opportunities to address some of these deficiencies. A more "active and constructive security policy," one capable of integrating the requirements for a higher international military profile with those necessary to deal with closer regional sources of military (and naval) apprehension in Northeast Asia, was to be pursued.[38] The 1994 North Korean nuclear crisis as well as the 1995 and 1996 Chinese military exercises near the Strait of Taiwan represented key events shaping the views of Japanese strategic planners in this regard. In the official defense establishment jargon, the Japanese armed forces had to become "streamlined, effective and flexible."[39]

For the JMSDF, the new security requirements demanded the enhancement of its ability to offer "agile" and "accurate" responses for new missions, though national naval strategy remained substantially unaltered. An expeditionary dimension was needed to meet new international missions, but "the defence of adjacent seas and the securing the safety of maritime traffic [were] essential in order to secure the foundations of national survival."[40] Compared to the force level established by the 1976 NDPO, the JMSDF could not prevent reductions to its pennant list, but by the end of the decade, the service had commissioned three large amphibious ships, the sumi class, that provided an expeditionary capability. In the uncertain and austere atmosphere of the 1990s, naval policy rapidly adapted to the new circumstances.

In 2004, whilst the structural changes initiated in the 1990s were being implemented, Japanese strategic planners decided to embark on a new policy revision that could account for the systemic transformations brought about by the 9/11 attacks to the United States, North Korea's political brinkmanship, missile tests and nuclear program, and China's double-digit investments in military modernization. The new document, which was approved in December 2004 as National Defence Programme Guideline, partly reviewed previous emphasis on multilateral cooperation, though it sought to maintain an overall balanced approach for the military to complete its transition towards a "multi-functional flexible defence force."[41] In the new document, Chinese military modernization, especially in the realm of naval and air power, was regarded as a source of increasing concern. This was because the Chinese navy represented a more sophisticated competitor than its Soviet counterpart, one whose steady rise was entwined with China's increasing economic interests at sea and their protection in contested areas like the East and South China Seas.[42] For the JMSDF, however, this new policy shift rewarded the ongoing transformation from a Cold war ASW force to one tailored for sea control in Japan's home waters and in the East China Sea (to defend Japan's maritime space within its exclusive economic zone – EEZ), expeditionary missions (to contribute to international security) and "good order at sea" (to contribute to the safety of maritime activities).

In Japan's post-9/11 defense posture, the naval service's efforts to balance its fleet with enhanced air and expeditionary capabilities were coupled with increased operational experience on the high seas. Between 2001 and 2010, Japanese units were deployed in the Indian Ocean for a refueling mission to support of the international anti-terrorism operations in Afghanistan. Throughout the mission, the JMSDF's replenishment ships refueled coalition vessels 794 times providing a total of 490,000 kl. In the last tour of duty in the summer of 2008, the newest addition to this type of logistical ship, the 13,500-ton *Mashu* conducted more than 20 refueling activities providing more than 3,600 kl to coalition forces.[43] At the same time, the escorting destroyer had an opportunity to tests systems and sensors, and exchange information with coalition and USN forces in the area. Meanwhile, in 2007, the JMSDF commissioned the lead ship of a class of two 13,500-ton flat-top DDH, *Hyuga*, designed to empower the fleet with a more independent air defense cover as well as provide command functions in case of deployments overseas in support of relief actions. Together with the fleet of modern destroyers and submarines, including the Aegis-equipped Kongō and Atago classes and the new air-independent-propulsion (AIP) Sōryu class, the JMSDF made sure to possess the credentials to be a major naval force in North East Asia and to continue to protect Japanese unaltered maritime economic interests. The commissioning in March 2011 of *Hyuga*'s sister ship, *Ise*, and the intention of the JMSDF to order two other flat-tops of approximately 26,000 tons of displacement each further confirm the service's long-term trajectory to empower the Japanese government with the strategic flexibility to decide how and to what extent deploy naval power. Such a strategic flexibility is pursued by means of a balanced and flexible fleet, designed to meet conventional as well as new threats, in the region and overseas.

## Conclusion: the emergence of a "Britain of the Far East?"

The defeat in the Pacific War brought Japan to the brink of economic, social and military collapse. In the post-war, strategists and policy-makers processed that dramatic experience and the reasons behind it. The latest Japanese maritime strategy, published in November 2008, is a testimony of

Japan's post-war journey to assess its experience as a maritime country. It articulated the role of Japan's future sea power into a "commitment" and a "contingency response" strategy. The former pertained to the wide-ranging sets of missions the naval service should be capable of undertaking within the core strategic triangle Tokyo–Guam–Taiwan (TGT), ranging from missile defense to sea control, to maritime security, enhancing in particular its intelligence, surveillance and reconnaissance (ISR) capabilities.[44] Far from Japanese shores, the commitment strategy is identified as one of support to multilateral efforts against threats to the disruption of trade and of terrorist activities in formats such as the Proliferation Security Initiative (PSI). Equal emphasis is put on capacity building of regional naval forces.[45] In this field, the Japan Coast Guard paved the way, enjoying considerable success in providing training, equipment and funding to countries in Southeast Asia, notwithstanding initial opposition from Indonesian and Malaysian authorities. In the contingency response strategy, provided the direct link between Japan's energy security requirements and the stability of areas in the Middle East and in Southeast Asia, the service advocated to maintain the capabilities necessary to perform missions like those conducted in the Indian Ocean, and presently, in the Gulf of Aden against pirate activities. Enhanced readiness for maritime interdiction operations and extended operational radius of ISR capabilities represented the service's top priorities.

The extent to which the JMSDF's strategic vision will find political support is difficult to say, especially in light of the current transitional phase of Japanese politics with new Prime Minister Kan Naoto struggling to maintain cohesiveness within the ruling party, and his predecessor resigning after just nine months at the helm of the government. What is certain is that the ruling party has expressed its intention to expand Japan's international profile as a security provider, and the release by the end of 2010 of a new national strategy should shed light on the country's future military posture accordingly. Recently released information from the Ministry of Defence seemed to confirm that whilst the budget will not receive a financial boost, core capabilities, including the navy's submarine force, are set to expand. The current fleet of 16 boats (18 including two training submarines) might be expanded to 22 units by 2015, a goal to be easily achieved by maintaining the current submarine procurement process unaltered and extending the life of the newer submarines in the fleet to 25 years.[46] All this suggests that naval power will continue to remain firmly at the heart of national security.

In October 2000, a study chaired by former American Secretary of State Richard Armitage envisaged for Japan a role as the "Britain of the Far East." In drawing this analogy, the document sought to point to the trans-Atlantic relationship as a template for the future development of the US–Japan security alliance.[47] What the document did not capture, however, were the more fundamental similarities that Japan shares with Britain. Sitting at the opposite ends of the Eurasian continent, Japan, like Britain, is an industrialized country, poor in primary resources, with economies highly dependent on trade and maritime transport. Today, like Britain, Japan maintains independent military capabilities for its basic security requirements, complementing their reach with ad hoc strategic partnerships and diplomatic and economic actions. Like Britain, Japan has a military posture with a strong maritime balance. This is a strategic imperative functional to empower its governments with the possibility to deploy forces wherever core economic interests demand. In this respect, Japan is the "Britain of the Far East" and for this reason, its maritime future is unlikely to dramatically change from its recent past. A maritime strategy seeking to protect crucial sea lanes and to contribute to international efforts to secure key flashpoints will continue to guide national policy. Concurrently, Japan will use the inherent flexibility of sea-based platforms to address both conventional concerns in North East Asia and ensure its contribution to international stability. Today, learning from its past offers Japan the best guarantee for its future.

## Notes

1 In this chapter, phonetic transcriptions of Japanese words follow the revised Hepburn Romanization system. Macrons are used to indicate long vowels in Japanese, except for place names (e.g. Tokyo) of common use in English language publications. Japanese names are given with family names preceding first names. In bibliographical references, names of Japanese authors are given according to Western practice. Names of Japanese authors in English language publications are reported according to the original text and therefore appear in some cases without macron or with different spelling.
2 Philippe Pelletier, *La Japonésie. Géopolitique et Géographie Historique de la Surinsularité au Japon* (Paris: CNRS, 1997), 24.
3 Matsuki Satoru, "Fune to Kōkai wo Suitei Fukugen Suru [Hypothetic Reconstruction of Ships and Navigation]" in Ōbayashi Taryō (ed.), *Kodai Nihon, Sankan: Umi wo Koetai Kōryū* [Ancient Japan, vol. iii: Maritime Activities, Tokyo: Chūōkōronsha, 1995], 123–170.
4 François Gipouloux, *La Méditerranée Asiatique. Villes Portuaires et Réseaux Marchands en Chine, au Japon et en Asie du Sud-Est, XVIe-XXIe Siècle* (Paris: CNRS, 2009), 78–87.
5 Accounts of the activity of the *wakō* are often reported by Western traders and missioners like the Italian Jesuit Matteo Ricci. Cf. Franco Mazzei, "Il Giappone nelle Opere di Matteo Ricci" in *Atti del Primo Convegno Internazionale di Studi Ricciani* (Macerata, IT: Biemmegraf, 1984), 152.
6 Arthur J. Marder, "From Jimmu Tennō to Perry: Sea Power in early Japanese History," *American Historical Review*, 1945: 1, 9–10.
7 Information gathered during the author's visit to the *Murakami Suigunjō*, Innoshima, Japan, 9 August 2010.
8 G. A. Ballard, *The Influence of the Sea on the Political History of Japan* (London: John Murray, 1921), 42–72; Marder, "From Jimmu Tennō to Perry," 19–31; The policies of sakoku were enacted in the 1630s and banned the construction of ocean-going vessels whilst strictly regulating foreign trade. For a general historical overview, cf. Andrew Gordon, *A Modern History of Japan. From Tokugawa to the Present Times* (Oxford: Oxford University Press, 2003), 17.

9 Naoko Sajima and Kyoichi Tachikawa, *Japanese Sea Power: A Maritime Nation's Struggle for Identity* (Canberra, AU: Sea Power Centre, 2009), 18–20.
10 Seymour Broadbridge, "Economic and Social Trends in Tokugawa Japan," *Modern Asian Studies*, 1974: 3, 353–356.
11 Robert K. Sakai, "The Satsuma–Ryukyu Trade and the Tokugawa Seclusion Policy," *Journal of Asian Studies*, vol. 23, 1964: 3, 391–403.
12 Pelletier, *La Japonésie*, 115.
13 On the influence of the Satsuma maritime tradition on the imperial navy's ethos, cf. Alessio Patalano, *Kaiji: Imperial Traditions and Japan's Post-war Naval Power* (unpublished PhD dissertation, King's College London, 2009), 45–54.
14 For a comprehensive presentation of the Satsuma faction and his main leaders, cf. David C. Evans, *The Satsuma Faction and Professionalism in the Japanese Naval Officer Corps of the Meiji Period, 1868–1912* (unpublished PhD dissertation, Stanford University, 1978), 114–151. Biographical details concerning these three characters can be found also in Charles J. Schencking, *Making Waves. Politics, Propaganda, and the Emergence of the Imperial Japanese Navy, 1868–1922* (Stanford, CA: Stanford University Press, 2005), 3, 14–16, 32.
15 Schencking, *Making Waves*, 33.
16 In the 1870s, the IJN was occasionally deployed overseas as well. In 1874, naval assets were engaged to transport troops in a punitive expedition against Taiwan, and subsequently deployed for "gunboat diplomacy" off the coasts of China and, later in 1875 against Korea.
17 Vice Admiral Yoji Koda, JMSDF, "The Russo-Japanese War. Primary Causes of Japanese Success," *Naval War College Review*, vol. 58, 2005: 2, 14.
18 Kaigun Rekishi Hozonkai (ed.), *Nihon Kaigunshi, II* (Japanese Naval History, vol. II, Tokyo: Daiichi Hōki Shuppan, 1995), 349–350. On the subject of the sinking of submarines there is disagreement between Japanese and German sources.
19 This subject is treated exhaustively in David C. Evans, Mark R. Peattie, *Kaigun. Strategy, Tactics and Technology in the Imperial Japanese Navy, 1887–1941* (Annapolis, MD: Naval Institute Press, 1997), chapters 7 and 8. For a brief overview, see Hirama Yōichi, Rear Admiral JMSDF (Ret.), "Japanese Naval Preparations for World War II," *Naval War College Review*, vol. 94, 1991: 2, 63–81.
20 Hirama, "Japanese Naval Preparations for World War II," 63–64; Captain Yoji Koda, JMSDF, "A Commander's Dilemma: Admiral Yamamoto and the 'Gradual Attrition' Strategy," *Naval War College Review*, vol. 46, 1993: Autumn, 66; Evans and Peattie, *Kaigun*, 479–482.
21 Hirama, "Japanese Naval Preparations for World War II," 64–71; Koda, "A Commander's Dilemma," 66–69; Evans and Peattie, *Kaigun*, 282–295.
22 For instance, the IJN was ahead of its peer competitors in the development of long-range torpedoes (a key weapon in night attacks). In 1935, it developed an oxygen torpedo, the Type 93 which, with 40,000 meters range at 36 knots, was superior to all other existing torpedoes. For an overall presentation of Japanese naval constructions in the interwar period, cf. Mark Peattie, "Japanese Naval Construction, 1919–1941," in Phillips P. O'Brien (ed.), *Technology and Naval Combat in the Twentieth Century and Beyond* (London: Frank Cass, 2001), 93–108.
23 Christopher Howe, *The Origins of Japanese Trade Supremacy* (London: Hurst & Co, 1996), 121.
24 Atsushi Oi, "Why Japan's Antisubmarine Warfare Failed" in David C. Evans, *The Japanese Navy in World War II: In the Words of Former Japanese Naval Officers* (Annapolis, MD: Naval Institute Press, 1986 [1969]), 385–414. For a comprehensive treatment of Japan's wartime sea lanes defense problem, cf. Minoru Nomura, *Kaisenshi ni Manabu* [Learning from the History of Naval Battles, Tokyo: Bungei Shunjū, 1985], 236–250; Graham, *Japan's Sea Lane Security*, Euan

Graham (New York, Abingdon, Oxon: Routledge, 2006) 77–89. On the problem of Japan's wartime merchant shipping, cf. Mark P. Parillo, *The Japanese Merchant Marine in World War II* (Annapolis, MD: Naval Institute Press, 1993); on the USN's submarine campaign in the Pacific War, Clay Blair Jr., *Silent Victory: The US Submarine War against Japan* (Annapolis, MD: Naval Institute Press, 1975).

25 Paul S. Dull, *A Battle History of the Imperial Japanese Navy* (Annapolis, MD: Naval Institute Press, 1978), 353–354.
26 James E. Auer, *The Post-war Rearmament of Japanese Maritime Forces, 1945–1971* (New York, Washington, London: Praeger, 1973), 154.
27 Military Assistance and Advisory Group Japan (MAAG-J), "Requirements for the Naval Defence of Japan," 14 November 1956, in Osamu Ishii, Naoki Ono (eds), *Documents on the United States Policy towards Japan. Documents related to Diplomatic and Military Matters 1956, Volume 4* (Tokyo: Kashiwashobo, 1999), 398–405.
28 Graham, *Japan's Sea Lane Security*, op. cit. 100.
29 Japan Maritime Self-Defence Force (JMSDF), *Kaijōjieitai Gojū Nenshi* [JMSDF's Fifty Year History] (Tokyo, 2003), 27.
30 Yoshida's moderate views, though not officially formalized, substantially informed his successors' policies and for this reason, they are frequently referred to as the "Yoshida Doctrine," or "Yoshida's Line." Christopher W. Hughes, *Japan Re-Emergence as a "Normal" Military Power* (Adelphi Paper 368–369, London: IISS/Oxford, 2004), 21–27; Richard J. Samuels, *Securing Japan. Tokyo's Grand Strategy and the Future of East Asia* (Ithaca, NY: Cornell University Press, 2007), 29–37; Shingo Nakajima, *Sengo Nihon no Bōei Seisaku. "Yoshida Rosen" wo Meguru Seiji, Gaikō, Gunji* [Japan's Post-War Defence Policy. Politics, Foreign Policy and Military Affairs about the "Yoshida's Line"] (Tokyo: Keiō Gijuku Daigaku Shuppankai, 2006), 5–14.
31 Masataka Kōsaka, "Kaiyō Kokka Nihon no Kōsō [The Concept of Japan as Maritime State]," *Chūō Kōron*, 1964: 9, 48–80; Masataka Kōsaka, "Tsūshō Kokka Nippon no Unmei [The Fate of Japan as a Trading State]," *Chūō Kōron*, 1975: 11, 116–140.
32 Masataka Kōsaka, *Options for Japan's Foreign Policy* (Adelphi Papers, no. 97, London: International Institute for strategic Studies, 1973), 3.
33 Japan Defence Agency (JDA), *Defence of Japan 1977* (Tokyo: Japan Defence Agency, 1977), 100.
34 JMSDF, *Kaijōjieitai Gojū Nenshi*, 31.
35 JDA, *Defence of Japan 1977*, 64–65.
36 Hiroshi Kimura, "The Soviet Military Build-up: Its Impact on Japan and its Aims" in Richard H. Solomon, Masataka Kōsaka (eds), *The Soviet Far East Military Build-up: Nuclear Dilemmas and Asian Security* (Dover, MA: Auburn House Publishing Company, 1986), 107.
37 For a good summary of the development of the JMSDF's capabilities in the Cold War cf. the study by Michishita Narushige in Kyōichi Tachikawa, Tomoyuki Ishizu, Narushige Michishita, Katsuya Tsukamoto (eds.), *Seepawa* [Sea power] (Tokyo: Fuyō Shobō, 2008), 230–253.
38 Advisory Group on Defence Issues, *The Modality of the Security and Defence Capability of Japan* (Tokyo, 1994), 6; Japan Defence Agency (JDA), *Defence of Japan 1996. Response to a New Era* (Tokyo: *Japan Times*, 1996), 70, 78–79. Captain Katsutoshi Kawano, JMSDF "Japan's Military Role: Allied Recommendations for the Twenty-First Century," *Naval War College Review*, vol. 51, 1998: Autumn, 9–21.
39 Japan Defence Agency (JDA), *Defence of Japan 1996. Response to a New Era* (Tokyo: *Japan Times*), 81.
40 Advisory Group on Defence Issues, *The Modality of the Security and Defence Capability of Japan*, 22.

41 The Council on Security and Defence Capabilities, *Japan's Visions for Future Security and Defence Capabilities* (Tokyo: 2004), 11–13; The National Institute for Defence Studies (NIDS), "Japan – Responding to the Changing Security Environment," *East Asian Strategic Review* (Tokyo: *Japan Times*, 2007), 228–229.
42 In September 2010, the subject of Sino-Japanese maritime disputes in the East China Sea has returned at the forefront of international media attention as a result of the collision between a Chinese fishing trawler and units of the Japan Coast Guard. The subsequent temporary detention of the captain of the trawler by Japanese authorities brought Sino-Japanese relations into a renewed state of tension, with consideration concerning national pride and international status overlapping with wider strategic considerations on the importance of this area in terms of natural resources, shipping lanes and (in the case of the Chinese navy) access to the ocean. For an overall view of the disputes, cf. Reinhard Drifte, *Japanese-Chinese Territorial Disputes in the East China Sea – Between Military Confrontation and Economic Cooperation* (Asia Research Centre Working Paper 24, London: London School of Economics and Social Science, 2008).
43 Data by the Japan Ministry of Defense (JMoD), online, available at: www.mod.go.jp/e/d_policy/ipca/refueling.html, accessed 20 March 2010.
44 Tomohisa Takei, "Kaiyō Shinkindai ni okeru Kaijōjieitai [The JMSDF in the New Maritime Era]," *Hatō*, 2008: 11, 16–18.
45 Ibid., 20–21.
46 Editorial Department, "Japan to Expand Submarine Fleet to 22 from 16," *Japan Today*, 21 October 2010, online, available at: www.japantoday.com/category/national/view/japan-to-expand-submarine-fleet-to-22-from-16, accessed 28 October 2010.
47 INSS Special Report, *The United States and Japan: Advancing toward a Mature Partnership* (Washington, DC: National Defense University, 2000), 3–4.

# 7 India's growing naval power
## Indian Ocean in focus

*Harsh V. Pant*

In February 2008, India hosted naval chiefs from around the Indian Ocean in what was named the Indian Ocean Naval Symposium (IONS), highlighting the role of the Indian Navy as an important instrument of the nation's foreign and security policy. It was also an attempt by India to promote a multilateral approach in the management of the security of the Indian Ocean. India signalled that as a rising power it is willing to fulfil its maritime responsibilities in the region but unlike in the past when India had been suspicious of what it saw as 'extra-regional navies' it is now ready to cooperate with other navies in and around the Indian Ocean. The IONS is now an annual feature of Indian naval diplomacy. Whether India's leadership will be enough to promote genuine maritime multilateralism in the region, however, remains to be seen.

The Indian Ocean has long been the hub of great power rivalry and the struggle for its domination has been a perennial feature of global politics. It is third-largest of the world's five oceans and straddles Asia in the north, Africa in the west, Indo-china in the east and Antarctica in the south. Home to four critical access waterways – the Suez Canal, Bab-el Mandeb, Strait of Hormuz and Strait of Malacca – the Indian Ocean connects the Middle East, Africa and East Asia with Europe and the Americas.[1] Given its crucial geographical role, major powers have long vied with each other for its control though it was only in the nineteenth century that Great Britain was able to enjoy an overwhelming dominance in the region. With the decline in Britain's relative power and the emergence of two superpowers during the Cold War, the Indian Ocean region became another arena where the United States and the former Soviet Union struggled to expand their power and influence. The United States, however, has remained the most significant player in the region for the last several years.

Given the rise of major economic powers in the Asia-Pacific that rely on energy imports to sustain their economic growth, the Indian Ocean region has assumed a new importance as various powers are once again vying for the control of the waves in this part of the world. Nearly half of the world's seaborne trade is through the Indian Ocean and approximately 20 per cent of this trade consists of energy resources. It has also been estimated that around 40 per cent of the world's offshore oil production comes from the Indian Ocean, while 65 per cent of the world's oil and 35 per cent of its gas reserves are found in the littoral states of this Ocean.[2] Unlike the Pacific and Atlantic Oceans, almost three-quarters of trade traversing through the Indian Ocean, primarily in the form of oil and gas, belongs to states external to the region. Free and uninterrupted flow of oil and goods through the ocean's sea lines of communication (SLOC) is deemed vital for the global economy and so all major states have a stake in a stable Indian Ocean region. It is for this reason that during the Cold War years when US–Soviet rivalry was at its height, the states bordering the Indian Ocean sought to declare the region a 'zone of peace' to allow for free trade and commerce across the lanes of the Indian Ocean. Today, the reliance is on the United States for the provision of a 'collective good': a stable Indian Ocean region.

This chapter examines the emerging Indian approach towards the Indian Ocean in the context of India's rise as a major naval power. It argues that though India has historically viewed the Indian Ocean region as one in which it would like to establish its own predominance, its limited material capabilities have constrained its options. With the expansion, however, of India's economic and military capabilities, Indian ambitions vis-à-vis this region are soaring once again. India is also trying its best to respond to the challenge that growing Chinese capabilities in the Indian Ocean are posing to the region and beyond. Yet, preponderance in the Indian Ocean region, though much desired by the Indian strategic elites, remains an unrealistic aspiration for India given the significant stakes that other major powers have in the region. In all likelihood, India will look towards cooperation with other major powers in the Indian Ocean region to preserve and enhance its strategic interests.

## The Indian Ocean: India's backyard?

As India's global economic and political profile has risen in recent years, it has also, not surprisingly, tried to define its strategic interests in increasingly expansive terms. Like other globalising economies, India's economic growth is heavily reliant on the free flow of goods through the Indian Ocean SLOC; especially as around 90 per cent of India's trade is reliant on merchant shipping. Given India's growing reliance on imported sources of energy, any disruption in the Indian Ocean could have a potentially catastrophic impact on Indian economic and societal stability. India's exclusive economic zone (EEZ) in the Indian Ocean, that according to the Law of the Seas runs 200 nm contiguous to its coastline and its islands, covers around 30 per cent of the resource abundant Indian Ocean Region.[3]

Any disruption in shipping across the important trade routes in the Indian Ocean, especially those passing through the 'choke-points' in the

Strait of Hormuz, the Gulf of Aden, the Suez Canal and the Strait of Malacca could lead to serious consequences for not only Indian but global economic prospects. Unhindered trade and shipping traffic flow is a sine qua non for the implementation of India's developmental process. Non-traditional threats in the form of organised crime, piracy and transnational terrorist networks also make it imperative for India to exert its control in the region.

Indian strategic thinkers have historically viewed the Indian Ocean as India's backyard and so have emphasised the need for India to play a greater role in underwriting its security and stability. India's strategic elites have often drawn inspiration from a quote attributed to Alfred Mahan: 'Whoever controls the Indian Ocean dominates Asia. The ocean is the key to seven seas. In the twenty-first century, the destiny of the world will be decided on its waters.' This quote, though apparently fictitious, has been highly influential in shaping the way Indian naval thinkers have looked at the role of the Indian Ocean for Indian security.[4] While sections of the Indian foreign policy establishment considered India the legatee of the British rule for providing peace and stability in the Indian Ocean, India's neighbours remain concerned about India's 'hegemonistic' designs in the region.

Underlining the importance of the Indian Ocean for India, K. M. Pannikar, a diplomat-historian, called for the Indian Ocean to remain 'truly Indian.' He argued that

> To other countries the Indian Ocean could only be one of the important oceanic areas, but to India it is a vital sea because its lifelines are concentrated in that area, its freedom is dependent on the freedom of that coastal surface.[5]

Pannikar was strongly in favour of Indian dominance of the Indian Ocean region much in the same mould as several British and Indian strategists viewed India's predominance of the Indian Ocean as virtually inevitable.[6] It has also been suggested that given the role of 'status and symbolism' in Indian strategic thinking, India's purported greatness would be reason enough for Indian admirals to demand a powerful Navy.[7]

In view of this intellectual consensus, it is surprising that India's civilian leadership was able to resist naval expansion in the early years after independence. India took its time after independence to accept her role as the pre-eminent maritime power in the Indian Ocean region and long remained diffident about shouldering the responsibilities that come with such an acknowledgement. The focus remained on Pakistan and China and the overarching continental mindset continued to dictate the defence priorities of the nation with some complaining that the Indian Navy was being relegated to the background as the most neglected branch of the armed services.[8] As the great powers got involved in the Indian Ocean during the Cold War years, India's ability to shape the developments in the region got further marginalised. India continued to lag behind in its ability to project power across the Indian Ocean through the early 1990s primarily due to resource constraints and a lack of a definable strategy. It was rightly observed that 'if the Indian Navy seriously contemplates power projection missions in the Indian Ocean, [the then Indian naval fleet] is inadequate ... it has neither the balance nor the required offensive punch to maintain zones of influence.'[9] India, for its part, continued to demand, without much success, that 'extra regional navies' should withdraw from the Indian Ocean, which met with hostility from the major powers and generated apprehensions in India's neighbourhood that India would like to dominate the strategic landscape of the Indian Ocean. India's larger non-aligned foreign policy posture also ensured that Indian maritime intentions remained shrouded in mystery for the rest of the world.

It has only been since the late 1990s that India has started to reassert itself in the Indian Ocean and beyond. This has been driven by various factors – the high rates of economic growth that India has enjoyed since early 1990s have allowed the country to invest greater resources in naval expansion; the growing threat from non-state actors that has forced India to adopt a more pro-active naval posture; and, a growing realisation that China is rapidly expanding its influence in the Indian Ocean region, something that many in the Indian strategic community feel would be detrimental to Indian interests in the long term. India has a pivotal position in the Indian Ocean as, unlike other nations in the region with blue-water capabilities such as Australia and South Africa, India is at the centre and dominates the SLOC across the ocean in both directions. There are now signs that India is making a concerted attempt to enhance its capabilities to back up its aspiration to play an enhanced naval role in the Indian Ocean.

## Expanding resource base

Sustained rates of high economic growth over the last decade have given India greater resources to devote to its defence requirements. In the initial years after independence in 1947, India's defence expenditure as a percentage of the gross domestic product (GDP) hovered around 1.8 per cent. This changed with the 1962 war with China in which India suffered a humiliating defeat due to its lack of defence preparedness and Indian defence expenditure came to stabilise around 3 per cent of the GDP for the next 25 years.[10] Over the past two decades, the military expenditure of India has been around 2.75 per cent but since India has been experiencing significantly higher rates of economic growth over the last decade compared to any other time in its history, the overall resources that it has been able to allocate to its defence needs have grown significantly. The armed forces for long have been asking for an allocation of 3 per cent of the nation's GDP to defence. This has received broad political support in recent years. The Indian prime minister has been explicit about it, suggesting that 'if our economy grows at about 8 per cent per annum, it will not be difficult for [the Indian government] to allocate about 3 per cent of GDP for national defense.'[11] The Indian Parliament has also underlined the need to aim for the target of 3 per cent of the GDP.

India, with the world's fourth-largest military and one of the biggest defence budgets, has been in the midst of a huge defence modernisation programme for nearly a decade that has seen billions of dollars spent on the latest high-tech military technology. This liberal spending on defence equipment has attracted the interest of Western industry and governments alike and is changing the scope of the global defence market.

As for the share of the three services, during the ten-year period between 1996–97 and 2005–06, the average share of the expenditure on the army, navy, and air force was 57 per cent, 15 per cent and 24 per cent respectively. Though the navy's share is the smallest, it has been gradually increasing over the years whereas the share of other services has witnessed great fluctuations. The Indian Navy saw its allocation going up by 10.5 per cent and procurement spending rising by 17 per cent in 2007.[12] In 2008–09, the navy's share 18.47 per cent of total defence allocation compared to 46.62 per cent of the army, and 53 per cent of the air force.[13] In the overall defence expenditure for the services, the ratio of revenue to capital expenditure is most significant in assessing how the services are utilising their allocated resources. Capital expenditure is the element that is directed towards building future capabilities. While the ratio of revenue to capital expenditure has been around 70:30 for the defence forces as a whole, there is huge variation among the services with the ratio of navy being 48:52. Of the three services, it is the only one that is investing in future capabilities to a greater extent than current expenditure.[14] Capital expenditure determines the trend of modernisation and with 52 per cent of its allocation going toward capital expenditure, the Indian Navy is ahead of the other two services in its endeavour to modernise its operations. Three key acquisitions by the Indian Navy – long range aircraft, aircraft carriers and nuclear submarines – are intended to make India a formidable force in the Indian Ocean. While India's global aspirations are clearly visible in the modernisation activities of the Indian Navy, nonconventional threats to Indian and global security have also risen in recent times, which might result in a change of priorities for the defence forces.

## Growing threats from non-state actors

Non-traditional threats to global security have grown exponentially and maritime terrorism, gun-running, drug trafficking and piracy are the major threats that India is facing across the sea-borders of the country.

With vital shipping lanes passing through the area, India has been emphasising the importance of maritime security in the Persian Gulf and the Gulf of Aden. Various terrorist organisations from Al Qaeda to Jammah Islamiah use maritime routes around India in the Indian Ocean region for narcotics and arms trafficking through which they finance their operations. Indian intelligence agencies have warned the government that India might face seaborne attacks by terrorist groups against nation's oil rigs, involving both production and support platforms, along both the coasts of India.[15] Piracy in various parts of the Indian Ocean such as the Malacca Straits and Horn of Africa is rampant, requiring a strong Indian maritime presence. In line with this perception, the Indian maritime doctrine states: 'The Indian maritime vision for the twenty-first century must look at the arc from the Persian Gulf to the Straits of Malacca, as a legitimate area of interest.'[16]

Most of the attacks and hijackings on the high seas are clustered in three areas: the Gulf of Aden and the eastern coast of Somalia; the coast of West Africa, particularly off Nigeria; and the Indonesian archipelago. In the first quarter of 2008, more than half of all attacks took place in the Gulf of Aden.[17] In 2008, at least 92 ships were attacked in and around the Gulf of Aden, more than triple the number in 2007 and an estimated $25 million to $30 million were paid in ransom to Somali pirates.[18]

Following the hijacking off the coast of Somalia in September 2008 of the merchant vessel MT *Stolt Valor* owned by a Japanese company with 18 Indian crew members on board, the Indian government authorised the Indian Navy to begin patrols in the Gulf of Aden and escort Indian merchant vessels. India has an economic interest in ensuring the protection of even non-Indian owned cargo ships in the Gulf of Aden shipping lanes as around 85 per cent of India's sea trade on the route is carried by foreign-owned ships while around one-third of India's total fleet of 900 cargo ships deployed in international waters are at risk.[19] Patrolling by the Indian Navy is intended to protect the nation's sea borne trade and instil confidence in the sea-faring community as well as functioning to deter pirates. Russia, NATO (North Atlantic Treaty Organization) and the EU forces have also started patrolling the region but efforts remain disjointed. India has made a case that a peacekeeping force under a unified command is needed to provide security to international shipping in pirate-infested regions.[20] In a first operation of its kind since the 1971 war with Pakistan, India's stealth frigate, INS *Tabar*, shot at and sank a pirate 'mother vessel' in the Gulf of Aden which later turned out to be a Thai trawler. Since the trawler was under the command of the pirates who refused to surrender, the Indian Naval vessel claimed to have fired in self-defence. This incident once again highlighted the Indian Navy's capability on the high seas, witnessed earlier by the world in the conduct of tsunami relief operations and during the evacuation of Indian nationals in the Lebanon War of July–August 2006. Moreover, the Indian Navy asserted its autonomy and ability in the service of a collective good – the protection of global maritime trade. India used this act of its navy to project India as a country capable of protecting its maritime interests and commercial sea routes in international waters.

While on the one hand the Indian Navy demonstrated its might on the high seas, on the other, its ability to tackle terrorism on the homeland has come under scrutiny after terrorists managed to hoodwink the Indian Navy and Coast Guard to launch a severe assault on Mumbai in November 2008. The terrorists managed to enter Mumbai by using a trawler, indicating a systemic failure of the Indian security agencies. It is the responsibility of India's Coast Guard to secure India's EEZ, up to 200 nm whereas the blue water beyond is the navy's responsibility. Though dangers of terror attacks from the sea have long been apparent to Indian policy-makers, no action was taken to strengthen the anti-terror defences. India's long coastline with its inadequate policing makes it easy to land arms and explosives at isolated spots along the coast. This was how explosives were smuggled into India in 1993 for the bomb blasts that crippled the Indian financial capital. The same method was used again by the terrorists to attack Mumbai in 2008. The Indian naval chief took responsibility for inaction and underlined weak infrastructure for patrolling and surveillance of coastal areas. Despite clear intelligence inputs the coast guard and the navy failed to either spot or interdict the Pakistani ship that carried terrorists from an Indus creek near Karachi in Pakistan.[21]

It is clear that global threats from non-state actors are multiplying. India will have to work with other major naval powers not only to tackle problems such as piracy but also deal with the larger issues of security for seagoing commerce. Because the navy has proven itself adept at giving the Indian government sufficient leverage in operational situations in the Indian Ocean, its utility for India in projecting power and protecting its interests is only going to increase. Yet the biggest challenge to the Indian Navy might come from the expansion of the prowess of that other Asian giant in the Indian Ocean: China.

## China's foray in the Indian Ocean

China emerged as the biggest military spender in the Asia-Pacific in 2006, overtaking Japan, and now has the fourth-largest defence expenditure in the world. The exact details about Chinese military expenditure remain contested, with estimates ranging from the official Chinese figure of $35 billion to the US Defense Intelligence Agency's estimate of $80 billion to $115 billion.[22] But the rapidly rising trend in Chinese military expenditure is fairly evident, with an increase of 195 per cent over the decade 1997–2006. The official figures of the Chinese government do not include the cost of new weapon purchases, research or other big-ticket items for China's highly secretive military. The Chinese Navy, according to the

Defence White Paper of 2006, will be aiming at a 'gradual extension of the strategic depth for offshore defensive operations and enhancing its capabilities in integrated maritime operations and nuclear counter-attacks.'[23]

China's navy is now considered the third-largest in the world behind only the United States and Russia and superior to the Indian Navy in both qualitative and quantitative terms.[24] The Peoples' Liberation Army (PLA) Navy (PLAN) has traditionally been a coastal force and China has had a continental outlook to security. But with a rise in its economic might since the 1980s, Chinese interests have expanded and have acquired a maritime orientation with an intent to project power into the Indian Ocean. China is investing far greater resources in the modernisation of its armed forces in general and its navy in particular than India seems either willing to undertake or capable of sustaining at present. China's increasingly sophisticated submarine fleet could eventually be one of the world's largest and with a rapid accretion in its capabilities, including submarines, ballistic missiles and GPS-blocking technology, some are suggesting that China will increasingly have the capacity to challenge America.[25] Senior Chinese officials have indicated that China would be ready to build an aircraft carrier by the end of the decade as it is seen as being indispensable to protecting Chinese interests in oceans.[26] Such an intent to develop carrier capability marks a shift away from devoting the bulk of PLA's modernisation drive to the goal of capturing Taiwan.

With a rise in China's economic and political prowess, there has also been a commensurate growth in its profile in the Indian Ocean region. China is acquiring naval bases along the crucial choke-points in the Indian Ocean not only to serve its economic interests but also to enhance its strategic presence in the region. China realises that its maritime strength will give it the strategic leverage that it needs to emerge as the regional hegemon and a potential superpower and there is enough evidence to suggest that China is comprehensively building up its maritime power in all dimensions.[27] It is China's growing dependence on maritime space and resources that is reflected in the Chinese aspiration to expand its influence and to ultimately dominate the strategic environment of the Indian Ocean region. China's growing reliance on bases across the Indian Ocean region is a response to its perceived vulnerability, given the logistical constraints that it faces due to the distance of the Indian Ocean waters from its own area of operation. Yet, China is consolidating power over the South China Sea and the Indian Ocean with an eye on India, something that comes out clearly in a secret memorandum issued by the Director of the General Logistic Department of the PLA: 'We can no longer accept the Indian Ocean as only an ocean of the Indians ... We are taking armed conflicts in the region into account.'[28]

China has deployed its Jin class submarines at a submarine base near Sanya in the southern tip of Hainan Island in the South China Sea, raising alarm in India as the base is merely 1,200 nm from the Malacca Strait and will be its closest access point to the Indian Ocean. The base also has an underground facility that can hide the movement of submarines; making them difficult to detect.[29] The concentration of strategic naval forces at Sanya will further propel China towards a consolidation of its control over the surrounding Indian Ocean region. The presence of access tunnels on the mouth of the deep water base is particularly troubling for India as it will have strategic implications in the Indian Ocean region, allowing China to interdict shipping at the three crucial choke points in the Indian Ocean. As the ability of China's navy to project power in the Indian Ocean region grows, India is likely to feel even more vulnerable despite enjoying distinct geographical advantages in the region. China's growing naval presence in and around the Indian Ocean region is troubling for India as it restricts India's freedom to manoeuvre in the region. Of particular note is what has been termed as China's 'string of pearls' strategy that has significantly expanded China's strategic depth in India's backyard.[30]

This 'string of pearls' strategy of bases and diplomatic ties include the Gwadar port in Pakistan, naval bases in Burma, electronic intelligence gathering facilities on islands in the Bay of Bengal, funding construction of a canal across the Kra Isthmus in Thailand, a military agreement with Cambodia and building up of forces in the South China Sea.[31] Some of these claims are exaggerated as has been the case with the Chinese naval presence in Burma. The Indian government, for example, had to concede in 2005 that reports of China turning Coco Islands in Burma into a naval base were incorrect and that there were indeed no naval bases in Burma.[32] Yet the Chinese thrust into the Indian Ocean is gradually becoming more pronounced than before. The Chinese may not have a naval base in Burma but they are involved in the upgrading of infrastructure in the Coco Islands and may be providing some limited technical assistance to Burma. Given that almost 80 per cent of China's oil passes through the Strait of Malacca, it is reluctant to rely on US naval power for unhindered access to energy and so has decided to build up its naval power at choke points along the sea routes from the Persian Gulf to the South China Sea. China is also courting other states in South Asia by building container ports in Bangladesh at Chittagong and in Sri Lanka at Hambantota. Consolidating its access to the Indian Ocean, China has signed an agreement with Sri Lanka to finance the development of the Hambantota Development Zone which includes a container port, a bunker system and an oil refinery. It is possible that the construction of these ports and facilities around India's periphery by China can be explained away on purely economic and commercial grounds but for India this looks like a policy of containment by other means.

China's diplomatic and military efforts in the Indian Ocean seem to exhibit a desire to project power vis-à-vis competing powers in the region such as the United States and India. China's presence in the Bay of Bengal via roads and ports in Burma and in the Arabian Sea via the Chinese built port of Gwadar in Pakistan has been a cause of concern for India. With access to crucial port facilities in Egypt, Iran and Pakistan, China is well-poised to secure its interests in the region. China's involvement in the construction of the deep-sea port of Gwadar has attracted a lot of attention due to its strategic location, about 70 km from the Iranian border and 400 km east of the Strait of Hormuz, a major oil supply route. It has been suggested that it will provide China with a 'listening post' from where it can 'monitor US naval activity in the Persian Gulf, Indian activity in the Arabian Sea and future US–Indian maritime cooperation in the Indian Ocean.'[33] Though Pakistan's naval capabilities do not, on their own, pose any challenge to India, the combinations of Chinese and Pakistani naval forces can indeed be formidable for India to counter.

It has been suggested that the Chinese government appears 'to have a very clear vision of the future importance of the sea and a sense of the strategic leadership needed to develop maritime interest.'[34] This is reflected in the attempts that China has made in recent years to build up all aspects of its maritime economy and to create one of the world's largest merchant fleets with a port, transport and ship-building infrastructure to match. In this respect, the Indian Ocean has an important role to play in the Chinese efforts towards establishing its predominance as the main maritime power in the region. And this is resulting in Sino-Indian competition for influence in the Indian Ocean and beyond. Despite a significant improvement in Sino-Indian ties since the late 1990s, the relationship remains competitive in nature and using its rising economic and military profile, China has been successful in containing India within the confines of South Asia by building close ties with India's key neighbours, in particular with Pakistan.[35]

Yet, the notion that China aspires to naval domination of Indian Ocean remains a bit far-fetched. China would certainly like to play a greater role in the region, protect and advance its interests, especially Chinese commerce, as well as counter India; but given the immense geographical advantages that Indian enjoys in the Indian Ocean, China will have great difficulty in exerting as much sway in the Indian Ocean as India can. However, all the steps that China is taking to protect and enhance its interests in the Indian Ocean region are generating apprehensions in Indian strategic circles about her real intentions, thereby engendering a classic security dilemma between the two Asian giants. And it is India's fears and perceptions of the growing naval prowess of China in the Indian Ocean that is driving Indian naval posture. Tensions are inherent in such an evolving strategic relationship as was underlined in an incident in January 2009 when an Indian Kilo class submarine and Chinese warships, on their way to the Gulf of Aden to patrol the pirate-infested waters, reportedly engaged in rounds of manoeuvring as they tried to test for weaknesses in others' sonar system. The Chinese media reported that its warships forced the Indian submarine to the surface which was strongly denied by the

Indian Navy.[36] Unless managed carefully, the potential for such incidents turning serious in the future remains high, especially as Sino-Indian naval competition is likely to intensify with the Indian and Chinese navies operating far from their shores.

## India responds to the Chinese challenge

The augmentation of China's capabilities in the Indian Ocean has alarmed India and has galvanised it into taking ameliorative measures. Underscoring India's discomfort with China's 'string of pearls' strategy, the Indian naval chief has argued that 'each pearl in the string is a link in a chain of the Chinese maritime presence' and has expressed concern that naval forces operating out of ports established by the Chinese could 'take control over the world energy jugular.'[37] India views Chinese naval strategy as expansionist and intent on encircling India strategically. The current Indian naval strategy is being driven by the idea 'that the vast Indian Ocean is its *mare nostrum* ... that the entire triangle of the Indian Ocean is their nation's rightful and exclusive sphere of interest.'[38] Just as the PLAN seems to be concentrating on anti-access warfare so as to prevent the United States Navy from entering into a cross-Straits conflict, the Indian Navy is also working towards acquiring the ability to deny China access through the Indian Ocean.[39] While the Indian Maritime Doctrine of 2004 underlined 'attempts by China to strategically encircle India,' the Indian Maritime Strategy released three years later emphasised attempts by the Chinese Navy to emerge as a blue-water force by pursuing an ambitious modernisation programme, 'along with attempts to gain a strategic toe-hold in the Indian Ocean Rim.'[40]

India's projection of naval power into the Indian Ocean and beyond is an outcome of India's increasingly outward looking foreign policy posture in line with its growing economic prowess. Through joint exercises, port visits and disaster relief missions, the Indian Navy has dramatically raised its profile in the Indian Ocean region in the last few years. India's rapid response to the December 2004 tsunami was the largest ever relief mobilisation by its naval forces and underlined India's growing role in the Indian Ocean as well as its ability to be a net provider of security in the region. India was one of the few nations affected by the tragedy that was able to respond relatively effectively and also lend a helping hand to neighbouring countries by sending its naval ships and personnel. The Indian Navy also demonstrated its rapid response capability when it evacuated a large number of Indians and other nationals from Lebanon during the 2006 Israel–Lebanon conflict.

## Diplomatic initiatives

India is using its naval forces to advance its diplomatic initiatives overseas and in particular towards shaping the strategic environment in and around the Indian Ocean. Indian interests converge with those of the United States in the Indian Ocean region and it is trying to use the present upswing in US–India ties to create a more favourable strategic environment for itself in the region despite its historical sensitivities to the presence of US forces in the Indian Ocean.[41] The US has also recognised the importance of India's role in the region as was evident in Colin Powell's contention that it was important for the United States to support India's role in maintaining peace and stability in the Indian Ocean and its vast periphery.[42] In its first maritime service strategy update in 25 years, the United States views its sea power as the primary instrument in the US defence arsenal to deter conflict with China, and cooperation with other countries' naval services, including India's, is recognised as crucial to fulfilling the strategic imperatives in the region.[43] The US and Indian navies have stepped up their joint exercises and the United States has sold India the USS *Trenton* (renamed INS *Jalashwa*), the first of its class to be inducted into the Indian Navy and marking a milestone in the US–India bilateral ties. The United States would like India to join its Container Security Initiative (CSI) and Proliferation Security Initiative (PSI) but India remains reluctant. PSI is viewed as a US-led initiative outside the United Nations' mandate while the CSI would result in the presence of US inspectors in Indian ports, making it politically radioactive. However, India has indicated that it would be willing to join the US-proposed 1,000-ship navy effort to combat illegal activities on the high seas, given the informal nature of the arrangement.[44] India is seen as a balancer in the Asia-Pacific where the US influence has waned relatively even as China's has risen. India's ties with Japan have also assumed a new dynamic with some even mooting a 'concert of democracies' proposal involving the democratic states of the Asia-Pacific working towards their common goals of a stable Asia-Pacific region.[45] While such a proposal has little chance of evolving into anything concrete in the near term, especially given China's sensitivities, India's decision to develop natural gas with Japan in the Andaman Sea and recent military exercises involving the United States, Japan, India and Australia does give a sense of India's emerging priorities.[46]

India's decision to establish its Far Eastern Command in the Andaman and Nicobar Islands in the Bay of Bengal is aimed at countering China's growing presence in the region by complicating China's access to the region through the Strait of Malacca, the main bottleneck of oil transit to China. India has launched Project Seabird, consisting of India's third operational naval base in Karwar on the nation's western seaboard, an air force station, a naval armament depot, and missile silos, aimed at securing the nation's maritime routes in the Arabian Sea.[47] India is set to establish a monitoring station in Madagascar, its first in another country, as it is deemed vital to guard against the terrorist threat emanating from East Africa as well as to keep an eye on China's plan in the region. India also has its eyes on Mauritius for developing a monitoring facility at an atoll and has strengthened its naval contacts with Mozambique and Seychelles. India responded to Chinese President Hu Jintao's offer of military assistance to Seychelles by donating one of its patrol aircraft to the Seychelles Navy. India's support in the building of Chahbahar port in Iran as well as the road connecting it to Afghanistan is an answer to the Chinese-funded Gwadar port in Pakistan. India's air base in Kazakhstan and its space monitoring post in Mongolia are also geared primarily towards China.

Competition between China and India is also increasing for influence in Burma as the Andaman Sea off Burma's coast is viewed as crucial energy lifeline for China while India also needs Burma for meeting its energy requirements. India will be rebuilding Burma's western Sittwe port and is one of the main suppliers of military hardware to the ruling junta. China's growing penetration of Burma is one of the main reasons India is reluctant to cease its economic and military engagement with the Burmese junta despite attracting widespread criticism from both outside and within India.

India's 'Look East' policy, originally aimed at strengthening economic ties with India's Southeast Asian neighbourhood, has now led to naval exercises with Singapore, Thailand and Indonesia. The ASEAN (Association of Southeast Asian Nations) member states have joined the Indian Navy in policing the Indian Ocean region to check piracy, trafficking and other threats to sea-lanes. India has also accelerated its naval engagement with a number of Persian Gulf states, making port calls and conducting exercises with the navies of Kuwait, Oman, Bahrain, Saudi Arabia, Qatar, United Arab Emirates and Djibouti as well as engaging with the navies of other major powers in the region such as the United States, the United Kingdom and France. It has also been suggested that to more effectively counter Chinese presence in the Indian Ocean and to protect its trade routes, India will have to seek access to the Vietnamese, Taiwanese and Japanese ports for the forward deployment of its naval assets.[48] India is already emerging as an exclusive 'defence service provider' for smaller states with growing economies that seek to strengthen their military capabilities in Southeast Asia and West Asia, such as Vietnam, Indonesia, Malaysia, Singapore, Qatar and Oman, providing it access to ports along the Arabian coast, Indian Ocean and South China Sea.[49]

## Naval platforms and doctrine

The Indian Navy is aiming for a total fleet of 140–145 vessels over the next decade, built around two carrier battle groups: *Admiral Gorshkov* which will now be handed over to India only by 2013 and the indigenous carrier, the 37,500-tonne STOBAR (short take off but arrested recovery) Air Defence Ship likely to be completed by 2014. India's ambition to equip its navy with two or more aircraft carriers over the next decade as well as its decision to launch its first indigenous nuclear submarine in 2009 is seen as crucial for power projection and to achieve a semblance of strategic autonomy. India's emerging capability to put a carrier task force as far as the South China Sea and the Persian Gulf has given boost to Indian Navy's blue-water aspirations and India hopes to induct a third aircraft carrier by 2017, ensuring that the Indian Navy has two operational carriers at any given point.[50] The deployment of the Jin class submarine at Hainan by China will also force India to speed up its indigenous nuclear submarine project that has been in the making for more than a decade now with the Indian Navy, rather ambitiously, aiming at the induction of five indigenous ATV (advanced technology vehicle) nuclear submarines. But with the first trials of the submarine already underway, India will be leasing an Akula II nuclear attack submarine from Russia for personnel training. A submarine-based nuclear arsenal is considered critical by Indian strategists to retain a second-strike capability. Despite some attempts at diversification of sources, India's dependence on Russia for military equipment remains acute and has resulted in bilateral tension in recent times. The Indian military, in particular, has been critical of an over-reliance on Russia for defence acquisition which was reflected in the Indian naval chief's view that there should be rethink on India's ties with Russia in light of the Russian demand of an additional $1.2 billion for the aircraft carrier, *Admiral Gorshkov*, purchased by India in 2004.[51] The Indian Navy is now actively looking to other states, particularly the United States, for its new acquisitions.

While a focus on augmenting its platforms, systems and weapons is clearly visible in the Indian Navy, concomitant changes in doctrine and organisation have been relatively slow to come by. It was only in 2004 that India released its first maritime doctrine since independence. The determination to establish its pre-dominance in the Indian Ocean region comes across quite categorically in the Indian maritime doctrine. The maritime doctrine underlines four roles for the Indian Navy: military/strategic; political; constabulary; and benign agent of humanitarian assistance. The doctrine emphasises the shift for the Indian Navy from conventional combat to include non-traditional threats and underscores the role of the Indian Navy in the nation's trade and energy policies. The doctrine calls for exercising sea control in the designated area of the Arabian Sea and the Bay of Bengal and urges the navy to contribute towards strengthening India's credible minimum nuclear deterrent in the form of nuclear submarines equipped with nuclear missiles. It emphasises Indian concerns about growing Chinese naval capabilities by underlining the allocation of a 24 per cent share of China's defence outlays to its navy compared to 16 per cent in India's case and the Chinese plans to configure its force levels around two-carrier groups. The doctrine, however, is a very ambitious document for a service that has always complained about lack of resources and it does not seem to offer a clear vision for the future. The challenge for the Indian Navy in the coming years will be to synergise its doctrine effectively with force planning and acquisitions.

Organisational changes have been even less visible. It has become imperative for the three services to cooperate more closely if the desired effects are to be achieved in contemporary warfare. 'Jointery' or 'jointness' is the new buzzword and the distinctions between sea, land and air are becoming increasingly redundant for the conduct of expeditionary operations. Integration is essential not only for operational effectiveness but is also a force multiplier and a measure of efficiency. And in this era of 'jointness,' of all the major armed forces in the world, India is probably the only one not fully integrated. India has taken some baby steps towards jointery though inter-services rivalry continues to plague Indian defence forces. The Indian Army continues to insist that it should be seen as the most important element while the navy and air force continue to resent and resist the domination of the army. The result is that while an integrated defence staff has been set up, the move towards a chief of defence staff has come to naught as the inter-services bickering gives the government an excuse to drag its feet on this issue essential for streamlining decision-making on defence issues. Lack of cooperation among the three services also leads to duplication of purchases, hindering efficient utilisation of precious resources. Yet, the acquisition and procurement processes continue to remain extremely complex and opaque. India's much-hyped defence modernisation programme is suffering because of delays in the procurement of major weapon systems.

## Conclusion

With its rise as a major power in the region, India has been forced to shed some of the reticence that has characterised the conduct of its foreign policy in the post-independence period, and the country has been called upon to provide security in its neighbourhood, including the Indian Ocean region. Given India's geographical coordinates, it will always have a pivotal role in the Indian Ocean and its littoral. Indian policy-makers have only just begun to recognise the importance of the Indian Navy as a powerful tool in the pursuit of their nation's foreign policy objectives. The Indian Navy's ambitious modernisation programme is geared towards its emergence as a world-class blue-water navy, equipped and willing to meet regional challenges, and become a guarantor of regional peace and stability. India is looking at its navy not only as an instrument of war fighting but also as an effective police force in the region as well as contributing to benign and coercive diplomacy in the littoral. Though the Indian and Chinese navies are usually placed on par with each other as 'medium regional force projection navies' when attempts are made to classify world navies, the pace of their recent growth might soon call for a re-evaluation.[52] Indian naval strategists warn that despite all the talk of quality and capability-based platforms, the Indian Navy is actually shrinking in size and that a ten-year strategic maritime gap has emerged between China and India which will be difficult to close without radical actions to upgrade shipbuilding and port infrastructure.[53] Though Indian naval aspirations are growing, the emphasis placed upon India's sea power has not been commensurate with the nation's growing maritime commitments and the ever-more sophisticated threats emerging in the waters around it. India's reluctance, primarily due to domestic political considerations, to conclude the logistics support agreement with the United States is also constraining the Indian Navy's ability to compete with the Chinese thrust into the Indian Ocean.

Both China and India would most certainly like to acquire the potential to project power and operate interpedently far from their shores. Yet, it is China that as of now seems more willing to actually commit to the expense of building up its fleet with a clear strategic agenda as to how its wants to utilise its naval assets. The ability of Indian policy-makers to think strategically on national security and defence issues has been questionable at best. Ad hoc decision-making has been the norm leading to a situation where long-time observers of India argue that it is likely that 'India will be among the medium powers ... a country of great economic capabilities but limited cultural and military influence.'[54] With policy-makers in New Delhi far removed from the nation's sea frontiers, there is an even less understanding of maritime issues. This political apathy has led to the nation's armed forces operating in a strategic void. The Indian Navy's attempt to come up with its own strategy and doctrine, though welcome in many respects, has little meaning in the absence of a national security strategy from the Indian government.

Despite the fact that some in India would like their nation to achieve preponderance in the Indian Ocean region, it remains an unrealistic aspiration as other major powers have significant stakes in the region and so will continue to operate and shape its strategic environment. A rising India is beginning to discover that major global powers have stakes in far-flung corners of the world and this realisation has allowed India to shun its fundamentally flawed original argument about the need for 'extra-regional navies' to withdraw from the Indian Ocean region. India's bilateral and multilateral naval exercises with major naval powers has helped in reducing the misperceptions about India's maritime intentions and has brought Indian Navy's capacity to contribute to peace and stability in the Indian Ocean littoral to the forefront. India, therefore, will look towards cooperating with other major powers in the region to secure common interests that include safeguarding the SLOC, energy security, and countering extremist and terrorist groups.

However, Asia is witnessing the rise of two giants, China and India, simultaneously and this will cause some inevitable complications. It has been suggested that much like the Japanese–American rivalry in the Pacific during the first half of the twentieth century over overlapping

SLOC, a similar degree of mutual suspicion and insecurity haunts Sino-Indian relations in the Indian Ocean.[55] While the costs of not cooperating will be too high for both China and India, the struggle for power and influence between the Asian giants will continue to shape India's naval posture as well as the strategic environment of the Indian Ocean region in the coming years.

## Notes

1 For details, see *CIA World Factbook*, online, available at: www.cia.gov/library/publications/the-world-factbook/geos/xo.html.
2 P. K. Das, 'Maritime Dimensions of India's Security,' *Indian Defence Review*, vol. 18 (2), pp. 43–47.
3 *Indian Maritime Doctrine*, Integrated Headquarters, Ministry of Defence (Navy), 2004, p. 56.
4 Rahul Roy-Chaudhury, *Sea Power and India's Security* (London: Brassey's, 1995), p. 199.
5 K. M. Pannikar, *India and the Indian Ocean: An Essay in the Influence of Sea Power on Indian History* (London: George Allen & Unwin, 1945), p. 45.
6 David Scott, 'India's "Grand Strategy" for the Indian Ocean: Mahanian Visions,' *Asia-Pacific Review*, vol. 13 (2), 2006, pp. 98–101.
7 George Tanham, *Securing India* (New Delhi: Manohar Publishers, 1996), p. 59.
8 N. Palmer, "South Asia and the Indian Ocean,' in A. Cottrell and R. Burrell, eds, *The Indian Ocean: Its Political, Economic, and Military Importance* (New York: Praeger, 1972), p. 237.
9 Ashley Tellis, 'Demanding Tasks for the Indian Navy,' *Asian Survey*, vol. 25 (12), December 1985, p. 1204.
10 Jasjit Singh, *India's Defence Spending: Assessing Future Needs* (New Delhi: Knowledge World, 2001), pp. 22–23.
11 'India Plans to Spend More on Defense if Economy Grows,' *Agence France-Presse* (New Delhi), October 20, 2005.
12 *The Military Balance*, The International Institute for Strategic Studies, 2008, p. 336.
13 Annual Report, 2007–08, Ministry of Defence, Government of India, p. 14.
14 V. N. Srinivas, 'Trends in Defence Expenditure,' *Air Power Journal*, vol. 3 (1), Spring 2006, pp. 64–73.
15 Arun Kumar Singh, 'The Next Terror Attack could be From the Sea,' *Asian Age*, May 18, 2008.
16 *Indian Maritime Doctrine*, p. 56.
17 Mark McDonald, 'Maritime Hijackings Decrease in Asia,' *New York Times*, November 19, 2008.
18 Hari Kumar and Alan Cowell, 'Indian Navy Strikes Pirate Ship,' *New York Times*, November 20, 2008.
19 Emily Wax, 'Indian Navy Sinks Suspected Somali Pirate Mother Ship,' *Washington Post*, November 11, 2008.
20 'UN force needed to prevent piracy: India,' *Indian Express*, November 14, 2008.
21 Shishir Gupta, 'Coast Guard Moved on LeT Alert but was All at Sea,' *Indian Express*, December 11, 2008.
22 Petter Stålenheim, Catalina Perdomo and Elisabeth Sköns, 'Military Expenditure,' in *SIPRI Year Book 2007: Armaments, Disarmament and International Security* (London: Oxford University Press, 2007), pp. 289–290.
23 Ibid.

24 Anthony H. Cordesman and Martin Kleiber, *The Asian Conventional Military Balance in 2006*, Centre for Strategic and International Studies, June 2006, p. 32.
25 Robert D. Kaplan, 'Lost at Sea,' *New York Times*, September 21, 2007.
26 *The Military Balance* (London: IISS, 2008), pp. 360–361.
27 Thomas Kane, *Chinese Grand Strategy and Maritime Power* (London: Frank Cass, 2002), p. 139.
28 Youssef Bodansky, 'The PRC Surge for the Strait of Malacca and Spratly Confronts India and the US,' Defense and Foreign Affairs Strategic Policy, Washington, DC, September 30, 1995, pp. 6–13.
29 Manu Pubby, 'China's New N-Submarine Base sets off Alarm Bells,' *Indian Express*, May 3, 2008.
30 Bill Gertz, 'China Builds Up Strategic Sea Lanes,' *Washington Times*, January 18, 2005.
31 For a detailed explication the security ramifications of the Chinese 'string of pearls' strategy, see Gurpreet Khurana, 'China's "String of Pearls" in the Indian Ocean and Its Security Implications,' *Strategic Analysis*, vol. 32 (1), January 2008, pp. 1–22.
32 For a nuanced analysis of this, see Andrew Selth, 'Chinese Military Bases in Burma: The Explosion of a Myth,' Griffith Asia Institute, Regional Outlook Paper 10, 2007.
33 Ziad Haider, 'Oil Fuels Beijing's New Power Game,' Yale Global Online, Online, available at: http://yaleglobal.yale.edu/display.article?id=5411.
34 Geoffrey Till, *Seapower: A Guide for the Twenty-First Century* (London: Frank Cass, 2004), p. 102.
35 Harsh V. Pant, 'India in the Asia-Pacific: Rising Ambitions with an Eye on China,' *Asia-Pacific Review*, vol. 14 (1), May 2007, pp. 54–71.
36 Manu Pubby, 'Indian Submarine, Chinese Warship Test each other in Pirate Waters,' *Indian Express*, February 5, 2009.
37 Quoted in Gavin Rabinowitz, 'India, China Jostle for Influence in Indian Ocean,' *Associated Press*, June 7, 2008.
38 E. Margolis, 'India Rules the Waves,' *Proceedings*, US Naval Institute, vol. 131 (3), March 2005, p. 70.
39 Sam J. Tangredi, 'The Future of Maritime Power,' in Andrew T. H. Tan, ed., *The Politics of Maritime Power: A Survey* (London: Routledge, 2007), pp. 143–144.
40 *Freedom to Use the Seas: India's Maritime Military Strategy*, Integrated Headquarters Ministry of Defence (Navy), 2007, p. 41.
41 On the recent trends in US–India ties, see Harsh V. Pant, *Contemporary Debates in Indian Foreign and Security Policy: India Negotiates Its Rise in the International System* (New York: Palgrave Macmillan, 2008), pp. 19–38.
42 Colin Powell, 'US Looks to its Allies for Stability in Asia and the Pacific,' *International Herald Tribune*, January 27, 2001.
43 'United States: New Naval Strategy,' *International Herald Tribune*, October 25, 2007.
44 Sandeep Dikshit, 'Join Global Policing of Sea Lanes, US asks India,' *Hindu*, April 19, 2007.
45 On India–Japan maritime cooperation, see Gurpreet Khurana, 'Security of Sea-Lanes: Prospects for India–Japan Cooperation,' *Strategic Analysis*, vol. 31 (1) January 2007, pp. 139–150.
46 On India's strategic priorities in the Asia-Pacific, see Pant, 'India in the Asia-Pacific: Rising Ambitions with an Eye on China,' pp. 54–71.
47 Yevgeny Bendersky, 'India's Project Seabird and the Indian Ocean's Balance of Power,' *Power and Interest News Report*, July 20, 2005.
48 Mohan Malik, 'Chinese Strategy of Containing India,' *Power and Interest News Report*, February 6, 2006.

49 Pranab Dhal Samanta, 'Start Getting Used to DSP: Defence Services Provider,' *Indian Express*, January 1, 2008.
50 Manu Pubby, '3rd Aircraft Carrier to be Inducted by 2017: Antony,' *Indian Express*, May 17, 2007.
51 Sandeep Unnithan, 'Battle over Gorshkov,' *India Today*, December 7, 2007.
52 On the classification of world navies along various axes, see Eric Grove, *The Future of Seapower* (London: Routledge, 1990), pp. 231–240.
53 Arun Kumar Singh, 'Navy Coast Guard Must Get More Funds, Powers,' *Asian Age*, June 2, 2008.
54 See Stephen Cohen's interview with Pragati, online, available at http://pragati.nationalinterest.in/wp-content/uploads/2008/06/pragati-issue15-jun2008-communityed.pdf.
55 John W. Garver, *Protracted Contest: Sino-Indian Rivalry in the 20th Century* (Seattle: University of Washington Press, 1989), p. 285.

# 8 Singapore and sea power

*Joshua Ho**

## Introduction – Singapore as a sea power

Before we embark on a description of the relationship between Singapore and sea power, it would be appropriate to look at what Alfred Thayer Mahan has to say about sea power in general since he is recognised as the first person to have coined the term. To be sure, his ideas are not easy to summarise accurately. He was concerned about the widespread ignorance about the role and importance of sea power even amongst experienced sea-faring peoples. To him, in peacetime, national power, security and prosperity depended on the sea as a mode of transportation and in wartime, sea power resulted from naval supremacy which provided the means of attacking the enemy's trade and threatening his interests ashore whilst protecting your own. In Mahan's mind, these advantages were so great that the sea powers would prosper in peace, prevail in war and dominate world events. However, Mahan was careful to say that the importance of sea power can be exaggerated and is only one factor in the rise and fall of nations. Sea power therefore revolved around a simple connection, in that trade produces wealth that leads to maritime strength. Naval strength protects trade, and in turn depends on geography, physical conformation, extent of territory, population, character of the people and the character of the government.[1]

In pre-modern times, sea power played a major role in the rise and fall of Singapore, or Temasek as it was earlier known, as a major port. Temasek became a major port when a regional polity was able to defend it and its trade routes by sea and even force ships to call at her port. When the dominant polity could not defend the port, as proved to be the case when the Dutch arrived, the significance of Temasek waned as ships called on the Dutch designated port instead, namely Batavia (Jakarta).

However, in modern times, the role of sea power, or naval supremacy, was less important in determining the role of Singapore as a major port. More important were the location, the existence of free trade in and around the port area, and a primary producing hinterland covering modern Malaysia and Indonesia. Due to its strategic location, Singapore quickly became a major maritime hub and a sea power in the sense that civil maritime capabilities and commercial operations were the major determinants of sea power rather than merely military maritime capabilities or the conduct of naval operations alone.[2]

This chapter thus describes the rise and fall of Temasek as a hub port during pre-modern times and the subsequent re-emergence of Singapore as a hub port founded on the principles of free seaborne trade during the modern era. The chapter goes on to describe how Singapore, being a sea power, has adopted a comprehensive approach to maritime issues, to include safety, security and environmental protection and how it has developed an integrated response to maritime issues in order to defend its maritime interests. The chapter then concludes by stressing the need for a continued emphasis on developing and maintaining the stable maritime regime necessary for seaborne trade to flourish and consequently for prosperity to pervade both regionally and globally. Let us first begin then with the rise and fall of Temasek as a trading port in pre-modern times.

## Temasek

Temasek was a trading settlement that began to form in Singapore in the late thirteenth century and grew in importance in the fourteenth century. The people were Malays, *Orang Laut* and Chinese. The Malays were rulers who opened the port for trade to generate revenue and attract foreign traders and people, all of which contribute to the wealth and prestige of their kingdom. The *Orang Laut*, Malay for "Sea People", were directed by the Malay rulers and chiefs to man war fleets and to harvest produce from the resource-rich marine environment which had a market in China. The trade of Temasek also depended on imports of Chinese silks, cottons, ceramics, iron cauldrons and other goods brought by the junks of the "Chuan-chou traders".[3] Temasek also had resident Chinese merchants interested in, among other items, the "black wood" found on the island.

Despite being a centre for trade, the people of Temasek were aware of their vulnerability in the region, as to the north the Siamese kingdom of Sukothai was in an expansionist mode, and to the south, the Javanese empire of Majapahit listed Temasek as amongst its vassals in 1365. Malay annals ascribed to Temasek the reigns of five rulers, the last of whom came under attack from Majapahit. Differing from this account, Portuguese sagas described how around 1300, a Malay prince by the name of Seri Teri Buana, of Palembang, southeast Sumatra, came to Temasek and took over the kingdom, which he renamed *Singapura*, "lion city", by murdering its ruler. Then, in 1396, he was driven out by an expedition sent by the King of Siam, to whom the murdered ruler was related by marriage, and probably by vassalage as well. As a result the Seri Teri Buana had to relocate his kingdom northwards to Malacca.

## Malacca

Malacca was founded at the beginning of the fifteenth century. The Chinese from the reigning Ming dynasty immediately dispatched a mission to open relations with the port arising in a region vital to the passage of Chinese shipping and trade. Representatives from the Malay prince who founded Malacca also presented themselves before the Chinese court.

The rulers of Malacca forcibly diverted ships to Malacca that used to call at Temasek. Naval power was a complement to trade, used to compel passing ships to stop over as well as to maintain security on the sea route. This consideration drove Malacca to establish control over both sides of the Straits of Malacca, bringing under its suzerainty certain parts of east coast Sumatra and the west coast of the Malay Peninsula. The king of Sukothai, who had been concerned over the loss of revenue due to the decline in trade receipts at Temasek, entered into an agreement with the ruler of Malacca to address the situation. Temasek was eventually ceded to Malacca in return for an annual payment of a stipulated amount of gold. Temasek's existence as an autonomous port-settlement thus came to an end after a little more than 100 years.[4]

But Malacca was not the only port-polity in the region. By the early sixteenth century, Aceh, a rival port-polity located at the northern tip of Sumatra had emerged to challenge the dominant position of the Johor court, whose sultans had shifted their capital to Johor following their retreat from Malacca in the face of a Portuguese attack on the port-city in 1511. Hence, Johor, Portuguese Malacca and Aceh contested for supremacy over the Straits of Malacca. However, Aceh's expansionist tendencies ceased with the death of its most powerful ruler in 1636. By this time, the Dutch had also entered the picture and Johor court formed an alliance with the Dutch to fend off the Portuguese. So for the next century, the Portuguese and the Dutch contested waters around Singapore. The Dutch wanted to establish a presence at the southern end of the Malay Peninsula but its plans were not well received by the Johor Sultanate. Because of this, by the second half of the seventeenth century, fewer and fewer Dutch ships were calling at Johor and the Dutch increased their focus on Batavia (Jakarta), which quickly became the centre of Dutch operations in East Asia. Consequently, the Johor River estuary became increasingly unattractive as a trading port and as a result in 1618, the Johor Sultanate moved its court to Lingga Island. Dutch hostilities undermined the Portuguese economic interests in Asia, leading to difficulties in maintaining its commercial operations in the Malacca Straits, and forcing the Portuguese to rely on the port of Makassar as their base of operations. In 1640, the Dutch captured Malacca and in 1667, the Dutch also captured Makassar and put an end to the Portuguese empire in maritime Southeast Asia.[5]

The emergence of the Dutch as the pre-eminent European power in maritime Southeast Asia by the second half of the seventeenth century, their concentration on the control and usage of the Sunda Straits over the Malacca Straits, and the shift of the capital of the Johor Sultanate from the southern end of the Malacca Straits to the Lingga Archipelago, led to a southward shift of the strategic maritime area that linked the South China Sea and the Indian Ocean, from the southern end of the Malacca Straits and the waters around Singapore to the west Java Sea and the Sunda Straits. The strategic significance of the Malacca Straits appears to have declined through the course of the eighteenth century and had become redundant in the maritime order that emerged from the conflict of the late sixteenth and seventeenth centuries. Even ports that had once been strategically important, such as Malacca and Singapore, were left on their own and consequently declined in importance.

## The re-emergence of Singapore as an entrepôt port

Stamford Raffles was a servant of the English East India Company with a keen interest in Malay studies and in natural history. He engineered the succession to the Johor Sultanate and established him in Singapore in order to establish a trading base in Singapore conceived on geopolitical and commercial principles. He managed to conclude an agreement with the Sultan on the 6 February 1819, which entitled the East India Company to use a defined area as a port and settlement.

Singapore possessed an advantageous location the potential of which was vastly enhanced by the application of free trade principles and advances in technology. Raffles thought of free trade for Singapore as a way to beat the competition from ports under indigenous rulers, such as Riau, or under the Dutch, notably Batavia (Jakarta), where traders were encumbered by all sorts of taxes and restrictions. Free trade except where Raffles decreed it was "virtually unknown" in the region, and he scored handsomely by being the first to deliver it.[6] Yet his move was also dictated by necessity as, apart from its geographical position, Singapore had few natural resources and no products to tempt the trader. Singapore's trade, as the British merchants coming long after Raffles realised, "was an artificial creation".[7]

This artificial creation was entrepôt trade which means that the goods transacted were not produced in the island but brought in from outside. The British merchants believed that free trade was essential to keep the Singapore entrepôt going. These merchant pioneers were not only opposed to the imposition of duties on imports and exports, they were also against the fees normally charged at any port, namely, tonnage and port dues, pilotage, wharfage and anchorage duties and port clearance fees.[8] Revenue was raised through excise duties, licences and property taxes.

The geographical location of Singapore became more important with the opening of the Suez Canal in 1869. Steamships began to call more often and used it as a coal bunkering centre. Then in 1871, telegraphic communications linked Europe, Australia and Hong Kong. Tin from Malaya and the Sumatran islands of Banka and Billiton made Singapore a world market for this mineral. Trade in rubber also produced more linkages, in particular with the Chinese, and between the traders in Singapore and the growers in remote rivers and jungles in Netherlands India.[9] Singapore also hosted the oil industry and the oil companies chose Singapore because it was well connected by shipping routes to the world and the region, and it was where they could store, blend, distribute and ship the oil, all at one convenient centre.[10] Singapore gained from the sheer volume of oil handled, the repair of oil tankers and the bunkering of oil-fired ships. In addition to being a staple port, Singapore was also a centre for the import and distribution of manufactures, in particular textiles where the British and European agency houses were supreme but where the Japanese also competed successfully based on price.

In 1960, Singapore began to refine oil sent from the Middle East, but Indonesia and Malaysia also sent their crude to be processed. Eventually Indonesia started to refine its own oil in 1985[11] and Malaysia followed suit with a refinery in Malacca.[12] These developments did not affect Singapore too much as Middle East and Chinese crude were also the basis of Singapore's oil refinery business. What mattered was that Singapore had the best refineries in the region as the multinational oil companies located in Singapore had seen to this, making it the Houston of Asia. Hence in summary, three things, namely location, free trade and a primary producing hinterland covering British Malaya (the Malay States) and "even more, Netherlands India" had come together to make Singapore so important.[13] This importance continues today.

The port of Singapore is a central node, a maritime hub, that sits astride the Straits of Malacca and Singapore, which link the Indian Ocean and the South China Sea, and which provide the main artery through which a huge proportion of global trade and energy flow. Tankers and bulk carriers move vast quantities of oil, coal, iron ore and minerals to the manufacturing centres of Southeast and Northeast Asia, while millions of containers flow in the opposite direction to feed consumer markets all over the world. Singapore has today become the world's top container port and is a major transhipment port, with 80 per cent of its container cargo transhipped, the world's top bunkering port, the world's third-largest oil refining centre, a thriving international centre for shipbuilding, ship repairs and conversions, and a regional cruise centre.[14] Because of the importance of the sea to Singapore's material well-being, it has adopted a comprehensive approach to maritime security, and developed an integrated response that is meant to promote Singapore's maritime interests in the Malacca and Singapore Straits.

## Adopting a comprehensive approach to maritime security

A comprehensive approach to maritime security addresses not only traditional inter-state conflict and tackling the challenge of maritime terrorism, but also includes the prevention of illicit smuggling of weapons of mass destruction and items needed to develop nuclear weapons by sea. In the past, it was normal in the shipping sector to make a distinction between safety and security, but now there is also recognition of the close relationship between maritime safety and maritime security. Even the International Maritime Organisation (IMO) has changed its motto from "safer ships, cleaner oceans" to "safe, secure and efficient shipping on clean oceans" to reflect the close relationship between safety and security.[15] Maritime safety is part of a comprehensive concept of security that includes maritime safety services, marine aids to navigation and services, and hydrographic surveying. However the linkages do not stop at just safety and security as the new IMO motto also emphasises the protection of the marine environment as an important goal. Hence, a comprehensive approach to maritime security has emerged which includes issues relating to maritime safety, security and environmental protection that is addressed both from the perspective of the users of the seas, comprising the ships, their owners and operators, and the provider of services, comprising the port and terminal operators, the maritime authorities, navies and coast guards.

With the increased scope of what maritime security means comes the need for an integrated response. At the national level, these developments have brought more agencies into play with responsibilities for maritime security. While navies see their business as protecting the nation and national interests at sea, most are not responsible for the security of port facilities or ships in port. These activities are the responsibilities of the national maritime authorities or marine departments, and the marine police or coast guard. The wider definition of maritime security puts a premium on inter-agency coordination both at the national and regional levels and the lack of this coordination will be a barrier to effective maritime security in the region. Already we are witnessing trends in the region where the need for an integrated approach has resulted in the setting up of new organisations or the implementation of new coordinating mechanisms. For example, in Singapore, this comprehensive approach and integrated response is termed as the "whole of government" approach and Singapore has a high-level committee that coordinates the activities of the three agencies in Singapore with responsibilities for maritime security, namely the Maritime and Port Authority (MPA), the Police Coast Guard (PCG) and the Maritime Security Task Force (MSTF) of the Republic of Singapore Navy (RSN).[16] The committee looks at ways to enhance maritime security and promote Singapore's broader maritime interests even as the individual agencies continue to exercise responsibility within each of their functional areas. Similarly, Malaysia has established the Malaysian Maritime Enforcement Agency (MMEA) and Indonesia's Marine Security Coordination Agency the BAKORKAMLA, or the Indonesian Maritime Security Coordinating Board (IMSCB), in response to similar concerns.[17]

Singapore's maritime interest can be defined as the minimisation of disruption to shipping and port activities and ensuring secure access to sea lanes through active policy prescription in the areas of maritime safety, security, environmental protection and international law. As disruptions can come in the form of armed conflict, piracy and armed robbery, maritime terrorism, restrictions to transit passage, accidents and marine pollution, Singapore has adopted various measures to enhance the safety, security and environmental protection of the Straits of Malacca and Singapore.

## Measures to enhance maritime safety

*Providing adequate aids to navigation.* Ensuring the navigational safety of the 70,000 ships that ply the Singapore Straits annually is an important task.[18] With the approval of the IMO and with the cooperation of Malaysia and Indonesia, a routeing system and traffic separation scheme (TSS) was implemented in the Malacca and Singapore Straits to enhance the safety of navigation. A mandatory ship reporting system has been implemented in the Straits with effect from 1 December 1998. This system, known as STRAITREP, requires ships proceeding through the Singapore Straits to report to the Vessel Traffic Services (VTS), in this case the MPA, on designated communications channels so that the authority can track its movements for safety purposes. A Vessel Traffic Information System (VTIS) comprising a chain of radar stations along the Singapore coast has also been developed to monitor shipping traffic and its operators, located at the port operations control centre (POCC), can contact the vessel concerned directly to advise if there is an impending close-quarter situation developing that might result in a collision. However, the collision avoidance directions are only advisory in nature and the ship's captain retains final responsibility for his actions.

Other measures to improve safe navigation in the Singapore Straits include the launching of electronic navigation charts (ENC) and the implementation of the differential global positioning system (DGPS) which improve the accuracy of position information to the metre-range. With the increased usage of the electronic chart display and information system (ECDIS), shipmasters can know their ship's positions accurately at a glance and be pre-warned of any close-quarter situation. Singapore has also implemented IMO-mandated automatic identification system (AIS) for ships above 300 gross tonnes, which has improved safety of navigation tremendously as ships' identities, position, course and speed information are now displayed on the radar of nearby ships and the VTS stations, and the ships can be contacted immediately for collision avoidance should the situation warrant it. With all these measures in place, the MPA's safety record continues to stand at a very low 0.03 incidents per 1,000 vessel movements.[19]

*Providing search and rescue services.* Besides preventive measures to ensure the safety of navigation, Singapore has also implemented search and rescue arrangements to facilitate the recovery of personnel should an accident happen in its Search and Rescue Region (SRR).[20] Singapore has promulgated the Singapore Plan for Search and Rescue (SAR) Services, and the Maritime Rescue Coordination Centre (MRCC) in Singapore coordinates the SAR effort by utilising the assets of the Singapore Armed Forces (SAF) and the PCG. The assets include Super Puma helicopters from the Republic of Singapore Air Force (RSAF), maritime patrol aircraft (MPA) and patrol vessels (PV) from the RSN as well as patrol craft from the PCG. Singapore has also implemented a bilateral SAR arrangement with Indonesia and has conducted SAREX Indopura with Indonesia on a regular basis. Singapore has also ratified the 1979 Convention on Maritime Search and Rescue (SAR Convention) which encourages cooperation between parties and SAR organisations with regard to SAR operations at sea.

## Measures to enhance maritime security

*Protection of critical maritime infrastructure.* Being the world's top container port, Singapore is a major node that sits astride the Malacca Straits, is a top bunkering port and a major oil refining centre. To ensure that Singapore's connection to the global maritime system continues uninterrupted and free of disruption, there is a need to physically defend the extensive maritime infrastructure that has been developed.[21] Protection is provided by the PCG and the RSN, with the army in support, against both state and non-state threats. The PCG and the RSN conduct continuous and extensive daily patrols as deterrence. The army also conducts land at Singapore's key petrochemical complex on Jurong Island. As maritime terrorism has become a threat since 9/11, actions have been taken to mitigate vulnerabilities to three scenarios: (*a*) the turning of hijacked container ships into Trojan horses for dirty-bombs; (*b*) the turning of hijacked ammonium nitrate carriers, LPG and LNG carriers by turning them into floating bombs; and (*c*) the use of bomb laden small boats to attack shipping.

For example, the Accompanying Sea Security Teams (ASSeT) board selected merchant ships that are deemed more vulnerable to hijacks when they enter and leave the port of Singapore. Selected merchant ships are also escorted by PVs along the Straits of Singapore. To reduce the threat posed by small boats, dedicated ferry routes have been mandated that avoid the anchorages and sensitive installations, like naval bases, and the

VTIS radars continuously monitor the movements of these vessels within the port limits. The identities of small craft are also facilitated through the mandatory installation of the harbour craft transponder system (HARTS), an AIS, for the 3,000 small harbour and pleasure craft that are licensed to operate in Singapore. The requirement to fit the HARTS is over and above the requirements of the Safety of Life at Sea (SOLAS) Code which only mandates that ships above 300 gross tonnes are to fit an AIS transponder for identification purposes. In addition, the port of Singapore has installed scanning machines to detect illicit material transported in containers, implemented the International Ship and Port Facility Security Code (ISPS), and participated in the Container Security Initiative (CSI) and Radiation Detection Initiative. Singapore has also ratified major counter-terrorism conventions like the 1988 Convention for the Suppression of Unlawful Acts against the Safety of Maritime Navigation (SUA Convention)

*Defending secure access to sea lanes.* Besides the protection of critical maritime infrastructure, there is also a need to defend the sea lanes that lead to the port.[22] As a result, extensive seabed surveillance has been conducted in the waters around Singapore to ensure that any anomalous mine-like objects can be detected quickly when required. Bilateral mine clearance exercises and coordinated patrols have also been conducted with both the Royal Malaysian Navy (RMN) and the Indonesian Navy (TNI-AL). In addition, the RSN, with the RSAF, has the capability to protect and ensure access to its sea lanes up to a considerable range from Singapore. This is achieved through extensive surveillance provided by MPA and airborne early warning aircraft coupled with a lethal ship strike capability provided by stealth frigates and submarines, and supported by advanced strike aircraft with air-to-air refuelling capability.

Singapore also jealously guards its continued access to the sea lanes and stoutly defends the transit passage regime in straits used for international navigation enshrined in the United Nations Convention on the Law of the Sea (UNCLOS). Singapore opposes any action taken by coastal states to impose regimes over straits used for international navigation which has the effect of hampering the right of transit passage. It views such actions as excessive coastal state interference in an area where the coastal state does not have jurisdiction under UNCLOS and is the reason why it has opposed Australia's pilotage system in the Torres Strait.[23]

*Delimiting maritime boundaries.* However, ensuring physical security through law enforcement action by the national security agencies is only one aspect to maritime security. The other aspect is to ensure that law enforcement can be exercised within areas where the legal jurisdiction is clear. As a result, Singapore has sought to delimit its maritime boundaries with its neighbours as it realises that without a clear delineation of jurisdictional responsibilities, malevolent individuals and organisations can exploit the legal grey zones to perpetrate their criminal activities.

Singapore opts to delimit its maritime boundaries with its neighbours through bilateral and, if necessary, trilateral negotiations and has had success in delimiting most of the maritime boundaries with both Malaysia and Indonesia. What remains in the Singapore Straits are areas where the maritime boundaries of the three countries of Singapore, Indonesia and Malaysia meet, which require trilateral negotiations and currently forms the next stage of the negotiation process. Where an issue cannot be negotiated bilaterally, Singapore has opted to commit such territorial differences to third party dispute settlement, an example of which was the referral of the dispute between Singapore and Malaysia over the ownership of Pedra Branca, Middle Rocks and South Ledge to the International Court of Justice (ICJ) for binding dispute settlement after almost 30 years of bilateral exchange of letters, documents and negotiations.[24]

## Measures to enhance marine environmental protection

Besides the threat of physical attacks, the port of Singapore and its surrounding waters are extremely vulnerable to oil pollution due to the high number of shipping activities within its port limits. Singapore has adopted a comprehensive approach to dealing with marine pollution that begins with prevention, implementation of strict regulations and putting in place emergency plans for quick and effective clean-up operations when cases of pollution occur. There is also a mechanism to ensure that adequate compensation for pollution clean-up cost is recoverable from the perpetrators. The measures can be classified into legislative and contingency plans to deal with a pollution situation.

*Implementation of legislative measures.* Singapore has put in place appropriate legislation to take polluters to task, as well as to prepare and respond to oil pollution incidents and obtain compensation.[25] The Prevention of Pollution of Sea Act was enacted in 1971 and updated in 1990 when Singapore acceded to the MARPOL 73/78 Convention which deals with the prevention of pollution of the sea by oil, chemicals, garbage, and sewage from ships. One significant feature of the Act was that it provides for a penalty of up to S$1 million and/or a maximum prison term of two years for a person found guilty of polluting Singapore's waters. The Act was amended again in 1999 when Singapore acceded to the 1990 International Convention on Oil Pollution Preparedness, Response and Cooperation (OPRC). Singapore has also acceded to Annexes I, II, III, V and VI of the MARPOL 73/78, to the OPRC-HNS 2000, and to international conventions established for oil pollution claims such as CLC 92, the 1992 Protocol to the International Convention on Civil Liability for Oil Pollution Damage; Fund 92, the 1992 Protocol to the 1971 International Convention on the Establishment of an International Fund for the Compensation for Oil Pollution Damage; and LLMC, the International Convention on Limitation of Liability for Maritime Claims, 1976 – all of which ensure that

Singapore would have access to sufficient compensation for the cost of the pollution clean-up operations and possible damages and losses from marine incidents.

*Developing contingency plans.* Despite the best preventive and legislative measures in place, pollution incidents can still occur and robust contingency arrangements are required. The private sector in Singapore has taken several measures that facilitate oil spill response. The first measure is the establishment of the East Asia Response Private Limited (EARL). The shareholders of EARL include BP Singapore, Caltex, Esso, Eastern, Mobil, Shell and BHP Petroleum. EARL has its regional centre in the western part of Singapore (Jurong) where it stores and maintains a wide range of oil spill response equipment. EARL has also entered into a global alliance with Oil Spill Response Limited (OSRL) of Southampton, United Kingdom. The alliance enables both companies to pool their resources and expertise and make the combined resources available to all their customers when required.[26]

The second measure is an oil spill response programme undertaken by the Petroleum Association of Japan (PAJ) since 1993. PAJ's programme consists of stockpiling and lending oil spill response equipment free of charge to government agencies or parties upon their request. This stockpile is kept by the Singapore Oil Spill Response Centre (SOSRC).[27]

The SOSRC was set up by SembCorp Logistics Limited in 1994.[28] The SOSRC, together with its parent company, is able to deal with almost any type of marine accident or emergency and many companies have signed contracts with SOSRC to ensure a rapid response. Not only does SOSRC maintain its own stockpile of oil pollution response equipment, it is also involved in the maintenance of equipment belonging to the PAJ. Singapore is well prepared to tackle oil pollution in and around its waters through careful planning and regular exercises directed by Singapore's MPA and involving other government agencies, local oil companies and pollution response companies.

The MPA is capable of coordinating various national agencies, foreign agencies and companies in response to a clean-up effort. For example, the MPA led clean-up effort arising from the collision of the *Orapin Global* and the *Evoikos* in October 1997 involved a total of 16 ministries/agencies, oil terminals, salvage companies, oil spill response companies, and one foreign agency with the involvement of some 80 craft and 650 personnel. Fortunately for Singapore, the impact of the spill was well contained as shipping traffic in the Singapore Straits was not disrupted and the straits remained open. Singapore's container terminals, oil and petrochemical complexes and power stations were also able to continue their operations without disruption. Damage to sensitive areas and the mainland was prevented and adverse ecological effects were limited to some small uninhabited offshore islands that were immediately hit in the initial aftermath of the spill due to their close proximity to the location of the incident.[29]

## Creating a stable maritime regime

The Asia-Pacific century is poised to begin, with China, India and Japan leading the way. Fuelling the Asia-Pacific engine will be the continued economic growth of China, as well as India, Japan and the United States. As a by-product of regional economic growth, trade and energy flows into and within the Asia-Pacific will continue to grow, leading to an increasing reliance on the sea as a mode of transport since the sea continues to be the most economical transport mode. Already, the trend of increasing shipping traffic is apparent from the traffic data reported via STRAITREP (Mandatory Ship Reporting System in the Straits of Malacca and Singapore), where traffic has increased by 74 per cent over the ten-year period from 1999 to 2008.[30] A study completed by the Ministry of Land, Infrastructure and Transport of Japan has also projected that the volume of ships through the Malacca Straits will increase from 94,000 in 2004 to 117,000 in 2010 and would further increase to 141,000 in 2020.[31] This surge in the use of the sea means that it is ever more crucial to safeguard the sea lanes and critical port infrastructure that lie along them by enhancing their safety, security and environmental protection.

Because countries in the region share significant maritime interests, the creation of a stable maritime regime through bilateral and multilateral cooperation needs to remain high on the regional political agenda. However, in pursuing cooperative initiatives, it is important to keep in mind the three broad principles espoused by Singapore's deputy prime minister and defence minister, Teo Chee Hean, at the March 2005 ARF Confidence Building Measure Conference on Regional Cooperation in Maritime Security and the 2005 Shangri-La Dialogue.[32] The three principles are that littoral states have the primary role in addressing maritime security issues, other stakeholders have important roles to play, and that consultation should be pursued and the rule of international law be observed in the implementation of any new initiatives.

## Notes

\* Joshua Ho is a Senior Fellow of the Maritime Security Programme at the S. Rajaratnam School of International Studies, Nanyang Technological University, Singapore.
1 Geoffrey Till, *Seapower: A Guide for the Twenty-First Century*, Second Edition (Abingdon: Routledge, 2009), p. 52.
2 Ibid., pp. 21–22.
3 John N. Miksic and Cheryl-Ann Low Mei Gek (eds), *Early Singapore 1300s-1879: Evidences in Maps, Text and Artefacts* (Singapore: Singapore History Museum, 2004), p. 44; Malcolm H. Murfett, John N. Miksic, Brian P. Farrell and Chiang Ming Shun, *Between Two Oceans: A Military History of Singapore from First Settlement to Final British Withdrawal* (Singapore: Oxford University Press, 1999), p. 20.
4 Kwa Chong Guan, Derek Heng and Tan Tai Yong, *Singapore, A 700-Year History: From Early Emporium to World City* (Singapore: National Archives of Singapore, 2009), pp. 31–32.

5 Niall Ferguson, *The Ascent of Money: A Financial History of the World* (London: Penguin Books Ltd, 2008), pp. 135–137.
6 Wong Lin Ken, "Commercial Growth before the Second World War", in Ernest C. T. Chew and Edwin Lee (eds), *A History of Singapore* (Singapore: Oxford University Press, 1991), p. 47.
7 C. M. Turnbull, *The Straits Settlements 1826–67: Indian Presidency to Crown Colony* (London: Athlone Press, 1972), p. 190.
8 Ibid., pp. 190–191.
9 W. G. Huff, *The Economic Growth of Singapore: Trade and Development in the Twentieth Century* (Cambridge: Cambridge University Press, 1994), p. 204.
10 Ibid., pp. 236–243.
11 Fereidun Fesharaki, "Singapore as an Oil Centre", in Kernial Singh Sandhu and Paul Wheatley (eds), *Management of Success: The Moulding of Modern Singapore* (Singapore: Institute of Southeast Asian Studies, 1989), pp. 307, 309.
12 Ibid., pp. 307, 311.
13 Huff, *Economic Growth of Singapore*, p. 273.
14 "The World's Busiest Port", *MPA Corporate Information Kit*, 2009. Online, available at: www.mpa.gov.sg/sites/pdf/infokit2.pdf (accessed 1 June 2009).
15 Sam Bateman, Catherine Zara Raymond and Joshua Ho, "Safety and Security in the Malacca and Singapore Straits: An Agenda for Action", *IDSS Policy Paper*, May 2006, pp. 15–16.
16 National Security Coordination Centre, *The Fight Against Terror: Singapore's National Security Strategy* (Singapore: Atlas Associates Pte Ltd, 2004), p. 50.
17 Joshua Ho, "Piracy in the Gulf of Aden: Lessons from the Malacca Strait", *RSIS Commentaries 9/2009*, 22 January 2009. Online, available at: www.rsis.edu.sg/publications/Perspective/RSIS0092009.pdf (accessed 1 June 2009).
18 "A Safe, Secure and Clean Port", *MPA Corporate Information Kit*, 2009, pp. 2–6. Online, available at: www.mpa.gov.sg/sites/pdf/infokit3.pdf (accessed 1 June 2009).
19 Ibid., p. 2.
20 Sam Bateman, Joshua Ho and Jane Chan, "Good Order at Sea in Southeast Asia", *RSIS Policy Paper*, May 2009, p. 25.
21 National Security Coordination Secretariat, *1826 Days: A Diary of Resolve, Securing Singapore Since 9/11* (Singapore: SNP International Publishing, 2006), pp. 23–28.
22 Republic of Singapore Navy, *Onwards and Upwards: Celebrating 40 Years of the Navy* (Singapore: SNP International Publishing Pte Ltd, 2007), pp. 39–75.
23 Robert Beckman, "Australia's Pilotage System in the Torres Strait: A Threat to Transit Passage?" *IDSS Commentaries 125/2006*, 7 December 2006. Online, available at: www.rsis.edu.sg/publications/Perspective/IDSS1252006.pdf (accessed 2 June 2009).
24 The ICJ ruled that the sovereignty over Pedra Branca belongs to the Republic of Singapore whilst sovereignty over Middle Rocks belongs to Malaysia and that sovereignty over South Ledge belongs to the state in the territorial waters of which it is located. See S. Jayakumar and Tommy Koh, *Pedra Branca: The Road to the World Court* (Singapore: NUS Press, 2009).
25 A Safe, Secure and Clean Port, pp. 9–11.
26 Global Response Network Leaflet, April 2009. Online, available at: www.oilspillresponse.com/pdf/grn/grn_leaflet.pdf (accessed 2 June 2009).
27 "A Summary of Oil Spill Response Arrangements and Resources Worldwide, Country Profiles: Singapore", *International Tanker Owners Pollution Federation Limited (ITOPF)*, December 2007. Online, available at: www.itopf.com/_assets/country/singapore.pdf (accessed 2 June 2009).
28 Ibid.

29 A Safe, Secure and Clean Port, p. 9.
30 Data obtained from STRAITREP, a Mandatory Ship Reporting System proposed by the littoral states of Indonesia, Malaysia and Singapore, and adopted by the IMO on 1 December 1998. Ships of 300 gross tons and above and not less than 50 metres in length, vessels carrying hazardous cargo, passenger vessels and others entering a defined operational area are required to report to the vessel traffic station (VTS) authorities through very high frequency (VHF) radio channels.
31 Takashi Ichioka, "Traffic Patterns, Safety, and Security in the Straits of Malacca", in Hongyi Lai (ed.), *Asian Energy Security: The Maritime Dimension* (New York: Palgrave Macmillan, 2009), p. 164.
32 *1826 Days: A Diary of Resolve*, p. 23.

# 9 The sea power and navy of the Republic of Korea*

*Seong-yong Park*

Sea power is an ambiguous term. This is mainly caused by the fact that Mahan used the term in a broad sense and did not provide a clear and succinct definition in his work. According to Geoffrey Till, the difficulty in understanding sea power stems from three reasons: "the limits of the words to describe sea-related things", the diverse meanings of "power" and what people take the word sea power actually to cover.[1]

This ambiguity has fostered a variety of differing comprehensions of sea power by many analysts. Till explores sea power both as an input (such as "navies, civil-maritime industries and the contribution of other armed services") and an output ("the capacity to influence the behaviour of other people or things at or from the sea").[2] Gorshkov appreciates sea power as the focus on a nation's capability (including a merchant marine, fishing fleet and navy) to use the ocean for national interests.[3] To define sea power, the *Naval Terms Dictionary* focuses on a nation's ability to use and control the sea, and to provide a denial capability against an adversary's sea use.[4] The Korean National Defence University defines it as the overall capabilities of the use of the sea for national survival and prosperity.[5] From these conceptual approaches, it can be concluded that sea power revolves around a range of capabilities in the use and control of the sea and in the exertion of influence; its nature is both military and non-military.

The term sea power is rendered as *haeyangryuk* in Korean. Interest in sea power amongst Korean academic circles began to rise in the 1970s when some relevant books were translated into Korean. Before this, studies on maritime affairs did not feature prominently or attract much interest. With the introduction of the term, sea power was translated into variable terms such as *haesangseryok* [sea force], *haesangkwonryuk* [sea authority] or *haesangryok* [power at sea], and those were used as synonyms for shipping power or naval power. Since the 1990s, the term of *haeyangryuk* [sea power] has finally been agreed in Korean academic and general discourse. This shows that the comprehensive nature of sea power is understood in South Korea's debates on the subject.[6]

## Historical context and maritime dependency

Historically, political regimes in the Korean peninsula relied, both militarily and commercially, on the sea to a substantial degree for their prosperity and survival. In the era of three kingdoms, Koreans engaged in vigorous maritime activities. The Kokuryo kingdom (37 BC–AD 668) ruling the northern part of the Korean peninsula and parts of Manchuria confronted the Chinese dynasties militarily and its navy was a useful asset in the consequent conflicts. For instance, it conducted a successive amphibious operation on the Yaotong peninsula of China in the third century.[7] Paekche (18 BC–AD 660), as a prosperous maritime kingdom, acquired much wealth by trading with China and Japan in the fourth century. From 826 to 846, Bo-go Chang, the Sea Lord of Shilla (57 BC–AD 935), nearly monopolised the Northeast Asian transit trade in the sea by securing control over the region's shipping.

The Koryo dynasty (918–1392) energetically engaged in international maritime trade. By establishing an international port on the island of Byeokran, it traded with neighbouring countries and even with the merchants of Arabic lands. The modern English name Korea derives from Koryo, which was indebted to the Arabic introduction of her to the West. Koryo also had much interest in using the sea for military purposes. Koryo's navy made a great contribution to the defence of the country by resisting the several attacks of the Yuan dynasty and destroying Japanese and Manchurian pirates.[8] Notably, it carried out three huge-scale maritime expeditions. One was carried out to sweep Japanese pirates from their base in Tsushima (1389).[9] The other two were executed by the allied forces of Koryo and Yuan in order to invade Japan. The two expeditions were politically forced by the Yuan dynasty's desire to subjugate Japan but failed to realise the goal. Additionally, it is worth noting that domestically invented guns and gun powder were introduced to naval warfare in the late period of the Koryo dynasty.

In the Chosun dynasty (1392–1910), socio-political mood undermined the development of maritime industry. In that era, people involved in maritime industry were generally categorised as belonging to the lowest social class and often treated with contempt. In the early era of Chosun, its navy was strong enough to organise the naval expedition to subjugate Japanese pirates in Tsushima (1419). However, with the change of national defence strategy centred on land defence known as the Jinkwan system, the top-level politicians of the kingdom concluded that a naval force might be less effective than an army and so naval strategy was subjected to army strategy.[10] This led to a catastrophic result in the initial phase of the Chosun–Japanese War (1592–1598). In the meantime the Chosun Navy was reorganised and reinforced by the leadership of Admiral Sun-shin Yi. He defeated Japan's battle fleets, broke up their maritime logistics, and finally forced Japan's expeditionary forces in the Korean peninsula to retreat, thereby leading to the end of the war. After this event, Chosun tried to maintain a strong maritime force although its maritime-despising tradition was still dominant.

From this context, one can see that the successive political regimes of Korea have been highly reliant on the sea for realising the country's interests and even securing its survival. These maritime characteristics, the constituents of Korean sea power, are also apparent in the policies of South Korea and have been amplified more than ever recently.

The Republic of Korea (hereafter ROK or South Korea) lies in the north eastern part of the Asian continent. The country is located between 33 degrees and 43 degrees north, and 124 degrees and 132 degrees east, has a population of about 48 million and her gross domestic product (GDP) is about US$832 billion.[11] The geo-political characteristics of the Korean peninsula and the location of North Korea (or Democratic People's Republic of Korea, DPRK) reinforce South Korea's reliance on the maritime dimension. Strategically, Northeast Asia is an essentially maritime environment and any country in the region has to use maritime routes to interact substantially with other states. In this condition, the DPRK's blocking the way to the continent of Asia forces the ROK to cultivate maritime passages. In this sense, the country can be regarded as an insular country and maritime factors will shape both her prosperity and survival.

With regard to the economic condition of the ROK, exports and imports play a significant role in its economic progress. Exports make up 70 per cent of the GDP and rely heavily upon maritime transportation systems. According to statistics from the ROK government, 809,829,604 tons of goods were exported and imported by shipping while 2,853,534 tons were carried by aviation in 2006.[12] This figure describes South Korea's absolute reliance on shipping for transportation. The fact that energy sources are mainly overseas is one of the factors to strengthen maritime dependency. South Korea ranks fifth in the import of crude oil and second in coal and liquefied natural gas (LNG) imports. The country has no international-connecting oil or natural gas pipelines, thus exclusively leaning on shipments in energy import.[13]

Her export-oriented economy structure and large import of energy raise the significance of sea lines of communication (SLOC). There are four major SLOC for the ROK. The first is the north-bound line including the routes accessible to Siberia, the North and South American continent, and also to the eastern areas of the American continent passing through the Panama Canal. The second is the Korean–Japanese route reaching major industrial areas and ports of Japan. The third is the Korean–Chinese line. The last is the South-bound line going to various destinations, including Southeast Asia, Australia, the Middle Eastern areas, and the European and African continents. Most resources including energy are imported to the ROK through this route.

Because of industrialisation and a growing consumption of sea food, it has been required for South Korea to have developed variable maritime industries. Accordingly, maritime transportation, shipbuilding, deep-sea fishery and marine food products are globally competitive. Especially, shipbuilding industry is one of the key business sectors in supporting Korean economic growth. As a result of domestic and foreign demand for merchant shipping, the ROK's shipbuilding industry has boomed although the recent world-wide economic crisis and the challenge from China have caused this to falter. In 2010 seven Korean companies entered the top ten shipbuilding companies in the world and six of these companies won first place to sixth place.[14] Bearing in mind the significant role of maritime industry in South Korea's development, the government has carried out Ocean Vision 2016 established in 2006. By increasing the contribution of maritime industries in the ROK GDP (about 7 per cent as of 2006) to 10 per cent, the vision has the goal to promote the ROK to be a top five maritime power in the world by 2016. Its comprehensive plan contains the development strategy for vulnerable sectors such as marine-scientific technology, maritime environment protection and maritime tourism as well as policies for reinforcing the competitiveness of Korea's major maritime industries such as fishery, shipbuilding, merchant shipping and port logistics.[15]

However, in comparison with vigorous debates and achievements on maritime economic (or commercial) development, the maritime military aspect has not attracted many except for Korean naval officers and a few scholars, and the naval development of the ROK has not kept step with the maritime economic progress. In view of the fact that naval power is closely related to the economic power of a country, it can be said that the Republic of Korea Navy (ROKN) is not competitive enough to support the ROK's economic activity and interest in the maritime dimension.[16] Namely, South Korea has developed her sea power disproportionately, with insufficient attention's being paid to its naval dimension

## The development of the Republic of Korea Navy

The ROKN comprises 68,000 personnel (including the Marine Corps). Under the navy headquarters, there are the Operations Command, the Marine Corps Command, the Logistic Command and the Education/Training Command.[17] The Operations Command is authorised to control maritime operations. Under its command there are: one submarine group, one naval aviation group and three fleet commands. These fleet commands, which are the backbone of combat missions, manage surface combat vessels and are responsible for each operational zone (First Fleet for the East Sea, Second for the West Sea and Third for the South Sea). The Marine Corps' missions are to conduct landing operations and to defend strategic islands including the island of Yeonpyeong, which the

North Korean artillery attacked on 23 November 2010. The ROKN contains 120 surface combatants including variable platforms, destroyers (from the KDX project phase I, II and III), frigates (Ulsan class), corvettes (Pohang and Donghae classes) and patrol craft (Chamsuri and Yoon Young-ha classes). The Navy also retains 12 SSKs (diesel powered 209 and 214 classes) and small submarines for special operations. In addition, about 60 naval aviation platforms are operating (P-3Cs and Lynx Mk. 99 and 99As) in order to execute anti-submarine and patrol operations.

The navy was the first armed service to be founded. Whereas the former organisation of the ROK Army was established in 1946 and the Air Force followed suit in 1948, the ROKN began in 1945 with the liberation of Korea from the Japanese 35-year colonisation. Admiral Won-il Sohn formed the Maritime Affairs Units on 21 August 1945 and integrated them with another maritime defence organisation, the Maritime Affairs Corps for Defence. The combination of the two organisations was renamed as the Maritime Affairs Association and later, on 11 November 1945, it was converted into the Coastal Defence Force. The Coastal Defence Force is recognised as the origin of the ROKN and accordingly, 11 November is commemorated as the anniversary of the navy's foundation.[18] Through the Korean War, the ROKN was able to make considerable progress in size and rapidly acquired modern naval knowledge, skill and tactics. However, the new navy's subsequent development was limited by the subsequent evolution of the national defence strategy after the war.

During the Cold War era, the national defence of the ROK put the main emphasis on its deterrent capabilities against the DPRK. This was one of the crucial factors shaping current ROK defence posture and resulted in the priority being given to ground forces. Regarding North Korea's typical continental force structure, the ROK developed its symmetrical defence posture with the focus on land-air operations. In order to cope with the envisaged threat from the North, the ROK-US alliance cultivated the system that South Korea made up major land deterrence and part of aerial containment, with American support focused on strategic and maritime deterrence. In this context, the ROK Army enjoyed priority in the defence budget while the ROK Air Force funding was secondary.

The symmetrical structure development and the shared defence system set up by the ROK-US alliance determined a limited role for the ROKN. In addition, the army-dominated tendency in the thinking of the ROK's political leadership, influenced by the two army-centred coups in 1961 and 1980 resulting in the army generals' assumption of power, restrained the development of the ROKN. As a result, dependent on the American naval presence, the navy only carried out a coastal defence mission to protect the flank and rear of the ROK ground forces from the possibility of a North Korean surprise seaborne assault. The ROKN also retained a limited amphibious warfare capability for supporting ground forces.[19]

With the conclusion of the Cold War, Northeast Asian security began to change fundamentally. As a result, South Korea has faced a reshaped regional security environment. As the strategic implication of Northeast Asia as the front line against the Soviet presence changed, so was the strategic status of the ROK–US alliance transformed, although its containment against the DPRK is still in the common interest of both nations. The United States has reduced her naval presence after the breakup of the USSR and the end of direct maritime confrontation against the Soviet forces in the region. China and Japan have boosted their military enhancement, especially naval and aerial forces, in order to counter amplified strategic uncertainty and increase their influence over the region.

In particular, maritime territorial and boundary disputes with Japan and the naval modernisation of China and Japan have added to the ROK's strategic concerns in the maritime dimension. Her economically-based maritime dependence fostered her increasing interest in maritime security. With the perception of these as concrete maritime security issues in national defence, the ROKN has begun to contemplate a blue-water future and has executed policies to realise this.

## Toward a blue-water navy

In the early post-Cold War era, whilst sustaining capabilities to contain the threat of North Korea at sea, it was necessary for the ROKN to respond to new maritime challenges. Throughout the defence enhancement programmes called the Yulgok Project from the 1970s to the early 1990s, the ROKN had acquired a deterrent capability based on qualitative superiority against the maritime forces of the north, except for submarine forces. However, this was not appropriate for the new strategic surroundings. The competitive atmosphere in the general security scene of Northeast Asia was increasingly visible. The naval strength and improvement of adjacent nations, particularly the PRC (People's Republic of China) and Japan, increased the strategic pressure on the ROK in realising and protecting her maritime interests. At that time, it was roughly estimated that the ROKN had 18.2 per cent of fighting strength compared to that of the JMSDF (Japan Maritime Self-Defense Force) and 22.4 per cent of the PLAN (People's Liberation Army Navy).[20]

Facing this unfavourable situation, instead of improving its capabilities only against North Korea, the ROKN, imbued with a vision of "Toward a Blue-water Navy", developed forces to build up effective capacities in response to comprehensive potential threats. The vision was officially advocated by Admiral Byoung-tac An (chief of naval operations, 1995–1997) in his inaugural address in the year of 1995 and has been succeeded by the following CNOs.[21] This policy has been fed by concerns from the top political level. The Dae-joong Kim Administration preserved the basic framework for a major naval development plan while other military projects were abolished or largely reduced by the economic crisis in the late 1990s. In particular, with the perception of the significance of maritime affairs (which might stem from the president's former duty as the Minister of Maritime Affairs and Fishing), the Moo-hyun Roh Administration fostered the favourable atmosphere for a naval leap toward a blue-water status by advocating ambitious naval projects and appointing Kwang-woong Yoon, a retired admiral, as the Minister of National Defence. Moreover, in the Roh Administration, the military reform called Defence Reform Plan 2020 (DRP 2020) was established with the intention of transforming the quantitative-intensive military structure to the qualitative-centred one and to implement balanced development among each armed service. However, the Myung-bak Lee Administration, which assumed office in 2008, has pursued the defence policy with relatively more emphasis on deterring the imminent menace from the DPRK than countering other potential security threats, which suggests that the ROK Army is likely to get priority again. Accordingly, the Lee Administration has been officially silent on the blue-water navy policy. The recent sinking of the ROKS *Cheonan* also makes the navy hesitate to use the term "blue-water navy". In the 2010 National Assembly's review of the ROKN, there was no mention of ambitions for an ocean-going navy or developing operational capability in deep waters through fear that this might be taken to imply a neglect of coastal defence. Nonetheless these ambitions still seem greatly dominant in guiding the ROKN's overall development and strategy.

What is the ultimate shape of the blue-water navy which the ROKN envisages? The term "blue" stems from the classification of navies by colour, which has the category of a brown-water navy standing for a navy capable of defending its coastal zone, a green-water navy for a navy competent to operate in regional sea and finally blue-water navy described as a navy with capability to operate across the deep waters. Although this typology provides a concise criteria in understanding naval hierarchy, it is rather ambiguous, particularly where referring to the wide coverage of a blue-water navy. In this criteria, both the French Navy and the United States Navy can be grouped as blue-water navies but the operation capability and geographic reach of both navies are definitely different.

For a fuller understanding of the ROKN's intention, operational reach and force projection capability, see Eric Grove's classification (expanded from Michael Morris' work) and the nine-rank naval hierarchy.[22]

This typology evaluated the ROKN as in Rank 5 (adjacent force projection navy) but as of 2010, it can be arguably categorised to Rank 4 (medium force projection navy). The ROKN wants a navy with the capabilities to execute high-endurance operations in deep waters, as well as adjoining waters in order to defend and realise national interests.[23] In the current maritime security environment, the enlarged maritime reliance of the ROK requires missions with an extended operational reach. At the same time, the ROKN has to consider that the modernisation of the PLAN followed by the expansion policy of China in the maritime dimension and the improvement of the JMSDF impose strategic concerns on the ROK.[24] Thus, it has to acquire the minimum level of capability to strategically check regional navies in order to protect national interests in the extended area. In this regard, it seems that the ROKN aims to position between Rank 3 and Rank 4. In the operational consideration, it can be arguably concluded that the blue-water navy the ROKN intends to be is more capable than the Rank 4 navy but does not fully satisfy with the criteria of Rank 3.

*Table 9.1* Nine-rank hierarchy of navies

| | Type | Operational characteristics | Nation |
|---|---|---|---|
| 1 | Major global force projection navy (complete) | All military roles of naval forces on a global scale | The United States |
| 2 | Major global force projection navy (partial) | Sea denial and limited power projection in oceanic range | The Soviet Union in the year of 1990 |
| 3 | Medium global force projection navy | One major operation out of area and high-level operations in closer ocean areas | The United Kingdom, France, China, Japan* |
| 4 | Medium regional force projection navy | Ability to project force to adjoining ocean basin** | Italy, Germany, India, |
| 5 | Adjacent force projection navy | Some ability to project force well offshore** | Israel, Portugal, South Africa, North Korea |
| 6 | Offshore territorial defence navy | High-level defensive capability up to about 200 miles from the shores | Norway, Egypt |
| 7 | Inshore territorial defence navy | Coastal combat capability | Oman, Singapore |
| 8 | Constabulary navy | The constabulary mission rather than combat | Mexico, Sri Lanka |
| 9 | Token navy | Symbolic naval role | Countries with a formal organisational structure and a few craft** |

Source: Eric Grove, *The Future of Sea Power* (Annapolis, MD: Naval Institute Press, 1990), pp. 236–240.

Notes
* Although China and Japan originally were in Rank 4, it was estimated by Grove that the PLAN and the JMSDF might promote to Rank 3. Regarding their force improvement by the recent time and possible acquisition of carrier-capability in foreseeable future, both can be arguably classified to Rank 3 or are transforming to the category of "medium global force projection navy".
** Grove's Quotations from M. A. Morris, *Expansion of Third World Navies* (London: Macmillan, 1987).

The ROKN's transformation toward an ocean-going navy has some implications in the national defence and regional maritime security. First, the introduction of the concept of a blue-water navy has to be sustained by an acceptance of the value of the maritime dimension and the importance of maritime strategy in the ROK defence. Second, the concept makes a paradigm-changing chance for future-oriented naval policy and strategy by providing specific objectives.[25] Last, it reflects the ROKN's strategic potential to take a balancing role in regional maritime security, significant if not on the scale of the United States Navy.

## Strategic mobile fleet plan

With the purpose of satisfying the ROKN's enthusiasm toward a blue-water navy, it was decided to build a force to carry out operations in deep waters in the mid-1990s. Unfortunately, as the economic crisis since late 1997 blew major defence projects out of the water, the strategic mobile fleet plan seemed to be stranded. However, the plan was aided by the resurrection of the major shipbuilding project in 1998.

The planned force was intended to become a "Strategic Mobile Fleet" under the control of Naval Operations Command. This plan is the centrepiece of the envisaged blue-water navy and it is expected that the planned fleet will enhance the operational range and strategic deterrence of the ROKN. A new base for this fleet will be constructed in the southern area of the Jeju Island by 2014.

The mobile fleet is based on a permanent establishment, but its function seems similar to that of the "Task Force". It is planned that the fleet will be responsible for strategic deterrence against neighbouring nations, SLOC protection from various threats and the backbone of maritime power projection in possible conflicts. However, the strong emphasis on the strict autonomy of the mobile fleet might hamper close cooperation at the strategic level with other regional fleets, reduce flexibility and so ultimately reduce the ROKN's efficiency, operational flexibility and response capability.

With regard to the size of the fleet, it seems that the navy originally intended to organise three flotillas for the fleet and distribute two Aegis, four multi-purpose DDGs, one LHD and one 20,000-ton logistics ship to each squadron, under the plan to acquire six Aegis, 12 multi-purpose DDGs and three LHDs.[26] The ROKN's intention to constitute three flotillas for the "Mobile Fleet" is based on the circulation (or *roulement*) of vessel deployment and maintenance. Normally, one squadron will be deployed while one is working up and the third is in maintenance and repair. Traditionally, the ROKN has tended to launch vessels in multiples of three, given its structure of three maritime districts each with a district fleet. In contrast to the original plan, it was announced in the early 2006 that one flotilla consisting of three squadrons would be acquired by 2012 with the next step being considered after 2020.[27] Actually, the ROKN will have acquired only six multi-purpose and three Aegis DDGs respectively from the Korean Destroyer Experimental (KDX) phase II and III by 2012. The Land Platform Experimental project ended with the introduction of only one LHD. Accordingly, the Seventh Mobile Flotilla was established with two squadrons, and the last one will be organised by 2012.[28] With these new ships, one squadron comprises one Aegis and two multi-purpose DDGs. After 2026 when the new project for six more 5,000-ton destroyers equipped with the downgraded version of Aegis system, the ROKN's strategic mobile fleet will be completely formed.

## Major improvement projects

*Korean Destroyer Experimental.* The ROKN started to build indigenous combat vessels in 1981 in accordance with defence enhancement programme planned in the 1970s. The Ulsan class frigates, Donghae class and Pohang class corvettes had been in commission by 1993. However, these ships, which were mainly based on preparations for littoral operations against the DPRK, could not be much help in solving the broader problems of the ROKN, such as its limited capability to execute multi-dimensional and long-range operations and the lack of large fighting platforms. Additionally, it was evidently required to replace the US-transferred Gearing class destroyers, which were built at the end of the Second World War and had been used over their expected service life.

In response, the ROKN considered the acquirement of the Korean-designed destroyer. The KDX project was designed in the early 1980s and significant research and development began in the mid-1980s.[29] The planned year for launching the Korean-designed destroyer was 1996, but in practice because of a delay in project definition it was seen in 1998. This project has been ambitiously boosted by the ROKN's ocean-going navy policy.

The KDX has three sub-programmes designed to launch three different classes of vessels. The KDX phase I was to build the destroyers of 3,000-ton displacement, which are used as the flagship in each regional fleet. This programme was completed in 2000 with the commission of three Kwanggaeto-the-Great class ships. The phase II was to construct six multi-role destroyers with 5,000-ton displacement, which are the practical strengths of the strategic mobile fleet. As the last ship of the Chungmugong Yi Soon-shin class was completed in 2006, the second phase programme was finished.[30] Phase III (the Sejong-the-Great class), the commissioning of three 7,000-ton destroyers equipped with the Aegis combat system is in progress. The two platforms are active and the last ship will be delivered to the ROKN by 2012.

The Sejong-the-Great class will provide high-end assets for the ROKN and the core fighting ingredients of the strategic mobile flotilla. The design of the class is basically influenced by the Arleigh Burke class DDG. One notable thing is the high possibility that the class will accommodate domestically-built Chonryong cruise missile with the maximum range of 500 km, which dramatically improves the long-range strike capability of the ROKN. The ships also provide competent air defence capability for a fleet and wider area cover too. In addition, if the ROK's attempt to introduce the SM-6 missile is realised, they can be used for theatre air defence to a limited degree.[31]

*Future Frigate Experimental (FFX).* In the 1990s, the ROKN planned the programme for a next-generation frigate. As asymmetrical build-up centred on submarines was embraced by the DPRK Navy with the recognition of disadvantages in symmetrical competition against its adversary and the ROKN pursued a blue-water navy policy, it considered constructing competitive frigate units with more enhanced anti-air and -submarine capability and expanded operational range than that of the existing Ulsan class frigates. This trial failed to take the next step because of the ROK's financial crisis in the late 1990s. This plan was resurrected, however, under the name of the FFX in the 2000s.

The main objective of the FFX is to replace the aging Ulsan class frigates, Donghae and Pohang classes corvettes. The Ulsan, Donghae and Pohang classes have limited combat capability and have almost reached at the upper limit of their service lives. Especially as seen in the sinking of the Cheonan (the fourteenth ship of the Pohang Class), the latter two classes lack proper ASW capability.

The FFX project seems set to produce platforms capable of mainly executing littoral operations but also vessels suitable for ocean-going missions. A likely role model for a future Korean frigate may be a frigate in the European navies, such as the Karel Doorman class of the Royal Dutch Navy and the Type 23 class of the Royal Navy. Given that the ROKN retains 38 FFs (fast frigates) and PCCs (Pohang class corvettes), the total number of ship through this project seems to be at least 20 plus, although a clear figure has not yet been revealed.[32] It is expected that six ships will be launched in the initial part of the project by 2015 and the first platform will appear in 2011.[33]

*Landing Platform Experimental (LPX).* The project codenamed LPX was to build new large amphibious assault ships. In order to improve amphibious assault capability limited by insufficient lift capacity, the defence reform plan aimed at promoting lift capability to brigade-level.

The Alligator class LSTs provide only limited carrying capability. They are the main platforms for the ROK's amphibious fleet and are suitable for approaching landing operations, but are not capable of multi-dimensional and "over the horizon" operations from the sea. Additionally, the increasing frequency for overseas expeditions such as the PKO missions has promoted the requirement for larger landing ships.

Practical ship design was assisted by Britain and her features are similar to that of HMS *Ocean*. The lead ship of new class, T(D)ok-do was launched in 2005 and came into service in July 2007.[34] It has been widely expected that two more ships will be launched by 2012 but the budget for extra ships has not been confirmed yet. Officially, the ROKN defines the Tok-do class into LPH (landing platform helicopter) category. However, the structure of the platform is more like that of an American Landing Helicopter Dock in practice.

*Korean Submarine Programmes.* The Korean submarine programme includes projects to provide diesel/electric-propelled attack submarines with the ROKN. The original plan to acquire submarines was initiated in the 1980s. Throughout modifications by the policies of the ROKN, a series of the project has been formed as the current three-phased appearance. For the ROKN, a submarine force will prove a valuable asset which can provide asymmetrical and strategic retaliatory measures against neighbouring navies in the current situation where they overwhelm the ROKN. Therefore, the submarine project will significantly enhance the ROKN's deterrent capability.

Phase I was designed to build the 1,200-ton Type 209 (Changbogo class). This phase finished with the completion of nine submarines of this class. Phase II was the plan to construct the 1,800-ton Type 214 (Sohn Won-il class) with air-independent-propulsion (AIP) systems. The ROKN originally intended to acquire three boats from phase II which was regarded as overarching project for the phase III. However, it was announced six more Type 214 would be acquired in order to achieve the overall level of 18 submarines in 2006; construction of the units for the second-batch is expected to begin in 2012 and they are likely to enter service by 2020.[35]

The KSS-III is the project to construct 3,000-ton submarines. Whereas the constructions of phase I and II has been managed overall by the technology from German submarine builder, Howaldtswerke-Deutsche Werft GmbH (HDW), the indigenous technology covering hull design, construction, command/control and sonar system will be applied to phase III.[36] It is believed that the ROKN will obtain nine boats from this project. The schedule for this project commenced in 2007 but the expansion of phase II delayed the projected commission of the first hull from the original year of 2012 to 2018.[37]

## The roles of the Republic of Korea Navy in national defence

The following can be identified as the tasks of the ROKN in national defence: strategic deterrence, front-line defence, sea control and sea denial, SLOC protection and maritime power projection. First, the ROKN provides deterrent power. The core concept of deterrence is to force adversaries to believe immense threats from retaliation or the overwhelming likelihood of damage to their interests through invasion or attack. Effective naval deterrence, Geoffrey Till has suggested, needs the following requirements: (*a*) "political will and clarity and consistency of aim"; (*b*) "the strategic mobility, flexibility and capacity to poise" of naval forces, which can generate enough attention from adversaries; and (*c*) "big powerful ships", which might mean sizable naval platforms with strong and destructive weapon systems.[38]

It can be argued that ROKN's deterrent capability is limited in effectiveness. Above all, the sizable platforms capable of delivering powerful weapon systems to achieve decisive impact on the adversaries are deficient in quantity. Comparing destroyers in other navies of Northeast Asia, the ROKN possesses 11 destroyers (as of 2009), while the PLAN retains 29 destroyers and the JMSDF does 44 destroyers (as of 2008).[39] Furthermore, the former has tried to acquire aircraft carriers and the latter has improved maritime power projection capability by launching the Hyuga class DDHs and planning the 22 DDH project.

Deterrence of the DPRK's submarine force would be reasonably assured, given the quality of that force; this would be more difficult against other neighbouring navies. However, against other neighbouring navies, there is less possibility to exercise effective deterrence.

For the ROKN, the available weapon option for deterrence is the cruise missile, with the view that conventional means against precision targets provides deterrent capability. It can use a designated Chonryong cruise missile with the range of 500 km. There have been plans to extend the range of this missile. It has been reported that the test and development of a cruise missile with 1,000 km-range and another version with 1,500 km have been in progress, although the ROK government and military have not officially offered confirmation or denial of this so as not to provoke regional countries.[40] Currently, only two platforms are in service (the Sejong-the-Great class destroyers), which can operate a cruise missile, but the commissioning of more of this class of destroyer and the installation of a cruise missile system on the Type 214 submarines will be carried out in the near future. In particular, a submarine armed with land-attack capacity is valuable retaliatory menace due to its stealthiness.

Second, the ROKN performs front-line defence.[41] That is, throughout forward deployment, it carries out surveillance of potential antagonists' activities in advance and is designed to neutralise their attacks before they directly reach the territory of the ROK. This role is valuable in that the sea provides prominent access to other regional countries in Northeast Asia and accordingly, most state-relevant threats that the ROK would face come from the maritime dimension. Even in managing the threat from North Korea, which mainly stems from massive ground forces, the front-line defence provided by the ROKN has an important role in suppressing the adversary's menace to the ROK's flanks in wartime and in cutting the north's infiltration of armed espionage groups by sea in peacetime.

Third, the ROKN must control the required sea areas and be able to deny an adversary's access to Korean maritime territory. Sea control and denial stems from the classical, but still valid concept of "command of the sea". The terminology "sea control" is helpful to acknowledge the transitoriness in time and limitation in area caused by the development of weapon systems. This new term with emphasis on relativities, however, does not undermine the basic implication of command of the sea as the concept was also relative, not absolute.[42] Whereas sea control focuses on using the sea for one's own purpose, sea denial is intended to forbid the adversary to use the sea for his own purpose. This concept can be implemented in two ways: one is an "alternative to sea control", which is suitable for navies with a defensive posture, and the other is "complementary to sea control", which is more active than the former.[43]

Confronting a stronger navy in possible conflicts, the ROKN has two possible options. The first one might be commerce raiding, which is likely to force the adversary to disperse its naval assets toward protecting merchant fleets and to make the ROKN realise sea denial and perhaps, assert control in some area of sea through the enemy's consequent inability to concentrate his forces. The second would be a "fleet in being" strategy, which is that the inferior fleet refuses the decisive battle but its existence hobbles the stronger fleet.[44] It poses a strong threat to the adversary that its passage of shipping would be interrupted by the possible movement of the inferior side in the absence of proper containment or blockade. Geographically, there are ports and sea areas directly accessible to a wider oceanic area, thus it is easy for ROKN fleets to operate with this effect. Close blockade by the enemy might hinder the ROKN's activities, but such would be vulnerable to the ROK's air cover. Accordingly, while avoiding battles, fleets or squadrons of the ROKN could participate in attacks on the enemy's commerce, or just pose the threat of aggressive operations.

With regard to a weaker naval adversary like North Korea, it is expected that the ROKN could pursue more active strategies in order to secure sea control and realise sea denial as "complementary to sea control". A fleet battle might be the first consideration. In battles, the ROKN based on qualitative superiority in surface combatants and cutting-edge weapons would enjoy some advantages over the DPRK Navy if the latter's abundant submarine forces could be properly neutralised. Nonetheless, to make any battle decisive is less probable in reality. The weaker side is likely to evade encounters with a superior adversary. Then, a blockade might be an alternative option to the ROK. In a possible conflict, the maritime forces of the DPRK are likely to attack the ROK's SLOC, which are vital for the latter's survival. In order to neutralise this strategy, a blockade would be required to some extent. The ROKN's blockade strategy against the DPRK

Navy could be supported by the geo-political characteristics of the Korean peninsula. The DPRK Navy operates two regional fleets as its main fighting power. One fleet is located in the West Sea and the other is based on the East Sea. For any joint operation or cooperation, they must pass through the south-bound routes. The ROK, however, is located in the southern part of the Korean peninsula and most of south sea areas are likely to be under the ROKN's supervision or control. In this context, the DPRK Navy is definitely at a disadvantage in joint operations or complementary cooperation between fleets. Accordingly, the best way for the ROKN might be to blockade both North Korean fleets in their respective areas, or if not possible, a plausible scenario might be to inflict a blockade on one of the DPRK's fleets in one region, thus weakening the DPRK effort in the other area.

Fourth, the ROKN secures the ROK's SLOC. Those are vital for the ROK as far as it depends for its survival and prosperity on import and export. The Korean interest in SLOC security began to be emphasised about two decades ago. Although the ROK had pursued an export-oriented policy for its prosperity since the late 1960s and this had enlarged the significance of shipping, the safety of its SLOC had been secured by the United States Navy during the Cold War. However, the start of the post-Cold War period changed the circumstances of the security of the SLOC, which has led the ROK to take proper measures on SLOC protection.

There are diverse possible menaces to the ROK's SLOC. They are exposed to the DPRK's naval threats. In addition, possible military dangers from neighbouring countries must be considered. Currently, non-conventional or non-state threats, such as piracy and armed robbery, are significant. For the safety of the SLOC, the ROKN has both relied on international cooperation and enhanced its naval capabilities. It has tried to improve international understanding on SLOC security and threats such as piracy and maritime terrorism by hosting bilateral or multilateral naval meetings and conferences, and participating in international maritime exercises. In the international context, to secure the SLOC, the ROK has deployed a destroyer to the Somali area where combined naval forces have been patrolling against pirates. Regarding naval force development for SLOC, making up a strategic mobile fleet would be a major leap for ROKN. It is expected that convoys for merchant ships could be a significant mission of the fleet. In order for it to protect the SLOC independently within 1,000 nm, one squadron of the mobile fleet should be able to guard effectively four shipping groups, each of which might consist of 50 50,000-ton ships.[45] However, the envisaged range the ROKN intends to secure has not been revealed officially and there are various opinions over which distance is suitable.

Last, the ROKN assaults the adversary's flank and rear areas by exercising maritime power projection from the sea in wartime. In peacetime, maritime power projection capability can take a role as a deterrence factor at a strategic level. Many wars in Northeast Asia and the Korean peninsula have been greatly influenced by power projection from the sea, for example the American naval attacks on Okinawa, Iwo Jima and the Japanese home islands in the Pacific War, and the Inchon landings in the Korean War.

The ROKN has developed a variety of means for the implementation of power projection from the sea. Against a weaker adversary, through coercive and decisive power projection, the ROKN could conclude a war in favour of the ROK. Regarding a more powerful opponent, this capability would provide some means of retaliation.

The ROKN's operational priority has traditionally been front-line defence and sea control and denial in adjacent waters. Its retention of a flotilla of small fast craft and coastal corvettes and frigates, and its recent decision to strengthen its submarine force reflects this littoral orientation. This operational priority has stemmed from the strategic situation of the ROK against the DPRK and the ROKN's limited position and capabilities within the framework of national defence. However, as the ROKN's role has been extended because of changes in the strategic environment, attention has been paid to developing other operational capabilities such as SLOC protection and power projection.

## The contribution of the Republic of Korea Navy in the international context

A stable maritime security environment, both in international areas in which it is interested as well as in its sovereign waters, is a crucial national interest to the ROK with its high level of maritime dependency. In Northeast Asia and Southeast Asia close to which the ROK's SLOC pass, there are a variety of threats at sea. Most threats in the maritime dimension require bilateral or multilateral cooperation. This cooperation ranges from traditional military interchanges to humanitarian as well as constabulary measures.

In order to enhance naval credibility and international understandings about the significant maritime issues of the region, and to mitigate possible confrontations at sea, the ROKN has made diverse contributions in international symposia and naval meetings. It has deployed its assets for peacekeeping operations, mutual ship visits and international naval exercises. The ROKN has regularly participated in RIMPAC which is the most sizable naval exercise in the region. Additionally, it has been associated with bilateral initiatives, for example Korean–Japanese exercises for maritime search and rescue since 1999. It has supported symposia such as "International Sea Power Symposium", every two years and regional naval meetings, mainly in bilateral contexts to discuss vital maritime issues of mutual concern. For the "Track One" naval effort, it has actively taken part in the Western Pacific Naval Symposium (WPNS). Together with these indirect endeavours, practical contributions have been made: the ROKN's two assets deployed to Southeast Asia in 2005 in the aftermath of the destructive tsunami, carried out disaster relief operations; the ROKN is also to participating in the anti-piracy cooperation of the international forces in Somali waters.[46]

In the strategic context of Northeast Asia, the ROKN has not so far been an influential entity shaping the regional maritime security environment. Nevertheless, although the ROKN is still weak compared to other regional navies, current and future force development will endow the country with more strategic options and competencies. In this regard, the potential role of the ROKN in the region is likely to be more important than in the past. It may well be able to take a balancing role in some situations. This does not mean the maintenance of a security order or stability by exercising overwhelming power over other players. Rather, the ROKN may be a factor to prohibit the balance of power from leaning too much to one side. In a particular context like the Sino-Japanese rivalry, this role is perfectly conceivable. Over the expansion of their influence in Northeast Asia, Japan and the PRC compete in some military fields, including the naval. By supporting a weaker naval power, the ROKN could neutralise the naval supremacy of a strong side.

Historically, the political regimes which stood in the Korean peninsula were maritime-dependent and actively used the maritime dimension to improve their national growth, wealth and security. With exception of the Chonsun dynasty whose maritime activity was very limited, generally speaking, sea power was influential under other dynasties. The ROK, with its tremendous reliance on the sea for its prosperity and survival, has developed maritime policies for both the military and non-military aspects of sea power. But security imperatives such as the confrontation with North Korea and the US–ROK mutual defence system, mean that sea power of South Korea has been cultivated in imbalanced way.

Until the end of the Cold War, the ROKN focused on controlling the ROK's surrounding waters and responding to threats from the North. Yet, in the post-Cold War era, new security challenges in the maritime dimension have forced it to take on further tasks. Accordingly, envisaging a navy capable of protecting national interests on the high seas as a future image, the ROKN initiated a transformation into a blue-water navy. This policy has been underpinned by political support but the recent mood of the Lee Administration may change given the sinking of the corvette, ROKN *Cheonan*.

The notable point of this transformation is the plan to establish a strategic mobile fleet which will be the backbone of the ROKN. The fleet is destined to carry out a variety of roles including strategic deterrence, merchant shipping protection and maritime power projection. Regarding the presently confirmed defence budget and plan, there is a gap between the plans of the ROK defence authorities and the ROKN itself and the size of the fleet. In the process of mediating this gap, the true possibility of a blue-water navy for the ROK will emerge. One cautious point is that the ocean-going development should be implemented with enhancing coastal defence against North Korea. The recent sinking of the ROKS *Cheonan* shows that the local provocation of the north is still threatening and dealing with it remains a high priority.

Together with the plan for the strategic mobile fleet, force development projects have been executed in almost every field. For a decade, a variety of fighting platforms for a high-end role have been launched. Surface forces have been especially enhanced in quality and quantity. Since the late 1990s, 11 destroyers including two with the Aegis combat system have been launched as parts of the KDX project. The FFX project is designed to replace the existing frigates and corvettes. For a projected force of 18 boats, the ROKN has completed the delivery of nine of 1,200-ton boats and plans to commission another nine 1,800-ton SSKs (ship submersible, conventional, diesel powered submarines). The LPX project for improving military lift capability has produced an LHD. However, regarding the modernisation phase of regional navies, such as the PLAN and JMSDF, more investment on improving the assets which can be strategic deterrence has to be made.

Looking at the current naval hierarchy in Northeast Asia, the ROKN is a relatively minor player. In order to protect and realise Korea's maritime interests in the future, an expanded role for the ROKN in both international and national defence contexts will be required. Furthermore, the naval development of the ROK has to look forward, to the era of a unified Korea when strategic forces to respond potential threats, such as navy and air force, might be even more important.[47]

## Notes

* This chapter was originally a part of the author's doctoral thesis at the University of Salford in 2009. For publication, it was re-organised, edited and supplemented with new content.
1 For more details of the difficulty in understanding sea power, see Geoffrey Till, *Seapower: A Guided for the Twenty-First Century*, second edition (Abingdon: Routledge, 2009), pp. 20–21.
2 Ibid., pp. 21–22.
3 S. G. Gorshkov, *The Sea Power of the State* (Annapolis: Naval Institute, 1979), pp. 1–2.
4 John V. Noel and Edward L. Beach (eds), *Naval Terms Dictionary* (Annapolis: Naval Institute Press, 1988), p. 247.
5 ROK National Defence University, *Anbokwangye Yongujip [Security Glossary]* (Seoul: Korean National Defence University, 2000), p. 138.
6 In-soo Lim, "Hankukui Mirae: Haeyangdaekukkwa Daeyang Haegun [The Future of Korea: Great Maritime Power and Blue Water Navy]", *Haeyang Hankuk [Monthly Maritime Korea]*, 285 (June 1997), pp. 97–98.

7 For more details, see Young-o Kang, "The Influence of Sea Power upon National Development", the Sejong Institute (ed.), *Korea's Seapower and National Development in the Era of Globalisation*, Proceedings of the Fourth International Sea Power Symposium (Seoul: the Sejong Institute, 1995), pp. 76–77.
8 For more details, see ibid., pp. 81–83.
9 During 1300–1600, Japanese pirates ravaged the coast of Northeast Asia and their activities reached even Singapore. At that time, they were too organised and well-equipped to be regarded as a mere group of criminals. They were organised and controlled by the Japanese feudal authorities. See ibid., pp. 81–82, a quotation from Edward Mead Earle, *Makers of Modern Strategy* (Princeton: Princeton University Press, 1971), p. 465.
10 Ibid., pp. 83–84.
11 World Bank, Data by Country, online, available at: http://data.worldbank.org/country/korea-republic (accessed 5 October 2010).
12 See the Statistics of Shipping and Aviation of ROK Ministry of Land, Transport and Maritime Affairs. Online, available at: http://english.mltm.go.kr/USR/BORD0201/m_18283/BRD.jsp (accessed 10 October 2010).
13 See US Energy Information Administration (EIA), Country Analysis Briefs: South Korea. Online, available at: www.eia.doe.gov/cabs/South_Korea/Full.html (accessed 5 October 2010).
14 "South Korea's Large Shipbuilding Industries Still Far Better than China", *Maeil Kyungje*, 23 September 2010. Online, available at: http://news.mk.co.kr/v3/view.php?year=2010&no=514366 (accessed 5 October 2010).
15 "'2016 Mirae Kuka Haeyangjeonryak' Juyonaeyong [The Main Content of 'Ocean Vision 2016']", *Haeyang Hankuk [Monthly Maritime Korea]*, 397 (October 2006), pp. 126–131.
16 For the relationship between naval power and economic power, see Choon-kun Lee, "National Economy and the Size of the Navy: A Case for the Republic of Korea", Choon-kun Lee (ed.), *New Ocean Era and Maritime Security*, Proceedings of the Fifth International Sea Power Symposium (Seoul: the Korean Institute for Maritime Strategy, 1998), pp. 273–292.
17 ROK Ministry of National Defence (MND), *Defence White Paper 2008* (Seoul: MND, 2009), p. 59.
18 Young-joo Cho, *The Naval Policy of the Republic of Korea: From Beginnings to the Twenty-First Century*, PhD Thesis (Hull: University of Hull, 2003), p. 25; Young-o Kang, "Hankukui Haekunryuk Bunsuk [The Analysis of the Korean Naval Power]", *Strategy 21*, 7 (KIMS, Spring/Summer 2001), p. 130.
19 Young-joo Cho, Ibid., p. 191.
20 James F. Dunningan, *How to Make War: Comprehensive Guide to Modern Warfare for the Post Cold War Era*, third edition (New York: William Morrow, 1993), pp. 604–605.
21 Ka-young Kim, "Chonryak Kidongryuk hwakbo: Daeyang Heagun Doyak [The Acquisition of Strategic Manoeuvring Power: a Leap to Blue Water Navy]", *National Defence Journal*, 378 (June 2005), p. 26.
22 Force projection means a capacity to engage in "sea control" and "sea denial" as well as "power projection". Eric Grove, *The Future of Sea Power* (Annapolis, MD: Naval Institute Press, 1990), p. 237.
23 Suk-joon Yoon, "Daeyanghaegun Gunseale Ddarun Haebyungdae Unyounggaenyum [Building an Ocean-going Navy and Employment Concepts of Marine Corps]", a paper presented at the Sixth Marine Development Symposium in Seoul, Korea, 25 September 2002, p. 26.
24 For the active maritime expansion of China, see International Institute for Strategic Studies (IISS), *Strategic Survey 2009: The Annual Review of World Affairs* (London: Routledge for IISS, 2009), pp. 329–332.

Sea power and navy of the Republic of Korea    163

25 Suk-joon Yoon, "Daeyanghaegun Gunseale Ddarun Haebyungdae Unyounggaenyum [Building an Ocean-going Navy and Employment Concepts of Marine Corps]" (2002), pp. 26–27.
26 "Gun, Haesangsusongro Terrosi Gunsajeak Daeung Ganggu [Considering Military Measures When Terrors on SLOC happen]", *Yonhap News*, 4 October 2004.
27 "2012nyonkaji Haegun 1gae gidongjeandan hwakbo [Navy to Acquire 1 Squadron by 2012]", *Yonhap News*, 21 April 2006.
28 "Navy Activates 1st Strategic Mobile Fleet", *Korea Times*, 1 February 2010.
29 ROK Navy, *Kukminkwa Hamkehanun Haegun [Navy with the General Public]* (Gyeryong, Korea: ROKN HQ, 2004), p. 35.
30 "Navy Launches New Destroyer", *Korea Times*, 20 October 2006.
31 It is reported that the ROKN has a plan to buy SM-6 ER missiles in order to equip the Sejong-the-Great class destroyers. See "Ties With US to Get Stronger", *Korea Times*, 30 January 2008.
32 *Jane's Fighting Ships 2008–2009*, pp. 454, 456.
33 "Defence Buildup Plan Unveiled", *Korea Herald*, 19 May 2006.
34 "Korean Navy Commissions New Assault Landing Ship", *Korea Herald*, 5 July 2007.
35 *Jane's Fighting Ships 2008–2009*, p. 450.
36 For phase-I, HDW launched the first boat and other boats were assembled with transferred-technology and help from HDW. Phase-II provided construction plans, materials and various equipments. Ibid., pp. 450–451.
37 "3,000t Jamsuham Saup 6-nyon Yongi [Six-year delay of 3,000t Submarine Project]", *Munhwa Ilbo*, 7 December 2006.
38 Geoffrey Till, *Seapower: A Guide for the Twenty-First Century*, first edition (London: Frank Cass, 2004), pp. 296–297.
39 ROK MND, *Defence White Paper 2008*, p. 314.
40 The ROK is a member of the MTCR (Missile Technology Control Regime) and its missile development is necessarily subject to the rule of the MTCR. However, the rule only regulates high-velocity and free flight ballistic missiles. Developing a surface-skimming cruise missile with slow speed does not violate the object of the MTCR. "Seoul Develops 1,000-KM Cruise Missile", *Korea Times*, 24 October 2006.
41 Tae-joon Kim, "Haegunui Gunsajeonryakkwa Moogichegye Baljeonbanghyang [The Development Direction of ROKN's Strategy and Weapon System]", *Gunsanonndan [Military Debate]*, 34 (Spring 2003), pp. 55–56.
42 Eric Grove, *The Future of Sea Power*, pp. 12–13.; Geoffrey Till, *Seapower: A Guide for the Twenty-First Century* (2004), pp. 149–157.
43 Geoffrey Till, ibid., p. 158.
44 Norman Friedman, *Seapower as Strategy* (Annapolis, MD: Naval Institute Press, 2001), p. 88.
45 For the reasoning behind 1,000 nm for SLOC protection and assertion of one squadron's capability to escort merchant shipping, see Jeong-kyu Park, "Hankukui Haesanggyotongro Bohoe Kwan Erongeok Gochal [Theoretical Consideration of Protection of the Korean SLOC]", *Haeyanggeonryak Yongu Nonchong [Collection of Treatises about Maritime Strategy]*, 4 (ROK Naval College, January 2003), pp. 129–130, 136.
46 Since 2009, the ROKN has deployed one destroyer to Somali waters. Currently, the fourth ship of the Chungmugong Yi Soon-shin class, Wanggun is operational.
47 Chung-min Lee, "The Future of Korea's Defence Strategy and the Role of Naval Forces", Choon-kun Lee (ed.), *New Ocean Era and Maritime Security* (1998), p. 248.

## Bibliography

Cho, Young-joo, *The Naval Policy of the Republic of Korea: From Beginnings to the Twenty-First Century*, PhD Thesis (Hull: University of Hull, 2003).
Dunningan, James F., *How to Make War: Comprehensive Guide to Modern Warfare for the Post Cold War Era*, third edition (New York: William Morrow, 1993).
Friedman, Norman, *Seapower as Strategy* (Annapolis, MD: Naval Institute Press, 2001).
Gorshkov, S. G., *The Sea Power of the State* (Annapolis: Naval Institute, 1979).
Grove, Eric, *The Future of Sea Power* (Annapolis, MD: Naval Institute Press, 1990).
*Haeyang Hankuk [Monthly Maritime Korea]*, 397 (October 2006).
IISS, *Strategic Survey 2009: The Annual Review of World Affairs* (London: Routledge for IISS, 2009).
Jane's Information Group, *Jane's Fighting Ships* 2008–2009.
Kang, Young-o, "Hankukui Haekunryuk Bunsuk [The Analysis of the Korean Naval Power]", *Strategy 21*, 7 (KIMS, Spring/Summer 2001).
Kim, Ka-young, "Chonryak Kidongryuk hwakbo: Daeyang Heagun Doyak [The Acquisition of Strategic Manoeuvring Power: a Leap to Blue Water Navy]", *National Defence Journal*, 378 (June 2005).
Kim, Tae-joon, "Haegunui Gunsajeonryakkwa Moogichegye Baljeonbanghyang [The Development Direction of ROKN's Strategy and Weapon System]", *Gunsanondan [Military Debate]*, 34 (Spring 2003).
Lee, Choon-kun (ed.), *New Ocean Era and Maritime Security*, Proceedings of the Fifth International Sea Power Symposium (Seoul: the Korean Institute for Maritime Strategy, 1998).
Lim, In-soo, "Hankukui Mirae: Haeyangdaekukkwa Daeyang Haegun [The Future of Korea: Great Maritime Power and Blue Water Navy]", *Haeyang Hankuk [Monthly Maritime Korea]*, 285 (June 1997).
Noel, John and Beach, Edward L. (eds), *Naval Terms Dictionary* (Annapolis: Naval Institute Press, 1988).
Park, Jeong-kyu, "Hankukui Haesanggyotongro Bohoe Kwan Erongeok Gochal [Theoretical Consideration of Protection of the Korean SLOC]", *Haeyanggeonryak Yongu Nonchong [Collection of Treatises about Maritime Strategy]*, 4 (ROK Naval College, January 2003).
ROK MND, *Defence White Paper 2008* (Seoul: MND, 2009).
ROK National Defence University, *Anbokwangye Yongujip [Security Glossary]* (Seoul: Korean National Defence University, 2000).
ROK Navy, *Kukminkwa Hamkehanun Haegun [Navy with the General Public]* (Gyeryong, Korea: ROKN HQ, 2004).
Sejong Institute (ed.), *Korea's Seapower and National Development in the Era of Globalisation*, Proceedings of the Fourth International Sea Power Symposium (Seoul: Sejong Institute, 1995).
Till, Geoffrey, *Seapower: A Guided for the Twenty-First Century*, first edition (London: Frank Cass, 2004), second edition (Abingdon: Routledge, 2009).
Yoon, Suk-joon, "Daeyanghaegun Gunseole Ddarun Haebyungdae Unyounggaenyum [Building an Ocean-going Navy and Employment Concepts of Marine Corps]", a paper presented at the Sixth Marine Development Symposium in Seoul, Korea, 25 September 2002.

*Yonhap news agency*
*Korea Herald.*
*Korea Times.*
*Munhwa Ilbo.*
*Maeil Kyungje*, online, available at: http://news.mk.co.kr/v3/view.php?year= 2010 &no=514366.
ROK Ministry of Land, Transport and Maritime Affairs, online, available at: http://english.mltm.go.kr/USR/BORD0201/m_18283/BRD.jsp.
US Energy Information Administration (EIA), online, available at: www.eia.doe.gov/cabs/South_Korea/Full.html.
World Bank, online, available at: http://data.worldbank.org/country/korea-republic.

# 10 Australia's maritime past, present and future

*Andrew Forbes*

All countries regard themselves as unique, Australia perhaps more so than others. This is particularly the case when examining Australian perceptions on, and the use of, sea power over the last century or so. The importance of sea power is inextricably 'linked' to Australia, because Australia was discovered, settled, protected and maintained through the use of British sea power exercised by the Royal Navy (RN). But forgotten today is that the fledging colonial economies (and later the federated Australian economy) were part of a world-wide economic system (the British Empire), whereby Australian raw resources were shipped to Britain with manufactured goods shipped in return. Thus all communication with Britain was by sea, people could only move between Britain and Australia by sea, trade moved by sea, and the RN protected this trade and could also bring additional military forces to Australia if required.

At the beginning of the twentieth century, as the colonies federated into the Commonwealth of Australia in 1901 and a few years later decided to create their own ocean-going navy, the new government had a good understanding of sea power and the importance of navies generally and the RN in particular. The public also understood the importance of shipping and the navy for their continued prosperity. The Royal Australian Navy (RAN) gained extensive operational experience in both world wars, albeit under RN command, and from the late 1940s when the RAN had Australian-born leaders, it also undertook operations in the Korean War, the Malayan Emergency, Confrontation, the Vietnam War and the two Gulf wars, as well as a number of other peacekeeping, diplomatic and constabulary tasks.

Notwithstanding this maritime history, it is the underlying assumption of this chapter that successive Australian governments, elements of the national security bureaucracy and more particularly the Australian public have forgotten what constitutes sea power, and its importance to Australia.[1] While no doubt this forgetfulness might cause concern in some naval circles and amongst the maritime theorists, should politicians be expected to know the ideas and concepts developed over a century ago by the classical naval strategists Mahan and Corbett, particularly in an area of globalisation where economic interdependence implies a level of safety for shipping – perhaps not?

Australia is a maritime nation; an obvious statement given it is an island, with numerous maritime interests ranging from ocean resources (fishing and seabed oil and gas) and seaborne trade to maritime security issues such as illegal fishing and immigration. The Australian government manages some of these maritime issues through an organisation known as Border Protection Command, and intuitively there is a limited understanding of the civil aspects of sea power (although not thought of in those terms).[2] Of course the government understands the broad utility of naval forces and how they might be used, but again this understanding is not in terms of sea power theory. This lack of understanding was highlighted in a parliamentary inquiry into a maritime strategy over 2003–2004, which failed to both understand and come to grips with the maritime issues facing Australia and the role of the navy in managing them.[3]

Knowledge of sea power amongst the Australian public is even lower, as Australia's maritime history has generally been forgotten as well as the basic facts of Australia's maritime geography. Indeed, the public's interest in 'maritime matters' only extends as far as the beach, and this is probably the best known physical attribute of Australia – the beach lifestyle. Knowledge of the RAN is also limited, as most of its activities occur not only offshore but generally far away from Australia. Combine this with a focus on the Gallipoli campaign in 1915 and the legend of the army 'digger', and the only visibility of the navy is well publicised search and rescue missions deep into the Southern Ocean, humanitarian assistance and disaster relief in Southeast Asia, or border protection in the exclusive economic zone (EEZ). More unfortunately, media focus on the navy today is generally based on scandals relating to sexual abuse and the misuse of drugs and alcohol, and the apparent mismanagement of the building or modernisation of ships and helicopters.[4]

How then to examine 'sea power' in an Australian context? At the outset, it can be said that the RAN firmly believes in the operational aspects of sea power and focuses on the need for sea control as a precursor for maritime power projection. The RAN understands the constituents of sea power but often these are outside its control, as well as understanding the distinctions between traditional and non-traditional concepts of maritime security that highlight civil aspects of sea power.

This chapter examines some of these issues and comprises four sections. The first section examines the development of the RAN, noting how this development has at times been driven more by Empire (and alliance) considerations, than by Australian national security considerations. The second section outlines relevant Australian maritime issues, which are predominantly civil in nature, and how the navy has been used by government to manage them. The third section outlines how the RAN thinks about sea power and what it is doing to promote not only its own role but also the general principles of sea power. A conclusion ends the discussion.

## The Royal Australian Navy

The creation of what is now the RAN is an interesting case study of colonial dependence evolving, albeit slowly, into an independent medium power navy.[5]

Colonial Australia could rely on the RN for maritime protection and this solidified in March 1859 with the creation of the Australia Station as a separate command.[6] Around this time, some of the Australian colonies purchased vessels to undertake a local maritime coastal defence role, but over time, both the colonial forces and the RN ships assigned to the Australia Station became obsolete. So we have an interesting situation where the various colonies rely on the RN for protection, but these protective forces are actually antiquated, while the occasional development of local maritime forces is resource constrained and not linked to RN forces. In the late 1880s, the British provided an auxiliary squadron to supplement the Australia Station, with the colonies contributing to its operating costs. With this augmented naval force, the colonies were able to step back and not worry about creating an independent navy.

Federation of the colonies into 'states' under a 'commonwealth' government, saw the colonial navies transfer to the Commonwealth as the Commonwealth Naval Forces (CNF), but by this time, they could not be regarded as any type of credible naval force. Again, this was not necessarily a problem as the RN continued to provide protection via the Australia Station, with Australia (and New Zealand) contributing to its costs. Control of this naval force rested with the Admiralty and was managed through the Commander-in-Chief China Station. So while Australia as part of the British Empire was provided with protection, the Australian government had no control over the force; which reoccurred numerous times in different circumstances for a further 40 years.

While the CNF made many acquisition plans for new warships, they initially came to nothing due to limited resources (as continues to this day for the RAN). It was not until 1909 that orders were placed for new vessels. Due to changing strategic circumstances in Europe, Britain also reversed its longstanding opposition to local, independent naval forces in its colonies, and encouraged Australia to create a navy based on the concept of a 'fleet unit' comprising a battle cruiser, three cruisers, six destroyers and three submarines. The Australian government agreed, drafting the necessary legislation and ship orders were placed in British shipyards. Significantly, in the creation of an Australian Navy, it relied heavily on the RN for all types of assistance. In 1911 the prefix 'Royal' was granted to the Australian Navy, the fleet unit entered Australian waters in 1913 and the British Commander-in-Chief Australia Station hauled down his flag.

The RAN fought in a number of theatres in the First World War, growing in size from 16 ships in 1914 to 37 in 1918, albeit under RN command and with many of the senior positions of the RAN filled by RN officers. As Sears has noted:

> The RAN emerged from World War I in what seemed a strong position. It had a large balanced fleet with proven equipment operated by well trained and experienced ships companies. It was intimately linked to the world's most powerful navy yet could operate as an independent unit when necessary.[7]

The financial costs of the First World War were a drain on the Australian economy for decades and the Great Depression also limited the funding that was available for 'defence' in general and for the navy in particular.[8] By 1932, the RAN had only three ships in full commission, with a destroyer in partial commission and two light cruisers in reserve.[9] Fitting into empire defence policy, the development of the RAN was based on cruisers for the protection of imperial shipping and not the balanced force needed for national defence. It was with a force of two heavy cruisers, four light cruisers, five old destroyers (and two being built) and two sloops (with another two under construction) that the RAN entered the Second World War.

RAN forces were again under the command of the RN, but this time, the Australian government was far more assertive about where its units might be deployed; with forces moving to the Pacific from Europe when Japan entered the war. But notwithstanding the diverse areas of operation, the main task of the RAN was clear: The experience also reinforced the reality that the primary task of the navy in this war was the protection of shipping.[10] By the end of 1941, all major Australian warships were commanded by Australians, while those vessels assigned to the Pacific Ocean came under United States command.

The Second World War can be regarded as the beginning of the split between Australia and Britain, mainly because of the British priority given to the European theatre rather than the Pacific. Notwithstanding the United States' role in 'protecting' Australia from the Japanese and that RAN forces in the Pacific theatre were under US command, Australia chose to remain within the British Commonwealth as the United States drew down its military forces in the region.

Post-war naval policy focused on the protection of shipping, albeit within a commonwealth framework, while defence policy was based on the foreign policy of collective defence and the need for expeditionary forces. Since the 1940s it had become increasingly clear that regional insurgencies might require a long-term army commitment (moved, supported and supplied by the navy) and that these naval forces would need to protect themselves from submarine attack.

The growing RAN desire for aircraft carriers did not fit the sea lines of communication problem, but did fit in with an expeditionary force. The post-war policy direction for the RAN was: the provision of a balanced task force as Australia's contribution towards collective defence; providing a sea frontier force of escorts, minesweepers, harbour defence and survey craft; and providing assault shipping for combined operations with the army.[11]

Until 1955, RAN operational planning was conducted within the confines of imperial defence and focused on the Middle East. During the 1950s the Australian government became more interested in Southeast Asian regional security, and for the RAN, its role was the regional protection of shipping. This open-ocean anti-submarine warfare (ASW) was the major allied naval planning issue in the Cold War, and as early as 1951, the Radford–Collins Agreement between the RAN and United States Navy was signed to manage this role in the Pacific Ocean.[12]

In June 1947, the Australian government approved the purchase of two light aircraft carriers and an independent fleet air arm, against opposition from elements in the Department of Defence (which continued, in conjunction with the Royal Australian Air Force (RAAF) until the last carrier decommissioned in the early 1980s). But military technology was changing rapidly so the first carrier, HMAS *Sydney*, was accepted in 1949 with obsolete capabilities, and the second, HMAS *Melbourne*, was delivered in 1955 as an up-to-date vessel. The cost of this capability was very expensive (not least for the aircraft), which had financial ramifications for any notions of a 'balanced fleet'. Post-war, the RAN made numerous plans for evolving its force structure but most came to nothing due to severe financial constraints, serious productivity problems in naval dockyards where its ships might be built or modernised, as well as the operating costs of running two aircraft carriers. Notwithstanding the delivery of HMAS *Sydney* in 1949, during the 1950s she was relegated to a variety of training roles and then placed into reserve in 1958.

By 1954 the Australian government tried to scale back and reorient its defence policy, and by implication, lower the funding allocated to the military. By this time, Australian defence policy focused on Southeast Asia in general and on Malaya in particular, to provide a concept of defence in depth; where forces would operate 'forward' to forestall any threat reaching Australia. The financial focus of the government on defence policy was on the RAAF at the expense of the army and navy. The task of the RAN was to undertake ASW to protect shipping and the sea lines of communication. With a focus on air power (delivered solely by the RAAF) the RAN was directed not to maintain a strike capability. So, power projection as a role disappeared but as ASW was a global issue it enabled the RAN to continue with its international engagement. More significant was the fact that ASW was an expensive 'capability' to maintain, so the navy retained fewer ships to remain within its financial allocation. Significantly, as ASW was a specialised task, it made it very difficult for the RAN to easily switch roles to meet emerging threats, as could be done with a balanced fleet.

The focus on Southeast Asia saw a RAN operational commitment to the region generally under the South-East Asian Treaty Organization (SEATO), and specifically to Malaya and Singapore under the Far Eastern Strategic Reserve, with two destroyers (or frigates) provided as well as the annual deployment of an aircraft carrier. SEATO enabled the RAN to operate with many developing navies in the region. Facing both alliance and non-alliance requirements, from the 1950s the RAN was well aware of the need for a balanced fleet, notwithstanding government defence policy.

At the strategic level, Australian foreign and defence policies were to maintain Commonwealth links but also to get the United States engaged in Southeast Asia. Unfortunately for Australia, it discovered that issues it thought critical were not necessarily so in the eyes of either Britain or the United States, leaving Australia stranded on occasion.

In 1959 the government announced that due to its high operating costs, naval fixed wing aviation would be abolished when HMAS *Melbourne* went into major refit in 1963. But with this pivotal decision, and with HMAS *Sydney* already in reserve, the RAN had lowered its operating costs. It was therefore able to consider the issue of a balanced fleet, and what types of capabilities Australia might acquire: up to eight Australian-built submarines, more auxiliaries, coastal minesweepers and guided missile destroyers (DDGs). As the British were facing their own financial problems and were not overly helpful, the RAN turned to the United States Navy for its surface combatants, but remained with Britain for submarines. And in answer to the long running planning conundrum of how to move and supply forces based overseas long-term, HMAS *Sydney* was brought out of reserve and became a fast transport ship. A fleet tanker was built in a British yard as was an escort maintenance vessel – all enabling improved power projection by improving range, endurance and maintenance support. A minesweeping force was also created.

The 1950s decision to fund the RAAF over the army and navy was an indication that Australian defence would be based on air power rather than sea power. But the limitations of the RAAF were obvious and became more pronounced over time, as it could not provide prolonged and extended air cover to the fleet on operations (and under 'forward defence' the navy was continuously committed to activities overseas). The purchase of US-built DDGs in the 1960s overcame this limitation and provided the ability to manage an air threat. Similarly, the advent of Soviet fast attack submarines saw plans for HMAS *Melbourne* to become a helicopter carrier with Wessex helicopters for ASW, but the government decided in 1964 to purchase Tracker aircraft for surveillance and ASW tasks, as well as the Skyhawk fighter-bomber to conduct strike. The long term funding problem for the government had been the age of HMAS *Melbourne* and the cost of replacing her and her air wing. But as the reasonably modern Tracker and Skyhawk could operate from HMAS *Melbourne* costs were considerably cheaper. Of course the RAAF was concerned with the Skyhawk purchase as the RAN wanted to use it for both air defence and strike, and the RAAF regarded the latter role as one solely for the, still to be delivered, F-111 long range bomber. The RAN was allowed to keep the Skyhawk and by not proceeding with the option of the seventh and eighth submarines, was able to purchase more aircraft. These decisions allowed the development of a real power projection capability using a small carrier, sea control with the DDG and sea denial with the submarines.

But at the strategic level in the late 1960s, things were unravelling quickly for the Australian government. In 1967 Britain announced its withdrawal 'East of Suez' by 1975 and in 1969, US President Nixon announced his Guam doctrine, where allies had to do more for their own defence. Thus Australia had to become more 'independent' in its defence arrangements. Moreover, the end of the Vietnam War saw a thawing of Cold War relationships and the strategic situation appeared more benign. In the early 1970s, a new government came to power vowing that Australia would not operate in other countries, thereby ending the policy of forward defence. The government also began a major restructuring of the defence bureaucracy through centralisation that continues to the present. The significance of this restructuring, commencing with the Tange Reorganisation (1973–1976) is that the three Armed Services lost their respective boards, their ministers, and became part of the Department of Defence. Further restructuring saw them lose the ability to develop their own force structures, this now being conducted in a joint organisation.

As an example of the political tin ear of the RAN, as the government was making these significant changes, it developed proposals for a much expanded role, with two new aircraft carriers, eight submarines, 17 destroyers, an amphibious helicopter assault ship, an amphibious transport ship, two maintenance ships and ten patrol boats. However, the naval staff work was not up to standard and the plans were rejected. Looking at these events today, it is hard to think that with the continuous battle by the RAAF to get rid of the carrier, and the high costs for its operation, why the RAN thought it could get two new aircraft carriers as well as an expanded amphibious capability? But the RAN was still attempting to evolve from an ASW force to a balanced fleet, and sought the modernisation of a range of vessels, as well as new destroyers, but the naval dockyards were not up to any of these tasks; instead the government turned to US dockyards to build four guided missile frigates (FFGs).

The RAN continued to seek a replacement for HMAS *Melbourne* throughout the 1970s and early 1980s, but after many hopes and promises, political reality intervened and a new government in 1983 announced HMAS *Melbourne* would not be replaced. The demise of fixed wing aviation saw a transition to rotary wing aviation from surface combatants and a rethink of how the fleet would be structured and would operate. With the loss of HMAS *Melbourne* and dreams for an amphibious force dashed, the

RAN had no power projection capability in the early 1980s, but could deliver sea control through the DDGs and FFGs and sea denial with its submarines.

The centralisation occurring in the Department of Defence saw the primacy of 'white papers' as the key policy document for developing the Australian Defence Force (ADF). The 1980s were a watershed in the development of an independent Australian defence policy. Unfortunately, the Department of Defence was unable to reach consensus on an overall defence policy, so in 1985 the government commissioned an external review by Paul Dibb to assess Australia's forward planning, determine defence capability requirements and develop a costed force structure plan for the next ten years; his *Review of Australia's Defence Capabilities* (the *Review*) was released in 1986.

The *Review* noted that a fundamental security interest was for a stable region free of external pressures. Indonesia was assessed as Australia's most important neighbour, as the Indonesian archipelago was a protective barrier to the Australian north, while Australia was a stable and non-threatening country on Indonesia's southern flank. This relationship was important, as any major threat to Australia would have to come through the Indonesian archipelago.[13] The *Review* proposed a strategy of denial that was, in essence, a defensive policy that would seek to deny any enemy the ability to cross the sea–air gap surrounding Australia and to prevent the landing of any forces on Australian territory. The denial strategy would involve a series of layered defences through which an enemy would have to pass before reaching Australia: Namely,

- Intelligence and surveillance to know about regional military developments and to detect any threat approaching Australia.
- A maritime force of air and naval assets to destroy an enemy in the sea–air gap; this means a refocusing to the north, and for a higher level of conflict, the ability to strike an adversary's bases and interdicting his lines of supply.
- Defensive capabilities close to Australian shores to prevent enemy operations in our focal areas or shipping lanes or on our territory; this might include surface ships, mine countermeasures capabilities, air defence assets and mobile land forces.
- Highly mobile and dispersed ground forces to deny population centres and military infrastructure if an enemy force landed.[14]

The resulting Defence White Paper, *The Defence of Australia 1987* accepted most of the *Review* recommendations, but adopted the terminology of defence in depth rather than layered defence. The new policy was based on the notion of self-reliance within a framework of alliances. It identified areas of primary strategic interest as being Southeast Asia, the South West Pacific and the east Indian Ocean. The two most important priorities for

Australia's national interests were: the defence of Australian territory and society from threat of military attack; and the protection of Australian interests in the surrounding maritime areas, its island territories, and its proximate ocean areas and focal points.[15]

The reorientation of defence policy in 1987 saw the 'defence of Australia' as the primary force structure determinant for the ADF, and given the maritime nature of Australia's geography, a maritime strategy of denying the sea–air gap in the northern approaches was adopted. While this strategy led to a policy that favoured the RAN and RAAF over the army, it looked like a continentalist strategy, focusing on the territorial defence of Australia, and in the maritime environment, it was essentially a strategy of sea denial. Even with the loss of the carrier, the RAN could manage local sea denial, as well as local sea control. In conjunction with a defence policy of self-reliance, it was also government industry policy to build the planned new ships locally to revitalise the Australian shipbuilding industry (this aspect will be examined in the next section).

Two subsequent white papers in 1994 and 2000 had difficulty reconciling the territorial defence of Australia with the reality of deployments into the region and far offshore to meet valid international obligations and Australia's foreign policy requirements.[16] Aspirational in the 1994 policy was a more considered power projection role with the acquisition and modification of two second-hand training and helicopter support ships into amphibious transports (landing platform amphibious, LPA). Similarly the 2000 policy looked at three DDGHs (destroyer guided missile with helicopter) and two LHDs (landing helicopter dock) to provide a major sea control and power projection capability for the mid-2010s (although this familiar terminology was not used).

The 2009 policy was a radical departure from previous policy statements, because it identified China as a possible threat to regional stability.[17] Significantly, the policy emphasised the importance of sea lines of communication and the need to reinvigorate ASW, and proposed 12 new submarines and eight replacement frigates configured for ASW. Clearly this new policy is focused on sea control and power projection.

### Assessing RAN sea power capabilities

As the RAN inventory has changed over time, so obviously have the capabilities possessed and how they might be used by the government of the day. The RAN always has ships at sea conducting maritime patrol and response, but the ability to generate sea control and power projection capabilities were determined by the DDGs and aircraft carrier in the first instance. Their loss saw a lessening of local sea control and a change in the type of power that might be projected, from naval airpower with an ability to conduct limited strike, to the limited support of land forces.

Historically the primary RAN role has been on the protection of shipping and sea lines of communication, with the planning issue being whether this is done close to Australia or further afield. Transportation of and supply to land forces operating offshore has impacted on the level and style of power projection but the policy to do these types of operations rests with government, with obvious delays in the development of such capabilities (and more interestingly, their retention even if there is a change in policy – thus the usefulness of a balanced fleet).

Over the past 25 years the RAN inventory has changed markedly as the policy of self-reliance was adopted, and with many of the ships in those original plans due for decommissioning over the next decade or so, new plans are being developed, at the joint level, for the future structure of the RAN.

Table 10.1 outlines the RAN inventory from 1980 to 2010. It shows the impact of the decommissioning of the aircraft carrier HMAS *Melbourne* and how the ability to conduct sea control through the DDG, and power projection first with HMAS *Melbourne* and later with the LPAs has waxed and waned. Importantly however, inventory should not be confused with availability and there have been major problems delivering a power projection capability with the LPAs, while sea denial has been compromised with the very low availability of submarines.

In 1987, the RAN inventory comprised three DDGs, four FFGs and five DEs (destroyer escort), an oiler and destroyer tender; six submarines; a heavy lift ship and four heavy landing craft; a MCM trials support ship (the coastal minesweeper) and two minehunters; 20 patrol boats; two hydrographic survey ships, two interim survey ships (landing craft heavy, LCH) and an oceanographic ship, and a training ship. There were also three aviation squadrons for ASW, training, electronic warfare and utility roles.[18] Future procurement plans outlined in *The Defence of Australia 1987* included eight light patrol frigates (fast frigate helicopter, FFH), six new submarines, improved MCMs, a second replenishment ship, four survey motor launches and a laser airborne depth sounder. Of greater significance, the new policy of self-reliance saw the RAN begin planning for two-ocean basing, with a fleet base to be constructed in Western Australia.[19]

The RAN inventory in 1994 comprised three DDGs, six FFGs and two DEs; a fleet oiler and auxiliary tanker; four submarines; a heavy lift ship, six LHCs and two training and helicopter support ships (that would be converted into LPAs); two inshore minehunters and five auxiliary minesweepers; 15 patrol boats; two hydrographic survey ships and four survey motor launches; and one trials and safety vessel. There were also three aviation squadrons, including the new Seahawk helicopter.[20] According to *Defence Australia: Defence White Paper 1994* the FFGs were to undergo an upgrade, while (Super Seasprite) helicopters were to be purchased for the FFH; there were also plans to replace the DDGs which would reach the end of their service lives around 2000. In addition, six coastal minehunters

Table 10.1 RAN inventory 1980–2010

| | 1980 | 1985 | 1990 | 1995 | 2000 | 2005 | 2010 |
|---|---|---|---|---|---|---|---|
| Aircraft carrier | 1 | – | – | – | – | – | – |
| Destroyer | 3/6/1 | 3/6/1 | 3/5/– | 3/2/– | 1/–/– | – | – |
| Frigate | 4 | 4 | 4 | 6/1 | 6/2 | 5/7 | 4/8 |
| Submarine | 6 | 6 | 6 | 3/1 | 1/3 | –/6 | –/6 |
| Amphibious | 6/–/– | 4/1/– | 4/1/– | 6/1/2 | 6/1/2 | 6/1/2 | 6/1/2 |
| Mine countermeasures | 1/2 | 1/– | –/2 | –/2 | 2/2 | 6/2 | 6/– |
| Patrol boat | 12/1 | 5/15 | 3/15 | –/15 | –/15 | –/10/3 | –/–/14 |
| Afloat support | 1 | 1 | 1/1 | 1/1 | 1/1 | 1/1 | 1/1 |
| Hydrographic | 2 | 2/2 | 2/4 | 2/4 | 2/4 | 2/4 | 2/4 |
| Aviation (sqn) | 6 | 3 | 3 | 3 | 4 | 4 | 3 |
| Oceanographic | 1 | 1 | – | – | – | – | – |
| Training ship | 2/2 | 2 | 1 | – | – | – | – |

Sources: Department of Defence, *Defence Report 1980*, *Defence Report 1986–87*, *Defence Report 1990–1991*, *Defence Annual Report 1995–1996*, *Defence Annual Report 2000–01*, *Annual Report 2005–2006 Volume One* – Department of Defence, *Defence Annual Report 2009–10 Volume 1* Department of Defence, *Defence Capability Plan 2009* (December 2010 update).

Notes:
Aircraft Carrier: HMAS *Melbourne*, decommissioned 1983.
Destroyer: DDG/DE/Tender; currently building three DDGHs.
Frigate: FFG/FFH; future plans: FFG decommission as DDGH commission, FFH to be replaced (2027–2030).
Submarine: Oberon/Collins; future plans: Collins to be replaced with 12 submarines from 2025.
Amphibious: LCH/LST/LPA; future plans: LPA to be replaced with two LHDs under construction, LST to be replaced with a strategic lift ship (2022–2024), LCH replaced (2022–2024).
Mine countermeasure (MCM); patrol boat (Attack/Fremantle/Armidale); hydrographic (survey ships/survey motor launches); future plans: 20 offshore combatant vessels (2021–2024).
Afloat Support; AO/AOR (fleet oiler/replenishment oiler); future plans: AOR replaced (2021–2023).
Aviation: transitioned from fixed wing to rotary, current capability is 16 Seahawks, six Sea Kings, and Squirrel for training; future plans for 24 helicopters to replace abandoned Super Seasprites and Sea Kings.

were to be built, and one of the new amphibious ships would replace the heavy landing ship. The patrol boats would also be replaced with an enhanced offshore patrol vessel that was being developed in conjunction with Malaysia.[21]

This force structure could still undertake a local sea denial task as well as a more enhanced sea control role with better frigates equipped with a Seahawk helicopter. Only aspirational at this stage is a more considered power projection role with the modification of the LPAs.

In 2000, the RAN inventory comprised a DDG, six FFGs and two FFHs; a fleet oiler and an auxiliary tanker; three submarines (plus one on 90 days' notice); a heavy landing ship, two LPAs, six heavy landing craft and a leased high-speed catamaran; two coastal minehunters; 15 patrol boats; two hydrographic survey ships, four motor survey launches and a laser airborne depth sounder. There were also four aviation squadrons with the new squadron including three Super Seasprite helicopters.[22] Future plans outlined in *Defence 2000: Our Future Defence Force* included the continuation of the FFG upgrade, but also an upgrade for the FFH. When the FFGs were to decommission from 2013, they would be replaced with three DDGHs. The auxiliary tanker would be replaced with a commercial tanker, and the patrol boats would also be replaced.[23]

The defence strategy envisaged in *Defence 2000* implied both sea control and power projection roles, although neither term was used. Achievement of these roles was implicit in the capabilities of the RAN, which could conduct local sea denial, local sea control and had an increasing power projection capability (albeit 'unprotected' as will be discussed below).

The RAN inventory in 2009 comprised four FFGs and eight FFHs; a fleet oiler and auxiliary tanker; six submarines; a heavy landing ship, two amphibious ships and six LHCs; six coastal minehunters and two auxiliary minesweepers; 14 patrol boats; two hydrographic survey ships, four survey motor launches and a laser airborne depth sounder. There were now three aviation squadrons, as the Super Seasprite helicopter had been abandoned as a technological failure.[24]

*Defending Australia in the Asia Pacific Century: Force 2030* confirmed the acquisition of three DDGHs with SM-6 (plus an option for a fourth ship) and eight larger frigates optimised for ASW; two large amphibious ships (landing helicopter docks, LHDs) and six new LHCs; 12 submarines also with a strike capability; 24 combat naval helicopters; a new oiler; and offshore combatant vessels to replace the existing patrol boats, hydrographic vessels and MCM vessels.[25] The strategy envisaged in *FORCE 2030* is clearly focused on sea control and power projection. The upgraded FFG and FFH can now provide an area rather than point defence capability and thus can better exercise local sea control, while providing protection to amphibious ships when they are in a power projection role.

## Australia's maritime interests

As an island, Australia adjoins the Pacific Ocean in the east, the Indian Ocean in the west, faces the Southeast Asian archipelago in the north and faces the Southern Ocean in the south. Except in the Torres Strait region, it is separated from its neighbours by a sea–air gap that is hundreds if not thousands of kilometres wide. Australia also has a number of offshore territories deep in the Indian and Southern oceans:

- In the Indian Ocean are Christmas Island and the Cocos (Keeling) Islands, 2,800 km and 3,700 km west of Darwin respectively; and Heard and McDonald Islands, about 4,000 km southwest of Perth.
- In the Pacific Ocean are Lord Howe Island, 700 km north east of Sydney, and Norfolk Island, about 1,500 km east of Brisbane.
- In the Southern Ocean is Macquarie Island about 1,500 km south of Hobart.
- There is also the Australian Antarctic Territory (AAT) comprising 42 per cent of the Antarctic landmass.

Such geography requires a defence policy that is predominantly naval. But what are some of the maritime issues facing Australia?

### The importance of seaborne trade

Australia is heavily reliant on seaborne trade for its economic survival. Historically this trade was focused on Britain as part of the empire and enhanced under the Ottawa Agreement in 1936, ensuring preferential trade within the Commonwealth. It was only in the 1950s that Australia began to focus on Asia, particularly Japan, and with Britain entering the Common Market in the early 1970s, Australia had no choice but to focus her trade elsewhere.

In 2008–2009, Australia's total seaborne trade was valued at $368 billion, with exports valued at $202 billion and imports at $166 billion.[26] Australia's largest regional trading partners for imports were Southeast Asia and East Asia at around $36 billion each followed by Europe at $33 billion and Japan and North Asia at $22 billion. Looking at regional export partners, Japan and North Asia was the biggest at $70 billion, followed by East Asia at $48 billion and Southeast Asia at $23 billion.[27] Given this level of trade, political and economic stability in Asia is critical for Australian economic security, and Australian defence relationships will be discussed later.

Curiously the majority of this seaborne trade is carried in foreign owned and foreign flagged ships, as the Australian 'national fleet' has been progressively run down over decades by numerous governments, while civil shipbuilding has also been small with the removal of bounties encouraging the building of an Australian fleet. The Australian government in 2010 has begun the discussion process with industry on how to reinvigorate the Australian national fleet.[28] There is also a tenuous link between the RAN and the Australian shipping industry – which is a one-way movement of RAN personnel into the shipping industry as RAN seafaring skills have been nationally accredited.[29]

If seaborne trade was disrupted or attacked, how might the RAN respond? The Radford–Collins Naval Control of Shipping Agreement (NCS) was signed in 1951 as a navy-to-navy arrangement to cover such issues as escort, convoy routing and diversion of traffic; reconnaissance; local defence ASW and search and rescue. The signatories were the United States, United Kingdom and Australia.[30] With the end of the Cold War in 1989, NCS gradually evolved into Naval Cooperation and Guidance of Shipping (NCAGS), based on developing and implementing measures to facilitate the conduct of military activity at sea either involving, or in the presence of, merchant shipping.[31]

There are also two international naval trade protection fora known as Shipping Working Groups: the North Atlantic Treaty Organization (NATO) and the Pacific and Indian Oceans Shipping Working Group, which are designed to ensure that participants of each group know how each views trade protection, to develop common strategic and operational level concepts and annually to test communications links.

Although the protection of shipping and sea lines of communication has long been a role of the RAN, its planning and conduct is undertaken by naval reserves, while operationally, the navy is focused on border protection operations as a major constabulary role, and maritime security operations and counter-piracy in the Middle East and the Gulf of Aden respectively.

Clearly the RAN would seek to provide local sea control to protect its trade, in the first instance, and failing that, local sea denial. The creation of a substantial mine countermeasures force took some time, and was based on the assessed vulnerability of Australian ports and channels to mining, which would disrupt Australia's critical seaborne trade.[32] But while Australian seaborne trade is extensive and valuable, the small national fleet means this shipping cannot be controlled by the government nor by the RAN. However, the relationships developed with regional navies through exercises, port visits and training provide the opportunity for regional cooperation to protect shipping, as all countries will be affected if there are disruptions to seaborne trade.

### Border protection

Australia has long been active in the international negotiations concerning the development of law of the sea issues, and progressively declared 'maritime zones' over time. Australia signed the *United Nations Convention on the Law of the Sea 1982* on 10 December 1982, and it has moved slowly to incorporate these concepts into its domestic legislation:

- under the *Fisheries Act 1968*, Australia legislated for a 12-nm Declared Fishing Zone (DFZ) on 30 January 1968;
- declared a 200-nm Exclusive Resources Zone (ERZ) in early 1977;
- declared a 200-nm Australian Fishing Zone (AFZ) on 1 November 1979;
- extended its territorial sea from 3 nm to 12 nm on 20 November 1990;
- declared a 200-nm EEZ and a continental shelf are between 12–200 nm from the Australian coastline on 1 August 1994;
- proclaimed a 200-nm EEZ and claimed the continental shelf associated with the Australian Antarctic Territory in December 1999;
- in 2008 the United Nations Commission on the Limits of the Continental Shelf extended Australia's continental shelf by 2.5 million sq km.

Australia has extensive boundary agreements with its neighbours, of which one negotiated with Indonesia is unique. Under the Perth Treaty, signed in 1997 and not yet ratified by both countries (but effectively implemented), Indonesia has sovereign rights for the water column (fisheries), while Australia has sovereign rights to the sea bed (oil and gas).

These various zones allow for sovereign rights to ocean and sea bed resources; an ability to enforce obligations is also necessary and this generally falls upon the navy.[33] While the navy has done occasional border protection tasks since its inception, a major focus, for the patrol boats at least since 1968, has been on stopping both illegal fishing and illegal immigration in Australia's EEZ.[34] But to protect Australian fisheries deep in the Southern Ocean, surface combatants and tankers have been used.[35]

The resources devoted to border protection operations over the past decade were considerable as the influx of asylum seekers by sea reached very high levels. At its peak, most of the RAN was conducting border operations, including the hydrographic ships which were painted grey rather than white, and for a considerable period, two coastal minehunters were tasked to this type of operation as well.

### Naval cooperation in Southeast Asia

Given Australia's geographic locations and colonial history, there has always been strong focus on Southeast Asia. Elements of the RAN have operated there since 1955 through deployments as part of the Far Eastern Strategic Reserve, and such deployments have continued until the present, albeit under differing regional security arrangements and exercise regimes, such as the Five Power Defence Arrangements.

Australia conducts a significant military exercise programme – bilateral, multilateral or held under specific arrangements – in South East Asia. Exercising is critical to the development and maintenance of sea keeping and warfighting skills. The training regime for all navies begins with individual training (does the individual have the skills and training necessary for the job), before progressing to collective training where a ship's company trains to operate and fight as a unit. Depending on the navy, training will then progress to operating at a task group level, which is a number of ships working together. Exercises practice and hone these skills at varying levels, depending on strategic requirements.

The RAN conducts regular port visits to Malaysia and Singapore, about every 4–6 months, and irregularly to the Philippines and Thailand, aiming to visit about once a year. The purpose of the port visit is to 'show the flag', demonstrate the Australian government's friendship with the country visited, while providing an opportunity for locals to visit the ship and for RAN personnel to absorb the local culture to gain an understanding of their regional neighbours.

## Naval shipbuilding

Mahan considered naval shipbuilding to be an essential component of sea power, but how is the industry viewed in Australia?

For most of the twentieth century, the naval shipbuilding industry was essentially government owned, but was progressively privatised or commercialised from the mid-1980s in conjunction with an extensive re-equipping of the RAN.

Australia had three major naval dockyards during the twentieth century, Cockatoo Island Dockyard and Garden Island Dockyard in Sydney, and Williamstown Naval Dockyard outside Melbourne. The Australian government assumed control of Cockatoo Island Dockyard in 1912, after purchasing the island and dockyard from the New South Wales government; it was the principal naval dockyard, although it had been leased to the private sector since 1933 and built warships under contract, as well as undertaking the repair, refit and modernisation of the Oberon submarines. In 1913 the British Admiralty transferred Garden Island Dockyard to the Australian government and it was predominantly involved in converting merchant ships to warships, and repair, refits and modernisation of Australian and allied naval ships. The Australian government purchased Williamstown Naval Dockyard in 1942 to provide the capacity to undertake both construction and repair activities.

The long history of Australian naval shipbuilding is a mixture of local and overseas construction, with government policy after the Second World War being one of maintaining the nucleus of a naval shipbuilding capability, which could be expanded in an emergency. This was put into practice by splitting construction orders between Cockatoo and Williamstown

Naval Dockyard, starting in 1944 and continuing for about 30 years. But both dockyards suffered from large cost overruns on projects as well as lengthy delays in delivering ships, and the government decided that its reorientation away from British to US warships in the early 1960s would need to include the ships being built in US yards. Occasionally the government would use a civilian yard for building auxiliaries, but the cancellations of a number of warship projects in the 1970s left the naval shipbuilding industry in disarray and no warships were built in Australian yards for 15 years, with the exception of a switch to auxiliaries being built in naval dockyards. But there were substantial cost overruns and delays in delivery. After having four FFGs built in US yards, in 1984 the government decided that the next two warships should be built in Australia, as they were a mature class of ships, and it was thought their construction at Williamstown Naval Dockyard should be a straightforward task. However, there were, again, substantial cost overruns.

In May 1986 the government announced a restructuring of operations at Williamstown Naval Dockyard and Garden Island Dockyard as they were overstaffed, their productivity had fallen and heavy subsidies were needed to keep them going.[36] Notwithstanding the contract to build two FFGs being given to Williamstown Naval Dockyard, its operations were still inefficient and there were cost overruns and extensive delays. Accordingly, the government announced its sale in 1987. The sweetener for the sale was the continuation of the FFG construction contract and the ability to bid for the impending FFH contract; the sale was completed in 1988.

In April 1987 the government announced it would not renew the lease of Cockatoo Island Dockyard (the lease terminated on 31 December 1992) and that it proposed to sell the island. In March 1989 the government commercialised its remaining assets, including Garden Island Dockyard, creating the 100 per cent government-owned company Australian Defence Industries, which would have to bid for defence (and commercial) work on its own merits.

The traditional reason given for the low productivity, cost overruns and lengthy delays in the naval dockyards is the intransigence of the trade unions and their demarcation disputes. This is partially true, but the RAN was equally to blame in that dockyard management was invariably in the hands of a RAN admiral, and little was apparently done to manage and stop these union practices. As a result, the RAN lost its dockyards.

Beginning in 1987, the government signed a $3.9 billion contract with the Australian Submarine Corporation (now ASC) to build six Collins class submarines in Adelaide. This project involved a 'section' build of the submarine, and introduced advanced welding techniques to Australia. A $3.6 billion contract with Tenix followed in 1989, which saw ten Anzac class frigates built at Williamstown (eight for Australia and two for New Zealand), and introduced local industry to modular warship construction. Five years later, a $917 million contract with Australian Defence Industries resulted in the building of six Huon class minehunters at Newcastle. This project introduced advanced fibreglass construction to Australia, and although the first hull was produced in Italy, the remaining five, plus systems integration occurred locally. Following on from construction of 14 Fremantle class patrol boats in the 1980s, a $175 million contract with NQEA in Cairns in 1996 produced two Leeuwin class hydrographic ships. This project involved the integration of multi and single beam echo sounders, towed and forward-looking sonars, and satellite and terrestrial position fixing equipment into a complex survey system suite. In 2003 a $553 million contract was signed with Defence Maritime Services (DMS) for 12 (later 14) Armidale class patrol boats. Sub-contracted to Austal at the Australian Marine Complex at Henderson, WA, these vessels were built using civilian rather than military specifications, and introduced the notion of contractor provided, long-term logistic support to the RAN.[37]

As part of the next re-equipment program for the RAN, in late 2007, the government signed two major contracts to begin the next phase of Australian naval shipbuilding. First, an $8 billion contract was signed with ASC and Raytheon to build three Hobart class DDGHs in Adelaide. Although the ship's AEGIS-combat system has been purchased from the United States, there will be at least 55 per cent Australian industry involvement in the project. Second, a $3 billion contract was signed with Tenix for two Canberra class amphibious ships (LHDs). Although the hulls will be built in Spain, about $500 million will be spent in Williamstown on superstructure construction and fit-out, while up to $100 million will be spent in Adelaide on combat system design and integration work, employing more than 2,500 people directly and indirectly.[38]

However, shipbuilding is just the beginning of developing naval capability, and the ship must be maintained, supported, repaired and modernised over its service life. A local build, combined with the retention of industrial capacity normally allows for through life support at a lower cost than if the vessels had been built overseas; primarily because the parts and expertise are located in Australia and can be provided much faster than from an overseas supplier. DMS has a contract to provide logistic support to the Armidale patrol boats throughout their service life. In December 2003, ASC signed a $3.5 billion contract for 25 years for through life support for the Collins submarines. And the logistic support arrangements for the Anzac frigates are based on a 70 per cent local content requirement. With a ship's lifespan likely to exceed 30 years, there will obviously be ongoing work for Australian industry.[39]

While the commercialisation and privatisation of the naval dockyards, led to savings on future shipbuilding contracts due to radically changed management practices, something important was lost. Notwithstanding their inefficiencies the dockyards had the skills to do practically anything ship-related, and more importantly, they could 'surge' when required. However, the writing of 'peacetime' contracts, whether for shipbuilding, repair or logistics support has backfired over the past decade when the operational tempo of the fleet has increased, leading to increased operational wear and tear and greater costs.

## Promoting and understanding sea power

The introduction to this chapter claimed that the RAN is a keen believer in sea power, but how do we know this?

Some 20 years ago, the then Chief of Naval Staff created what is now called the Sea Power Centre – Australia, to conduct research on naval and maritime issues, with a particular focus on promoting sea power. There were a number of reasons for this decision, including a recognition that naval staff work for defence policy – and planning was generally poor; an increasingly international relations focus for the navy through the revamped Five Power Defence Arrangements and the Australian creation of the Western Pacific Naval Symposium; and a recognition that there was limited or no understanding of sea power in government, the national security bureaucracy, the general public and more disturbingly, within the navy itself.

### How has the centre undertaken this task?

Looking first at the naval aspects of sea power, both strategic and operational doctrines have been written and distributed widely in Australia and overseas. *Australian Maritime Doctrine* first issued in 2000, explains why a country would have a navy and what it can be used for.[40] It is here that sea power terms are explained and historical examples given of where the RAN has developed and practiced sea power. It is of course interesting that the RAN waited nearly a century before drafting its own doctrine, relying on RN doctrine in the interim. In order to 'sell the message' to a wider audience, a video was also made explaining the basics of doctrine. This was followed in 2005 with *The Navy Contribution to Australian Maritime Operations*, which is operational level doctrine that explains how navies do things.[41] This focuses on how the RAN is structured, what capabilities it has, how they are generated and how they are used. *Australian Maritime Doctrine* was updated over 2009–2010 and a second edition published in mid-2010, with more Australian historical examples of sea power, as well as fine tuning the structure of the book. A complete rewrite of *The Navy Contribution to Australian Maritime Operations* has begun and the second edition is expected to be published mid-2012.

Lectures on sea power are provided to various RAN training schools, defence colleges, to the RAAF, to universities, and to the Indonesian and Malaysian navies through their staff colleges. The centre also produced the RAN Reading List in hard copy in 2006 with an online supplement published each year.[42] The simple aim is to improve professional mastery in the RAN by providing a guide to the relevant books for those interested in naval affairs.

Looking at the civil aspects of sea power; in its early days, the centre focused on providing navy input to government agencies and universities as they considered various maritime issues and non-traditional maritime security issues; including: environmental issues, maritime confidence building measures, ship security and safety, fishing and law of the sea issues. The corollary of this input was that the navy also gained a good understanding of these issues for policy, planning and educative purposes. When the then Environment Australia was developing government policy on oceans usage, the navy was heavily involved, ensuring all members of the inter-departmental committee understood the enforcement role and capabilities of the navy.[43]

While many of the centre's early activities were published by universities, an internal publications programme commenced based on three individual titles: *Semaphore* – a two-page analysis of relevant naval and maritime issues, both historical and contemporary; Working Papers – up to 15,000 word papers looking at historical and contemporary naval and maritime issues; and Papers in Australian Maritime Affairs – over 15,000 word volumes looking at historical and contemporary naval and maritime issues (including postgraduate theses).

The centre runs a biennial King-Hall naval history conference that attracts international speakers, publishes books and articles on RAN history, as well as manages the RAN's historical written record; it also runs a biennial sea power conference which examines naval and/or civil aspects of sea power. The centre also has very strong relationships with counterpart institutions in the United States, United Kingdom, Canada, Malaysia, Singapore, Indonesia, India and South Korea, enabling the exchange of publications and collaborative research.

## Conclusion

Over the past 25 years, the RAN has been deployed around the world on a variety of diplomatic tasks (and occasional military tasks) all the while maintaining an extensive commitment to border protection and other constabulary operations. At the high-end of naval capability, the RAN deployed to the 1991 and 2003 Gulf wars, and after each commitment, then made regular deployments to undertake diplomatic operations enforcing UN sanctions on Iraq; the naval commitment to the Middle East has been consistent for nearly 20 years.[44] This commitment was extended a few years ago to enable the frigate deployed to the Gulf to also undertake counter-piracy operations. Using the amphibious transports, the RAN has increasingly been involved in providing support to the army in East Timor, Bougainville and the Solomon Islands, as well as humanitarian assistance and disaster relief, particularly after the 2004 Indonesian tsunami. What is most interesting about these deployments is that they often appeared counter to priority tasking contained in successive Defence White Papers. So, while the defence of Australia was the highest priority and the planning determinant for determining military capabilities, the RAN could be deployed into the near region or as far afield as the Middle East.

The latest Defence White Paper, of 2009, proposed a stronger and more powerful navy, clearly focused on sea control and power projection. But an important consideration is the lack of apparent funding to bring these capability proposals into effect. Under the Strategic Reform Program, the Department of Defence is to save $20 billion over ten years from its administration to invest in future capabilities, but this is not enough. The DDGH and the LHD are in contract and under construction, so they appear safe; but decisions on the FFH replacement and the 12 submarines are a few years away, so while the Department of Defence is assessing the options for these capabilities, future governments have the opportunity to walk away from the 2009 promises.

So, in 2010 the RAN can be seen as a force in transition, which is the natural order of events for a balanced force that evolves to accommodate new technology within a limited service life for platforms and equipment. Proposed plans announced by the previous government suggest a bright future for the RAN – but only if they can be funded; if they are, the ability of the RAN to conduct sea control, sea denial and power projection is assured.

## Notes

1 Forgotten may be too strong a term as the teaching of sea power is limited to military staff colleges.
2 See the Border Protection Command website for more information, online, available at: www.bpc.gov.au/ (4 January 2011).
3 One of the reasons for this outcome was that the RAN was not allowed to make a submission, instead a bland Department of Defence submission was delivered late to the committee (and had not arrived by the time defence officials were being questioned by committee members). See Joint Standing Committee on Foreign Affairs, Defence and Trade, *Australia's Maritime Strategy*, Parliament House, Canberra, 2004.
4 But in fairness to the RAN, procurement and maintenance is outside its control, with responsibility residing with the Defence Material Organisation.
5 The historical narrative that follows is based on David Stevens (ed.), *The Royal Australian Navy*, Australian Centenary History of Defence, Volume III, Oxford University Press, Melbourne, 2001; the analysis is my own.
6 David Stevens, '1901–1913: The Genesis of the Australian Navy', in Stevens (ed.), *The Royal Australian Navy*, p. 6.
7 Jason Sears, '1919–1929: An Imperial Service', in Stevens (ed.), *The Royal Australian Navy*, p. 55.
8 As part of the Washington Five Power Treaty 1922, the RAN battle cruiser HMAS *Australia* was included as part of British force reductions.
9 Glenn Kerr, 'The Decline of Australian Naval Deterrence 1919–1939', *Semaphore*, Issue 5, Sea Power Centre – Australia, Canberra 2003.

10 James Goldrick, 'World War II: The War against Germany and Italy', in Stevens (ed.), *The Royal Australian Navy*, p. 105.
11 Alastair Cooper, '1945–1954: The Korean War Era', in Stevens (ed.), *The Royal Australian Navy*, p. 162.
12 See Andrew Brown, 'The History of the Radford–Collins Agreement', *Semaphore*, Issue 15, Sea Power Centre – Australia, Canberra, 2007; and for the declassified versions of the 1959 and 1967 agreements, see Andrew Forbes and Michelle Lovi (eds), *Maritime Issues 2006: SPC-A Annual*, Papers in Australian Maritime Affairs No. 19, Sea Power Centre – Australia, Canberra 2007, pp. 47–70.
13 Paul Dibb, *Review of Australia's Defence Capabilities*, Canberra, 1986, pp. 48–49.
14 Dibb, *Review of Australia's Defence Capabilities*, pp. 50–51.
15 Department of Defence, *The Defence of Australia 1987*, Canberra, 1987, pp. 12, 22, 24–25.
16 Department of Defence, *Defending Australia: Defence White Paper 1994*, Canberra, 1994; and Department of Defence, *Defence 2000: Our Future Defence Force*, Canberra, 2000.
17 Department of Defence, *Defending Australia in the Asia-Pacific Century: FORCE 2030*, Canberra, 2009.
18 Department of Defence, *Defence Report 1986–87*, Canberra, 1987, pp. 93–95.
19 Department of Defence, *The Defence of Australia 1987*, Canberra, pp. 40, 43–49, 62–63.
20 Department of Defence, *Defence Annual Report 1994–95*, Canberra, 1995, pp. 185–187.
21 Hector Donohue, 'A Naval Perspective' in Jenelle Bonner and Gary Brown (eds), *Security for the Twenty-First Century? Australia's 1994 Defence White Paper*, Australian Defence Studies Centre, Australian Defence Force Academy, Canberra, 1995, pp. 129–131; Department of Defence, *Defending Australia*, pp. 42–44. However, when Malaysia decided on a German designed boat rather than the Australian design, the OPV did not eventuate, and the extant patrol boats remained in commission.
22 Department of Defence, *Defence Annual Report 2000–01*, Canberra, 2001, pp. 76, 98–105.
23 Department of Defence, *Defence 2000*, pp. 89–91.
24 Department of Defence, *Defence Annual Report 2008–09*, Volume I – Department of Defence, Canberra, 2009, pp. 76–77.
25 Department of Defence, *Defending Australia in the Asia-Pacific Century*, pp. 70–74.
26 Bureau of Infrastructure, Transport and Regional Economics, *Australian Sea Freight 2008–09*, Canberra, 2010, p. 1.
27 Bureau of Infrastructure, Transport and Regional Economics, *Australian Sea Freight 2008–09*, Canberra, 2010, p. 8.
28 See Department of Infrastructure and Transport, *Reforming Australia's Shipping – A Discussion Paper for Stakeholder Consultation*, Canberra 2010, online, available at: www.infrastructure.gov.au/maritime/shipping_reform/files/Position_paper_shipping_reform_final.pdf (4 January 2011).
29 See Jane Landon, 'Civilian Accreditation of RAN Sea Training', *Semaphore*, Issue 13, Sea Power Centre – Australia, Canberra, 2007.
30 Each signatory has a specified area of responsibility, and Australia's area is south of the equator to Antarctica at 3°S and from 60°E in the mid-Indian Ocean to 16°W in the mid-Pacific Ocean. The aim of the agreement is to coordinate efforts at protecting merchant shipping and ASW operations during periods of tension or war. Under the agreement, the parties periodically exercised either in the context of larger multinational exercise or with specific

command post exercises such as the appropriately named RIPCORD, ROLLER COASTER and ROLL CALL series. More recently exercises have been conducted as part of the EXPANDED SEA and (the current) BELL BUOY series. See T. D. Young, 'Australia bites off more than the RAN can chew', *Pacific Defence Reporter*, March 1986, p. 15; Andrew Brown, 'The History of the Radford–Collins Agreement', *Semaphore*, Issue 15, Sea Power Centre – Australia, Canberra, November 2007.

31 NCAGS concerns military cooperation, guidance, advice, assistance and supervision to merchant shipping to enhance the safety of merchant shipping that has agreed to be under navy supervision. In this context, naval supervision includes mandatory rerouting, control of movement and/or convoy of merchant shipping. The protection of merchant shipping involves the employment of military forces or procedures to prevent or defend against offensive actions directed at merchant ships. The benefits of NCAGS to merchant shipping are: an improvement in safety and security in the crisis area; minimised disruptions to passages through areas where military operations are being conducted; maintenance of seaborne trade; quicker reaction to changing threats; better understanding of military constraints; the potential for stabilising insurance costs; minimising disruptions to commercial schedules; and improved support for maritime counterterrorism and anti-piracy activities.

32 See Joint Committee on Foreign Affairs, Defence and Trade, *The Priorities for Australia's Mine Countermeasure Needs*, Parliament House, Canberra, 1989.

33 Although now dated, see Andrew Forbes, *Protecting the National Interest: Naval Constabulary Operations in Australia's Exclusive Economic Zone*, Working Paper No. 11, Sea Power Centre – Australia, Canberra, 2002.

34 See David Stevens, 'The Special Cruise of HMAS *Gayundah* – 1911', *Semaphore*, Issue 10, Sea Power Centre – Australia, Canberra, 2006. Fisheries production in 2008–2009 was valued at $2.2 billion, employing approximately 15,000 people, and with exports valued at $1.53 billion; see D. T. Wilson, R. Curtotti and G. A. Begg (eds), *Fishery Status Reports 2009: Status of Fish Stocks and Fisheries Managed by the Australian Government*, Australian Bureau of Agricultural and Resource Economics – Bureau of Rural Sciences, Canberra, 2010, pp. 40, 42, 43.

35 See Andrew Forbes, 'RAN Activities in the Southern Ocean', *Semaphore*, Issue 18, Sea Power Centre – Australia, Canberra, 2006 and Andrew McCrindle and Rebecca Jeffcoat, 'The Effects of Weather on RAN Operations in the Southern Ocean', *Semaphore*, Issue 13, Sea Power Centre – Australia, Canberra, 2006.

36 See Robert J. Cooksey, *Review of Australia's Defence Exports and Defence Industry: Report to the Minister for Defence*, Canberra, 1986, p. 9; and Department of Defence, *The Defence of Australia 1987*, p. 83.

37 This is taken directly from Andrew Forbes, 'The Economic Benefits of Naval Shipbuilding', *Semaphore*, Issue 9, Sea Power Centre – Australia, Canberra, August 2008.

38 Forbes, 'The Economic Benefits of Naval Shipbuilding'.

39 Forbes, 'The Economic Benefits of Naval Shipbuilding'.

40 RAN, *Australian Maritime Doctrine*, Sea Power Centre – Australia, Canberra, 2000.

41 RAN, *The Navy Contribution to Australian Maritime Operations*, Sea Power Centre – Australia, Canberra, 2005.

42 RAN, *Royal Australian Navy Reading List*, Sea Power Centre – Australia, Canberra, 2006.

43 Environment Australia, *Australia's Oceans Policy*, two volumes, Canberra, 1998.

44 For details, see Greg Nash and David Stevens, *Australia's Navy in the Gulf: From Countenance to Catalyst, 1941–2006*, Topmill, Sydney, 2006; and John Mortimer and David Stevens (eds), *Presence, Power Projection and Sea Control: The RAN in the Gulf 1990–2009*, Papers in Australian Maritime Affairs No. 28, Sea Power Centre – Australia, Canberra, 2009.

# Part II
# Transitions

## Adapting to change: the British experience

So far this book has largely been about the role of sea power in the rise of the countries of the Asia-Pacific region, about the nature of their maritime preoccupations, and about the consequential effects on their naval policies. One of the issues that has emerged from all this has been the fact of constant change in the interactions between these countries, about, in fact, their relative rise and fall. The spectacular growth of the Imperial Japanese Navy (IJN) in the interwar period, its complete destruction during the Second World War and its reinvention as the Japan Maritime Self Defense Force afterwards is a dramatic example of the rise and fall, and perhaps rise again, of naval powers. But how and why do these processes of transition come about, how in general are they handled and what might be the pattern in the future?

While the last issue will be investigated in the final chapter of the book, the next two chapters will explore the transition of naval power from one country to another, specifically from Britain, which despite its geographic position was a Pacific power to a perhaps surprising degree, to the United States. In contrast to the Homeric and deadly struggle for supremacy between Japan and the United States, this process of transition, this passing of the sceptre, was a gentle one, if not without its tensions.

At the beginning of the twentieth century, British naval power seemed unassailable. Its naval building capacity had seen off the challenge of Germany and other European competitors and when in 1917, the American Sixth Battle Squadron joined the Grand Fleet it came very much as a junior partner, anxious to learn from British experience.[1] But even then, there were many on both sides of the Atlantic who could discern the likely trend of the trajectories of the two countries in the future. By their historic alliance with the Japanese in 1902, and the Entente Cordiale with the French in 1904, the British had already signalled recognition of the fact that only by seeking the strategic assistance of others could they hope to narrow the widening gap between their resources and their commitments.

One other major resource was the naval strength of their empire, particularly, in the Pacific, Australia, New Zealand and Canada. Against this background, the empire was asked to do more – and did. As Earl Grey, the

Governor General of Canada remarked in 1909, 'the offer of gallant New Zealand, with a population equal to half that of the province of Ontario, had caused the blood of every Briton in all parts of the world to pulse more buoyantly in his veins'.[2] There *were* hesitations on the part of the dominions however. Strategic realties conflicted with political ones. Strategically the empire faced a threat that required a strong centralised imperial navy; but politically that was not acceptable to the dominions, which, led by Canada were concerned that their *local* strategic interests might suffer. This showed itself as a difference of opinion as to whether the dominions ought to provide fleet units capable of looking after local interests or Capital ships to join the main British battlefleet wherever it happened to be operating, or some compromise between the two. In the end an acceptable compromise was duly arrived at, but the centrifugal tendency was apparent from the start.[3]

The United States was the other source of potential help. In the interwar period, the strategic interests of the two countries came more and more to coincide, mainly because both were faced with a challenge from the resurgent power of imperial Japan. But there was reluctance on both sides to encourage and sometimes even acknowledge this slow process of strategic convergence, and it certainly had not gone far enough to deter Japan from its sequence of assaults at the end of 1941.

Both, but particularly the British, were then constrained by the absolute priority of the European theatre and it was only towards the end of 1942 that British began seriously to think about the effort to recover lost ground in the Pacific. The issue was whether to do so in an independent campaign to recapture Southeast Asia fought in only roughly coordinated parallel with the American advance across the Pacific and up along the archipelagos of the South West Pacific – or to join forces with the Americans in the central Pacific.

In the end the British did both to the extent they could, but Chapter 12 concentrates on the decision for, and the operations of, the British Pacific Fleet in the central Pacific campaign. The situation was almost the complete reverse of the position in 1917 when the American Sixth Battle Squadron joined the British Grand Fleet. Accepting this secondary role was not an easy process but was unavoidable for the imbalance in industrial capacity, resources and experience in oceanic carrier operation was very great.[4] Command and supply arrangements proved complicated and politically sensitive. Unlike in 1917, there was a really serious shooting war to be fought for command of the sea against a most determined adversary willing to engage in full-scale battle. Not all Americans wanted the British to help share the burden; not all Britons wanted, at this stage of the war, to share this last and final effort, or much later to serve as junior partners to the United States. But with all its difficulties, the transition process worked, the sceptre in effect was handed over. The result was a strategic combination that proved unbeatable in the Pacific, that re-appeared in miniature during the Korean War of 1950–3 and that dominated the strategic fortunes of Europe during the Cold War. As a model of the peaceful transition of maritime power, in short, it has no equal – or at least not yet.

## Notes

1 Michael Simpson (ed.) *Anglo-American Naval Relations 1917–1919* (London: Scolar Press for the Navy Records Society, 1991) especially pp. 325–94. His follow-up volume *Anglo-American Naval Relations 1919–1939* extends the story through to the outbreak of the Second World War.
2 Speech of 21 May 1909 at a dinner in Ottawa. 1A 71-1-1913/1661 Pt I, NZ Archives.
3 This may be tracked through Nicholas Tracy (ed.), *The Collective Naval Defence of the Empire, 1900–1940* (London: Ashgate for the Navy Records Society, 1997).
4 One of the trickiest aspects of the campaign as far as the British were concerned, was their having to develop an independent fleet train to support the unfamiliar oceanic scale of the British Pacific Fleet's theatre of operations. Peter V. Nash, *The Development of Mobile Logistic Support in Anglo-America Naval Policy* (Gainesville, FA: University Press of Florida, 2009), pp. 21–46.

# 11 British sea power and imperial defence in the Far East

Sharing the seas with America

*Greg Kennedy*

The British Empire was a global maritime phenomenon. The wealth, the markets, the raw materials needed to create and sustain industrialization, as well as the military power needed to protect and enforce the rules of the international system that allowed the empire to flourish, were all linked to the use and control of the sea.[1] Dominions and colonies around the world gathered the raw materials and created markets within the internal imperial economic system, producing wealth through both actions, and provided the global system with basing and logistics needed to sustain the world's only truly global navy.[2] Inculcated into the national identity of the nation and empire as a whole, the Royal Navy (RN) was intellectually, physically, symbolically and intuitively regarded as the embodiment of the martial aspect of imperial defence.

Yet, despite the dominance of the British Empire in many of these areas of maritime power, the empire could not achieve all that was necessary for its survival without alliances and coalitions with other maritime powers. It is that link, between the British control of the sea, maritime power, diplomacy, trade, economics and the British utilization of maritime alliances, that is the key feature of this study. Given the limited space available, the chapter will use the Far Eastern part of the empire as the geographic focus. Given the scale and speed of the changes in the nature of the international system in that region, it represents the most illuminating and comprehensive theatre for an exploration of how was the empire defended by maritime power. To achieve that objective, the chapter will concentrate on five stages of the British imperial maritime condition in the century under review: the post-Crimean era, 1856–1889; the period of Great Power maritime re-alignment, 1890–1913; the First World War and its immediate aftermath, 1914–1929; the rise of naval rivalry and the Second World War, 1930–1945; the post-Second World War world and British Imperial Defence, 1946–1956.

Technological change for the RN, in the post-Crimean period, consisted of several things. The change from sail to steam, from wooden hulls to iron, of more powerful and diverse weaponry, more sophisticated methods of creating wealth through industrialization and a revolution in communications, were just some of the adjustments the RN had to make due to technological advancement.[3] These changes also created a number of issues related to supply, sustainment and basing. In the Far East, the development of Australia, New Zealand, Hong Kong and Singapore as bases to support the British regional maritime presence created a number of new strategic situations. These maritime interests accompanied the trade interests associated with the development of China as a source for raw materials, as well as a vast market, and the growth of the white colonies as a similar internal imperial asset.[4] Expansion and consolidation of the British possessions in the Far East brought economic and fiscal progress, but at the same time the colonies and naval infrastructure in that far flung part of the empire, by their very existence, created vulnerabilities that required protection, something that had to be weighed against home waters defence at all times.[5] And while there was a certain aspect of European Great Power rivalry at work in the Far East, with France, Germany and the United States having some naval presence in the region, the main dynamic of the balance of power in the region was the maritime power of the British Empire balanced against the military power of the Russian Empire.[6] The cost of trying to maintain a dominant position in such a balance, one that was linked to both the European and Far Eastern theatres, was immense.[7] As a result of that growing financial cost, Britain began to explore two options for defraying some of that expense: the contribution of the colonies themselves toward the defence effort, and, a quest for regional allies who would support British strategic interests.[8] However, in light of the fact that there was no substantial maritime threat to British supremacy in the area, there was little need to expend too much effort in finding collective security solutions to the problems in the region. Great Britain's defence of the realm, and by default its Far Eastern interests, was delivered by a naval supremacy in the home waters off the coast of Europe. If the French, German or Russian navies were blockaded and prevented from gaining access to the high seas, then all British global interests would be protected. Therefore, the primary method from 1856 to 1890, by which British imperial security was provided in the Far East, was through the maintenance of naval numerical and technological supremacy in the Channel, North Sea and Mediterranean waters.[9] This system was very effective so long as there was no threat to the empire that originated outside European waters. The rise of America, Russia and Japan, as substantial maritime powers in the Far East, created the strategic need for British strategic policymakers to re-evaluate this European-centred approach to imperial defence.

While the RN still needed to respect the ability of the Russian Fleet to operate against British imperial interests in the post-Crimean War era, particularly in the Far East, that threat was nothing that the world's most powerful navy could not deal with on its own. The RN kept a wary eye on Russian developments in the northern Saghalien, Tsushima Island and

Hokkaido areas, performing hydrographic surveys there in 1855, 1859 and 1860. British trade was protected by treaties with the Tokugawa shogunate, rather than by military alliances.[10] France, too, was seen by such British policymakers as permanent under-secretary of the Foreign Office Edmund Hammond as being a rival power in the Far East. However, diplomacy and loose alliance relations with that European power meant that Britain could limit France's immediate desires in that region and protect its own interests, without having to rely on naval power threatening the French Fleet. For Hammond, France was a manageable concern. The more serious threat was Russia, with whom, he predicted, Britain would one day have to compete for naval supremacy and political influence in the Far East.[11] So, while trade links with Japan grew and the exploration and exploitation of China became an ever-expanding part of the British imperial system in the mid- to late nineteenth century, so too did the difficulties and costs of providing security for the empire in that region.

The growth of trade and commerce from the Asiatic nations and the white colonies in the region meant there was an increase in a reciprocal need to find allies in the region, unless the British wished to base and supply a permanent and sizeable naval force in the Far East.[12] The Carnarvon Commission of 1882 clarified the linkage between increasing global trade and the need for an investment in military infrastructure. That growth required more coaling bases, the fuel of the new steam-powered, armoured navy, as well as supply and communications facilities, working to form a coherent imperial defence network. It pointed out that:

> Not until the important coaling stations shall have been made secure can the strength of the British Navy be adequately exerted at sea. When, however, this has been accomplished, no other power will posses equal facilities for keeping fleets at sea, or equally good lines of communication.[13]

For the Far East in particular, the Indian Ocean was being tied more closely to the home waters of Europe, both through the new strategic route of the Suez Canal, and through the string of bases that stretched from the Cape of Good Hope to Australia. And, while coaling and repair facilities were the primary concern of the military for such an investment, the Carnarvon Commission also recognized the greater role of the other attributes of maritime power:

> It appears to us that direct communication should be kept up by British vessels with all the important parts of your Majesty's Empire.... A line of steamers carrying both passengers and mails, a direct line of telegraph, is not only important from a military point of view, but must exercise a great and probably an assimilating influence upon the relations of any two peoples.[14]

This expense of reconfiguring the British global basing system to be able to support operations in the Far East, as well as installing or upgrading new steamer, telegraph and port facilities, combined to make the task of maintaining the imperial presence in the region a thorny fiscal problem. Linked to this internal problem of financing the empire was the fact that local regional navies, such as Japan, China and the Russia Far Eastern fleet, were all increasing in size and technical proficiency.[15] No longer was it merely a case of small, relatively lightly armed and inexpensive cruiser fleets being able to subdue Asian fleets or bring pirates to justice. As the Far East entered into the naval arms race of the late nineteenth century, improving fighting power and capability now meant that more advanced, capable RN main fleet units would need to be sent to the region if sea control was to be assured. Under such conditions the obvious answer was therefore to increase the overall size of the fleet, ensuring through superior numbers that the right balances of forces were available in both home and imperial waters. Such an increase in costs for maintaining naval supremacy was not an attractive option.[16]

The path lying before British strategy policy-makers towards the latter half of the nineteenth century was clear, as far as defence of the Far Eastern parts of the empire was concerned. The desire to keep defence costs to a minimum compelled the British policymakers to begin the quest for reliable security partner states in the region.

The Spanish-American War of 1898 created new dynamics in the balance of power at work in the Far East. American interests in China had always caused the North American power to have some interests in the region, but the acquisition of actual territorial possessions in the form of the Philippines added a new dimension to the American presence.[17] Even before the outbreak of the war between the declining European and the upstart North American powers, President McKinley and his administration had been approached by the British government about the possibility of an agreement on Far Eastern matters being reached between the two nations.[18] However, while formal, strategic maritime links between Britain and the United States were not approved, events from the war itself had forged closer professional bonds between the RN and the United States Navy (USN). The hero of the American naval campaign against the Spanish in the Philippines, Admiral Dewey, was adamant in his praise of and gratitude to the RN and the British Commander-in-Chief of the Far Eastern Squadron, Admiral Chichester, for having assisted the American naval forces in Manila. At one point during the conflict the German Far Eastern Squadron arrived in Manila harbour, where the American and British were already anchored. On entering the harbour the German units took up anchorages which brought their guns to bear on the American ships, a worrying and aggressive act for Admiral Dewey to have to contend with. Upon seeing this activity, Admiral Chichester immediately weighed anchor and interposed himself between the two contending fleets, providing a veritable shield for the American warships. Chichester was under no formal obligation or orders to interfere in any operations in that area, but was certainly aware that British interests would be best safeguarded by supporting American activities, short of outright war, in the region. When the German commander enquired if it was Chichester's intention to aid the Americans, the reply encapsulated much of what were to be the Anglo-American maritime relationship in the Far East for the next 50 years: "Captain, that is only known between Admiral Dewey and myself."[19]

Such a masterful manipulation of the power of perception and doubt were to prove to be an integral part of how British strategic foreign policymakers played the Anglo-American relationship in the Far East: preying on the belief of other nations that Anglo-American strategic relations were closer than was the reality.[20] Nevertheless, there was a growing, grudging admiration for the way in which the "new" USN had performed during the conflict, as well an appreciation for the USN's level of technological achievement, seamanship and professional conduct. More important was the demonstration of willingness shown on the part of the United States to use its naval forces outside of Atlantic waters. This was a decisive change from previous American international engagement in the violent affairs of the Great Powers, a condition that was noted and appreciated by Great Britain. Finally, despite the American government declining the offer of collaboration in the region, the twin forces of trade and security were pushing the English-speaking countries closer and closer in general, a condition that would influence how readily the two nations were willing to cooperate on strategic issues in the Far East.[21] The cooperative nature of that relationship was reinforced, for the British, by the more dominant Japanese naval position that was a reality after the successes of that nation in the prosecution of the Sino-Japanese War, as well as the increased naval presence of Russia and Germany in the region through their acquisition and development of permanent naval bases.

In 1899, a series of incidents that challenged the European nation's right to control Chinese trade, markets and finances caused instability in the status quo in Northern China. Sections of the population formed themselves into the Boxer Association, a movement originating in Shantung Province aimed at keeping foreigners and foreign ideas from penetrating too far into that area's way of life. In the summer of 1900, following the murder of a Church of England missionary the international community used its naval and military presence to create an international force at the mouth of the Peiho river.[22] The involvement of not only the United States, but other European nations, in helping to quell the uprising and protect their interests in China, resulted in the growth of non-British naval power in the region. For the British, these events also highlighted the need for regional allies to help maintain security not only with regard to events in China, but also against a growing Russian presence, if costs for the defence of empire were to be kept to a minimum.[23] The question was who would be the RN's partner in the Pacific as the twentieth century began? Both Japan and the United States had grown in naval capability, each signalling its intent to establish itself as an important naval power in China and the Far East in general.

The Japanese, with their own problems regarding Russian expansion into Port Arthur, and increasing trade and military ties with Britain, was the first extra-European naval ally utilized to safeguard British interests in the Far East.[24] This coincided, in the final years of the nineteenth century, with a British imperial strategic position that was being made less secure due to the manifestation of dual threats in European waters, in the form of increasing German naval power and the prospect of a Franco-Russian combined fleet in the Mediterranean. The need to be able to concentrate the more capable and expensive major fleet units in home waters became a growing imperative for the British system of imperial defence. Soon added to these influences were the significant costs of the Boer War and an ever increasing military expenditure for operations in China itself.[25] With such operational demands on the RN as well as the costs of increasing and maintaining the appropriate level of naval forces both on the rise, there was little choice for a reluctant British strategic policymaking elite. Despite a disinclination to tie themselves to what was seen as a possibly expansionistic ally, whose ambition could possible result in the British finding themselves embroiled in a Far Eastern conflict not of their making or choosing, the British signed the naval alliance with Japan in January 1902.[26] The alliance was created, therefore, with two British objectives in mind: keeping the rising costs of naval power projection down and securing a reliable partner to assist in deterring Russia from taking any destabilizing action in the region. Almost immediately following the signature, however, the outcome of the Russo-Japanese War of 1904–1905 created the strategic conditions which made the utility of the agreement much less necessary.

Despite being a naval ally of Japan, Great Britain was not dragged into the Russo-Japanese conflict. Due the vagueness of the agreement and the trigger for activation of the agreement being a condition that was "life or death" for the existence of Japan, the need for the British to have to participate in the conflict was never deemed to have been arrived at.[27] After the decisive defeat of the Russian naval forces at the Battle of Tsushima in May 1905 and the ultimate victory in Manchuria of the Japanese military forces, there was no longer any Russian threat to British maritime interests in the Far East. This radical shift in the balance of power in the region, along with the overall military embarrassment, political strife and financial woes of Russia, combined swiftly after the end of the war to create a new international strategic condition. Without a strong Russia as an ally, and faced with the growing military and naval power of a now more assertive Germany, both France and Russia became agreeable to the idea of a loose strategic understanding with Great Britain. This entente was the second significant strategic shift which made the need for any Anglo-Japanese alliance less necessary.[28] The third strategic factor affecting the British imperial position in the Far East was the continued growth in the belief of the United States to be a potentially useful ally, or, at least a benevolent neutral.

British policymakers had not worried about America during the negotiation and signing of the Anglo-Japanese treaty. Because the treaty would be a support to the security required in the region to provide for the "Open Door" in China, and because of similar America disapproval of Russian actions in China, Lord Lansdowne and the Foreign Office saw no reason for America to object to or feel threatened by the treaty.[29] Those sentiments in London were reinforced by close observations of the United States machinery of government in Washington. In April 1905, Sir Mortimer Durand, the British Ambassador to the United States, wrote to the Secretary of State for Foreign Affairs, Lord Lansdowne. Included in Durand's letter was an end-of-term report by Captain Dudley De Chair, the RN's naval attaché. De Chair was coming to the end of his time as the RN's representative in America. After a number of years of unparalleled access to and insight into the USN, De Chair had taken it upon himself to provide a summary of all he had observed. The report focused on what he believed was the state of the strategic relationship between not only the two naval services, but the nations themselves. Durand fully endorsed the views and recommendations put forward by De Chair:

> Captain De Chair has had favourable opportunities of studying the American Navy, and his views regarding it are of much value. I have reason to believe that he has succeeded in gaining to an exceptional degree the confidence of American Naval Officers, and that he is treated by them in a very friendly manner. As your Lordship is aware, I do not believe that there is any likelihood of an Anglo-American alliance in the near future, even if we desire it; but the cooperation of the two Navies in peace or war is always a possibility, and undoubtedly it may be of much advantage to us that our officers and those of the United States should cultivate friendly relations. The more this can be done without arousing suspicion the better for us. I say without arousing suspicion, for it must always be remembered that Americans are sensitive about us to a curious degree, and we should not run the risk of seeming to court them unduly.[30]

The American press, as well as key individuals within the USN and American political elite, had been approaching De Chair favouring the idea of the two English-speaking navies cooperating during a time of war, if one ever came, in the Far East. His report emphasized the fact that, although there was a cultural and professional closeness and relationship between the two services, there was little or no practical knowledge of one another's tactics, communications or manoeuvring at sea. Despite all the good will and friendship in the world, however, without precise operational and tactical knowledge the likelihood of the two services being able to operate effectively together was minimal. De Chair emphasized the need for the RN to take every opportunity to expand its knowledge in these areas, as well as to press the USN to allow such information to be released. His view was that the USN had applied engineering and new sciences to naval warfare in a way that made them equals to the British in this regard and, indeed, in readiness to experiment and take bold innovative conceptual risks, superior to the Admiralty. While the RN still held the advantage in discipline, organization and training, the American navy possessed an intelligence and vigour that was "most uncommon," in partnership with a strength, courage and endurance in their physical abilities that were the equal of the RN. Possessed of such a view of the USN and its relationship to the RN, he recommended that,

> I therefore have the honour to suggest that if it is considered desirable at any time to think of Naval Cooperation with the United States that now is decidedly the time to act, and the following reasons and suggestions are submitted with that end in view.[31]

The list of reasons for such an accommodation with the United States was extensive. Apart from the personal views of powerful and important individuals, the US press had itself been proposing the instigation of joint naval exercises between the RN and the USN. De Chair was fully aware of the limits in place that prevented a full, formal, active military alliance from being formed between the two nations, but believed that a gradual, incremental approach, brought about by such limited activities as joint exercises, would be successful in establishing common national interests and the sentiment of cooperation. Such sentiments were especially important given the pressure Germany was putting on the United States and President Theodore Roosevelt to come into a closer international relationship with that nation.[32] De Chair also recognized the powerful anti-British sentiments of some American politicians, such as the New England bloc of Senators Hale, Frye and Cabot Lodge. Their ability to create problems for closer Anglo-American maritime relations would not be easily overcome. But, nevertheless, the bulk of the people of the United States were more inclined to a better maritime understanding with the British Empire. Events in the Far East were particularly important for this:

> It is felt therefore in the United States that although an alliance between Great Britain and the United States may be very far ahead a Naval cooperation for any definite and special purpose is by no means unlikely. Americans daily recognize that no imaginable grounds exist

for war between Great Britain and the United States. Lord Salisbury's wise and conciliatory attitude in the Venezuelan affair of 1895, our benevolent neutrality in their war with Spain, the Alaskan boundary adjustment, the general absence of irritating questions and the immense commercial interests between the two countries, have reduced almost to a vanishing point, undoubtedly among the majority of Americans the enmity of 1776, 1812, and 1864. Feelings of kinship have replaced bitterness, respect and good will have largely taken the place of hatred and contempt, and it is almost certain that Naval cooperation between Great Britain and the United States would be as welcome in certain contingencies as is the present political cooperation between them in East Asiatic affairs. These causes tend steadily towards encouraging the idea that united action between the fleets of Great Britain and the United States is one of the possibilities of the future and if such be the case it behoves Great Britain especially in regard to her Navy to make such preparations that in the event of a sudden cooperation between the two Navies no time shall be lost in assembling and wielding the two fleets as one.[33]

This call for nurturing Anglo-American maritime relations, in order to promote closer overall strategic relations, also was made by other influential British naval actors.

Julian Corbett, historian, author and respected maritime advisor to the Admiralty, held a similar opinion. He believed that in the future Britain's ability to wage a large-scale European war would be linked to relations with the United States. It was the case, he wrote, that:

Our great danger in case of war is the stoppage of our food and raw material and especially that which comes across the Atlantic. Now if this trade is to be in the hands of an Anglo-American syndicate how is a European army to stop it? By a stroke of the pen such ships as may remain under the English flag could be transferred to the American with perfect plausibility and if the European enemy refused to recognize the transfer it would mean almost certain war with America as well as ourselves. The Atlantic trade is certainly something they would fight for. They nearly did in 1794 while their debt to France was still warm. France had to give way or they would have fought her by our side, over this very question. The rule would apply vice versa for America's benefit and then I see in it not only our capital coming back to us after many days but also the first step to our real angle. Saxon kriegbund – not depending on a mere treaty but on commercial unity, which once formed in this way can never be broken. If one is hit both must be hit and hard enough for both hitting back. That is the general idea ... I see America not conquering us but binding herself to the wheels of our chariot and bind away say I.[34]

This sort of maritime imperialism, with strong elements of both racial and economic determinism, was echoed in the writings of Mahan in the United States and taken up by such important political figures as President Theodore Roosevelt. The closer the transatlantic ties became, the greater the ability for some coordinated action in the Far East appeared.

Despite Roosevelt's hard feelings towards Lansdowne, Durand and the British in general, for not assisting him during the negotiations at Portsmouth to end the Russo-Japanese war (Roosevelt wanted the British to help limit the Japanese demands and attempts to annihilate the Russian presence in the Far East, which made reaching a conclusion in the peace negotiations much more difficult.), Anglo-American maritime relations concerning the Far East had become closer than ever before.[35] That relationship was consolidated by the 1907 sailing of the American "Great White Fleet." Without British support and supply, through its system of bases in the Far East, this first modern demonstration of the USN's ability to project and sustain naval power in the Far East would not have been possible. The Great White Fleet's presence created a closer operational understanding of the American navy on the part of the RN, as well as gave a tangible reality to the United States being a true Far Eastern naval power.[36] British strategic policymakers recognized that such a presence meant greater trade and market competition from the Americans. Those interests were the reasons for the American presence. Having another non-regional power with security interests in the region, especially the democratic, capitalist United States, meant, even though the American presence threatened more competition on an economic level, greater security for British interests overall. As American and British interests were parallel in nature; both wanting free, unhindered trade and no use of military force to influence markets, there was every reason to expect that the American strategic relationship would grow only stronger. Upon the outbreak of the First World War in 1914, the combination of growing Anglo-American trade links, financial ties and common interests in the maintenance of the "Open Door" in China, saw this close, competitive/cooperative relationship become a reality.[37]

Events of the First World War did nothing to drive Anglo-American strategic relations in the Far East any further apart. In fact, the British reliance on America for money, manpower and munitions during the war had created a strategic situation wherein Great Britain could no longer act without recognizing that American opinions and desires in foreign affairs were now critical factors that needed to be taken into consideration at all times.[38] The permanent under-secretary for foreign affairs, Sir Charles Hardinge, summed the situation up precisely in October 1916, when he pointed out that "we cannot get on without America either during or after the War."[39] However, the same could not be said for Anglo-Japanese relations during that period. Indeed, the Japanese actions during of the war, demanding a greater role in directing how the "Open Door" in China would be managed, acted as a catalyst for closer Anglo-American relations, as both Western nations eyed the more aggressive Japan carefully in China.[40] In 1918, as the aims and objectives of the post-war peace settlements began to be considered, the question of whether or not the Anglo-Japanese Alliance would be renewed in 1922 was a key feature of the British strategic policymaking situation. With Russia now torn apart by revolution, Germany no longer a naval threat, France, America, Italy and Japan all allied with Great Britain, what was the need for a formal bi-lateral maritime arrangement to safeguard imperial interests in the Far East?[41]

Those interests were to be protected by a combination of post-1918 collective security institutions and agreements. The first of these was the newly-formed League of Nations. As the international overseer of the rights of all nations to self-determination and the right to exist without fear of military aggression, the league's collective security approach was based on a combination of potential economic sanctions, military force and international moral suasion. Japan, as a member of the League of Nations, was now obliged to regulate its actions in China in accordance with the league ideals, as were all other members of the Nine Power Treaty. That treaty, signed in 1922, formed the basis of the other pillar of security in the Far East in the 1920s: the Washington Treaty System.[42] This system involved an arms limitation agreement, with the nine main powers involved in the division of China into spheres of influence agreeing to abide by a set of rules of conduct. Signatories to this agreement were to accept an agreed definition of China's sovereignty, independence, administrative and territorial rights and to maintain the concept of "the Open Door." In other words, the Washington Treaty System was a formalized set of guidelines constructed for the orderly post-war development of China, in order to ensure that a "scramble for China" did not end in conflict. Its purpose was to ensure a status quo in the region.[43]

Inter-linked to this Nine Power Treaty was the Four Power Treaty, which limited Japan, Great Britain, the United States and France as to where and what fortifications they could build in support of their various fleets. Great Britain could finish the base at Singapore but could increase the fortifications of no other base east of Singapore. The United States could develop its facilities at Pearl Harbor and maintain its installations in the Philippines, but could not build any new naval bases west of Hawaii. France was allowed to keep what minimal facilities it had, but was to build no more. Japan was, therefore, given effective regional dominance, as it was the nation whose main naval bases were closest to the area. It, too, was limited as to how much further west it could build future naval facilities, but, given its natural geo-strategic advantages in basing and port facilities, this restriction was unimportant. What was more important for the naval balance of power in the Far East was the Five Power Naval Treaty, which was at the core of the Washington system.[44]

The Five Power agreement saw Britain, the United States and Japan agree to a capital ship ratio of 5:5:3 (France and Italy were the other signatories to this agreement with a ratio of 1.75 each). This agreement, based on the main naval weapon of the period, the battleship, ensured that none of the nations would have to build any new types of those most expensive of naval weapons. Simultaneously, it allowed for security in terms of planning and anticipation, with each nation knowing exactly how many and what sort of battleships each would build. What was not resolved was the size and capabilities of the rest of the naval forces. These would be dealt with over the next decade. But, Japan believed that its allotted ratio was a denial of its rightful status in the world's international structure. To compound Tokyo's irritation, the creation of this Washington system called for the demise of the long-standing Anglo-Japanese alliance. This perceived combination of inferior naval status, a feeling of rejection by Great Britain and the newly-realized American strength in Far Eastern affairs, sowed seeds of discord between Japan and the two English-speaking nations.[45]

Throughout the 1920s the Washington Treaty system appeared to keep the balance of power stable in the Far East. Issues of trade competition, immigration and the continual build-up of a strong military presence on the Chinese mainland created disputes and tension between Japan, China, the United States and Britain, but for the most part relations were viewed as amicable and normal, "for China." The USN, as well as the RN, based many of its peacetime war games on a scenario that involved a hostile Japan, but these were often seen as worst case planning exercises, with, as yet, little real political basis. It was the rise of Chinese nationalism in the 1920s that created areas of tension that eroded the status quo created between the Great Powers through the Washington system. As Chinese actions threatened the foreign interests and the operation of the "Open Door" policy, Japanese actions to protect its interests in China became more and more aggressive and reliant on the use of military power. Under such circumstances both Great Britain and America became more concerned about the potential threat Japan posed to their interests in the Far East.

By 1932, as Chinese and Japanese forces waged war in the international city of Shanghai, endangering the lives of British, American and European nationals, to say nothing of the extensive financial houses based in the city, the two Western powers were moving towards a closer strategic relationship. Despite a lack of coordination in their foreign policy concerning how to deal with Japan in China, Great Britain and America still were tied to a common set of interests. The realization of the unhappy truth of not being the dominant military powers in the region became a stark reality to both Western nations. Both Britain and the United States instead evoked the Japanese obligation under the Kellogg–Briand agreement of 1928 not to use force for its own gain, as well as its participation in the Washington System and its requirement to allow the concept of the "Open Door" to exist. In light of a League of Nations declaration of its aggression towards China, Japan refused to abide by the league's findings and in March 1933 left the league. As events in China grew into a period of calm in the spring of 1933, both Great Britain and America were compelled to take stock of their own strategic position in the region.[46]

Great Britain was caught in a difficult middle ground. Torn between a desire to support the League of Nations to deter Japan and the realization that public opinion and a weak military presence in the Far East limited its ability to coerce Japan into a less threatening position, British policy was a combination of appeasement and resistance. To some in London, Russia's growing fear of Japanese intentions in Manchuria was a beacon of hope at a time when British imperial defence planning in the region called out for the need to find a counter-weight to the growing Japanese menace. However, the counter-weight of the Soviet Union to Japanese expansion in the Far East was not a very reliable strategic tool in which to place much faith. A more useful option was to entangle British and American strategic interests in the region to such an extent that even though the two pursued separate policies towards Japan, the aims and objectives were so similar that their strategic policies regarding Japan were parallel, if not identical.[47]

By March 1932, many Foreign Office officials, such as Sir Robert Vansittart, the permanent under-secretary, were exasperated by the Japanese attitude towards foreign powers in China, fearful of further, bolder attacks on British interests by either Chinese or Japanese forces and desperate to find some leverage or ally that might deter any further Japanese invasion of China. In this balance of power dynamic, the British were sceptical about the usefulness of the new American president, Franklin Delano Roosevelt, and his administration. The question for British strategic foreign policymakers was: what worth were the Americans in the Far East. America, like Great Britain, did not have the same military power in the region as the Soviet Union, and the United States, like Britain, was forced to try to find leverage through international agreements and trade in its attempts to deter Japan.[48] Throughout 1934 and 1935, both the United States and Great Britain viewed the chance of a clash between the Soviet Union and Japan as being highly probable. Such a clash could work to both London's and Washington's advantage by weakening each of the two potentially dangerous powers while leaving British and American interests relatively unharmed. When no such war occurred, however, it was left to both Western nations once more to attempt to limit Japanese naval power in the hope that some stability could still be achieved.[49]

Throughout the period from 1935–1939 the RN became more and more reliant for its security in the Far East on the growing American maritime power. This reliance was not simply a need for ships and naval forces to be assigned by treaty or pact to act in the defence of British imperial interests in the Far East. Instead, fearful of provoking the IJN (Imperial

Japanese Navy) into an even more hostile position with regard to Western powers by maintaining substantial naval forces in the Far East, the RN increased its informal ties to the USN. By creating these informal ties, through shared intelligence, codes, technology, plans, ship designs and political information, the RN used its perceived close relationship with the USN in an attempt to deter the Japanese from a continued use of naval power to change the balance of power in the Far East. As tensions in the Far East grew throughout 1938 and 1939, the RN became even more anxious to ensure American naval support if Japan were to attack British interests in the region. While Australia, India, New Zealand and South Africa were asked to prepare their naval forces for a higher level of operation with the RN, in order to protect the Indian Ocean and Pacific sea lines of communication, it was American naval power that was seen as being more important for any RN success. This was especially true for offensive–defensive operations, such as blockade or the protection of sea lines of communication, if British forces were forced to meet the IJN while the RN was involved in operations in Europe.[50] Plans for allowing the American Far Eastern Fleet to use Singapore in time of war, as well as requests for American naval units to openly operate from the British base in time of peace (acting as a signal to the Japanese of the closeness of the Anglo-American naval relationship), were all part of the RN's attempts to bolster its ability to safeguard Britain's Far Eastern position.[51] By March 1939, the American chief of naval operations (CNO) was reported to the Admiralty as declaring,

> He [CNO] does not consider it likely that the United States would be at war with Japan without the United Kingdom being equally at war with the Japanese, this perhaps explains why the Navy Department do not seem particularly nervous about fortifying Guam.[52]

This perception was borne out by events of the Second World in the Pacific.

The Japanese decision to attack the USN at rest in Pearl Harbor on December 7, 1941, signalled two things. The first was the success of the British strategy to create the image of a united Anglo-American maritime front to Japan, thereby ensuring it did not face the Japanese maritime threat on its own. Second, the involvement of the United States as a full and formal part of the war effort brought the transatlantic maritime power bloc into open and full effect, creating a globally dominant maritime coalition, a reality that would be the centre of gravity for the Western allies' war effort.

In the post-Second World War world the RN once more found itself working in a changed international system: the Cold War. Questions of the utility naval power in the atomic age, as well as the uncertainty of just what the British Empire was to be after 1945 created much uncertainty for the

RN: where was it to operate; what missions would it perform; and what were the objectives in imperial defence to be achieved through the use of maritime power?[53] By 1956, with the loss of India, the British withdrawal from the Middle East underway and British imperial interests in the Far East in dispute, the RN had come to the end of its time as the protector of formal empire. However, defence of global interests, of an empire, was not a dead concept in the RN by 1956. Indeed, the idea of empire, the values of law, order, justice and righteousness were as strong as ever for the senior service and its sense of what it was defending.

The British Empire was not just a territorial or geographic possession for the RN. It was as much an intellectual and philosophical belief system as anything, and it was that image of values, of good, that the RN still saw itself as defending in 1956. Vital for this approach was the fact that what had also not changed was Great Britain's maritime relationship with the United States. In 1956, that maritime alliance was present not only in the Far East, but globally, still operating and protecting the Western allies' centre of gravity, the free and open utility of all the world's oceans. And the protection of such a use of the oceans was the protection of British national interests.[54]

From 1856 to 1956, Great Britain's strategic interests in the Far East have been inextricably linked to the maritime power of the United States. In that century the linkage between closer general Anglo-American relations and the specifics of their maritime relationship in the Far East have been absolute. Once America was engaged and committed to a permanent strategic presence in the region, Great Britain obtained a valuable strategic option: to be able to use a non-regional power, with similar trade, economic, cultural, social and political perspectives that made working in tandem a more attractive and useful option than having to tie themselves to either a European or regional power to achieve the same level of security. As the twentieth century progressed and American and British strategic interests moved closer and closer together in general, the Far East was the theatre where those relationships were strongest. Both wanted to project power and protect interests in the region. Both wanted to achieve this at a minimal cost. And both were determined not to be forcefully ejected from their Far Eastern possessions without a fight. Commanding the world's largest navies, the world's largest economies, the world's strongest currencies and banking centres, and the world's strongest technical/industrial complexes, the combination of Anglo-American maritime power in the Far East was a force no regional power could withstand. Rarely formalized, but in a theatre of interaction as important (if not more so – particularly in times of peace), as Europe, the British strategic entanglement and linkage of American strategic fortunes for the defence of the empire must surely go down as one of the most successful and prescient demonstrations of the utility of maritime power in modern history.

## Notes

1 Walter Russell Mead, *God and Gold: Britain, America, and the Making of the Modern World* (New York, 2007); John Charmley, *Splendid Isolation? Britain and the Balance of Power 1874–1914* (London, 1999); Lawrence James, *The Rise and Fall of the British Empire* (London, 1994); Anil Seal, ed., *The Decline, Revival and Fall of the British Empire: The Ford Lectures and Other Essays* (Cambridge, 1982); Niall Ferguson, *Empire: How Britain Made the Modern World* (London, 2004); C. J. Lowe, *The Reluctant Imperialists: British Foreign Policy, 1878–1902*, vol. I and II (London, 1967); W. C. B. Tunstall, "Imperial Defence, 1815–1870," vol. 2, pp. 807–841; "Imperial Defence, 1870–1897," vol. 3, pp. 230–254; "Imperial Defence, 1897–1914," vol. 3, pp. 563–604, all in the E. A. Benians, J. R. M. Butler and C. E. Carrington, eds., *Cambridge History of the British Empire* (Cambridge, 1940, 1959); Keith Neilson, *Britain and the Last Tsar: Anglo-Russian Relations, 1894–1917* (Oxford, 1995); D. C. Watt, "Imperial Defence Policy and Imperial Foreign Policy, 1911–1939: A Neglected Paradox," *Journal of Commonwealth Political Studies*, vol. 1, 1963; John Kent, *British Imperial Strategy and the Origins of the Cold War, 1944–49* (Leicester, 1993).

2 Donald M. Schurman, John Beeler, ed., *Imperial Defence, 1868–1887* (London, 1997); Eric A. Walker, *The British Empire: Its Structure and Spirit* (Oxford, 1943); Keith Neilson and Greg Kennedy, eds., *The British Way in Warfare: Power and the International System, 1856–1956: Essays in Honour of David French* (Farnham, 2010).

3 John F. Beeler, *British Naval Policy in the Gladstone and Disraeli Era, 1866–1880* (Stanford, 1997); C. I. Hamilton, *Anglo-French Naval Rivalry, 1840–1870* (Oxford, 1993); Andrew Lambert, *The Creation of the Steam Battlefleet, 1815–1860* (London, 1984); Andrew Lambert, *The Crimean War: British Grand Strategy against Russia, 1853–56* (Manchester, 1990).

4 "Milne Memorandum on the State of the Navy, April–May 1858," pp. 685–695, in John Beeler, ed., *The Milne Papers: The Papers of Admiral of the Fleet Sir Alexander Milne, 1806–1896*, vol. 1 1820–1859, Naval Records Society (Aldershot, 2004).

5 "Drummond Memorandum on the State of the Navy, May 1858," pp. 695–700, ibid.

6 "Saunders Dundas Memorandum on the State of the Navy, June 1858," ibid., pp. 702–717.

7 Ibid.; Andrew D. Lambert, "The Royal Navy, 1856–1914: Deterrence and the Strategy of World Power," in Keith Neilson and Jane E. Errington, eds, *Navies and Global Defence: Theory and Strategy* (Westport, 1995), pp. 69–92; John F. Beeler, "A One Power Standard? Great Britain and the Balance of Naval Power, 1860–1890," *Journal of Strategic Studies*, vol. 15, no. 4, 1992, pp. 548–596.

8 P. J. Cain and A. G. Hopkins, *British Imperialism, 1688–2000*, second edition (London, 2000); Andrew Lambert, "The Royal Navy and the Defence of Empire, 1856–1918," in Greg Kennedy, ed., *Imperial Defence: The Old World Order, 1856–1956* (London, 2008), pp. 111–132.

9 "Corry Memorandum on the State of the Navy" July 29, 1858, in Beeler, ed. *The Milne Papers*, pp. 733–748.

10 Hamish Ion, "Towards a Naval Alliance: Some Naval Antecedents to the Anglo-Japanese Alliance, 1854–1902," in Phillips Payson O'Brien, ed., *The Anglo-Japanese Alliance, 1902–1922* (London, 2004), p. 28.

11 Keith Neilson and T. G. Otte, *The Permanent Under-Secretary for Foreign Affairs, 1854–1946* (London, 2009), p. 21.

12 John B. Hattendorf, R. J. B. Knight, A. W. H. Pearsall, N. A. M. Rodger and Geoffrey Till, eds, *British Naval Documents, 1204–1960* (Aldershot, 1993), "Draft

by H. C. E. Childers for a Letter to the Earl of Clarendon, 23 January, 1869, pp. 593–595; ibid., "Memorandum by Colonel Sir William Jervois, 1 January, 1875," pp. 595–598.
13 *British Naval Documents, 1204–1960*, "The Carnarvon Commission, 1882," pp. 601–604.
14 Ibid.
15 *British Naval Documents, 1204–1960*, "The 'Truth about the Navy', 1884, *Pall Mall Gazette*, 18 September, 1884," pp. 604–607.
16 *British Naval Documents, 1204–1960*, "Minute for the Board of Admiralty by Admiral Sir Frederick Richards, First Naval Lord, 31 October 1895," pp. 699–701; Jon T. Sumida, *In Defence of Naval Supremacy: Finance, Technology, and British Naval Policy 1889–1914* (London, 1989); Nicholas A. Lambert, *Sir John Fisher's Naval Revolution* (Columbia, 1999).
17 Bradford Perkins, *The Great Rapprochement: England and the United States, 1895–1914* (London, 1969), p. 59.
18 Ray Ginger, *The Age of Excess: The United States from 1877 to 1914* (London, 1975), p. 197.
19 Admiral Dudley De Chair Papers, in Possession of Colin De Chair, Grove Cottage, Wood Dalling, Norfolk, UK, Folder Two.
20 For concepts of the idea of the informal strategic alliance and use of uncertainty in Anglo-American relations as a form of deterrence and coercion see, Greg Kennedy, *Anglo-American Strategic Relations, 1933–1939: Imperial Crossroads* (London, 2002).
21 Iestyn Adams, *Brothers across the Ocean: British Foreign Policy and the Origins of the Anglo-American "Special Relationship" 1900–1905* (New York, 2005).
22 Hamish Ion, "The Idea of Naval Imperialism: The China Squadron and the Boxer Uprising," in Greg Kennedy, ed., *British Naval Strategy East of Suez, 1900–2000: Influences and Actions* (London, 2005), pp. 35–61.
23 Ibid., pp. 55–56; also, Neilson and Otte, *The Permanent Under-Secretary for Foreign Affairs*, pp. 75–76; Thomas G. Otte, "'Floating Downstream': Lord Salisbury and British Foreign Policy, 1878–1902," in T. G. Otte, ed., *The Makers of British Foreign Policy From Pitt to Thatcher* (Basingstoke, 2002), pp. 98–127; Keith Neilson, *Britain and the Last Tsar: British Policy and Russia 1894–1917* (Oxford, 1995).
24 Keith Neilson, "The Anglo-Japanese Alliance and British Strategic Foreign Policy, 1902–1914" in O'Brien, ed., *The Anglo-Japanese Alliance*, p. 49; Ian Nish, *The Anglo-Japanese Alliance. The Diplomacy of Two Island Empires, 1894–1907* (London, 1966).
25 T. G. Otte, *The China Question: Great Power Rivalry and British Isolation, 1895–1905* (London: Oxford University Press, 2007); ibid., "'Wee-Ah-Wee'? Britain at Weihaiwei, 1898–1930," in Kennedy, ed., *British Naval Strategy East of Suez*, pp. 4–34, p. 15; Neilson and Otte, *The Permanent Under-Secretary for Foreign Affairs*, pp. 109–122.
26 Neilson, "Anglo-Japanese Alliance," pp. 52–53.
27 Neilson, "Anglo-Japanese Alliance," pp. 55–56.
28 Zara Steiner and Keith Neilson, *Britain and the Origins of the First World War* (Basingstoke, 2003); T. G. Otte, "The Fragmenting of the Old World Order: Britain, the Great Powers and the War," in R. Kowner, ed., *The Impact of the Russo-Japanese War* (London, 2007), pp. 95–121; David G. Herrman, *The Arming of Europe and the Making of the First World War* (Princeton, 1996).
29 Perkins, *The Great Rapprochement*, pp. 217–219; Otte and Neilson, *The Permanent Under-Secretary*, pp. 117–119.
30 Papers of Admiral Dudley De Chair, in Possession of Rodney De Chair, Oakplace, Chichester, UK, Family Record Folder, vol. 2, Confidential Letter from Durand to Foreign Secretary, April 22, 1905.

31 Ibid.
32 Ibid.; Kathleen Dalton, *Theodore Roosevelt: A Strenuous Life* (New York, 2002), pp. 282–290.
33 Papers of Admiral Dudley De Chair, in Possession of Rodney De Chair, Oakplace, Chichester, UK, Family Record Folder, vol. 2, Confidential Letter from Durand to Foreign Secretary, April 22, 1905.
34 Sir Julian Stafford Corbett Papers, Queen's University, Kingston, Ontario, Folder 3, Corr. with Newbolt, Letter from Corbett to Newbolt, May 3, 1902.
35 Perkins, *The Great Rapprochement*, pp. 223–240.
36 James R. Reckner, *Teddy Roosevelt's Great White Fleet* (New York, 1988); Kenneth Wimmel, *Theodore Roosevelt and the Great White Fleet: American Sea Power Comes of Age* (Washington, 1998); Nathan Miller, *Theodore Roosevelt: a life* (New York, 1992); Daniela Rossini, *From Theodore Roosevelt to FDR: Internationalism and Isolationism in American Foreign Policy* (Boston, 1999); William N. Tilchin and Charles E. Neu, eds., *Artists of Power: Theodore Roosevelt, Woodrow Wilson, and their enduring impact on US foreign policy* (Westport, 2006).
37 Michael J. Hogan, *Informal Entente: The Private Structure of Cooperation in Anglo-American Economic Diplomacy, 1918–1928* (Columbia, 1977).
38 K. M. Burk, *Britain, America and the Sinews of War 1914–1918* (London, 1988).
39 Quoted in Neilson and Otte, *The Permanent Under-Secretary for Foreign Affairs*, p. 155.
40 Peter Lowe, *Great Britain and Japan 1911–1915: A Study of British Far Eastern Policy* (London, 1969); Keith Neilson, "'For Diplomatic, Economic, Strategic and Telegraphic Reasons': British Imperial Defence, the Middle East and India, 1914–1918," in Keith Neilson and Greg Kennedy, eds, *Far Flung Lines: Studies in Imperial Defence in Honour of Donald Mackenzie Schurman* (London, 1997), pp. 103–123.
41 Keith Neilson, "'Unbroken Threat': Japan, Maritime Power and British Imperial Defence, 1920–32," in Kennedy, *British Naval Strategy East of Suez*, pp. 62–72.
42 Emily O. Goldman, *Sunken Treaties* (Pennsylvania, 1994); Christopher Hall, *Britain, America, and Arms Control* (New York, 1987); Malcolm H. Murfett, "Look Back in Anger: The Western Powers and the Washington Conference of 1921–1922," in B. J. C. McKercher, ed., *Arms Limitation and Disarmament* (New York, 1992), pp. 83–104; Stephen W. Roskill, *Naval Policy Between the Wars*, vol. 1 (London, 1968), pp. 70–75; J. Kenneth McDonald, "The Washington Conference and the Naval Balance of Power, 1921–22," in John B. Hattendorf and Robert S. Jordan, eds., *Maritime Strategy and the Balance of Power* (London, 1989), pp. 189–213; Ian H. Nish, *Alliance in Decline* (London, 1972); Erik Goldstein and John Maurer, eds, "Special Issue on the Washington Conference, 1921–22: Naval Rivalry, East Asian Stability and the Road to Pearl Harbor," *Diplomacy and Statecraft*, 4 (1993); Roger Dingman, *Power in the Pacific: the Origins of Naval Arms Limitation* (Chicago, 1976); William R. Braisted, *The United States Navy in the Pacific, 1909–1922* (Austin, 1971).
43 The best general survey of the international situation in the Far East in the period from 1919–1933 is provided in the relevant chapters of Zara Steiner, *The Lights That Failed: European International History, 1919–1933* (Oxford, 2005). See also, Walter LaFeber, *US–Japanese Relations Throughout History* (London and New York, 1997).
44 Chris Bell, *The Royal Navy, Seapower and Strategy Between the Wars* (London, 2000); Arthur Marder, *Old Friends, New Enemies: The Royal Navy and the Imperial Japanese Navy* (Oxford, 1981).
45 Keith Neilson, *Britain, Soviet Russia and the Collapse of the Versailles Order, 1919–1939* (Cambridge, 2005); Antony Best, *Britain, Japan and Pearl Harbor: Avoiding War in East Asia, 1936–41* (London, 1995).

46 Keith Neilson, "Perception and Posture in Anglo-American Relations: The Legacy of the Simon-Stimson Affair, 1932–1941," *International History Review*, vol. 29, 2007, pp. 313–338.
47 Kennedy, *Anglo-American Strategic Relations and the Far East*; ibid., "1935 A Snapshot of British Imperial Defence in the Far East," in Kennedy and Neilson, eds., *Far Flung Lines*, pp. 190–216.
48 Greg Kennedy, "What Worth the Americans? The British Strategic Foreign Policy-Making Elite's View of American Maritime Power in the Far East, 1933–1941," in Kennedy, ed., *British Naval Strategy East of Suez*, pp. 90–118.
49 Keith Neilson, "The British Way in Warfare and Russia," in Neilson and Kennedy, eds, *The British Way in Warfare*, pp. 7–28.
50 Ian Cowman, *Dominion and Decline: Anglo-American Naval Relations in the Pacific, 1937–1941* (Oxford, 1996); Ashley Jackson, "The Colonial Empire and Imperial Defence" in Kennedy, ed., *Imperial Defence*, pp. 234–250; Brian P. Farrell, "Coalition of the Usually Willing: the Dominions and Imperial Defence, 1856–1919," in Kennedy, ed., *Imperial Defence*, pp. 251–303.
51 Greg Kennedy, "Symbol of Imperial Defence: The Role of Singapore in British and American Far Eastern Strategic Relations, 1933–1941," in Brian P. Farrell and Sandy Hunter, eds, *Sixty Years On; The Fall of Singapore Revisited* (Singapore, 2002); J. Neidpath, *The Singapore Naval Base and the Defence of Britain's Eastern Empire, 1919–1941* (Oxford, 1981).
52 Kennedy, "What Worth the Americans?," p. 103.
53 Eric Grove, *Vanguard to Trident: British Naval Policy Since World War II* (London, 1987); Ian Speller, *The Role of Amphibious Warfare in British Defence Policy, 1945–1956* (Basingstoke, 2001); Matthew Uttley, *Westland and the British Helicopter Industry, 1945–1960* (London, 2001); K. Hack, *Defence and Decolonisation in Southeast Asia: Britain, Malaya and Singapore, 1941–68* (Richmond, 2001); M. H. Murfett, *In Jeopardy: The Royal Navy and British Far Eastern Defence Policy, 1945–1951* (Kuala Lumpur, 1995).
54 S. Dokrill, *Britain's Retreat from Suez: The Choice Between Europe and the World?* (Basingstoke, 2002); Ashley Jackson, "Imperial Defence in the Post-Imperial Era," in Kennedy, ed., *Imperial Defence*, pp. 303–332.

# 12 The British Pacific Fleet and the decline of empire?

Adaptations to change

*Jon Robb-Webb*

On 15 December 1944, Commander-in-Chief British Pacific Fleet (CINCBPF), Admiral Sir Bruce Fraser arrived in Hawaii for a meeting with Commander-in-Chief Pacific Ocean Area (CINCPOA), Admiral Chester Nimitz. In many ways this was a historic event. It had been a historic flight from Colombo, the first ever by a land-based aircraft to Perth and then on from Australia to Pearl Harbor, via the New Hebrides and the Phoenix Islands. Fraser had taken with him a small staff which included the first Wrens to serve in the Pacific.[1] This little band was in the hands of the US Naval Air Transport Service (NATS). Although the majority of this epic flight was taken up with preparations for the talks ahead, Admiral Fraser had time to chat to the American air crew and commented to his Flag Lieutenant with mock indignation that a Master Sergeant earned more than he did.[2]

But the meeting itself has a stronger claim on history's attention. It could well be argued that it represented the passing of Neptune's Trident from one navy to the next. The discussions undertaken by the two Admirals and their respective staffs concerned what has been described as the most powerful fleet the Royal Navy (RN) ever put to sea.[3] It was certainly the first time that the principal British fleet passed under the command of an allied navy.

This chapter is about the way in which the British adapted to changing strategic and power relationships. In particular it demonstrates the way in which naval force and sea power was utilized to underpin the emerging international system. Furthermore it illustrates how the British and Fraser in particular utilized the meeting at Pearl Harbor to cement a new relationship between the two allies and their navies.

Until October 1944 Britain did not have a Pacific Fleet. It is true that the British Empire did indeed span the globe. It was naval strength that permitted, fostered and sustained British commercial, resource and dominion interests. Use of the sea knitted together British interests. It was the shield, trident and progenitor of British power, and linked far flung colonial out-posts into a network of imperial interests that centred on London. But this network flowed across the North Sea to the Baltic and

Northern Europe, across the Bay of Biscay and into the Mediterranean or down the west coast of Africa to Cape Town; out from Britain to Gibraltar, Alexandria, Bombay, Basra, Sydney, Singapore; west across the Atlantic to the Americas. But for Britain the Pacific was a vast and peripheral ocean, more barrier than connection. It is not unreasonable to argue that the great idea of the nineteenth century, Darwin's theory of evolution, was shaped by this ocean and that whalers created a significant revenue stream but Britain's interests were located along the Pacific's margins not spanning it. From Hong Kong and Singapore shipping flowed west across the Indian Ocean, linking the sub-continent through the Suez Canal and the Mediterranean back to Britain. Britain had significant interests along the South American Pacific coast; Australia, New Zealand and Canada all had Pacific coasts; the one serious strategic threat outside Europe, Japan, was obviously a Pacific power; the empire's possessions in the Pacific had increased numerically after the First World War but all the same, it would be hard to argue that Britain was a natural Pacific power. For Britain the gravest threat was Germany and though the *Germany first* strategy also made sense in terms of America's security priorities, it was to be source of lingering tension between them. This chapter concerns the relatively brief period in which this position was reversed, when the Pacific became central to British foreign policy and future security policy.

This story also reveals much about the way in which navies are utilized to underpin strategic relationships. As Nicholas Sarantakes urged in *Joint Forces Quarterly* 'Present day warfighters, quartermasters, strategists and commanders should keep this case study in coalition operations in mind when dealing with allies, since the operational distribution of power is similar.'[4]

## The origins of the British Pacific Fleet

The shifting power relationship between the major Western allies is well illustrated by the discussions and arguments over British participation in the final operations against Japan. Some unlikely partnerships emerged during this period of domestic and international debate. Before delving into the details of the December meeting it is important to review how the BPF came into being.

At the SEXTANT conference in November 1943, the British high command accepted as a basis for examination the deployment of a fleet to the Pacific, the establishment of its main base in Australia and its advance base in the Solomon and Bismarck islands. The Admiralty had first considered Australia as a base for a fleet as early as 27 December 1941.[5] However the pressures in the Mediterranean, in the Atlantic and in home waters had compelled the RN to stand on the defensive and adopt a fleet in being strategy in the Indian Ocean based in Ceylon. Britain had prevailed in getting her 'Germany first' grand strategy adopted by the allies but despite this the United States had effectively been on the offensive in the Pacific since August 1942. The United States, unlike the British, had the economic and military capacity to wage a two hemispheric war. If Britain wanted to regain her position with Australia, in Hong Kong, in Singapore and Malaya she would also have to participate more fully in the defeat of Japan. The deployment of a fleet to operate alongside the United States Navy (USN) offered the possibility of meeting such a commitment.

The following spring, however, Churchill presented a paper to the Chiefs of Staff arguing that the British effort should be focused on an amphibious strategy in the Indian Ocean. This was in part prompted by the desire to regain Malaya and Singapore through her own efforts before the Americans completed the defeat of Japan. The prime minister sought to ensure that when the war ended Britain would be in possession of what, in his view, was rightfully hers and would not be dependent upon the Americans for the return of her lost colonies.

Correlli Barnet has argued that Churchill's idea for concentrating the British effort in Southeast Asia made far better politico-strategic sense. He argues that 'it would have enabled Britain to win her own, if peripheral, victory against Japan in her own theatre; to play a middle-sized fish in a middle-sized pond.' He went on to argue that operating in the Central Pacific under Nimitz, 'meant playing the sprat in the largest pond in the world [which] could only expose Britain's shrunken relative stature as a power and above all as a naval power.'[6]

The experience of the BPF did indeed reveal Britain's shrunken status. In that Barnet is right, but his analysis misses the point that such revelations would be exposed regardless. The fleet was utilized as more subtle expression of political power than Barnet acknowledges. At the grand strategic level the focus of British naval policy was as much, if not more, on American opinion rather than Japanese destruction. The fleet was a crucial tool for alliance building; nothing else in the British armoury offered the possibility of being deployed to a timetable set by political need. The British Foreign Office, the Chiefs of Staff and the American State Department all saw British participation as essential not just as a gesture of allied solidarity directed at Japan, but as crucial for the development of Anglo-American relations post war.

The major decision concerning British participation was taken in principle at the Octagon Conference, in Quebec, in September 1944. During the meetings not only was Admiral King forced to accept a British presence but Churchill also performed an about face over the substance and form of the contribution. Willmott has produced the most convincing explanation for the prime minister's change of heart. The available evidence supports the conclusion that the Chiefs of Staff opposed Churchill's advocacy for operations in the South West Pacific Area or Indian Ocean simply because resources made them impracticable.[7] The Chiefs of Staff had been pressing their case with Churchill for most of the preceding summer, arguing that Britain could not mount an amphibious operation because of manpower overstretch. Churchill eventually agreed that planning for a British commitment would have to be focused around a naval force but he continued to be vague concerning where exactly it would operate.

Admiral King recalled after the war that the prime minister urged that the RAF and the RN be permitted to join the effort against the Japanese as soon as possible.[8] Roosevelt asked King whether 'he needed any help from the Royal Navy,' which King declined, arguing that the best occupation for any available British troops, plane and ships would be the recovery of Singapore. He went on to argue that UK forces should be employed to assist the Dutch in the recovery of the chain of islands from Sumatra through Java to Borneo. Having had to change his mind, such arguments clearly did not please the prime minister.

Nimitz also noticed that the prime minister was clearly agitated by a Combined Chiefs' proposal that the RN would not operate north or east of the Philippines.[9] The CINCPOA recognized that the British, with many political and economic interests in the Far East, 'needed a victory in that part of the world to erase from the minds of the Orientals the effect of the crushing defeats of 1941 and 1942.' He believed that Churchill would not be content with the prospect of minor successes in some out-of-the-way corner of the Pacific theatre. The prime minister by now wanted British forces clearly and visibly involved in the final defeat of the Japanese homeland. King, too, was aware of the political motivations behind the British position. In his autobiography he makes it clear that he was suspicious of the offer of British assistance, precisely because he feared that any combined effort would have political strings attached. In particular he was concerned that it would oblige the USN to reciprocate with help clearing the Japanese out of the Malay States and the Netherlands East Indies, in effect a distraction from the main task before the United States.

Attempting to deflect the issue, King reported that a paper was being prepared for the Combined Chiefs of Staffs on possible employment of British forces in the Pacific.[10] Churchill raised the question of whether it would not be better to employ the new British ships in place of the 'battle worn' vessels of the USN. King could only respond by saying the matter was under active consideration but Churchill continued to press the issue. Nimitz recounts that Roosevelt eventually conceded saying that, 'I should like to see the British fleet wherever and whenever possible.' At which point Admiral King was visibly shaken. Nimitz also described the prime minister's reaction.

> Churchill was offended. To him it was inconceivable that an offer of the fleet of Drake and Hawke and St. Vincent and Nelson should not be instantly and gratefully embraced. 'The offer of the British Fleet has been made,' growled Churchill. 'Is it accepted?'
> 'Yes,' said Roosevelt.[11]

The issue emerged again the following day when the Combined Chiefs of Staff met without their political masters and King attempted to upset the applecart in the words of Samuel Morrison by letting it be known that he wanted no part of the British Navy in the Central Pacific.'[12] Admiral King argued that the president's acceptance of the offer did not mean what the British thought it had meant. He conceded that it was of course essential to have sufficient forces for the war against Japan but that he was not prepared to accept a British fleet which he could not employ or support. 'In principle he wished to accept the British fleet in the Pacific, but it would be entirely unacceptable to him for the British main fleet to be employed for political reasons in the Pacific, and thus necessitate the withdrawal of some of the United States fleet.'[13]

The discussion began to get more and more heated with the chief of naval operations (CNO) berating not only his supposed allies but his fellow members of the Joint Chiefs. King, having vociferously argued with General Marshall (US Army Chief of Staff), was finally called to order by Admiral Leahy, the President's Chief of Staff, with the remark: 'I don't think we should wash our linen in public.' King, with the other American Chiefs of Staff against him, eventually gave way; but with very bad grace.[14] The following afternoon the British and American Chiefs of Staff reconvened and although it was apparent that King was now resigned to the use of a British fleet in the Pacific he made it quite clear that it must expect no assistance from the Americans.

The resultant insistence on separate logistic arrangements and complex command structures was to bedevil the BPF for much of its time on operations. Whilst this administrative compromise was necessary in order to achieve the political object the British desired and maintain a degree of acquiescence from Admiral King, it made Fraser's task that much more difficult.

The result of these grand and military strategic level discussions was that the BPF was formed in October 1944 alongside the East Indies Fleet (which operated in the Indian Ocean) on the dissolution of the Eastern Fleet which had been based in Ceylon (now Sri Lanka). When Fraser raised his flag as CINCBPF he was both fully aware of Admiral King's reluctance accept a RN contribution to the main operations against Japan and determined to do just that.

## The Pearl Harbor meeting and beyond – matters of detail

For Admiral Fraser, any hope of achieving his strategic objectives of having the BPF operate alongside the USN in the most advanced operations against Japan, rested on securing excellent relations with Nimitz and his HQ staff. And for that the Pearl Harbor meeting was crucial. This was not the first time the two had met. They had encountered each other ten years earlier when Nimitz was captain of USS *Augusta*, part of the US Asiatic

Fleet and Fraser was in command of HMS *Effingham*. Fraser knew that the entire visit was an important demonstration of the fact that the British were serious about their commitment and willingness to get along in every way. For their part, the warmth of the American reception was clearly genuine. Commander Charles Sheppard, the BPF intelligence officer, commented that from the moment of touch down maximum cooperation was received. Sheppard put much of this attitude down to the rapport between the two Admirals and their similarities:

> I think the basis of the friendship between Admiral Fraser and Admiral Nimitz lay in the similarities of their characters. Both were 'quiet' men, both had a good sense of humour – Admiral Fraser's of an impish variety – and both were easily approachable.[15]

The meeting at Pearl Harbor and the relationship established between the two admirals and their staffs would set the tone for the cooperation between the two fleets. Indeed there was much to overcome. Just prior to the meeting Nimitz had written to Admiral King and commented that,

> I do not need Paul Revere (with his three [sic] lanterns) to tell me that the British are coming. The attached paraphrase of six Top Secret dispatches reads like an operation order for an occupation force. Perhaps it is intended to be an occupation force.[16]

King replied expressing his concerns over Fraser's appointment as CINCBPF. Fraser would have outranked both Admiral Spruance and Admiral Halsey.[17] The debate over command arrangements in the Pacific theatre were not helped by the absence of a supreme commander. The Americans had compromised between Nimitz and MacArthur's competing claims for seniority by creating two geographical commands; the South West Pacific Area for the later and the Central Pacific for the former. Fitting the British into this structure was not as easy as might be assumed. MacArthur was keen to have the British assigned to him as it would free him from dependence upon Nimitz for naval assets. The Admiralty were less keen on the idea but given the fact that Churchill had long desired to use the RN to reassert British rule in Singapore and Hong Kong, they informed Fraser that,

> Such arrangements might be considered convenient in the future, but unwelcome at present since it might result in British Forces being excluded from taking part in major operations in the Pacific. You should therefore neither discourage it, should it be brought up in discussions in Australia, or with Admiral Nimitz, but refer exact terms of any proposal made to Admiralty.[18]

Fraser, in contrast, was set against the idea of operating under MacArthur but he would have to get Nimitz's agreement if he were to operate the BPF in the most advanced operations against Japan. Although Admiral King retained the right to re-assign the British from the Central Pacific to MacArthur's South West Pacific Area the critical decision rested on Nimitz's recommendation to his boss. This was something that would only be forthcoming if the two admirals and their staffs could, not only agree on what to do with the BPF, but also how it would integrate with the USN.

The brief drawn up by Fraser's staff concerning the subjects for discussion at the meeting reveals much of the arguments that were being explored at his headquarters. The fundamental issue regarded where and how the BPF would operate. The first proposal was for entirely separate US and British strategic areas. The staff paper advanced two reasons in support of this idea; first, full operational control would be exercised by CINCBPF, and second, as a consequence of this, it was felt that the BPF would be easier to administer and operate. Against this three important points were highlighted. It was thought first that the BPF were unlikely to be allocated anything but an insignificant area of operations. This would clearly have been in conflict with Fraser's ideas of participating in the most advanced Pacific operations and would have failed to deliver the grand strategic objective of political leverage with the Americans. Second, the practicalities of a separate strategic area gave some concern. The BPF was not self sufficient in either shore facilities or harbour defence capabilities. Though reluctant to admit it at the military strategic level of command, the RN was conscious of their likely dependence upon the assistance of the USN at the operational and tactical levels.

The final argument against a separate strategic area was the recognition that any such arrangement would be uneconomical in overall naval power. The war in the Far East was highlighting the increasing inability of the British to sustain the war. Their best hope was to bring about as rapid a conclusion to hostilities as possible. Any diversion of military capability into subsidiary activities would therefore be counter-productive.

The alternative proposal under consideration from the British side was to establish combined US and UK strategic areas. The idea was that the BPF would operate as a strategic unit on specific 'missions as designated by the American High Command.' Fraser's staff suggested the example of operating from Manila to cut Japanese North–South supply routes in the South China Sea. This it was felt could be combined with other 'specific operations – for example, a Highball or XE attack on Japanese Fleet.'[19] Fraser's own his thoughts on these proposals were,

> I favour alternative (2) and it is particularly desired that the British Fleet should operate as near the heart of the enemy as possible. At the same time I want to emphasize that it is unreservedly at the disposal of

the American Command for the purpose of bringing the war to a conclusion at the earliest possible moment.[20]

In essence this is what took place during the invasion of Okinawa, operation Iceberg. The BPF, operating under Spruance and the Fifth Fleet participating in the main campaign, were allocated the task of neutralizing the Japanese air threat to the invasion that could be staged through Sakishima Gunto. However, this arrangement was not confirmed at the Pearl Harbor meeting. Nimitz refused to make any commitments to the British concerning operations. He suggested that they raid the Japanese-held oil installations on Sumatra and implied that, for the time being, the BPF could make its best contribution by attaching itself to Kinkaid's Seventh Fleet for operations in the South West Pacific Area. This was distinctly not what the British had in mind. When they objected, Admiral Nimitz said that he might be able to make use of their fleet in connection with the scheduled assault on Okinawa. He then turned the issue over to Admiral Spruance so that he and his staff could consider that possibility.[21]

It is clear that the British made a very different interpretation of these talks than the Americans. Fraser took them to mean agreement had been reached that the BPF would operate either under Spruance and the Fifth Fleet or Halsey, when the Third Fleet was formed, in the main operations against Japan. He reported reaching agreement to London, signalling 'I intend to operate the British Pacific Fleet to the best possible effect in the most advanced operations in the Pacific and Fleet Admiral Nimitz has agreed that I should do so.'[22] The Americans, however, continued to explore the possibility of transferring the BPF to MacArthur's South West Pacific command. This reassignment remained a distinct likelihood until August 1945.

The staff talks continued with discussions returning again to the tricky issue of basing requirements. At this stage of the BPF's build up, the aim was to operate, a fully self-supporting balanced fleet, from an advanced base as soon as possible and not to call upon the Americans for any support. However, due to the late arrival of some units, particularly shore based facilities, the British felt it would probably be necessary to call upon American assistance. This was something that Fraser wished to avoid if at all possible. He did feel, however, that it would be convenient if the BPF's first advanced base was also one used by the USN. Admiral Cunningham in London disagreed with Fraser. He responded to Fraser's letter of 2 July, arguing that Fraser only had a short term policy of bringing the greatest force to bear on the enemy as soon as possible. Cunningham's own view was,

> Where we differ, as far as I can see, is in our conception of what the course of the war in the Pacific will be ... we are strongly of the opinion that we must continue to press for some sort of forward base.

> The great difficulty that we are experiencing in getting our demands for the fleet train conceded also makes a forward base with some storage and aircraft facilities essential.[23]

Everything Fraser attempted was constrained by the limited logistics available. He argued with Cunningham's concept of an independent forward base because the BPF simply did not possess the resources to construct or man it.[24] The outcome of this debate left the BPF with rear bases in Eastern Australia and an intermediate base at Manus, a location Fraser described as 'a dismal place.'[25]

It was arranged for an experienced American carrier captain and several American communications teams to be assigned to the British fleet, which would be considered equivalent of a 'Fast Carrier Task Force' and that CINCBPF had the same status under CINCPAC (Commander-in-Chief Pacific) as Third or Fifth Fleet commanders.

Command arrangements between the United States and United Kingdom became embroiled in not just inter-allied relations but also those between MacArthur (Commander-in-Chief South West Pacific Area, CINC-SWPA) and Nimitz. At the end of December 1944 Fraser received a report via the Admiralty in London concerning comments made by General MacArthur to his British liaison officer, General Lumsden.[26] Lumsden had written to Lord Ismay, Chief of Staff, Minister of Defence and Deputy Military Secretary to the War Cabinet, informing him that MacArthur now wished the BPF to operate in the South West Pacific Area. This would provide him with a naval capability that was virtually independent of Nimitz. In his somewhat expressive style MacArthur told Lumsden, 'Were the British Fleet here now I could give them ample opportunities of gaining great renown for themselves and great credit to the British Empire.'[27]

The Admiralty advised Fraser in the report that though such arrangements might be 'considered convenient in the future' at the present the fear was that they would exclude the BPF from participating in the major operations planned for the Pacific. Fraser was instructed to discourage discussion of any such ideas, should they be brought up in discussions in Australia, or with Admiral Nimitz. If the Americans or the dominion brought the prospect up Fraser was to be non committal and refer the exact terms of any proposal made back to Admiralty.[28]

The effectiveness of the BPF as both a fighting force and as a tool of diplomatic alliance building was dependent up its smooth integration into the organization of the USN. In order to facilitate this process the RN and the USN exchanged officers. These liaison officers (LOs) were a vital mechanism by which information, intelligence, doctrine and tactical procedures were shared. In addition to this they played an important role in easing the understanding of each other. The Admiralty commented on their role and function writing:

Upon them, and them alone the Admiralty and the War Cabinet relied for information as to how far the war in the Pacific was keeping step with American official reports on its progress, and the truth about the methods and the efficiency of the US Navy. They were also envoys of the British Pacific Fleet. They were in a position to gather thorough and intimate knowledge of not only the organization and methods of the US Fleet, but the outlook and psychology of the officers and men of their Service, so that British ships and units on joining would be able to fit themselves harmoniously into service with our Allies.[29]

Although this exchange had been running in the Pacific since 1941, Fraser's visit to Pearl Harbor produced enhancements to the role of liaison officer. Agreement was reached concerning wider access to American intelligence as well as participation in Nimitz's planning. This later integration was initially the subject of debate between Nimitz and Admiral King, King and the Admiralty, as well as between Nimitz and Fraser.[30] A compromise was reached permitting access of RN LOs in order that Nimitz could be advised as to the capabilities of the BPF and Fraser kept abreast of developing USN plans so that he could adequately prepare the British fleet.

The USN was generous almost to a fault with the quantity of information and intelligence that they provided to the British.[31] Although there were difficulties in processing the quantity of material provided by the Americans, given the small number of personnel that the BPF had assigned to the task, this generous cooperation was essential to the fleet's efficient operation. The exchange of LOs between the USN and the RN was a vital mechanism for not only the sharing of information and intelligence but also for the wider interoperability of the two navies. LOs were pivotal in adapting carrier flight deck procedures so that cross decking could be undertaken, aligning radio frequencies, and possibly most significant, aiding the understanding of each other's psyche.

Not everybody appreciated the importance of understanding the Americans. Fraser had his difficulties with London; the Pacific was not only quantitatively different from the naval war in the Atlantic and Mediterranean but also qualitatively. Fraser recognized that the USN was conducting a revolutionary form of naval warfare; something only seen on paper in Whitehall. Fraser deployed the analogy of European war distances in the hope of bringing his predicament home in a signal to the First Sea Lord, Cunningham,

> When you also consider that our Fleet operations are equivalent in distances to:
> 
> i) A Fleet based on Alexandria under Egyptian control
> ii) An advanced anchorage at Gibraltar under Spanish control

iii) A fuelling service in the Azores, the Portuguese allotting the area
iv) Operating against Labradore [sic] under Canadian control
v) The Russian Admiralty assigning the units to the Fleet Train and controlling logistic support one can perhaps more readily understand the difficult nature of the problem. Perhaps the comparison to the Russian Admiralty is a little unfair, but they are fairly autocratic![32]

Fraser's little dig at the Admiralty at the end of his signal is quite revealing. There was a widespread feeling at all levels of the fleet that those back home, whether family or policymakers, did not understand the particular conditions of the Pacific. Fraser recognized that the duration of Pacific operations, their climactic conditions and their distances put an intense strain on his men. He tried to counter their incipient feelings of isolation with fleet newspapers. He pointed out to Cunningham in London that one of the keys to the USN's success lay in the morale of the crews. This was maintained by regular changes to cinema programmes aboard ship in order to manage the long periods of boredom, ice cream to relieve oppressive heat and humidity, and regular mail to counteract any feeling of their being forgotten. Cunningham's war had been fought in the Mediterranean and he doesn't appear to have shared Fraser's opinion as to the importance of such crew comforts. The First Sea Lord responded to Fraser's comments on maintaining morale with the following signal,

> I hope our people will not get too blinded by American lavishness. We cannot compete with them in either personnel or material, nor do I think we should train our men to expect the same waste as practiced in the American Navy. I am sure that soda fountains, etc. are very good things in the right place, but we have done without them for some hundreds of years and I daresay can for another year or two.[33]

Cunningham missed the point; the war in the Pacific was one that placed almost unbearable strain on men and material. Both needed to be sustained. The developments in the Fleet Train permitted the BPF to mount sustained operations off a hostile coast for periods of time not seen since the days of sail. They provided fuel, ammunition, victuals and most crucially mail. Perhaps more significantly the signal reveals something of the First Sea Lord's attitude toward the USN. A somewhat arrogant view that the United States and the USN were pampered, endowed with abundant resources and consequently inclined to wastefulness. The scale of operations in the Pacific, the vast distances over which these operations were conducted and their extended duration demanded resources of a quantity only the United States could provide. The BPF were only ever going to be a minor contribution to forces in the Pacific but they had to demonstrate an operational capability comparable to the USN to be accepted and that included cinema and ice-cream.

## The British Pacific Fleet arrives: further matters of detail

Admiral Rawlings understood the political significance of what his task force provided by tactical and operational capability:

> Just had a nice signal from Nimitz – what pleased me most about it is that so far there is nothing that they can poke Charlie at the White Ensign over. I do mind very much that we come through high in their opinion – it's so absolutely important for our future – indeed I feel it's the most serious side of my job far and away.[34]

By mid-February 1945, the BPF having arrived in Sydney following their strikes on Palembang, Fraser wrote to Nimitz concerned apparently about the future employment of his fleet. The issues of command arrangements had not been settled completely and the BPF found itself caught again in the middle of a jurisdictional dispute between Nimitz and MacArthur. Fraser found it difficult to plan the BPF's forthcoming operations because of the residual uncertainty over where, and under whose command, it would actually operate. He wrote to Nimitz in the middle of February concerned that the BPF had not yet been allocated to any command. The CINCBPF was proceeding on the assumption that the fleet would operate with the US Fifth Fleet in Operation Iceberg, the invasion of Okinawa. Fraser evidently believed that in so doing he was following Nimitz's instructions. Fraser also had concerns about the availability of his fleet if it was diverted to the South West Pacific Area. Admiral King in Washington had implied that Fraser should have no direct communication with Vice Admiral Thomas Kinkaid Commander of the Seventh Fleet. Fraser denied having any discussions about future operations with Kinkaid and so was left somewhat in the dark. Fraser's sense of frustration was obvious when he wrote to Nimitz clearly seeking a sympathetic ear.

> My only object is to try and bring the BPF into action on the dates you desired, but am beginning to feel a little frustrated. Time is getting short, the Fleet is in SYDNEY, and I have no airstrip allocations at MANUS. Can you help and advise me if we are doing wrong. It hardly seems to me to be practicable to be based in the command of CinC-SWPA without having communication on local matters.[35]

Fraser followed this up with three further signals. He informed Nimitz that his intention was to dispatch the BPF for Manus, MacArthur's command, in the first week of March. From there they would sail for the forward base of Ulithi. The CINCBPF believed that even if there were alterations to the planned British involvement in Iceberg the fleet would be more suitably deployed at Manus, though he would wait for confirmation before moving on. His other concern was that the delay in bringing his fleet into action was having a negative effect upon its morale. Fraser told Nimitz stating that he was sure the admiral would realize how important it was not to keep the fleet inactive at Sydney for a prolonged period. The few British facilities at Manus would not ease the difficult situation to any great degree. Ideally Fraser hoped to see the fleet actively employed as soon as possible.[36]

Fraser went on to explain that he regarded Nimitz as his effective Commander-in-Chief (CINC) although the complicated state of assignment did not make their relative positions quite clear at this time. Fraser's relationship with Nimitz was undoubtedly much better than that with King in Washington and it is probable that by treating Nimitz in this manner he was again seeking out a sympathetic ear to intercede with King on his behalf. Fraser was insistent in his desire that 'we might be assigned to your area at least for the start of ICEBERG if this is likely to take place before any operation for which we might be required in the South West Pacific Area.'[37]

Nimitz did indeed take the matter up with Admiral King in Washington. He wrote to King stating that in the absence of direct instructions or any other information concerning future operations of the BPF he proposed to support Fraser's move north to Manus.[38] CINCPAC was in a difficult situation. Admiral King retained the right to reallocate the British to MacArthur at seven days notice and had not yet authorized their participation in operations to take the Ryukyus. King's opposition to British involvement in the Pacific War was well known to Nimitz. Without clear authorization and with Fraser pressing the issue it is to Nimitz's credit that he managed very successfully to balance the complex interaction of political and operational matters.

Both Nimitz and Fraser needed to develop their planning and preparations. Without a clear idea of where and when the BPF might be committed, this was proving to be something of a problem. Nimitz referred the matter up the chain of command to Admiral King. King, a little surprised at Nimitz's need for clarification, informed CINCPAC

> I am at a loss to understand why there should be confusion as to status of British Pacific Fleet. All arrangements for basing British Pacific Fleet are in the hands of CinCPOA including CinCSWPA concurrence where appropriate and always bearing in mind that said Fleet is to be self supporting.[39]

King continued by reiterating that it was his authority to commit the BPF to action; 'Allocation of units of British Pacific Fleet for operations remains in my hands.' The COMINCH (Commander-in-Chief) explained the delay in reaching a decision as a consequence of a failure by the Joint Chiefs of Staff to agree on any other future operations.

> I cannot commit units of British Pacific Fleet to Iceberg (involving two to three months) or any other operation until Joint Chiefs of Staff decide what operations are due to be carried out other than those already approved. Prospects now are that such decision will be reached by middle of March.[40]

By the time the fleet left Australia for its intermediate base of Manus, however, a final decision as to where it would operate had still not been taken. This was only partially a result of American reluctance to sanction British participation in the main operations against Japan. It had almost as much to do with inter American disputes. The attempts to unite these two independent area commanders without appointing a supreme commander were doomed from the start. It is debatable, moreover, whether MacArthur would have co-operated fully with any other commander.[41] The tension between MacArthur and Nimitz was to cause difficulties for the BPF. The British were in the unenviable position of operating under Nimitz in the central Pacific, basing in MacArthur's area in Leyte and Manus and under the Australian government in Australia. Disagreements between Nimitz and MacArthur extended to the complicated issue of base facilities.

The problems of basing arrangements were extremely delicate issues in which operational and political considerations became inextricably linked. Despite initially advocating the establishment of their own separate base, Fraser demonstrated a flexibility of mind and eventually came to the conclusion a joint basing system was in the best operational interests of the fleet.[42] The CINC argued no operational intermediate base could be constructed in under a year that would make the fleet any less dependent on Australia.[43] The admiral had agreed the use of Manus as an advanced base with Nimitz but CINCPAC's (Commander-in-chief Pacific) fear that control of the island might pass to MacArthur if the BPF were reassigned continued to make operations, if not difficult, then less smooth than they could have been.[44] British basing requests were not welcomed by the USN who believed that they might result in a permanent post-war occupation – something that the prime minister certainly had in mind with his proposals for operations in Southeast Asia. These suspicions resulted in Admiral Somerville who headed the British Admiralty Delegation (BAD) in Washington receiving a less than sympathetic hearing from King when he tried to resolve this issue[45]

The BPF was eventually allocated to the US Fifth Fleet under Admiral Spruance. On the 17 March 1945 the BPF was designated Task Force 57 and sailed for its forward operating base of Ulithi for participation in Operation Iceberg, the invasion of Okinawa. The United States had begun preliminary air strikes against the Ryukyus and on 26 March British carrier borne aircraft attacked in the Pacific for the first time. Their allotted task was to neutralize the airfields of Sakishimo Gunto, to prevent interference with the landings at Okinawa from China and Formosa.[46] This was a significant moment; it marked the point when a principal, if not the principal, British fleet came under the command of a foreign navy. Although remarked upon at the time it appears to have been smooth and good natured transition on both sides at sea.[47]

At the end of May 1945 Nimitz again discussed proposals for the future employment of the BPF with Admiral King. Nimitz saw two options. First that the RN would continue to utilize Australia as a main base with an advance base at Manus and operate against Japan with the Third Fleet sharing anchorages (but with no British shore installations) at Ulithi and Eniwetok. In the second category they would operate to reopen the Malacca Strait and liberate the enemy-held areas in the British command area. This latter plan had been proposed by the Joint Chiefs of Staff. It was recognized that for this purpose they would need a base in the South China Sea for which Brunei Bay appeared the most appropriate.[48] Although the British had been arguing for basing facilities in the Philippines,[49] Nimitz disagreed

> I see no need for a base in the PHILIPPINES for either category of operations. If it later develops that the British ships operate against JAPAN with a line of supply through MALACCA STRAIT, ULITHI and LEYTE can be used as advanced anchorages. In the foregoing I do not regard temporary augmentation of United States carrier aircraft pools et cetera as constituting British shore installations.[50]

Although not privy to all these deliberations, the RN's liaison officer at Nimitz's headquarters was able to signal Fraser, with CINCPOAs approval, that the American timetable entailed TF38 (Halsey) commencing strikes on targets in Honshu, Hokkaido and Kuriles as early in June as possible after rest and replenishment at Leyte. Subject to their continued availability, which was not necessarily guaranteed, CINCPAC planned to include TF37 (BPF) in strikes when fleet returned from replenishment and battle damage repairs. It was anticipated that these offensive operations would be continued up to and including Operation Olympic (the invasion of Japanese home islands).[51] The situation had changed dramatically from that which existed before participation in Operation Iceberg when Fraser had to appeal to Nimitz for information.

The issue of basing, however, continued to dog cooperation and forward planning. As did the possibility of reallocation of the BPF, hence Nimitz's caveat regarding continued availability. Although plans were being prepared regarding the use of Eniwetok in the Marshall Islands as an anchorage from October, until such time the fleet would continue to use Leyte in MacArthur's command as an advanced base.

Nimitz informed Fraser directly a few days later when he signalled that, repairs to damage sustained during Operation Iceberg permitting, the BPF should anticipate sortieing Manus in early July for operations with Halsey against the Japanese home islands.[52] By this time it appears that the decision as to whether or not the British would participate in the Third Fleet's operations had been taken almost by default. Although Nimitz was less sure of the timetable of involvement the momentum of a British contribution seems to have carried the day.

The decision having been made that the BPF, designated Task Force 37, would operate in conjunction with the American Third Fleet under Admiral Halsey, Rawlings reported for duty at 06.45 on 16 July and took station astern TG38.4. British participation in Iceberg had avoided many of the issues of how closely the two navies should integrate and how this would affect command arrangements, as the BPF operated as a separate task force in support of the American landings on Okinawa. Matters now came to a head, however, when the BPF joined the TF38 for operations off Japan. Rawlings and Vian joined Halsey aboard USS *Missouri* for a conference on the forthcoming operations. The Americans were fuelling and Halsey used the opportunity to hold a staff conference and become acquainted with both Rawlings and Vian. Halsey describes the meeting in his memoirs,

> Reluctantly I opened the conference. I say 'reluctantly' because I dreaded it. When I was informed at Pearl Harbor that the British Pacific Fleet would report to me, I naturally assumed that I would have full operational control, but when I reread the plan at Leyte, I discovered that tactical control had been reserved.[53]

Halsey had raised this matter with Nimitz in a signal on 6 June and then again ten days later, a few weeks before sortieing from Leyte with the Third Fleet for operations off the Japanese coast. In his first signal Halsey wrote 'I tentatively plan to employ British group as tactical unit of TF38.'[54] He acknowledged that because of a difference in speed and technique the British Service Group would operate separately from their USN counterparts but in the same general vicinity. Halsey had concluding that 'British forces [could] be incorporated into our combat and service operation scheme at any time.' The idea in his mind was to operate TF37 in the same manner as a USN task group with the normal inter group interval. The British in TF37 would conform to the manoeuvres of CTF38. This would permit the RN to make a contribution to and benefit from the USN's defensive umbrella. Halsey argued that this made the most military sense and 'does not infringe on British position guaranteed by Nimitz-Fraser Agreement.'[55] The agreement reached had included the text 'to the maximum practicable extent the British ships will constitute a separate task force with no more direct tactical co-ordination with the US TF's than the situation requires.'[56] Commenting upon this in his dispatches to the

Admiralty, Fraser explained that he did not 'mean this to preclude the possibility of a British TG operating in an American Task force, but CinC Pacific appears to have taken it to mean that,'[57] Nimitz certainly did not concur with Fraser's interpretation. Caught between Halsey's desire for tactical unity and King's insistence upon separation he rejected the commander of the Third Fleet's proposal. Instructing him to 'operate TF37 separately from TF38 in fact as well as in name under arrangements which assign to Rawlings tasks to be performed but leave him free to decide upon his own movements and maneuvers.'[58]

This situation was of obvious concern to Halsey. The addition to fighting power that the BPF represented could easily be negated if co-ordination could not be agreed upon. At their first meeting Halsey presented Rawlings with three alternatives. First, the British in the shape of TF37 would operate close aboard, as another task group in TF38. It would not receive direct orders from Halsey, but it would be privy to the orders issued to TF38. These it would consider as a 'suggestion' to be followed to mutual advantage, thereby assuring a concentrated force with concentrated weapons. Halsey's second proposal envisaged TF37 operating semi-independently, some 60 or 70 miles away from the Third Fleet, thereby preserving its technical identity at the cost of a divided force. Halsey let it be known that he would consent to this choice only if the request were put in writing. The third option saw TF37 operating completely independently, against soft spots in Japan which the USN would recommend if so desired.[59]

Whereas Operation Iceberg had sidestepped these important issues as to how closely the two navies would integrate because of the detached nature of the BPF's task, matters had now come to a head. Rawlings had already expressed what he saw as the key role the BPF would play in forging Anglo-American naval relations when back in March he had signalled Fraser;

> My own feeling, for what it is worth, is that the really important side of what we do here is to end up with the White Ensign still looked up to by the Americans. I can not help feeling that in the long run it will do more for us than anything else.[60]

Indeed, mindful of Fraser's oft repeated intentions that the BPF were to operate in the most advanced operations against Japan, Rawlings had little time for Halsey's second or third option. Rawlings reported to Fraser that

> The principal points which were settled forthwith were the desire of the British Task Force to work in close tactical cooperation with TF38, conforming to their movements, and that we should take part in Battleship and Cruiser bombardments as well as surface sweeps.[61]

As Halsey recalled after the war; 'Bert Rawlings did not hesitate. He said, "Of course I'll accept Number 1." My admiration for him began at that moment. I saw him constantly thereafter, and a finer officer and firmer friend I have never known.'[62]

Ultimately Halsey directed all his forces, British and American, as one mutually supporting striking unit and although TF37 was weaker than one of the Third Fleet's task groups Fraser was able to report to London that:

> Task Force 37, of the BPF, operated in conjunction with the American Task Force 38 under orders of the commander of the United States Third Fleet, with the object of inflicting maximum destruction on Japanese airfields, aircraft and shipping, together with certain other important targets.[63]

The fleet was formed into four groups in the order from North to South TF37, TG38.1, TG38.4, TG38.3. This integration within the Third Fleet was something of an occasion and Rawlings noted that: 'It may well be that 4pm on 16 July 1945, will prove a not unimportant milestone on the long road of the world's history.'

The fact that Halsey operated TF37 as a tactical unit of TF38 in the same way as he did TF38's component task groups despite Nimitz's instructions does not appear to have caused the Admiral any serious concern. Fraser found such behaviour puzzling writing that;

> It is an interesting sidelight on the American way of thought – in particular on their rigid acceptance of the written word – that CinC Pacific considers it necessary to enforce this small restriction [integration of TF37 into TF38's defensive umbrella]. It is also interesting to note that ComThird Fleet, while accepting the restriction in its normal sense, in fact disregards it completely and continues to operate the British Task Group as a group as part of his own Task Force. Provided he obeys the letter of the law, even if he completely disregards its spirit, every American is quite happy that the right and sensible action has been taken.[64]

Such insights into the collective psychology of this most powerful of allies were to stand Fraser and many of his colleagues in good stead in the post war environment.

## Conclusion

For a brief period of time the Pacific became the focus of British grand strategy. The BPF was a symbol of the United Kingdom's commitment not only to the final defeat of Japan but more importantly to the country's most significant ally. It was less the damage that the fleet inflicted that reveals its strategic impact but rather the damage it received. By standing shoulder to shoulder with the USN in the main operations against Japan, by receiving Kamikaze hits during the invasion of Okinawa, by projecting the Fleet Air Arm over the Japanese home islands, the RN demonstrated that Britain was a steadfast partner.

As the new USN strategy[65] states so eloquently, trust is not something that can be surged in time of crisis. It has to be built up and sustained over time. It requires a persistence of commitment and this is what the BPF provided.

A naval commitment was all that the British could provide given her available military resources. Only it had the strategic reach, political presence and interoperability to achieve London's grand strategic objectives.

The establishment of close and ultimately intimate relations between the RN and the USN developed the habit of cooperation in the minds of both parties. In effect the BPF became theatre entry forces in a political, diplomatic sense; a kind of 'coalition entry force.' Although Britain's plans to further contribute both land-based airpower and ground forces came to naught as the war ended before the need for an opposed assault on Japan itself, the navy had laid the ground work for cooperation. Naval forces provided the British government with the only means of participating in the Central Pacific. The establishment of a good working relationship between Nimitz and his staff and Fraser and his at the December 1944 Hawaii meeting was critical to this process. The fleet was a self contained force that could be quickly deployed to achieve political objectives. This capability was founded upon a first rate war fighting ability. Although the political symbol of the fleet was paramount it would have been a hollow gesture if it had not been backed up by real and proven military capacity.

The fleet needed to demonstrate an ability to undertake long range persistent carrier strike operations. This they did neutralizing the air fields on Sakishima Gunto denying the Japanese the option of staging aircraft through them to attack the shipping intended for the Okinawa invasion. On the basis of such evidence Admiral Halsey was ultimately able to integrate the British task force tactically into the Third Fleet for the final USN attacks on the home islands; in the face of not inconsiderable opposition from Admiral King.

As the *Chicago Daily Tribune* reported in June 1945 'Cooperation in the Pacific between British and American forces is forging a new link toward permanent peace.' Admiral Rawlings was quoted at a news conference saying

> At the bottom of everybody's heart is the feeling that if the Americans and us stick together our children and grandchildren will not face another war like this. When you learn to be good fleet mates the stage is set for peace.'[66]

It is obvious from the foregoing that the RN's experience in the Pacific during the final stages of the Second World War did expose Britain's decline as a naval power when faced with the scale of the USN capabilities. But the central task of the RN's commitment to the Pacific at the military and grand strategic level was political. It wedded together the two navies despite the problems of an extremely complex command arrangement. The consequences of the British not participating in the final stages of the war against Japan, in the most advanced operations, would have been severe and long-lasting in the minds of those who had become their most important ally. As Rawlings summed it up to Admiral Fraser:

> I know that I've been inexcusably rude and brusque. But you know more of human nature than I do and so you will realise that for quite longish periods I have had but one anxiety – and that was that never under any circumstance must we fail to keep our undertakings and appointments with the Americans. For me that mattered far more than who won any battle or whether ships got hit ... I felt that if we did not emerge with the poor old White Ensign looked up to, respected and admired, that if we gave any part of the Americans any opportunity to say 'the British have quit' or 'can't take it' – then something might be lost that could perhaps never be regained.[67]

The British had sought to replace dominance at sea with influence on the dominant sea power. The country would remain a maritime dependent nation and the alliance under-pinned by the naval commitment of the BPF would form the bedrock of her post-war defence policy.

## Notes

1 The staff consisted of Flag Lt Vernon Merry, Fraser's CoS Cdre Evans-Lombe Asst CoS (Plans) Capt. Brown, Int Officer Lt Cdr Charles Sheppard, Gp Capt. Kearey RAF, Fraser's secretary Capt. Allfrey and the two Wrens, Second Officer Nancy Bond and Stella Brown.
2 R. Humble, *Fraser of North Cape*, Routledge & Kegan Paul Plc (London 1983), p. 251.
3 H. P. Willmott, *Just Being There*, Paper presented to the Institute of Historical Research for the Julian Corbett Prize in Modern Naval History 1986 p. 2.
4 N. E. Sarantakes, *The Short but Brilliant Life of the British Pacific* Fleet *Joint Forces Quarterly*, 40 (1) 2006, p. 85.
5 The National Archives (hereafter TNA) ADM 199/2376 Report of Experience of the BPF January–August 1945 15/3/46.
6 C. Barnett, *Engage the Enemy More Closely*, Penguin Books (London 2000), p. 877.
7 See H. P. Willmott, *Grave of a Dozen Schemes: British Naval Planning for the War Against Japan, 1943–1945*, Airlife Publishing (London 1996), pp. 111–134.
8 E. J. King and Whitehill W. M., *Fleet Admiral King: A Naval Record*, Eyre & Spottiswoode (New York 1953), p. 360.
9 E. B. Potter, *Nimitz*, Naval Institute Press (Annapolis 1976), pp. 323–324.
10 *Fleet Admiral King* op. cit. p. 361.
11 *Nimitz* op. cit. pp. 323–324.

12 S. E. Morison, *History of the USN in WWII, Vol. XIII The Liberation of the Philippines*, Oxford University Press (Oxford 1959), p. 257.
13 *Fleet Admiral King* op. cit. p. 361.
14 Admiral of the Fleet Viscount Cunningham of Hyndhope, *A Sailors Odyssey*, Hutchinson & Co. (London 1951), p. 612.
15 Cdr Charles Sheppard, quoted in Humble, *Fraser of North Cape*, Routledge (London 1983), p. 252.
16 *Nimitz* op. cit. pp. 347–348.
17 MS 83/158 File 20 Lord Fraser of North Cape Papers National Maritime Museum (hereafter Fraser Papers) Message from COMINCH and CNO 12-11-44.
18 MS 83/158 File 20 Fraser Papers, Admiralty Message December 44 – report of conversation between General Lumsden and MacArthur concerning British Fleet being assigned to SW Pacific.
19 Highball – a variant of the 'bouncing bomb' bomb, designed for use against shipping. No 618 Squadron RAF, flying Mosquito's, began trials in April 1943, finally reaching the Far East in January 1945. Highball was never employed and the squadron disbanded in July 1945. XE craft were a type of midget submarine, 33 tons submerged displacement, underwater endurance of 80 miles and a crew of five.
20 MS 83/158 File 20 Fraser Papers. Brief for CINCBPF. Subjects for Discussion at Pearl Harbor.
21 *Nimitz* op. cit., p. 347, 348–349.
22 MS 83/158 File 20 Fraser Papers CINCBPF to Admiralty following N/F1 Pearl Harbor Agreement.
23 MS 83/158 File 23 Fraser Papers Letter from First Sea Lord to Admiral Fraser 5/7/45.
24 MS 83/158 File 23 Fraser Papers Letter From CinCBPF to First Sea Lord17/7/45.
25 MS 83/158 File 23 Fraser Papers Letter from CinCBPF to First Sea Lord 14/3/45.
26 MS 83/158 File 20 Fraser Papers Report from Admiralty to CinCBPF December 1944.
27 TNA PREM 3/164/4 Lumsden to Ismay 30/12/44.
28 MS 83/158 File 20 Fraser Papers Report from Admiralty to CinCBPF December 1944.
29 TNA, ADM 223/494 US Intelligence Organization in the Pacific.
30 MS 83/158 File 20 Fraser Papers, see correspondence between British Admiralty Delegation (BAD) Washington and Admiralty contained in.
31 For a fuller discussion see J. Robb-Webb *Anglo-American Naval Intelligence Cooperation in the Pacific 1944–45 Intelligence and National Security*, vol. 22 no. 5, October 2007, pp. 767–786.
32 MS83/158 File 23 Fraser Papers Signal to First Sea Lord 17/7/45.
33 MS83/158 File 23 Fraser Papers, CinC Operational Correspondence with Flag Officers, Letter First Sea Lord to CinCBPF 19/1/45.
34 Rawlings to Cunningham April 1945, quoted in M. Robson *Not Enough Room to Swing a Cat*, Conway (London 2008), p. 133.
35 Nimitz Papers Serial 1 Command Summary Book 6, Washington Navy Yard, 12/2/45 12037 CINCBPF to CINCPAC.
36 Nimitz Papers Serial 1, Signals 190701, 190715 and 190720 CINCBPF to CINCPAC ADV HQ.
37 Ibid.
38 Nimitz Papers Serial 1, Signal 192306 CINCPAC ADV HQ to COMINCH 19/2/45.

British Pacific Fleet, the decline of empire? 235

39 Nimitz Papers Serial 1, 211635 COMINCH to CINCPOA info CINCBPF, CINCSWPA (Nimitz Only).
40 Ibid.
41 Douglas MacArthur's insistence that President Truman should visit him rather than him reporting to Washington during the Korean War perhaps gives some indication of how the general would have responded.
42 TNA ADM 199/118 op. cit., paragraph 32–48, in particular paragraph 41 details Fraser's change of mind over basing arrangements.
43 MS 83/158 File 23 Fraser Papers Letter from CinCBPF to Admiral Cunningham 2/6/45.
44 TNA, ADM 199/118 op. cit., paragraph 53.
45 The following extract from one of many letters sent to Fraser by Somerville gives something of an indication of BAD's difficulties. Fraser Papers MS 83/158 File 23 Somerville 25/4/45

> I had a hell of an argument on Saturday with Ernie King touching the matter of a base for the BPF, Ernie started off by flying into a rage and saying that the BPF had failed to implement the agreement that it should be self-supporting. I asked in what respect the Fleet had not been self supporting, and he barked in reply 'Food.' I told him I was surprised to hear this in view of the large quantities of food which Australia is supplying to the American Fleet, and I should have thought the BPF would not have had much difficulty in obtaining what they wanted from one of our own dominions. Ernie then became hotter than ever and asked if I wished an itemised list of deficiencies; I said yes, and went on to add that his general demeanour and violence seemed to suggest that he regarded the BPF as a pain in the neck to him, and that possibly he felt quite satisfied he could complete the war against Japan quickly and effectively without any assistance from the British. If he thought so he had better say so. Ernie then asked me if I expected him to give an answer to this, and I said 'No,' he wouldn't have the guts to do it. By this time the temperature having reached boiling point, I told Ernie it was a little odd that we should be fighting like this and suggested we might discuss this matter reasonably and with the heat turned off.

46 TNA ADM. 199/1457 British Pacific Fleet Brief Account of Activities paragraph 14.
47 TNA ADM 199/555 BPF Actions in Operation Meridian and Iceberg. Report from Office of Vice Admiral Second in Command BPF 9/5/45 covering initial stages of ICEBERG 26/3/45–20/4/45.
48 Nimitz Papers Serial 1, 30 May 300526 CINCPAC ADV to COMINCH and CNO.
49 TNA ADM 199/118 op. cit., paragraph 40.
50 Nimitz Papers Serial 1, 30 May 300526 CINCPAC ADV to COMINCH and CNO.
51 Nimitz Papers Serial 1, 30/5/45 301225 CINCPAC ADV to CINCBPF info CTF37 from BPFLO.
52 Nimitz Papers Serial 1, 5/6/45 050612 CINCPAC ADV to CINCBPF Info COMINCH CINCPAC PEARL COM3RDFLT COMSERON10.
53 Fleet Admiral W. F. Halsey and J. Bryan III, *Admiral Halsey's Story*, McGraw-Hill Book Company (New York 1947), p. 261.
54 Nimitz Papers Serial 1, 6/6/45 060611 COM3RDFLT to CINCPAC ADV.
55 Nimitz Papers Serial1, 16/6/45 160007 COM3RDFLT to CINCPAC ADV.
56 TNA ADM 199/118 CinCBPF Despatches November 1944–July 1945 para. 94.
57 Ibid., para. 95.
58 Nimitz Papers 17/6/45 170715 CINCPAC ADV to COM3RDFLT.

59 *Admiral Halsey's Story* op. cit. pp. 261–262.
60 MS83/158 File 23 Fraser Papers, 28/4/45 from V. Adm, 2CinC to CinCBPF CinC Operational Correspondence with Flag Officers.
61 TNA ADM 199/1478 Report to CinCBPF from Rawlings 1/10/45.
62 *Admiral Halsey's Story* op. cit. 1947 p. 262.
63 TNA ADM. 199/118 CinCBPF 31/10/45.
64 TNA ADM 199/118 paragraph 96.
65 General James T. Conway, Commandant US Marine Corps, Admiral Gary Roughead, Chief of Naval Operations and Admiral Thad W. Allen, Commandant US Coast Guard, *A Cooperative Strategy for 21st Century Seapower*, Department of the Navy (Washington 2007).
66 *Nimitz Visits British Pacific Fleet United States Naval Institute Proceedings* vol. 71, no. 7, July 1945, p. 866.
67 MS83/158 File 23 Fraser Papers CinC Operational Correspondence with Flag Officers. Undated letter from V. Adm 2CinC BPF to CinC BPF.

# 13 Conclusions

Transitions and futures[1]

*Patrick C. Bratton and Geoffrey Till*

The preceding pages have largely confirmed the Mahanian view that there is a direct linkage between sea power on the one hand and national power and prosperity on the other. Moreover, it seems this linkage is regarded as being of a particular significance in the Asia-Pacific region, and not least because maritime developments might well result in something of a security order significantly different in the future from what it is now. This raises, again, the notion of transitions in maritime power and related questions about what causes them, what forms do they take and what consequences do they have?

## The transition from British to American maritime supremacy

As Paul Kennedy established long ago in his seminal *The Rise and Fall of British Naval Mastery*,[2] the linkages between sea power and national power and prosperity go both ways. Kennedy showed how Britain's growing economic vulnerability, the rise of countries with greater resources and an unsustainable degree of 'strategical over-extension' combined to worsen Britain's position when considered from the viewpoint of the six general preconditions for success singled out by Mahan in his *The Influence of Sea Power on History*.[3] Britain's 'geographical position' was increasingly less advantageous especially with the advent of air and missile power and the shift of strategic weight to the Asia-Pacific. The 'physical conformation' and 'extent of territory' of post imperial Britain were dwarfed by new powers like Russia, the United States and China. Social and political changes have undermined the advantages that Mahan discerned in the 'number of the population' their seafaring 'national character' and even the 'character of the government' – certainly in comparison with the burgeoning economic and maritime powers of Asia.

From the start, the British realised that supreme sea power was not a permanent condition, and that it is not an independent variable, but on the contrary is constantly affected by changing conditions. As such, sea powers inevitably rise and fall as their circumstances change. Thus in the terms of one British government report of 1727: 'Command of the sea has frequently passed from one nation to another, and though Great Britain has continued longer in possession of the superiority than perhaps any other nations did, yet all human affairs are subject to great vicissitudes'.[4] In fact this report was unduly pessimistic as things turned out and British naval mastery had another 200 years or so to run, but the basic point was true enough.

The last two chapters have addressed the issue of how the British adapted to these vicissitudes, and so have provided something of a historical model against which contemporary development in the Asia-Pacific region may be assessed. As we have seen, the process of change, though emphatically less cataclysmic than Japan's doomed attempt to seize maritime supremacy by force from the United States and Britain simultaneously, was nonetheless not without its tensions and difficulties. The relationship was aggravated by America's blossoming national pride and consciousness of its superior economic power during and shortly after the First World War. The launch of the United States Navy's 1916 programme, when Britain was enmeshed in the costly travails of the First World War, was a clear bid for American naval supremacy, and shortly after the First World War, Navy Secretary Daniels threatened another round of naval construction with same aim, thus deeply alarming the British.

Common sense, the public hankering for naval disarmament on both sides of the Atlantic and the bite of economic cut-backs in a time of increasing financial instability had their effect and persuaded both sides to accept 'parity' instead under the Washington naval treaty of 1921–2. There remained, however, a competitive edge to their negotiations at Geneva in 1927 and London 1930 about what 'parity' actually meant in terms, particularly, of cruiser size and numbers. Both sides continued to include each other as putative adversaries in their war-gaming plans.[5] The competitive edge between the British and the Americans only mellowed in the late 1930s as they gradually drifted together in the face of the Japanese challenge. By the second London Conference of 1936, the British were persuaded into the necessity for compromise by an acute awareness of the gap between their resources and their strategic commitments, particularly as their European distractions grew. As Greg Kennedy has noted elsewhere, 'tellingly, in all legitimate British naval planning for the Pacific, the United States was factored in, either as a benevolent neutral or an ally of some degree'.[6] Moreover, the British found themselves operating alongside a navy based on the principle of acquiring overwhelming material superiority – and with the industrial resource to deliver it. This was aptly summed up by Admiral King:

> Naval accomplishments in this mechanized age are dependent upon production. The best officers and men can do little without an adequate supply of the highly specialized machinery of warfare. Our

guiding policy is to achieve not mere adequacy, but overwhelming superiority of material, thereby ensuring not only victory, but early victory with the least possible loss of American lives.[7]

Accepting the consequent role of junior partner was not an easy pill for the British to swallow, and they resented such apparent slights as the American reluctance on some occasions to pass classified operational and/or commercially sensitive material over to their closest ally, with quite the open-handed freedom that the British thought had characterised their own approach to their transatlantic partner.[8] There were significant ideological differences in the clash between the American insistence on the 'freedom of the seas' and Britain's equally determined insistence on 'belligerent rights'. There were even squabbles as late as 1937 over the ownership of remote Pacific islands of potential strategic value, such as Canton Island in the Gilbert and Ellis group.[9]

But, increasingly, the view that the two countries were, after all, 'Anglo-Saxon cousins' with many common political values, steadily developed; in fact neither side took war plans against each other as very much more than a heuristic device for preparing for an uncertain future. Common perceptions of Japanese aggression accelerated the strategic convergence of the two countries especially after the bombing of the USS *Panay* in 1937 when the pro-British American Commander-in-Chief China Harry E. Yarnell wrote that he was,

> Delighted that on completion of the present rearmament program the British navy will assume its proper role in the defense of the Empire. The safety of the Empire means too much in the maintenance of Anglo-Saxon ideals of liberty and good government to be jeopardised.

He later commented 'as for pulling chestnuts out of the fire, England stands to pull just as many out for us as we do for her. If these three[10] countries stand together they can dominate the situation in the Far East. If they do not', he added prophetically, 'they will be defeated singly and in detail'.[11]

The problem was that British enthusiasm for a closer deterrent alliance was not matched in the United States because of the strength of the country's isolationist sentiment in both the public and Congress – and for a certain distaste in being manoeuvred into propping up a decaying imperial construct. The result of this was reluctance to go much further in the period immediately before the further outbreak of hostilities in the Pacific, than for both sides to explore what cooperation between the two would mean in the event of war, with no firm decisions actually to do it being taken.

The British, for instance, were keen, should some kind of Japanese démarche seem imminent, that simultaneous naval 'demonstrations' of the British and American fleets from Singapore and Hawaii (or even better, Manila) respectively would be an effective deterrent, or if that failed, response, to Japanese aggression.[12] As things turned out, the two sides did not get close enough to have that deterrent and peace-keeping effect.[13]

Complacent assumptions about there being time enough to finalise such plans indeed could be said to have had a counterproductive effect, encouraging rather than discouraging the Japanese effort to seize the Trident from the British and Americans. First, the increasing cooperation between the two may well have fed Japanese perceptions of developing strategic encirclement and so contributed to their decision to strike when they did before it was too late. Second, the uncertainty of American support, significantly contributed to early and rapid Japanese success in the Malayan campaign in a variety of ways. For example it undermined the British Operation Matador plan for a pre-emptive invasion of Thailand before the Japanese landed Again, When Admiral Sir Tom Phillips arrived in Singapore with Force Z (the battleship HMS *Prince of Wales* and the battle-cruiser HMS *Repulse*) on 6 December 1941, the Japanese attack was already in train, so as a deterrent the enterprise was clearly a failure. It is possible, moreover, to argue that the Japanese destruction of that force was made more likely by Phillips having to fly straight to Manila to confer with his American opposite number, and the *Repulse* leaving for talks in Australia, so being off-station at the critical time before the Japanese actually struck. The Admiralty had been strongly opposed to the dispatch of such a weak force in the first place, but this was plainly Churchill's response to the pre-war American requirement that such an 'adequate token force' sent to Singapore should contain 'some capital ships'.[14]

But even if the process of strategic convergence was fatally limited by such tensions and hesitations, the groundwork for close cooperation between the two had certainly been laid. Agreement on many practical measures, such as planning transparency, the exchange of communications liaison staff, agreement on communication procedures, the exchange of technical information and so on.[15] By the end of the Pacific campaign in 1945, as we have seen this process of operational and strategic convergence had gone much further, but so also had the divergence in deployed and deployable strength between the United States Navy, the British and, indeed, everyone else. By that time, it was absolutely clear that the United States had taken over as the world's main naval power. From the start, though, it was a maritime supremacy that rested on much more than just American naval power. It also relied on the economic and naval capacities of the United States' leading partners, not least the British. The transition, in other words, developed into a partnership.

## A failed transition: the challenge of the Soviet Union

Almost immediately, though, another potential rival appeared – the Soviet Navy which by the later 1960s and early 1970s seemed to be acting as more and more of a constraint on America's freedom of action in the Mediterranean, the Atlantic and the Pacific. The Western allies took the lessons of the interwar period to heart and did their utmost to ensure that they were able to offer a sufficiently united and effective collective response to see off this maritime challenge, at acceptable cost and without conflict. Although this competition was largely conducted outside the Pacific and so does not constitute a major focus of this volume, it does nonetheless merit a brief review since the apparent strategic imperatives of the Cold War so influenced American policy towards the region in general and especially towards, China, Japan, Korea and Southeast Asia. Moreover, it provides another opportunity to review the causes and impact of superior sea power.

On the face of it, the victory of the West over the Soviet Union may seem, for latter-day Mahanians, to be yet another example of the inevitable triumph of the sea powers over a land-bound and constrained continental adversary. The Soviet Union had gone the way of Napoleon, Wilhelmine Germany and Hitler. NATO (North Atlantic Treaty Organisation), an alliance centred on an ocean, had been able to bring the full resources of overwhelming, global maritime power against an adversary constantly having to worry about its territorial borders, the inevitable inefficiencies of its economy, the political reliability of its allies and the moral resilience of its own people. In the long run, the maritime West was bound to win. Or at least that is what Mahan would probably have thought, had he been around at the time.

But that is *not* how it appeared to Western politicians, analysts and to the soldiers, sailors and airmen of the time – nor to their adversaries in the Soviet Politburo or General Staff during the Cold War. At the time, and indeed since, the 'terrible simplicities' of the Mahanian narrative could seem increasingly irrelevant in the strategic circumstances of the mid-twentieth century for three basic reasons.

First, as far as sceptics were concerned the sea power of a continental state in the form of a growing merchant marine and an increasingly powerful navy seemed likely to be able to exploit the inevitable vulnerabilities of a maritime alliance, especially its geographic dispersion and its total reliance on sea-borne communications. Second, sceptics thought the Western advantage in accumulated naval power could well be 'negated' by technological advance. Particularly during the Khruschev era from 1956 to 1964, they thought nuclear weaponry would render much of the West's naval arsenal obsolete at the level of grand strategy.[16] A Soviet Navy ability to operate a sea-based nuclear deterrent force would 'equalise' the two fleets strategically. Tactically and operationally, asymmetric technologies in the shape of anti-ship missiles and fast torpedoes possibly armed with nuclear warheads would prove a means for keeping Western striking fleets well away from the Soviet coast where they could do most harm. Third and finally, history was claimed to be on the side of the Soviet Union: the tremendous social, collective industrial and military resources of Mackinder's Heartland could therefore be fully mobilised in a way that would cancel out the advantages of Mahanian sea power and free-market economics.[17]

In the end though, the Mahanian narrative stood the challenge. The Western economic system proved much better able to sustain the levels of expenditure and technological effort required to win the military race for supremacy at sea; sea power held the alliance together in a manner which confronted the Soviet Navy not just with an accretion in the numbers and skills of their adversaries, but also by an extension in the range of the situations in which it would need to counter them in any strategic venture against the West. Moreover, The Maritime Strategy of 1986, despite its Western critics, convinced Soviet leaders that the initiative was being wrested from their grasp.

The purpose of The Maritime Strategy, as described by George Baer 'was to establish an internal consensus on the offensive value of the forward-deployed, big fleet triphibious Navy and, with Mahan's admonitions ever present, to engage public as well as professional support'.[18] It was an unashamedly offensive plan to seize the initiative by taking on the Soviet fleet in Europe's northern waters and the North West Pacific, thereby providing the conditions for the most effective defence of NATO's sea lines of communication (SLOC) across the Atlantic, strikes on the opponent's home territory and the support of forward allies like Norway, South Korea and Japan. The strategic aim was to improve the 'correlation of forces' on the central front, by posing an outflanking threat to the north and threatening the Soviet Union's all-important ballistic missile submarines.[19] No longer could the apparent superiority of their land forces on the Central Front be assumed to be the decisive factor.

Finally, Western sea power rescued the West from the prospect of being so pre-occupied with the defence of Europe that it ignored the fate of the outer world, where, in Mr Khruschev's opinion, the decisive struggle between socialism and capitalism was really going to be played out, not least because of the importance of the Third World as a market and a source of oil and other strategic materials.

Putting this all together, the Mahanian narrative would seem substantially to have prevailed. At the very least, the defensive and potentially offensive naval capabilities of what was essentially a maritime alliance helped prevent it from *losing* the strategic competition with a constrained landpower that had resolved to go to sea. But, by that very fact of not losing, the United States and the Western alliance, given its economic and industrial advantages, was likely in the end to prevail, and the challenge to

American sea power represented by the Soviet Navy to fail. Fortunately, in this case, it did not take a conflict to prove the point.

But now, in the early twenty-first century, some would argue, American sea power faces its biggest challenge in the putative rise of China in the developing security environment of the Asia-Pacific region. A host of questions arise. Are we witnessing another historic transition in the world's power balance? To what extent is this shift both caused and exemplified by sea power? If such a transition is indeed taking place, what will be its manifestations and its consequences both for the region and the world? Is China's rise simply the most obvious manifestation of a general shift in the strategic balance between East and West? It seems right to conclude this volume with a final review of some of these issues by considering two admittedly inter-related questions:

- Are we witnessing a new period of transition in which maritime power is transferred from West to East and from the United States to China?
- What form might such transition take and what consequences might it have?

## A transition from West to East, from the United States to China?

One of the great emerging issues in the political literature of the early twenty-first century is proving to be the contention that 'we are living through the end of 500 years of western ascendancy'.[20] There is a developing consensus that Asia-Pacific concerns will play a much more important role in shaping the international context than it has done for several centuries. Across the spectrum of debate there is little doubt that 'Asia is poised to increase its geopolitical and economic influence rapidly in the decades to come'.[21] This is an enormously complex, open-ended issue with inter-related economic, political, social, cultural and military dimensions which has yielded a vast literature ranging in both depth and support for the basic proposition from popular books such as Kishore Mahbubani's *The New Asian Hemisphere: The Irresistible Shift of Global Power to the East* and more scholarly, narrower books such as Yasheng Huang's *Capitalism with Chinese Characteristics* which looks just at economic aspects of the situation.[22] Some like Martin Jacques go on to argue that the long-term consequence of this will not be a world much like the present but with someone different at the head of the table but one based on a set of governing and operating principles more collective, less individual, more state-centric and less liberal system-centred, more authoritarian, less democratic; the Yuan will replace the dollar, Mandarin will take over from English. Globalisation with Chinese characteristics, in other words.[23]

Economic developments have been most responsible for this putative shift in the world balance. Compared to the United States or Europe the

Asia-Pacific region in general and China in particular appear to have survived the 2007–9 economic crisis in much better shape than either the United States or Europe, and indeed China has recently over-taken Germany as the world's largest exporter.[24] The increased visibility of the G20 (of which nine economies come from the Asia-Pacific) rather than the G8 in the resolution of the current recession exemplifies this shift in relative economic weight.

The growth of China's economic capacity is the clearest evidence of this. China's gross domestic product (GDP) growth rates have been fantastic, recording a tenfold increase between 1978 and 2004, compared to fourfold for the United Kingdom between 1830 and 1900. According to the World Bank, 'China and India have emerged in recent years as drivers of global economic growth, accounting for 2.9 percentage points of the 5 percentage growth in global output in 2007'. As a result, China accumulated a current account surplus of 10 per cent of GDP, while the United States on the other hand accounted for more than half the world's current account deficit at 6 per cent of GDP.[25] A highly effective government stimulus programme and massive credit expansion drawn from the world's biggest accumulated reserves (which is in turn have derived from high levels of both savings and foreign investment), meant it recovered quickly from the crisis of 2007–9, with export levels, 17 per cent higher in 2009 than for 2008.[26] In 2000, the US GDP was eight times larger than China's; now it is only four times larger, and, according to Jim O'Neill, Goldman Sachs' chief economist, will overtake the United States in 2027.[27] Many such as Professor Victor Sit of Hong Kong Baptist University indeed argue that China's economic achievements to date should be seen essentially as providing the foundation for a 'Second Global Shift' into a more sophisticated kind of economic prowess.[28]

These extraordinary rates of growth have been mirrored elsewhere in Asia and have resulted in increasing levels of economic inter-dependency. For the first time for very many years, Asia's future economic development is will be based on Asian money since eight of the ten biggest holders of reserve currencies are now to be found in the region. These facts seem bound to transform the nature of the world economy. The United States, India, China and Japan are projected by Goldman Sachs to be the world's four biggest economies by 2040, with extensive global interests based on the need for markets and for raw materials.[29] But this dependence cuts both ways. China for example has developed massive trade surpluses with most other areas and is now one of the world's biggest holders of reserve currencies. As a result, China is increasingly susceptible to systemic currency fluctuations and to major drops in demand for its goods from the United States and Europe. In all these ways the Asia-Pacific in general and China and India in particular[30] have become major determinants of the world trade system. The region's economic prowess is exemplified by new levels of confidence around the region as it bounces out of a recession that has left the West floundering. This optimism compares most strikingly with the general angst, for example, about American competitiveness.[31]

Much of this is due to the countries of the Asia-Pacific regions being increasingly able to exploit the sea as a means of transportation. The Asia-Pacific's geography, sea-based trade, energy flows and security concerns means that the region's strategic order is profoundly maritime. For this reason, 'geopolitically speaking, the maritime balance would appear to be the key to future stability in Asia',[32] especially now that India and China have rediscovered their maritime dimensions after centuries of comparative neglect. In May 2007, for the first time, the Chinese Navy helped rescue a valuable cargo of export and other Song dynasty treasures lost in the *Nanhai No 1* a ship wrecked 800 years ago.[33] This nicely illustrates China's re-discovery of a maritime past largely lost in the early part of the fifteenth century, after the epic voyages of the Chinese mariner Zheng He, when the Ming dynasty consciously turned away from the sea.[34] Aware of its absolute economic dependence on marine transport and animated by one of the world's most coherent long-term maritime plans, China has developed into an all-round maritime player. Some 90 per cent of the world's containers are manufactured in China.[35] Within the past decade, energetic state-led enterprise and the development of greenfield sites have led China to become the world's third-largest ship-builder after Japan and Korea. Chinese ports are expanding at a bewildering rate. Shanghai is now the world's largest cargo port and is putting considerable pressure on both Hong Kong and Singapore as container ports. Uncomfortable with an excessive reliance on foreign shipping, China first set up the China Ocean Shipping Company and then to provide internal competition and the efficiencies that come with it, China Shipping Container Lines. These have both become major international shipping concerns and operate on a global scale, being the sixth- and eighth-largest shipping companies in the world respectively.

Although the Chinese re-discovery of the critical importance of the sea is the most marked, much the same can said of India, Japan and the rest of the Asia-Pacific too. The percentage of the GDP of East Asia that derived from international sea-based trade rose from 47 per cent in 1990 to 87 per cent in 2006.[36] The raw energy of the new centres of industrial production in China are balanced by the more sophisticated marine services industry of Hong Kong and Singapore, places which still see a slow drift of European expertise out to these areas.

Historically, growth in GDP is strongly, though not inevitably, correlated with naval expenditure and, given the maritime basis of much of that growth, it is perhaps hardly surprising that there is remarkable expansion in the size, composition and operational aspiration of local fleets. Naval modernisation plans in the region were stalled by the Asian currency crisis of 1997–8, and their recovery further interrupted by the global credit crisis a decade later; even so, fleet re-construction is surging ahead. The

US-based naval consultancy firm AMI International anticipates a naval spend in the Asia-Pacific of US$173 billion by 2030; the Asia-Pacific naval market as a whole is 'expected to move past NATO countries to become the second-largest source of future naval spending after the United States'. Asia already spends more on defence in general than does Europe. According to the French naval armaments firm DCNS, the Asia-Pacific region was considered 'as a future centre for defence business ... The defence market in the Asia-Pacific should be, in about 2016, a major market – even above the United States'.[37]

This surge in naval spending is manifested by the acquisition around the region of such high-intensity capabilities as anti-submarine warfare (ASW) – especially of the blue-water kind – anti-air warfare, ballistic missile defence, the development or maintenance of sea-based strategic deterrent forces – all of which tend to make most sense when planners have relatively sophisticated conventional adversaries in mind. Well over 70 per cent of the Asia-Pacific's projected naval spending over the next 20 years will be taken up by submarines, destroyers, frigates and amphibious warfare vessels.[38] By contrast, the percentage of the projected total spend taken up by the kind of auxiliaries, OPVs and patrol craft associated with the maintenance of good order at sea is comparatively small at around 7 per cent.

In general, the region's navies are seeking much more advanced, first class platforms, weapons and systems, rather than the re-conditioned, second hand, or new but modest equipment they generally received in the past. Whether it is Korea's Aegis destroyers, Malaysia's Scorpene-class submarines or Indonesia's Sigma class corvettes, there is now a new insistence on high quality acquisitions. This kind of modernisation tends to produce navies that while not necessarily larger are certainly more powerful. While the tendency towards more powerful surface forces is the more obvious indicator of growth in aspiration, the region's development of submarines seems just as significant, not least for its force-equalisation potential. The growth of the region's interest in network-enabled operations may in the end prove even more significant in enhancing its naval power. Finally, another important aspect of the region's naval advance has been a determination to build up national capacities for indigenous production. In contrast to the Western climate of recession and retrenchment many countries of the area have significantly expanded their capacity to produce the naval platforms they need themselves.

With all this new technology comes an expanding operational reach. The South Korean, Malaysian, Singaporean navies have all participated for the first time in increasingly blue-water anti-piracy operations off the coast of Somalia, joining other smaller Asia-Pacific navies like the Australians and the New Zealanders, alongside the Americans, Chinese, Indians and Japanese. Singapore indeed has taken charge of Combined Task Force 151, operating in the Gulf of Aden, and participated for the first time in the US RIMPAC exercise off Hawaii in June and July 2008.[39] This has included a set of new and challenging missions, or old ones interpreted in more ambitious ways. The latter is perhaps most obvious in terms of the protection of national interests off-shore. The countries of South East Asia for example are showing more signs of taking the defence of good order in their territorial seas and Exclusive Economic Zones (EEZs) much more seriously than they used to by acquiring the necessary equipment, beginning to enact enabling legislation and cooperating amongst themselves.

Even the smaller navies of the Asia-Pacific region are demonstrating a new level of determination to develop both their concepts and their capabilities for traditional sea control and maritime power projection operations. Given such developments around the region, it is not surprising that of the world's 21 biggest navies no less than eight come from the Asia-Pacific (excluding Russia and the United States).

The growth of the navies of the Asia-Pacific seems to contrast most forcefully with the decline of those of the West and especially Europe, where the near universal story is of reducing budgets, smaller inventories and greater problems in meeting increasing commitments. The emerging naval balance between China and the United States is often presented as the starkest strategic consequence of such momentous developments. China's rise, not just as a continental power with a huge population, a vast geographic area, with nuclear weapons and relative imperviousness to large-scale overland attack, but as a developing naval and maritime power too, fundamentally changes things. Because of its growing and absolute dependence on overseas commodities, energy and markets, China, like the rest of the Asia-pacific region has little choice but to become more maritime in its orientation. Almost inevitably it is developing more ambitious naval forces, and even more significantly, the maritime industries that historically tend to go with it. Almost equally inevitably, these will challenge the strategic primacy of the United States in a geographic area hitherto dominated by American naval power; as such this momentous development could easily degenerate into the levels of competition and conflict that have until now often characterised great changes in the relative power of great states.[40] US sensitivity to these developments is reflected in the current US naval preoccupation with political, technological and operational ways of maintaining their current levels of access to the waters of the Western Pacific, in these new and more challenging circumstances.

But against all this, there is the argument that the current margin of superiority of the United States Navy is such that all these developments will not have material effect on the overall naval balance between East and West. Despite the narrowing of the gap indicated by simply measuring the reducing numerical margin of superiority enjoyed by the US Navy is still far ahead of all others in its size, technological sophistication and global reach. True though this is, current margins of superiority are likely to be reduced in the future by declining naval appropriations over the next few years. The navy currently has 280 ships and is aiming at the provision of

313 approximately to meet the future operational requirements of two medium wars against regional adversaries plus permanent presence levels of readiness recommended by the Bottom-up Review of 1993 and the QDRs (Quadrennial Defense Reviews) of 1997 and 2001. Estimates of the numbers of ships needed for this target have varied between 300 and 346.[41]

Over the past five years, naval appropriations have averaged at $11.1 billion per year, but the Congressional Budget Office has concluded that $20–22.4 billion per annum (nearly twice as much) would be needed to meet the navy's target of 313 ships. That target is therefore likely to be unaffordable, not least in view of the rising level of federal debt and projected US spending on social welfare.[42] Moreover, as many commentators have pointed out the existing force level of 280 ships is the smallest since 1916. Finally, the United States' capacity to stay in the maritime lead is conditioned by its industrial capacity to produce the necessary equipment but 'for the first time since 1890 ... the US Navy is faced with the prospect of competing against a potentially hostile naval power possessing a ship-building capacity that is equal to if not superior, to its own'[43] – in some respects at least.

Other factors have also to be entered into the calculation, most particularly a sense of what the United States Navy has to do with what it's got. The real strength of a navy, relative or otherwise is not the number of units that it has, or their relative sophistication, but how these compare to the requirements of the tasks that it will have to perform. In this more nuanced mode of assessment the sheer diversity of the United States Navy's capabilities will reflect the extraordinarily varied scenarios for which it feels it has to prepare. US naval planners base their acquisitions, among other things, on a need to conduct two medium scale conflicts with regional adversaries simultaneously, while maintaining combat credible presence in other areas of concern and sustaining an enduring counter-terrorism mission.

As a result of its diversity of missions naval planners have to prepare against a variety of asymmetric techno-tactical anti-access strategies ranging from terrorists on jet-skis to the anti-ship ballistic missile strategies of the Chinese:[44] 'Indeed Navy planners are so concerned about new anti-ship ballistic missiles that they have articulated the need for about ninety fleet ballistic defence ships'[45] while still satisfying the need to be able to cope with Iranian minefields and fast attack craft. With the same potential force dissipation effect, the United States Navy now feels required to maintain a significant and simultaneous presence in the very different conditions pertaining to the Western Pacific, the Indian Ocean, the Gulf and Red Sea, the Gulf of Aden, the Mediterranean, the Caribbean and to some extent the Atlantic theatres of operation. This all makes it extremely difficult for the United States Navy actually to assemble that concentration of force that Mahan advocated so strongly. This in effect reduces the relative weakness of lesser navies that are less subject to the centrifugal effects of global coverage, and suggests that US margins of superiority at what turns out to be the decisive point could be a good deal closer than a look at raw numbers of platforms would perhaps suggest.

So this, broadly, is the general hypotheses about the rise of Asia and the relative maritime decline of the West, and a quick review of some of the basic evidence adduced in support of the proposition. Because of the region's economic prowess it has both the incentive and the capacity to build up its commercial maritime capabilities and its naval power. The region is doing so very dramatically and with that comes such geopolitical clout that the strategic architecture of the twenty-first century is bound to be unfamiliar, very different and for the West, perhaps frightening.

There is, however, some cause to look a little more closely at this assumption that a major transition of power from West to East in general and China to the United States in particular *is* actually taking place. For a start, one obvious angle is to question the extent to which the Asia-Pacific region can be regarded as a strategic and cohesive entity like the West is often supposed, with rather greater cause, to be. 'When you want to talk to Asia', asked Kissinger famously, 'who do you call?' The geographic extent of the Asia-Pacific region and the huge variety of its countries, peoples, polities and strategic interest and indeed the apparently growing level of strategic competition *inside* the region would certainly appear to raise legitimate doubts about the strategic cohesiveness of the Asia-Pacific region as a whole.

Kishore Mahbubani in his claims for the new dominance of Asia has put considerable stress on the advantages Asia derives from the 'Asian way' of non-interference and the culture of peace. But there do remain significant rivalries in the area, not least between China, India, Japan and Korea. The so called 'trust deficit' between China and India, for example, remains because while bilateral trade is growing it is still very imbalanced and political tensions regarding the border, military modernisation, Pakistan and water supplies persist. As one respected commentator has argued: 'Over the next few decades, the mere avoidance of a major war, whether between China and America, or inside Asia, will require conscious effort and statecraft of a high order'.[46] The prospect of conflict would do particular harm in the Asia-Pacific region where as Mahbubani has pointed out, economic prosperity has depended in large measure on a, perhaps somewhat surprising, level of inter-state and intra-state strife lower than all areas other than Western Europe and North America. Given the extent to which this peace depends on increasing economic integration and prosperity and on the willingness of local states not to engage in potentially transformational arms races that destabilise local balances, a resurgence of nationalist emotions and inter-state competition in the Asia-Pacific region would do major harm to its prospects for global influence – and damage global prospects generally.[47] Accordingly, the notion that as a distinctive whole, the Asia-Pacific region can somehow take control of the world's destiny may seem implausible. The region is far too fragmented for that. Indeed it is possible to argue that much of the residual power of the United States when compared to that of China rests on its capacity to gain substantial support from a variety of other countries within the region.[48] Some have even gone further to argue that the essential role of the United States will be to moderate such tensions amongst the major players of the Asia-Pacific region.[49] In this sense, Asia's rise depends on the United States, the very country whose power it is supposed to supplant!

For all the caveats and nuances, moreover, the United States *is* still the world's main military power and seems likely to remain so for the foreseeable future. In some sense, the figures, impressive or depressing according to one's point of view, speak for themselves. At some US$700 billion in 2009, the United States spends nearly as much on defence as the rest of the world put together but this is still only some 4.4 per cent of GDP – more than most countries, but less than some and in strictly economic terms[50] easily affordable. Certainly even now the United States is nowhere near the level of defence spending that contributed to the fall of the Soviet Union. Moreover, the West, if construed as the United States and its NATO allies, still accounts for about 70 per cent of the world's global defence spending, and if allies such as Japan, South Korea and Singapore are factored in as well the total goes higher still. China's level of defence spending is notoriously hard to measure, but almost any calculation suggests that although China is catching up there remains a huge gap in military spending between the two countries.[51]

While the United States Navy's planned expansion to a future fleet of 313 ships may prove unaffordable, its *current* level of 280 ships seems overwhelming. In the heyday of its global power, the Royal Navy could sometimes achieve a two-power standard, that is, its forces were equivalent to the fleets of its next two rivals combined. In straight numbers of major combatant terms, the United States Navy also has a two-power standard over the Chinese and Russian fleets with 203 ships to their 205. But in themselves, numbers count for little. Indeed the Royal Navy was rarely able to achieve a two-power standard and for much of its period of dominance actually deployed fewer ships than its immediate adversaries.

Tonnage, is a better indication of strength since the offensive and defensive power of an individual unit is usually a function of its size. If we look instead at aggregate tonnage, the United States Navy has a 13-power standard, with a 2.63:1 advantage over a combined Russian–Chinese fleet, which in any case includes many ships and submarines that are not in fact combat-ready. Its 11 fleet carriers and ten light carriers provide a nine-power standard, and they operate 980 aircraft, twice as many as those carried on all 16 carriers of the next nine countries. In major surface combatants, factoring in the advantage that the United States Navy possesses through its below deck vertical launch missile systems, its 105 warships transform a comfortable numerical two-power standard into an effective 20-power standard. Its 56 SSN (nuclear attack submarine)/SSGN (nuclear guided missile submarine) fleet might on the face of it seem overpowered by the world's other 220 SSNs and SSKs (diesel submarine) but the qualitative advantages of the US submarine force are huge. It is much the same story in regard to the United States Navy's amphibious and crucial support fleets, in its capacity to support special forces operations, in its broad area maritime surveillance capabilities, in its US Coast Guard (the equivalent of many of the world's navies) and in the enormous advantages conferred by the experience of many decades of 24/7 oceanic operations.[52] It will be many years before this commanding global lead in deployable naval power is seriously compromised:

> The consensus of sources is that the size and level of operational experience of the US Navy and Air Force makes it nearly impossible for potential opponents to mount a serious challenge in the waters and air space over the world's oceans. This is likely to continue until 2035.[53]

Another factor often forgotten is that of the world's next 20 fleets in aggregate tonnage terms, no less than 18 are allies of the United States; of these 13 are formal allies, including nine from NATO Europe, the remainder being reliably friendly. NATO Europe's fleets already reach high levels of cooperation with the United States Navy and the latter's new maritime strategy, *A Co-operative Strategy for 21st Century Seapower*[54] is expressly designed to develop spread such levels of cooperation still further.

Turning to the wider maritime rather than largely naval scene, the counter-case to the 'Asia Rising' school of thought which Kishore Mahbubani exemplifies so well, is represented by Razeen Sally's devastating critique of India's economic performance and Minxin Pei's more general review of Asian prospects. Minxin Pei concludes: 'Don't believe the hype about the decline of America and the dawn of a new Asian age. It will be many decades before China, India and the rest of the region take over the world if they ever do'.[55] So, what are the issues of apparent contention?

Given the maritime emphasis of this volume, the maritime economy is the obvious place to start. There are several points to be made. First China's ship-building strengths are focused at the low end of the industry with the deficiencies in quality assurance, skills, innovation and experience to be expected from an industry in the first flush of youth. Outside expertise has still to be brought to bear. Second, things will of course get better, but then the main losers will not be Europe or the West which has already abandoned large-scale ship-building but other parts of the Asia-Pacific, specifically Japan and Korea. Third, there are areas where Western/European expertise is likely to remain for the foreseeable future, not least in the construction of passenger liners, specialist craft like dredgers, oil support ships and the like and in the support services like marine insurance, brokerage and chartering. Indeed in recent years Europe's marine industries have bottomed out, even showing signs of a modest recovery – until the recession that is. There has been a large increase in the proportion of the world's mariners that come from Eastern Europe, moreover. The conclusion that might emerge from all this is that the maritime drift from West to East may well have largely ended and in the future is likely to follow a different, less dramatic trajectory than it did in the past.

Moreover, many commentators on economic growth in the Asia-Pacific region, and most specifically in China have a tendency to confuse size with strength. Strength, as has already been remarked, is really the relationship between capacity on the one hand and on what needs to be done on the other. In China's case, questions may properly be asked about both.

First, the underlying strength of the Chinese economy is increasingly being questioned. Chinese manufacturing success for example relies on components and designs taken in from outside and seems to be mostly in labour-intensive, low priced consumer items of reasonable quality; China remains far behind Japan or Germany, when it comes to technological innovation, and the export of machinery and other high-value products. China has no brand in the world's top 100.[56] 'Chinese' products exported to Europe moreover are often manufactured in several different Asian countries, of which China is last in the chain, with comparatively low 'value-added' and correspondingly lower trading benefits, compared to other Asian countries.[57] All this bears a superficial resemblance to the relationship that Japan had to the United States in the 1960s, but China, according to Toshio Egawa, is unlikely to make the transition to advanced economy as the country's elite tend to go into bureaucracy rather than manufacturing industry.

Moreover, some would argue that much of this is based on a Yuan estimated by the *Economist*'s Big Mac Index to be 50 per cent undervalued and is sustained by a level of debt far higher than the $840 billion in public debt officially disclosed by the Chinese government economy, while the People's Bank of China and the Treasury are owed in an economy over-heated by easy credit, potentially $1.5 trillion by cities, provinces and the entities they control.[58] To a variety of academics and financial analysts this, described as 'growth on steroids', all looks disturbingly like Japan before the great fall: a bubble waiting to burst, and a dire threat not just to China but to the whole economy of the rest of the world, not least because China is far from being the only country saddled with threatening levels of debt.[59] But even if the predictions of such doomsters do prove wide of the mark, China is still clearly going to have problems trying to run an economy and a society of 1.3 billion people with authoritarian planned capitalism. For instance, there is still a long way to go before China enjoys the adherence to legality and transparency of information associated with economic advance, and which are the prime means by which market capitalism and democracy have interacted to produce an explosion in GDP between 1750 and 2000:[60] 'The dictates of modern economics demand that Chinese traders, entrepreneurs and bankers must have the same access to global information flows that their economic competitors in other modern societies have'.[61] This calls for transparency of information, and a greater adherence to legality but some would argue that China is moving away from such necessary standards rather than towards it in a manner which will constrain its future growth.[62]

On top of this, China certainly has a multitude of domestic problems to face – an aging population,[63] massive numbers of people moving from countryside to town, acute environmental hazards and lax standards, and gross administrative deficiencies, not least endemic corruption,[64] which the 2005 Transparency International Corruption Index measured as pushing China down to seventy-eighth position in the world, its worst ever performance.[65] A recent study by the World Bank claims that China has 16 of Asia's 20 most polluted cities and the UNDP 2005 *Human Development Report* showed that over the last 25 years, China's levels of social inequality have nearly doubled, fuelling domestic tensions, straining domestic harmony and resulting in locally destabilising explosions of wrath, that, according to official Chinese statistics, are ten times worse in number and seriousness than they were in 1993.[66] For all such reasons, 'China's present leadership is acutely aware that eventually China will have to move to democracy',[67] difficult though that will undoubtedly be.

Because the Chinese economy is increasingly integrated with that of the wider Asia-Pacific region, difficulties here will have widespread effects elsewhere, not least because other countries in the region have their economic, political and domestic difficulties too, which according to Minxin Pei include looming demographic problems, a lack of innovation, low per capita levels of GDP and earnings, deficiencies in the education system.[68] All this, at the very least, is likely to constrain Asian 'dominance' of the twenty-first century.

While there is little doubt that the maritime concerns and strengths of the Asia-Pacific region will be much more important relative to those of the West in the remaining decades of this century, the extent of that transition, its character and possibly its consequences consequently remain uncertain. But with that we should turn to the second and final question to be addressed in this chapter: how conflictual might this transition, should it indeed come to pass, prove to be?

## A conflictual transition from West to East, from the United States to China?

Again two relatively distinct schools of thought seem to be emerging about this. It is also worth making the point that this debate is equally vibrant in

China.[69] Optimists accept the notion of an end to Western maritime dominance but argue that the process need not be conflictual in form or in consequence and may to some extent at least mirror some of the characteristics of the transition from British to American maritime supremacy discussed earlier. Pessimists doubt this. We will start with the latter viewpoint.

Pessimists tend to argue that the notion that serious inter-state competition, and even conflict, is increasingly outmoded by the unifying consequences of a globalised system which emphasizes the common interest of the nations that constitute it, may prove something of chimera. Globalisation is undoubtedly under strain and has failed before, particularly in the period just before the First World War, and it might again, at least in terms of being an economic system that promotes prosperity, peace, stability and international harmony. Even attempts to resolve its economic and political problems, if mishandled, may become a major cause of instability and conflict.[70]

Protectionism is on the rise. Mahbubani cites the EU as being a particularly bad example with its agricultural subsidies.[71] George Soros worries that the current recession may well lead to financial protectionism in which governments are forced to adopt their own regulatory mechanisms, because as the United Kingdom found out in relation to Iceland, states cannot afford to rely on foreign-owned banks or the responsibility of overseas regulators.[72] Given the EU's difficulties in agreeing an international regulatory system, what hope for the rest of the world? Fuelled by such worries, concerns about the ultimate survivability of the current system, in the aftermath of the 2007–9 recession abound.[73]

Such a weakening of the system could well lead into a relapsing future world in which national interests *do* still matter at least as much as they used to, and in which competition and confrontation become more the order of the day than cooperation. Perhaps this was the real lesson of the Copenhagen climate control conference of 2009. Its failure to agree legally binding environmental regulations was, by many, specifically blamed on China's determined pursuit of its own national interests because of its perception that fixed long-term goals would jeopardize its economic growth.[74] It is easy to imagine a great range of other future quarrels, from the consequences of China's poor human rights record[75] to increased levels of rivalry over sources of energy and other raw materials, especially if China adopts the strategically mercantilist approach to such issues that some analysts foresee.[76] This may challenge the rather comforting assumptions of those who believe that a plenitude of key resources (energy, food, water) mean that the cake of the world economy will continue to grow in size, satisfying everyone, more or less. Instead we may be faced with a more turbulent future in which inter-state conflict cannot be ruled out.

Should this darker, bleaker world materialise, then the issues of transition become more problematic, especially given the particular issues that divide countries like the United States, China and India, this is likely to prove as difficult as it is necessary.[77] As Niall Ferguson succinctly comments, 'major shifts in the balance of power are seldom amicable'. In China, as elsewhere, there are hawks who most definitely do still think in old-fashioned great power politics terms.[78]

Those of a still more pessimistic disposition come to even bleaker assessments, more of Chinese intentions than of Chinese capabilities, although some of these, in the shape of the latest Chinese submarines and stealth fighter aircraft, together with the DF-21D anti-ship ballistic missile are potentially worrying enough. Pointing to such incidents as the harassing of the USNS *Impeccable* by a number of Chinese vessels and the ferocious political reaction to the prospect of the US carrier *George Washington* entering the Yellow Sea in support of South Korea after the sinking of the ROKS *Cheonan*, many commentators argue that China is attempting to assert its power over regional seas in a manner which will undermine the freedom of navigation and America's strategic interests in the region. If to this is added an apparently growing assertiveness in its claims to the islands of both the East and South China seas, and indeed a expanding level of competitiveness with Japan and India as well, a picture forms of an emerging naval hegemon bent on wresting naval supremacy from the United States and its allies.

Accordingly, the United States Navy still thinks of itself as navy under threat. It is not that American admirals believe themselves to be faced with the prospect of war with China; rather it is a matter of a declining ability though the use of its naval forces to shape events in the Western Pacific in the way that Washington would prefer, particularly in regard to the foreign policy choices made by other Pacific nations.[79]

The United States Navy in the Asia-Pacific considers the PLAN (People's Liberation Army Navy) to be 'much bigger and better-armed than necessary for the defense and security that China needs'.[80] In response it could deploy a number of obvious counters, not least significant forces in place, together with early reinforcements. Providing the necessary forwards-based roulement of ships, submarines and aircraft will clearly be a major determinant of the United States Navy's future acquisitions and deployment strategy. Moreover the same requirement accentuates the value of bases in Yokusuka, Guam and Diego Garcia plus available facilities in Singapore and elsewhere, and may lead to a re-allocation of US naval assets from the Atlantic to the Pacific above the current proportions of 58 per cent to the Asia-Pacific region and 42 per cent to the Atlantic.[81] 'They clearly have the potential to put some of our capabilities at risk' former US Secretary of Defence Robert Gates has admitted, 'and we have to pay attention to them. We have to respond appropriately with our own programmes'. The current US intention is to invest enough in programmes such as the much discussed but still uncertain 'air-sea battle concept' for the United States Navy to maintain its strategic edge.[82]

Given this possible range of US responses, the PLAN could not hope to overwhelm the United States Navy for the foreseeable future provided the United States were able to concentrate sufficient assets in the area of concern. But the PLAN would nevertheless seem able to hold the US Pacific Fleet at increasing risk. At the very least, the US Navy's capacity to provide 'dominance on demand' in the waters of Northeast Asia is going to be significantly harder to achieve in the future than it has proved in the past.[83] The need for the US Navy to concentrate its forces in this area is suggested in CS21 where 'combat credible forces' will be provided for the Gulf and Northeast Asia, but only 'globally distributed, mission-tailored forces' elsewhere.[84]

Pessimists tend to conclude, therefore, that there is precious little prospect of the kind of peaceful transition that characterised the transition of British maritime supremacy to the American. This was made possible by the fact that both faced the same clear-cut threats (successively, Germany, Japan and the Soviet Union), and both had substantial cultural, social, economic and historic linkages spanning several centuries. For this reason, the long period of British naval dominance was not thought of a military threat to the United States through the nineteenth century and into the early twentieth; conversely the rise of American power was never considered a *strategic* threat to British security thereafter. It was possible moreover for both countries, the now dominating power and the country it supplanted, to enter into an active and positive strategic partnership. It is by no means clear that much of this applies as yet to the currently strained relations between China and the United States or their shared future, for all their mutual trading interests.

Optimists, however, propose that the rise of China need not be a cause for concern, for China will not be an imperialist power like the Europeans were in the eighteenth and nineteenth centuries or Japan tried to be in the twentieth. Instead its policy will be based on 'an instinctive hierarchical order' with assumptions of a degree of deference from its neighbours but much less of a proclivity to intervene in their affairs or to project its power very far from Asian shores.[85] China is, such commentators argue, a different kind of non-Western 'civilisational' state, even if one distinguished by a marked 'superiority complex'.[86] China, in short, is said to be a different kind of state whose 'peaceful rise', were this to materialise, would not represent a strategic threat, even if it does continue to expect a degree of deference from its neighbours.[87] China in other words does not, according to this argument, 'do' dominance in the way the West has.

Provided the United States 'makes room' for an emerging China, according its interests the respect they deserve, there need not be anything like the strategic competition, and the disastrous consequences, that characterised the British triumph of sea power over the French in the eighteenth century or the failed twentieth-century attempts of Germany, Russia and Japan to wrest naval mastery from the leading maritime powers of the day.[88] Instead, the peaceful transitions and adjustments of the transition from British to American naval mastery might be more the order of the day.

In any case forecasts of the West's imminent doom seem often to reflect much exaggerated views of the actual extent of Western power, both maritime and economic in the past. The allegedly 'dominating power' has often proved more constrained and limited at the time than it does in nuanced retrospect. The European 'moment' of dominance for example was shorter and much less total, more conditional than often assumed. Its 'rise' was at least as much due to the transient passing weaknesses of others as it was to European strengths. Indeed as late as 1820, Western Europe's share of global GDP was just 23.6 per cent compared to Asia's 59.2 per cent. For centuries before that, in fact, Asia was the largest player in the world economy.[89] Europe's domination of the world system only came with the onset of industrialisation at the end of the eighteenth century, a sophisticated system of credit that could finance distant enterprise and, crucially, command of the sea.[90] Even then, trade was the objective, not the establishment of empire. Where they could, the British in particular were content to trade with advantage as in South America and China (with its treaty ports) without having to assume the burdens of empire. This phenomenon was the result of a unique combination of factors, one of them, the first industrialisation, being much more transformative, in effect, than anything else apparently on offer now.

The same point could be made about the 'American empire' or even of the very idea of empire itself. A few years ago, there appeared a shoal of books and articles arguing that the military and economic might of the United States, when compared to that of all other states made it, not just a superpower, but a hyper-power. As Hubert Vedrine, the former French foreign minister, once proclaimed: 'The United States today predominates on the economic, monetary [and] technological level and in the cultural area ... in terms of power and influence, it is not comparable to anything know in modern history'.[91] The un-admiring Erik Hobsbawm agreed that the United States now

> Occupied a historically unique and unprecedented position of global power and influence. For the time being it is, by the traditional criteria of international politics, the only great power; and certainly the only one whose power and interests span the globe.[92]

From this was born the notion that we were all living in an American empire, like it or not. This supposed fact of life was common ground, even if its consequences were not. Niall Fergusson wondered whether this new empire which dared not speak its name would prove as effective as the British one had been; some wondered whether 'such an empire would serve moral purposes and yet survive and prosper',[93] others just feared the worst.[94] But, in fact, this very recent example of group-think, quickly proved exaggerated, suggesting perhaps a need for caution with the still more confident and pervasive predictions of the 'Asia Rising' school and often about its alarming consequences too.

Moreover, just below the surface, there were and are real doubts about just how substantial *any* kind of empire actually ever was when looked at closely. British imperial historians have for years been making the point that empire rested essentially on sufficient consent of a sort. How else could the British 'rule' India, a region of 225 million to 250 million people with just 1,250 senior civil servants and at most 35,000 British troops?[95] Collaboration, concession and consent were an essential part of the imperial project, even one so apparently based on brutal military power as Spain's.[96] Without at least a degree of consent and collaboration no empire could survive for long. Since power will always beget counter-power,

> Better, and probably more economical in the long run, is a strategy that undercuts the incentives for ganging up [against the imperial power] – to soften the hard edge of [in this case] the US's overwhelming power with the soothing balm of trust.[97]

This requires the imperial power to attend seriously to the interests of others, as all of them sooner or later have had to do. And of course when that consent is gradually withdrawn, empires have collapsed, often because of their essential complexities and fragilities, with bewildering speed.[98] The American 'empire', if it existed at all, could have followed the same path.

Moreover, it was easy to point to the other limitations of power even at the time the critics of the United States were lamenting its extent most loudly. First, it was a democracy with all the constraints that a free press, a cumbersome division of powers, legions of lawyers and a marked reluctance to accept that it *was* an empire could bestow.[99] Accordingly other countries could genuinely wonder 'who rules in Washington?' Easily and often, this could mean the United States was incapable of wielding power as effectively as the more imperialist of its leaders might have wanted, or its opponents might have feared.

Second, the United States had a financial deficit – insufficient savings relative to investment and taxation relative to public expenditure.[100] The US economy, large though it was, was declining in relation to everyone else; it was no longer the centre of global manufacturing, and had stopped being a net exporter of capital, or indeed the main provider of foreign direct investment. Its financial deficit could only be stabilised by East Asian capital – a situation worsened by the sub-prime crisis of 2007, the credit crunch of 2008 and the 'Great Recession' of 2009. Its economic dominance was increasingly dependent on the views and policies of Europe and, especially, of the Asia-Pacific.

Third, the other main source of America's power lay in the military dimension where it seemed beyond competition. After its apparent definitive victories over the forces of darkness in Afghanistan and Iraq, subsequent events in those two unhappy countries cruelly demonstrated the limitations of even America's military prowess. No-one could doubt that prowess when measured in terms of capacity to project kinetic power, or the extent to which Donald Rumsfeld's faith in the Revolution in Military Affairs had indeed transformed the way in which that kinetic power could be dispensed. What was at issue was the extent to which military power of this sort enables the United States or indeed any other modern state to achieve even their most crucial objectives.

Weaknesses in the economic and military bases of America's power may to some extent be compensated for by the third element mentioned by Vedrine, the matter of culture and its attractiveness to others. This could be measured in the spread of McDonalds and Starbucks around the world at one level and, at another, in the global popularity, measured in opinion polls of 'the American idea' of free, democratic and prosperous societies, sometimes as strongly distinct from its leaders. This advantage, arguably, the United States retains, even in China, whose 'modernisation' at least superficially looks a good deal more Americanised, than American development looks 'Sinified'. In the rest of the world it is hard to imagine China's Confucian Institutes for example having the same impact on world consciousness as that enjoyed, for better or ill, by Starbucks or Hollywood.

Beyond the debate about who might dominate whom, there is cause to tackle the deeper issue of whether 'dominance' means much these days anyway. Interestingly the *Newsweek Special 2010* which focused on the issue of 'The End of US Dominance' has on its cover a picture of the huge statue of a dinosaur at Palm Desert, California; but the issue is not so much that the United States is the dinosaur but instead the whole concept of dominance. Many would say that the primacy of individual nations no longer makes sense in an era of globalisation when events are largely decided by economic forces above and beyond the remit of individual states.

In any case there will be other significant players, not least because other states are rising, as well as the India and China which have so captured the public imagination: Brazil, Mexico, South Africa, Saudi Arabia – and Russia. The expansion of the global market with total world output quadrupling since 1980 means that the increased economic weight of such emerging market economies has not come at the expense of the more developed economies. Instead, they are responsible for a bigger slice of a growing global pie.[101] Accordingly, 'there will be no *absolute* losses: most Western states will remain among the most affluent and well-endowed states. However there will be *relative* losses. The relative material superiority the West has enjoyed for centuries will gradually diminish'.[102] We seem, indeed, to be moving into a much less unipolar and more familiarly multipolar world in which responsibility for the direction of the world's affairs is rather more shared than it used to be. Mahbubani puts it like this: 'the world is returning to the historical norm in terms of the natural place of Asian societies in the hierarchy of societies and civilisations around the globe', warning that it would be best for all concerned if the West accommodated itself to that fact.[103] This might be an era of what Richard Haas calls 'non-polarity' a world of a dozen or so major actors, state and non-state 'ordered' by the links that join them.[104] In this conception, even potential global competitors such as China and the United States have things in common that are critical to the peace and prosperity of both; the cycle of China exporting to the United States and then lending it the proceeds that result, for example, has worked well so far and nicely demonstrates such linkages. All the same China and Russia both clearly want to 'facilitate the establishment of a multipolar world and [the] democratisation of international relations'.[105]

The maritime industries, which have been a focus of this volume, illustrate the same point. The merchant shipping industry is famously globalised. The ship's constructors, owners, operators may well come from quite different countries – its crew and cargo being totally international, its flag, chartering, brokerage and insurance insurance arrangements widely dispersed in accordance with commercial convenience. Shipping firms establish local regional offices to be near their customers, so will have a possibly shifting head office somewhere and regional offices spread strategically around the world to exploit taxation and exchange control regimes that make most commercial sense. It is often hard to establish where the centre of gravity or the prime beneficiaries of such global operations actually are. Accordingly, to talk of the manner in which maritime trade is shifting from one area to another is to miss the essential point. In this as in so much else, it is not a question of East versus West, or one part of the world 'against' another. Maritime industry operates over and beyond the purview of regions and still more of national governments; although no-one could doubt that they still influence the process.

From this perspective, transitions of power from West to East may well prove to be more gradual and much less confrontational in process, extent and consequence than is sometimes claimed. After all, China, the United States and all countries to a greater or lesser extent face the same range of problems – such as the financial crisis, organised crime, mass migration, global warming, pandemics and international terrorism which can only be addressed by serious collective action. More states have a significant share in the global economy and, in consequence, an interest in advancing solutions to global challenges. China, the United States, Europe and India all have common interests and consequently a significant stake in global governance and international security.

To the extent this is true, the rising power of one state relative to another will, the argument goes, matter much less than it used to in the pre-globalised world. This may particularly be the case where that power is essentially maritime in nature – and so usually deemed less threatening.[106] The real issue for concern and debate, instead would clearly be about threats to the prosperity and security of the entire international community and about how that community works to head off common challenges. Such problems demand strong and effective governance and international consent rather than dominion, but a degree of leadership, rather in the manner of a chairman of the board, is still likely to be required. At the moment, many would argue, while only the United States can provide this sort of consensus-building leadership, it must do so in partnerships with others, not least China.[107] Thus Henry Kissinger in his September 2010 address to the International Institute for Strategic Studies:

> Neither [the United States and China] has much practice in cooperative relations with equals. Yet their leaders have no more important task than to implement the truths that neither country will ever be able to dominate the other, and that conflict between them would exhaust their societies and undermine the prospects of world peace.[108]

Today, this kind of leadership is indeed exemplified in the critical maritime domain. The absolute dependence of today's globalised sea-based trading system on good order at sea and the safe and timely sailing of the world's merchant shipping means that the world's navies and coastguards need to cooperate against anything that threatens maritime security, whether that take the form of pirates and other forms of maritime crime, direct attack by forces hostile to the system, or from the incidental effects of inter-state and intra-state conflict. This is the burden of the US Navy's recent doctrinal statement *A Cooperative Strategy for 21st Century Seapower* with its avowed aim of helping to set up a 'global maritime partnership'. This emphasis on enhanced maritime cooperation in turn has led to two other US maritime policy responses. First, there has been a need, and corresponding action over recent years, to adapt major traditional US alliance relationships in the Asia-Pacific region – with Japan, South Korea and Australia (and to a lesser extent with the Philippines and Thailand) to the new maritime environment. This has led to much closer maritime cooperation (particularly in distant blue-water deployments, interoperability, and advanced air and missile defences) between the United States Navy and its allied counterparts in Japan, South Korea and Australia.[109]

In addition to adapting critical alliance relationships, the US policy emphasis on maritime cooperation has also spurred a growth in US maritime cooperation with other friends and partners in the Asia-Pacific region who are not formal allies. As part of a broader developing strategic relationship, the US Navy has developed through exercises and closer operational engagement (and now ship and maritime patrol aircraft transfers and sales), a new relationship with the increasingly influential Indian Navy. Further to the east, and beginning earlier in the past decade, the United States has developed closer maritime ties (and valuable facilities access) with Singapore, which has a growing, high-technology navy. Additionally, also beginning in the previous decade, the US Navy has gradually increased maritime operational exercises and exchanges in Southeast Asia with Malaysia, Indonesia, and even to a certain extent, Vietnam. The fact that this has generally been welcomed around the Asia-Pacific region suggests a general acknowledgement of the fact that for the moment at least, in Kishore Mahbubani's words,

> The real reason why most international waterways remain safe and open – and thereby facilitate the huge explosion of global trade we have seen – is that the American Navy acts as the guarantor of last resort to keep them open. Without the global presence of the US Navy, our world order would be less orderly.[110]

For the time being the US Navy seems likely to continue to be the indispensable power but it may well be that a relative shift in naval capacity will provide both the incentive and the opportunity for other navies and coastguards, most obviously those of the Asia-Pacific to take a bigger share in such activities If this does indeed turn out to be the way things go, then the majority of observers might well be tempted to conclude that a possible change in the nature of the naval balance, even if it happened, really wouldn't matter very much, and so is most unlikely to produce the kind of seismic tensions that such transitions have done in the past. Instead, what might be envisaged is more of a 'shared' type of maritime dominance, in which the main outlines of the Mahanian narrative are preserved but exercised by what he described as 'a community of commercial interests and righteous ideals'[111] but comprising a rather different set of navies than Mahan had in mind.

At the moment there are too many uncertainties for anyone to be able to predict reliably which of the two partially competing visions of a putative 'post American' world order will eventually come to pass, but one thing we can be certain of is that their maritime dimension will be crucial, and that naval activity will be both a determinant and an illustration of the result.

## Notes

1 We are indebted to Dr Stan Weeks for his help in the production of this chapter.
2 Paul M. Kennedy, *The Rise and Fall of British Naval Mastery* (London: Macmillan, 1983), pp. 347–349.
3 Alfred T. Mahan, *The Influence of Sea Power on History 1660–1783* (Sampson, Low, Marston & Co Ltd, 1897).

4 Cited in Kennedy, *Rise and Fall*, p. 349.
5 This story is authoritatively told in Stephen Roskill, *Naval Policy Between the Wars: The Period of Anglo-American Antagonism, 1919–1929* (London: Collins, 1968) especially pp. 204–233, 300–330, 433–466.
6 'What Worth the Americans? The British Strategic Policy-making Elite's View of American Maritime Power in the Far East, 1933–1941' in Greg Kennedy (ed.), *British Naval Strategy East of Suez 1900–2000* (London: Frank Cass, 2005), pp. 98–99.
7 Cited, in Peter V. Nash, *The Development of Mobile Logistic Support in Anglo-American Naval Policy 1900–1953* (Gainsville: University of Florida Press, 2009).
8 Ibid., pp. 100–101, 131–132.
9 Michael Simpson (ed.), *Anglo-American Naval Relations, 1919–1939* (London: Ashgate for the Naval Records Society, 2010), p. 235.
10 The third country in question was France.
11 Yarnell, letters of 28 November and 22 December 1937, cited in Simpson *Anglo-American Naval Relations 1919–1939* op. cit. pp. 256, 259.
12 Memorandum for the Chief of Naval Operations, January 1938, cited in Simpson *Anglo-American Naval Relations 1919–1939*, pp. 260–273. Meeting Report of 14 June 1939, cited in ibid., pp. 288–290.
13 Simpson *Anglo-American Naval Relations 1919–1939*, pp. 288–289.
14 Ibid. See my 'Churchill, Strategy and the Fall of Singapore' in Brian P. Farrell (ed.) *Churchill, Singapore and Empire* (Singapore: NUS Press, forthcoming).
15 Simpson *Anglo-American Naval Relations 1919–1939*, pp. 275–278ff.
16 James J. Tritten, *Soviet Naval Forces and Nuclear Warfare* (Boulder, CO: Westview Press, 1986), pp. 215–222.
17 This argument is taken much further in G. Till 'The Cold War at Sea' in Daniel Moran (ed.) *Maritime Strategy and Global Order* (Washington, DC: Georgetown University Press, forthcoming). This in many ways reflected the strange belief during the first decades of the Cold War that the Soviet Union and its allies would materially outpace the West and that it was hopeless to even try to match the Eastern bloc in terms of conventional military forces. For example, in the early 1950s when the number of Red Army divisions in Europe was assumed to be 175, NATO military plans to expand to even 50 divisions failed. Governments that had pushed for the expensive military buildup were forced from office by 1953 and the conventional wisdom took hold that it was impossible for the West to match the material might of the Eastern bloc, this led to the reliance of NATO on nuclear weapons to balance perceived Soviet conventional superiority. Of course in hindsight given the vast disparity of wealth between the West and the East and the great inefficiencies of the Soviet economy these beliefs seem strange or even fanciful. See P. Swartz, *NATO's Nuclear Dilemmas* (Washington, DC: Brookings, 1983), pp. 17–26; A. Tractenberg, *Constructed Peace: The Making of the European Settlement, 1945–1963* (Princeton: Princeton University Press, 1999), pp. 96–103; and Wallace Thies, *Friendly Rivals: Bargaining and Burden-Shifting in NATO* (Armonk: M & E Sharpe, 2003), pp. 64–72, 93–106.
18 George Baer, *The US Navy: One Hundred Years of Sea Power* (Stanford, CA: Stanford University Press, 1994), pp. 428–429; see also Norman Friedman, *Seapower as Strategy* (Annapolis, MD: Naval Institute Press, 2001), pp. 219ff. is a good introduction. For a variety of competing views, see Stephen E. Miller and Stephen Van Evera, *Naval Strategy and National Security* (Princeton, NJ: Princeton University Press, 1988), pp. 16–170. The definitive history of the development of The Maritime Strategy is Peter Swartz's unpublished Centre of Naval Analysis Study *The Maritime Strategy of the 1980s: Threads, Strands and Line*.

19 Christopher A. Ford and David A. Rosenberg 'The Naval Intelligence Underpinnings of Reagan's Maritime Strategy', *Journal of Strategic Studies*, April 2005, pp. 392–402.
20 Niall Ferguson 'The Decade the World Tilted East', *Straits Times*, 7 January 2010.
21 Minxin Pei 'Think Again: Asia's Rise', *Foreign Policy*, 22 June 2009, p. 5.
22 Kishore Mahbubani, *The New Asian Hemisphere: The Irresistible Shift of Global Power to the East* (New York: Public Affairs, 2008); Yasheng Huang, *Capitalism with Chinese Characteristics* (New York: Cambridge University Press, 2008).
23 Martin Jacques, *When China Rules the World* (New York: Penguin, 2009), pp. 409–413.
24 'China's Trade Figures Bounce Back from Crisis', *Straits Times*, 11 January 2010.
25 World Bank Development Indicators, 2008 to be found online, available at: http://sitesresources.worldbank.org/DATASTATISTICS/Resources/wdi09introch1.pdf accessed 12 February 2010.
26 'China's Trade Figures Bounce Back from Crisis', *Straits Times*, 11 January 2010.
27 Niall Ferguson, *The Ascent of Money: A Financial History of the World* (London: Penguin Books, 2009), p. 285.
28 Unpublished presentation paper at East Asia Institute, Singapore, 26 February 2010.
29 Jim O'Neal 'The BRICS Dream 2006', Economics Department, Goldman Sachs, online, available at: www2.goldmansachs.com/ideas/brics/index.html accessed 7 August 2009; for a counterblast to the proposition that the Asia-Pacific in general and China in particular will transform the world economy see, Minxin Pei, op. cit.
30 Pete Engardio (ed.), *Chindia: How China and India are Revolutionizing Global Business* (New York: McGraw Hill, 2007) is a good example of this line of thought.
31 See statement of Norman R. Augustine, Retired Chairman and CEO of the Lockheed Martin Corporation Before the Democratic Steering and Policy Committee, US House of Representatives, 7 January 2009.
32 Shiv Shankar Menon (Former Foreign Secretary, India) 'The Evolving Balance of Power in Asia' Address at IISS Global Strategic Review, Geneva, 13 September 2009, p. 4.
33 'Chinese Navy Dives to Save a Golden Junk', *Guardian*, 13 May 2007; 'Unusual Chinese Recovery', *Naval History*, August 2006.
34 This is still a neglected area. For an authoritative if difficult review, see Gang Deng *Chinese Maritime Activities and Socioeconomic Development c 2100 BC–AD 1900* (London: Greenwood Press, 1997).
35 Ian Storey 'China as a Global Maritime Power: Opportunities and Vulnerabilities' in Andrew Forbes (ed.) *Australia and its Maritime Interests: At Home and in the Region* (Canberra ACT: RAN Seapower Centre, 2008), p. 109.
36 World Bank, *World Development Indicators 2008* (Washington, DC: World Bank, 2008), p. 317.
37 Robert Karniol 'Boom Time Ahead for Asia-Pacific Navies', *Straits Times*, 9 November 2009. I am indebted to Bob Nugent Vice-President (Advisory) of AMI International (online, available at: http://aminter.com) for these figures and for his personal support of this project. 'DCNS Plans to Expand Business in Asia-Pacific', *Jane's Defence Weekly*, 11 November 2009.
38 Figures courtesy of AMI International.
39 'Singapore Navy's Inaugural Participation in Rim of the Pacific Exercise'. Online, available at: https://app-pac.mica.gov.sg accessed 7 August 2009.

40 For the dangers of such 'power transition' see Steve Chan 'Exploring Puzzles in Power-transition Theory: Implications for Sino-American Relations', *Security Studies*, 13: 3, pp. 103–141.
41 Robert O. Work *The US Navy: Charting a Course for Tomorrow's Fleet* (Washington, DC: CSBA, 2008), p. 14.
42 Ibid., pp. 14ff. 'America's Disastrous Debt is Obama's Biggest Test', *Financial Times*, 19 April 2010.
43 Work op. cit., p. 71. See Remarks by Dr Donald C. Winter, Secretary of the Navy at the Sea Air Space Exposition, Washington, DC, 3 April 2007.
44 Sam Tangredi *Futures of War: Towards a Consensus View of the Future Security Environment* (Newport, RI: Alidade Press, 2008), pp. 105–107. Andrew S. Erickson and David D. Yang 'Using the Land to Control the Sea: Chinese Analysts Consider the Antiship Ballistic Missile', and Eric Hagt and Mathew Durnin 'China's Antiship Ballistic Missile: Developments and Missing Links' both in *Naval War College Review*, Autumn 2009, pp. 53–86 and 87–116 respectively.
45 Work, op. cit., p. 71.
46 Timothy Garton Ash 'As Threats Multiply and Power Fragments, we need Realistic Idealism', *Guardian*, 31 December 2009.
47 Here see the arguments in Ross, Robert S. 'The US–China Peace: Great Power Politics, Spheres of Influence, and the Peace of East Asia', *Journal of East Asian Studies* 3(3), 2003, pp. 351–375 and Ross, Robert S. and Zhu Feng, eds, *China's Ascent: Power, Security and the Future of International Politics* (Ithaca: Cornell University Press, 2008); Buzan, Barry and Ole Waever *Regions and Powers: The Structure of International Security* (Cambridge: Cambridge University Press, 2003); Goldsmith, Benjamin E. 'A Liberal Peace in Asia?', *Journal of Peace Research*, 44(1), 2007, pp. 5–27.
48 This has been argued above, by Patrick C. Bratton in Chapter 2.
49 Robert Kaplan *Monsoon: The Indian Ocean and the Future of American Power* (New York: Random House, 2010), especially pp. 296–323.
50 The domestic and political costs of these levels of defence spending, on the other hand are more difficult to calculate and may prove significantly less easy to bear.
51 Eberhard Sandschneider 'Is China's Military Modernization a Concern for the EU?', in Marcin Zaborowski (ed) *Facing China's Rise: Guidelines for an EU Strategy* (Paris: Institute for Security Studies, Chaillot paper no 94, December 2006), pp. 40–41; Mahbubani (2008) op. cit., p. 105.
52 Work, report, pp. 7–12.
53 Tangredi, op. cit. p. 103.
54 General James T. Conway, Admiral Gary Roughead, Admiral Thad W. Allen, *A Cooperative Strategy for 21st Century Seapower* (Washington, DC: Department of the Navy, 2007).
55 Minxin Pei 'Think Again: Asia's Rise', *Foreign Policy*, 22 June 2009; Razeen Sally 'Don't Believe the India Hype', *Far Eastern Economic Review*, 1 May 2009; Minxein Pei 'Why China Won't Rule the World', *Newsweek Special Edition* 2010.
56 Will Hutton, T*he Writing on the Wall: China and the West in the 21st Century* (London: Abacus, 2008), p. 33. Toshio Egawa (MD Konica Corporation) 'Japan under the Democratic Party' MFA Diplomatic Academy, Singapore, 8 January 2010. Wang Gungwu and John Wong (eds) *Interpreting China's Development* (Singapore: World Scientific, 2007) is a useful introduction to the problem.
57 Duncan Freeman 'China's Rise and the Global Economy: Challenges for Europe' in Marcin Zaborowski (ed) *Facing China's Rise: Guidelines for an EU Strategy* (Paris: Institute for Security Studies, Chaillot paper no 94, December 2006), p. 15.

58 Much of this is the product of a huge increase in the paper value of property, creating a 'bubble' with which central government is beginning to grapple. 'China Takes More Steps to Cool Property Market', *Sunday Times*, 18 April 2010.
59 Gady Epstein 'Ponzi in Peking', *Asia Forbes Magazine*, January 2010; and William Pesek 'Headed for a Great Fall?', *Straits Times*, 15 January 2010. Amongst the worried experts quoted in these two articles are Victor Shih, Northwestern University; Andy Xie, Morgan Stanley Economist; Professor Michael Pettis at Peking University; Jim Chanos, the Head of Kynikos Associates in New York. If correct, these estimates suggest that China's real level of public debt is not the 20 per cent of GDP officially admitted but more than 70 per cent with another 30 per cent in hazard, significantly worse in fact than the US situation of 50 per cent direct debt and 18 per cent of shared debt. Japan at some 200 per cent however is worse than either. See also Niall Ferguson's warnings, 'Riots, Upheaval and States Gone Bust: The Price we could Pay for Forgetting History', *Guardian*, 26 May 2009.
60 'Mixed Views in China over Google's Exit Threat' and 'China Downplays Pullout Threat', *Straits Times*, 14 and 16 January 2010. Martin Jacques and Will Hutton 'Is Western Supremacy but a Blip as China Rises to the Global Summit?', *Guardian*, 23 June 2009.
61 Mahbubani (2008) op. cit., p. 139.
62 Timothy Garton Ash 'China's Economic Success may Soon Bring Trouble: It would be Ours Too', *Guardian*, 4 December 2008.
63 'China is Growing Old before Getting Rich', *Straits Times*, 14 January 2010.
64 'China to Stem Exodus of Corrupt Officials' and 'No Corrupt Official is Above the Law' in *Straits Times*, 12 and 13 January 2010.
65 Will Hutton *The Writing on the Wall: China and the West in the 21st Century* (London: Abacus, 2008), pp. 32–36; Peter Ferdinand 'The Challenge of Democratisation' in Zaborowski (2006), op. cit., pp. 32–34.
66 Ferdinand, op. cit.
67 Mahbubani (2008) op. cit., p. 143.
68 In per capita GDP terms, for example China currently ranks just 104th in the world. Lee Kuan Yew 'China and US Need Each Other' *Straits Times*, 8 April 2010. 'Chinese Varsities Growing Too Fast', *Straits Times*, 17 February 2010.
69 The internal Chinese debate about what Beijing's official 'Harmonious World' foreign policy after the era of US primacy actually means can be seen through a comparison between Professor Zhao Tingyang's *The Tianxia System* (2005) and Sen. Col. Liu Mingfu's *The China Dream* (2010). *The Tianxia System* uses traditional Chinese ideas to craft a new world order while *The China Dream* argues that the PRC needs to have a military rise to guard its economic rise. These two books are important because they became social phenomena and media events that put their authors into the spotlight. They provoked debates that spread their influence far beyond their core audiences of philosophers and military officers into China's broader civil society. The possibilities discussed range from a more modest pursuit of world harmony, to the more active project of harmonising the world – by force, if necessary. See William A. Callahan *China: The Pessoptimist Nation* (Oxford: Oxford University Press, 2010).
70 This is the burden of Joseph Stiglitz, chief economist at the World Bank 1997–2000 in *Globalisation and its Discontents* (New York: W. W. Norton & Co, 2002), pp. 12, 14, 15, 17. See also Francis Fukuyama 'History is Still Over' *Newsweek Special* 2010.
71 Mahbubani (2008) op. cit., pp. 27, 186.
72 George Soros 'Recovery could Run out of Steam', *Straits Times*, 7 January 2010.

73 Thus John Gray *False Dawn; The Delusions of Global Capitalism* (London: Granta, 2009), pp. 209–228. Mike Moore identifies areas urgently needing for reform in *Saving Capitalism: Why Globalisation and Democracy offer the Best Hope for Progress, Peace and Development* (Singapore: John Wiley, 2009), pp. 259–267.
74 Mark Lynas 'How do I Know China Wrecked the Deal? Because I Was There', *Guardian*, 23 December 2009. 'Don't Blame China for Flawed Copenhagen Outcome, says Prescott', *Guardian*, 28 December 2009.
75 'Fury at China over Refusal to Pardon Briton', *Guardian*, 29 December 2009.
76 Philip Andrews-Speed, Liao Xuanli and Roland Dannreuther 'The Strategic Impact of China's Energy Needs', *Adelphi Paper 346* (London: IISS, 2002) Kenneth Lieberthal and Mikkal Herberg 'China's Search for Energy Security: Implications for US Policy', *NBR Analysis*, vol. 17, no 1, 2006, pp. 5–42.
77 Lee Kuan Yew 'China and US Need Each Other', *Straits Times*, 8 April 2010; Wang Gungwu 'China Talks Tough but Policy Unchanged', *Straits Times*, 24 February 2010.
78 Niall Ferguson 'The Trillion Dollar Question', *Guardian*, 2 June 2009; 'China should Aim to be World No 1', *Straits Times*, 2 March 2010. This article discusses the recent book *The China Dream* by Professor Colonel Liu Mingfu of China's National Defence University.
79 Ronald O'Rourke *China Naval Modernization: Implications for US Navy Capabilities – Background and Issues for Congress* (Washington, DC: Congressional Research Service, June 2010), p. 25.
80 Vice Admiral John Bird, Commander US Seventh Fleet, Review Interview, *Straits Times*, 8 November 2008. Also Admiral Robert Willard, Commander US Pacific Command, quoted in 'China's Military Buildup Shows Need for US Dialogue: Admiral', *Agence France-Presse* (Seoul) 21 October 2009.
81 Ronald O'Rourke, *China Naval Modernization: Implications for US Navy Capabilities – Background and Issues for Congress* (Washington, DC: Congressional Research Service, June 2010), p. 37.
82 'US to Match China's Arms Build-Up: Gates', *Straits Times*, 10 January 2011.
83 Daniel Whiteneck, Michael Price, Neil Jenkins and Peter Swartz *The Navy at a Tipping Point: Maritime Dominance at Stake?* (Washington, DC: Center for Naval Analyses, March 2010), p. 16.
84 I am indebted to Captain Barney Rubel for this insight.
85 This is the burden of the argument presented in Martin Stuart-Fox *A Short History of China and Southeast Asia: Tribute, Trade and Influence* (Crows Nest, NSW, Australia: Allen & Unwin, 2003).
86 Dani Rodrik (Professor of Political Economy at Harvard) 'The World According to China', *Straits Times*, 15 January 2010. See also Jacques (2009), op. cit. pp. 414–439; Pen Shing Huei 'A More Assertive China won't Rock the Boat', *Straits Times*, 5 February 2010; William Choong 'House of Chimerica Still Standing', *Straits Times*, 5 February 2010.
87 This much discussed point depends on interpretations of the significance of Chinese history, another vast issue. For an introduction see Martin Stuart-Fox *A Short History of China and Southeast Asia: Tribute Trade and Influence* (Crow's Nest, NSW: Allen & Unwin, 2003), p. 155 and especially pp. 226–245. Stuart-Fox argues that China is the world's last empire but one notably constrained in its use of raw military power. The great debate about the extent, nature and purpose of Zheng He's famous voyages of the fourteenth century provide a useful maritime illustration of this crucial point. For this compare Geoff Wade 'The Zheng He Voyages: A Reassessment', Singapore NUS Asia Research Institute Working Paper 31, October 2004 with Johannes Widodo, *The Great Explorer Cheng Ho: Ambassador of Peace* (Singapore: Asiapac, 2005).

88 This argument is effectively made in Hugh White 'Power Shift: Australia's Future Between Washington and Beijing', *Quarterly Essay*, 39, 2010.
89 Mahbubani (2008) op. cit., p. 51.
90 Niall Ferguson (2009) op. cit., pp. 285–287.
91 Cited in Josef Joffe 'Power Lies in the Balancing', *Australian*, 6 August 2003.
92 Eric Hobsbawm 'America's Neo-Conservative World Supremacists will Fail', *Guardian*, 25 June 2005. See also V. G. Kiernan *America: The New Imperialism* (New York: W. W. Norton & Co., 2005) and Walter Nugent *Habits of Empire: A History of American Expansion* (New York: Random House, 2008).
93 Michael Ignatieff *Empire Lite* (New York: Vintage Books, 2003).
94 Hobsbawm, op. cit.
95 Angus Wilson *The Strange Ride of Rudyard Kipling* (London: Secker and Warburg, 1977), p. 137.
96 Henry Kamen *Empire* (New York: Harper Collins, 2003).
97 Joffe, op. cit.
98 Niall Ferguson 'Complexity and Collapse: Empires on the Edge of Chaos', *Foreign Affairs*, March/April 2010.
99 Nugent, op. cit., pp. 316–317.
100 Some have argued that in the long term this will make a close economic linkage of the United States and China which Niall Ferguson and Dr Moritz Schularick popularized as 'Chimerica' dangerously unsustainable. But see William Choong 'House of Chimerica Still Standing', *Straits Times*, 5 February 2010.
101 Martin Parkinson *The Role of the G-20 in the Global Financial Architecture*, Address to the Lowy Institute, Melbourne 9 October 2006.
102 Mahbubani (2008) op. cit., p. 102.
103 Mahbubani, op. cit. (2008), p. 52, 126.
104 Richard N. Haas 'The Age of Nonpolarity', *Foreign Affairs*, May–June 2008. The perceived rise of the BRICs (Brazil, Russia, India and China – the BRICs economies) and the 'Next 11' world economies can only accelerate this process. Jim O'Neill 'BRICs Are Still on Top, *Newsweek Special 2010*. See also Dilip Hiro 'After Empire; the Birth of a Multipolar World (New York: Nation Books, 2010) and 'A New Fluidity to Power Plays', *Straits Times*, 26 February 2010.
105 Xi Jinping, quoted in 'Putin, China's Xi Vow "Strategic" Support in First Meeting', *Agence France-Presse*, Moscow, 23 March 2010.
106 This notion is discussed more fully in Jack S. Levy and William R. Thompson 'Balancing on Land and at Sea: Do States Ally Against the Leading Global power?', *International Security*, vol. 35, no. 1, Summer 2010.
107 Fareed Zakaria *The Post American World and the Rise of the Rest* (London: Penguin, 2009), pp. 254–279; Timothy Garton Ash 'Only a Strategic Partnership with China will Keep this New Dawn Bright', *Guardian*, 27 November 2008.
108 Henry A. Kissinger, Address at the Eighth IISS Global Strategic Review Conference, Geneva, 10–12 September 2010, quoted in 'A World Full of Fault Lines', *Straits Times*, 7 December 2010.
109 For the responsible US regional military commander's official perspective, see US Pacific Command, USPACOM Strategy, November 2008/April 2009.
110 Mahbubani (2008) op. cit., p. 105.
111 A. T. Mahan *Retrospect and Prospect* (London: Sampson Low, Marston, 1902), pp. 177–178.

# Index

Page numbers in *italics* denote tables.

Aceh 132
Adams, John 47
Aegean Sea 11
Afghanistan 26, 29, 31, 64, 105, 123, 259
airborne warning and control system (AWACS) aircraft 63, 67
aircraft carriers 24, 56, 62, 69, 88, 100, 115, 118, 123–4, 169–72, 174, 250
Aleutian Islands 24, 57
Al Qaeda 116
American Association of Port Authorities 50
American Peace Corps 71
American Sixth Battle Squadron 191–2
AMI International 246
amphibious warfare 24, 62–3, 69, 104, 148, 154, 172, 246
Amsterdam 4
An, Admiral Byoung-tae 149
Andaman Sea 122
anti-ship cruise missile (ASCM) 59–60, 62, 80, 242
anti-shipping operations 33
anti-submarine warfare (ASW) 52, 59, 63, 67, 69, 101–5, 154, 170–2, 174–5, 179, 188n31, 246
ARF Confidence Building Measure Conference on Regional Cooperation in Maritime Security (March 2005) 141
Armitage, Richard 106
arms trafficking 116
Asia-Pacific Center for Security Studies (APCSS) 21
Asia-Pacific region 7, 8, 19–23, 29, 35–6, 46–7, 49–51, 53, 111, 117, 122, 141, 191, 237–8, 243–55, 258, 261–2, 264n29; maritime boundary and border disputes 37n4, 51, 149
Association of Southeast Asian Nations (ASEAN) 48, 50–1, 123; Declaration of Conduct Agreement with PRC 51; Defense Ministers Meeting (ADMM) 50
Arabian Sea 119, 122, 124
Australia 12, 34, 50, 82, 100, 114, 122, 134, 138, 146, 166–86, 191, 197, 208, 215, 219, 222, 227–8, 235n45, 240, 246, 261; *Australian Maritime Doctrine* (2000) 184; Border Protection Command 167; *Defence 2000: Our Future Defence Force* 177; *Defence Australia: Defence White Paper 1994* 175; *Defending Australia in the Asia Pacific Century: Force 2030* 177; Department of Defence 170, 172–3, 186; *Fisheries Act 1968* 180; *Review of Australia's Defence Capabilities* (1986) 173; naval dockyards 181–4; Strategic Reform Program 186; Tange Reorganisation (1973–1976) 172; *The Defence of Australia 1987* (Defence White Paper) 173; *The Navy Contribution to Australian Maritime Operations* (2005) 184
Australian Antarctic Territory (AAT) 178
Australian Defence Force (ADF) 173–4
Australian Defence Industries 182
Australian Fishing Zone (AFZ) 180
Australian Marine Complex 183
Australian Submarine Corporation (ASC) 182

# 270  Index

Australia, New Zealand, United States Security Treaty (ANZUS) 34, 40n42
automatic identification system (AIS) 136

Bab-el Mandeb 111
Bahrain 123
Balkans 10
Bangladesh 119
Barnet, Corelli 216
battleships 23, 30, 100, 206, 230
Battle of Dannoura (1185) 95
Battle of the Yalu (17 September 1894) 99
Battle of Tsushima (27 May 1905) 99, 200
Bay of Bengal 119, 122, 124
Beiyang Fleet 99
Bismarck Islands 215
Black Sea 11
Boer War 200
Bougainville 186
Boxer rebellion 99, 199
Braudel, Ferdinand 95
Brazil 29, 259, 268n104
Britain *see* Great Britain, United Kingdom
British Admiralty Delegation (BAD) in Washington 227
British East India Company 133
British Empire 166, 168, 195–6, 209, 214
British Foreign Office 197, 201, 207, 216
British Grand Fleet 191–2
British Pacific Fleet (BPF) 192, 193n4, 214–33, 235n45
Busan 50
Bush, George H.W. 26
Bush, George W. 27, 38n18

Cape of Good Hope 197
Cambodia 119
Canada 12, 185, 191–2, 215
CARAT naval exercise 53, 55n24
Carter, James 29
Cartiglione, Giuseppe 1
Carnarvon Commission of 1882 197
Center for Excellence in Disaster Management and Humanitarian Assistance (COE) 21, 27
Center for Strategic and Budgetary Assessment (CSBA) 81
Chichester, British Admiral 198–9

China 1, 3, 4, 6, 11–12, 13, 19, 22, 25, 35, 45n119, 47, 51, 56, 57–62, 69–72, 73n42, 75–81, 84, 86, 93–4, 97–9, 101, 112–13, 117–27, 131–2, 134, 141, 145, 147, 149, 151, 174, 196–200, 204–7, 228, 237, 241, 243–61, 264n29, 266n59, n68, n69, 267n87, 268n100, n104; anti-satellite technology 33; Declaration of Conduct Agreement with ASEAN 51; defence expenditure 117; economic growth 57–8; National Security Strategy 67; People's Bank of 252; People's Republic of (PRC) 27, 48, 51, 66, 76, 78, 80, 149, 160, 266n69; Song dynasty 3, 4, 11, 245; US and 26–31
China Ocean Shipping Company 245
China Shipping Container Lines 245
Chinese Central Military Commission (CMC) 79, 83, 86; *Military Strategic Guidelines* 86
Chinese Communist Party 83
Chinese Defense White Paper 2004 78
Chinese Defense White Paper 2006 84
Chinese Defense White Paper 2008 85, 91n27
Chinese People's Armed Police Coast Guard 85
Chinese People's Liberation Army (PLA) 58, 64–5, 67, 75–86, 89n8, 118; Dalian Naval Academy 84; Dalian Vessel Academy 86; Military Operations Other Than War (MOOTW) 76–7, 85, 87–8; *New Historic Missions* 83–5, 87; *Science of Military Strategy* 81
Chinese People's Liberation Army Air Force 58–9, 63, 76, 78, 81
Chinese People's Liberation Army Navy (PLAN) 33, 57–71, 75–89, 89n8, 90n13, 118, 121, 149–50, 151n 156, 161, 255–6; aviation 63, 69; bolstering national pride 66–7; naval infantry 63–4, 69; Sanya submarine base 118–19; ships: *Peace Ark* (hospital ship) 66; *Qiangdao* 65; *Taicang* 65; *Zhen He* 64; South Sea Fleet 66–7; training 64, 68
choke points 33, 50, 112, 118–19
Chosun dynasty 145–6
Chosun–Japanese War (1592–1598) 145
Christmas Island 178

Index  271

Churchill, Winston 216–17, 219, 240
climate change 26
Clinton, William 26
Clinton, US Secretary of State Hilary 48
Cobra Gold naval exercise 53
Coco Islands 119, 178
Cold War 9, 24–6, 49, 102–3, 105, 111–12, 114, 148–9, 160, 172, 179, 193, 208, 241, 263n17
Combined Chiefs of Staff 217–18
Commonwealth Naval Forces (CNF) 168
Constantinople 11
Container Security Initiative (CSI) 122, 138
Convention for the Suppression of Unlawful Acts against the Safety of Maritime Navigation (SUA Convention), 1990 138
Convention of Kanagawa (1854) 97
Convention on Maritime Search and Rescue (SAR Convention), 1979 137
Convoy Act of 1650 (British) 47
Copenhagen Climate Summit 28, 254
Corbett, Sir Julian 2, 8, 166, 203
corvettes 148, 153–4, 159, 161, 246
Cox, James 1
Cromwell, Oliver 47
cruisers 23, 30, 168–9, 198, 230, 238; Aegis-class 60, 152–3
Cunningham, Admiral (RN) 221–4
cyberwarfare 33

Dae-jung, Kim 34, 149
Darwin, John 13
De Chair, RN Captain Dudley 201–2
Defence Maritime Services (DMS) 183
de Lanessan, J.I. 6
democratic alliances 35
Democratic People's Republic of Korea (DPRK) 146, 148, 150, 153–4, 157–9; Navy 157–8; submarine force 156–7; see also North Korea
Deptford 4
Desert Storm 58
destroyers 59–60, 69, 88, 104–5, 148, 152–3, 156, 161, 168, 171–2, 174–7, 246; destroyer guided missile with helicopter (DDGH) 174, 177, 186; helicopter-carrying (DDH) 104–5; Russian Sovremenny-class DDG 59; US Arleigh Burke-class DDGs 60, 154
Dewey, US Admiral 198
Dibb, Paul 173

Diego Garcia 255
differential global positioning system (DGPS) 136
disaster relief 26–7, 121
Djibouti 123
drug trafficking 26, 85, 115–16, 123
Dull, Paul 100
Durand, Sir Mortimer 201, 204
Dutch see Netherlands

Earl Grey 191–2
East Asia Response Private Limited (EARL) 140
East China Sea 51, 57, 78, 80, 94, 103, 105, 110n42, 255
East Indies 22
East Timor 186
East–West Center 21
Economic Exclusion Zone (EEZ) 51, 67, 80, 85, 105, 112, 117, 167, 180, 247
Egawa, Yoshio 252
Egypt 56, 65–6, 120, *151*
electronic chart display and information system (ECDIS) 136
electronic navigation charts (ENC) 136
Ethiopia 8
European Economic Community 25
European Union (EU) 28, 29
*Evoikos* 140
Exclusive Resources Zone (ERZ) 180

Ferguson, Niall 8, 255, 257
First Sino-Japanese War (1894–5) 99
First World War 8, 30, 99, 168–9, 195, 204, 215, 238, 254
Five Power Defence Arrangements 180, 184
Five Power Naval Treaty 205–6
Four Power Treaty 205
France 6, 28, 47, 54n7, 58, 123, *151*, 196–7, 200, 203, 205–6, 256, 263n10
Fraser, Commander in Chief British Pacific Fleet (CINCBPF) Admiral (RN) Sir Bruce 214, 218–33, 235n45
free trade 10, 26
frigates 148, 153–4, 159, 161, 171–2, 174–7, 182, 186, 246; guided missile (FFG), 59–60, 69, 172, 182; stealth 138
Fund 92, 139
Fuquan, Tang 86

Gallipoli 167
Gates, Robert 31, 255

## Index

Gempei War 95
Germany 10, 28, 54n7, 68, 99–100, 108n18, *151*, 191, 196, 199–200, 202, 215, 241, 252, 256
German Far Eastern Squadron 198
globalization 1, 8, 10, 166, 254, 259–60
Gogol 10
Gorshkov, S. 144
Great Britain 5, 7, 8, 12, 19, 28, 46–7, 54n7, 58, 68, 77, 99, 106–7, 111, 133–4, *151*, 155, 166, 169, 171, 178, 182, 191–2, 195–209, 214–33, 237–40, 256–8; *see also* United Kingdom
Grove, Eric 150–1
Guam 23, 57, 208, 255
Gulf of Aden 48, 76, 87, 89n8, 106, 113, 116, 120, 179, 246, 248
Gwadar 120, 123
Gwangju massacre 34

Haas, Richard 260
Hainan Island 67, 118, 124
Halsey, Admiral (USN) 219, 221, 228–32
Hambantota Development Zone 119
Hammond, Edmund 197
harbour craft transponder system (HARTS) 138
Hardinge, Sir Charles 204
Hart, Liddell 6–7
Hawaii 23, 43n86, 51, 64, 205, 214, 232, 240, 246
Hean, Teo Chee 141
Heard and McDonald Islands 178
He, Zheng 11, 15n34, 56, 70, 245, 267n87
Henley, Captain John 47
Hobsbawm, Erik 257
Hokusai 94
Hong Kong 50, 134, 196, 215, 219, 245
Howaldtswerke-Deutsche Werft GmbH (HDW) 155
Huang, Yashen 243
Huaqing, Liu 76, 90n14
humanitarian assistance 21, 52–3, 62, 66, 85, 87, 124
Hun, Roh Moo 34, 150

Imperial Japanese Navy (IJN) 10, 79, 99–102, 108n16, n22, 191, 207–8
Inchon 159
India 5, 11, 13, 19, 25, 26, 27, 29–32, 35, 40n48, 62, 77, 87, 111–27, 141, *151*, 185, 208–9, 244–5, 249, 251, 255, 258–60, 268n104; defence spending 114–15; Malabar naval exercise 53; Project Seabird 122
Indian Army 12
Indian Coast Guard 117
Indian Maritime Doctrine of 2004 121, 124
Indian Navy 111, 113, 115–18, 120, 123–6, 262; ships: *Admiral Gorshkov* 123–4; INS *Tabar* 116; INS *Jalashwa* 122; STOBAR (short take off but arrested recovery) Air Defence Ship 123
Indian Ocean 11, 26, 27, 31, 66–7, 88, 105–6, 111–22, 125–7, 133–4, 178, 197, 216, 248
Indian Ocean Naval Symposium (IONS) 111
Indian Oceans Shipping Working Group 179
Indonesia 32, 34, 116, 123, 130, 134, 136–7, 139, 173, 180, 185, 246, 262; Marine Security Coordination Agency 136
Indonesian Maritime Security Coordinating Board (IMSCB) (BAKORKAMLA) 136
Indonesian Navy (TNI-AL) 138
Inland Sea (Japan) 94, 96
intelligence, surveillance and reconnaissance (ISR) 106
International Convention on Limitation of Liability for Maritime Claims 1976 (LLMC) 139
International Convention on Oil Pollution Preparedness, Response and Cooperation (OPRC), 1979 139
International Court of Justice (ICJ) 139, 142n24
International Institute for Strategic Studies 261
International Monetary Fund (IMF) 27, 28
International Maritime Organisation (IMO) 135–6
International Sea Power Symposium 159
International Ship and Port Facility Security Code (ISPS) 138
Iran 32–3, 120, 123
Iraq 29, 31, 185, 259
Israel 121, *151*
Italy *151*, 182, 205–6
Iwo Jima 159

Jacques, Martin 243
Jakarta 132–3
Jammah Islamiah 116
Japan 1, 4, 5, 9, 12, 20, 23, 24, 25, 26, 27, 28, 32–5, 47, 50–3, 67–8, 77–8, 80, 82, 89n11, 93–107, 122–3, 134, 140–1, 145, 149, *151*, 159, 169, 191–2, 196–8, 200, 202, 204–7, 215–16, 229, 231–2, 238–42, 244–5, 249–52, 255–6, 261, 266n59, 2004 National Defence Programme Guideline 104; Combined Fleet 98; Defence Agency 102; Ministry of Land, Infrastructure and Transport 141; Ministry of the Navy 98; National Defence Programme Outline (NDPO) 103–4; ships: *Hyuga* 105; *Ise* 105; *Mashu* 105; *Yamato* 100; Systems Investigative Committee (SIC) 102; Tokyo–Guam–Taiwan strategic triangle (TGT) 106
Japan Coast Guard 106, 110n42
Japan Maritime Self Defense Force (JMSDF) 102–6, 149, 151, 156, 161, 191
Java Sea 133
Jeju Island 152
Jeou, Ma Ying 35
Jiangxi, Huang 66–7
Jingdezhen 1
Jintao, Hu 83–4, 86, 123
Johor 132
*Joint Forces Quarterly* 215
Jun, Zhai 71, 74n57

Kadena Air Force Base (US) 81
Kazakhstan 123
Kellogg–Briand Agreement (1928) 206
Kennedy, Paul 12, 237–8
Kenya 71
Khan, AQ network 32
Khan, Genghiz 9–10
King, Admiral (USN) Ernest J. 216–19, 223, 226–8, 232, 238
Kinkaid, Vice Admiral (USN) Thomas 225
Kissinger, Henry 249, 261
Kipling, Rudyard 9
Kiribati 52
Klinberg, Frank 29, 42n68
*Kobukson* ("turtle ships") 96
Korea 10, 31, 53, 71, 94, 96–7, 99–100, 108n16, 144, 161, 241, 245–6, 249, 251

Korean Destroyer Experimental (KDX) 153, 161
Korean National Defence University 144
Korean War (1950–3) 159, 166, 193, 235n41
Koryo dynasty 145
Kuwait 123

League of Nations 205, 207
Lebanon 65, 116, 121
Liaotung Peninsula 99
liberalism/liberal values 3, 4, 10, 11, 13, 21
Libya 32
Linn, Brian 23–4
Lombok Strait 48
London Conference (1936) 238
Lord Howe Island 178
Lord Ismay 222
Lord Lansdowne 201, 204

Macao 8
MacArthur, General Douglas 220–2, 225–7, 235n41
Macartney, Lord 11
Mackinder, Halford 9, 10, 242
Madagascar 122
Maer, George 242
Mahan, Alfred Thayer 1–2, 5, 7, 8, 9, 12, 13, 46, 48, 53, 56, 113, 130, 144, 166, 181, 204, 237, 241–2, 248, 262; *The Influence of Sea Power on History* 237
Mahbubani, Kishore 243, 249, 251, 254, 260, 262
Majapahit 131
Makassar 132
Malacca 132, 134
Malacca Straits 33, 48, 111, 113, 116, 118–19, 122, 132–4, 136–7, 141, 228
Malaya 134, 170–1, 216
Malayan Emergency 166
Malaysia 82, 123, 130, 134, 136, 139, 177, 181, 185, 187n21, 246, 262; Malaysian Maritime Enforcement Agency (MMEA) 136
Manchuria 99, 145, 200
Macquarie Island 178
Marianas Islands 100
MARPOL 73/78 Convention 139
Marshall, General George C. 218
Marshall Islands 100, 228
Marshall Plan 24

Masataka, Kōsaka 103
Masayoshi, Ōhira 103
Mauritius 122
McKinley, US President 198
Mead, Walter Russell 13
Mediterranean Sea 11, 46, 48, 66, 95, 100
Mercantile finance 5–6
Mexico 39n28, 40n50, 55n21, *151*, 259
Mongolia 123
Mongols 9–10, 11
Montesquieu 3
Morris, Michael 150
Morrison, Samuel 218
Mozambique 123
Mughal Empire (India) 11
Mumbai attacks (November 2008) 117
Munemori, Taira no 95
Murakami *suigun* 95–6
Muscovy 10
Myanmar (Burma) 32, 51, 71, 119, 123
Myung-bak, Lee 35, 150

*Nanhai No 1*, 245
Naoto, Kan 106
Naval Cooperation and Guidance of Shipping (NCAGS) 179, 188n32
Netherlands 3, 5, 9, 14n11, 97, 130, 132, 217
New Guinea 24
*Newsweek Special 2010* 259
New Zealand 12, 34, 52, 100, 168, 182, 191, 196, 208, 215, 246
Nicobar Islands 122
Nigeria 116
Nimitz, Admiral Chester 214, 216–31
Nine Power Treaty (1922) 204
Nine-rank hierarchy of navies *151*
Nixon, Richard 29, 172
Nobunaga, Oda 96
Non-Governmental Organizations (NGOs) 53
Norfolk Island 178
North Arabian Sea 76
North Atlantic Treaty Organization (NATO) 9, 24, 25, 26, 30, 116, 179, 241–2, 246, 250–1, 263n17
North Korea 26, 31, 32, 35–6, 51, 104, 146, 148–9, *151*, 156–7, 160–1; *see also* Democratic People's Republic of Korea (DPRK)
Norway *151*, 242

O'Neill, Jim 244
Obama, Barack 27, 31, 38n18
Oceania 22
Octagon Conference 216
Oil Spill Response Limited (OSRL) 140
Okinawa 35, 81, 159, 221, 225, 227, 229, 231–2
Oman 6, 123, *151*
Operation Iceberg 221, 225–30, 232
Operation Matador 240
Operation Olympic 228
Opium Wars 12, 77, 82
OPRC-HNS 2000 139
*Orang Laut* ("Sea People") 131
*Orapin Global* 140
Ottawa Agreement (1936) 178
Ottoman Empire 11

Padfield, Peter 3, 10
Pannikar, K.M. 5, 113
Pacific Reach 53, 55n23
Pakistan 24, 25, 29–32, 34–6, 64, 113, 116–17, 119–20, 123, 249
Panama Canal 146
pandemic diseases 26–7, 36, 260
Paracel Islands 80
Pearl Harbor 30, 100, 205, 208, 214, 218, 221, 223, 229
Pei, Minxin 251, 253
Perry, Commodore Matthew 38n23, 47, 97
Persia 10
Persian Gulf 26, 57, 64, 66, 86, 116, 119–20, 123
Perth Treaty 180
Peter the Great 4
Petroleum Association of Japan (PAJ) 140
Philippines 23, 25, 32–5, 43n86, 50–2, 181, 198, 205, 217, 228, 261
Philippine Sea 80
Phillips, Admiral (RN) Sir Tom 240
piracy & anti-piracy 4, 11, 26, 36, 46, 48, 51, 65–6, 68, 73n43, 84, 87–8, 113, 115–17, 123, 136, 158, 160, 162n9, 188n32, 246, 261
port operations control centre (POCC) 136
Portugal 8, *151*
Portuguese navy 2–3
Powell, Colin 122
Pratas Islands 80
Prevention of Pollution of Sea Act 139
Proliferation Security Initiative (PSI) 21, 106, 122
propulsion systems 59–61

## Index 275

Protocol to the 1971 International Convention on the Establishment of an International Fund for the Compensation for Oil Pollution Damage 1992 139
Protocol to the International Convention on Civil Liability for Oil Pollution Damage 1992 139
Pyongyang 34

Qatar 123
Qingdao 99
Quianlong, Emperor (Calm Sea Palace) 1, 11–12

Radford–Collins Naval Control of Shipping Agreement (NCS) 170, 178
Radiation Detection Initiative 138
Raffles, Stamford 133
Rawlings, Admiral (RN) 225, 229–32
Raytheon 183
Republic of Korea (ROK) 146–51, 154, 156, 160–1; Defence Reform Plan 2020 (DRP 2020) 150; *see also* South Korea
Republic of Korea Air Force (ROKAF) 148
Republic of Korea Army (ROKA) 148, 150
Republic of Korea Navy (ROKN) 147–61; Chonryong cruise missile 156; Future Frigate Experimental (FFX) 154, 161; Land Platform Experimental project (LPX) 153–4, 161; Naval Operations Command 152; Seventh Mobile Flotilla 153; ships: ROKS *Cheonan* 150, 154, 160–1, 255; Strategic Mobile Fleet 152, 161; Yulgok Project 149
Rim of the Pacific (RIMPAC) Exercise 52, 159, 246
Rodger, Nicholas 4
Rome 10
Roosevelt, Franklin Delano 207, 217
Roosevelt, Theodore 23, 39n28, 202–3
Royal Air Force (RAF) 217, 234n19
Royal Australian Air Force (RAAF) 170–2, 174, 184
Royal Australian Navy (RAN) 166–77, 179–86; RAN inventory 1980–2010 *176*; *Semaphore* (publication) 185; ships: HMAS *Melbourne* 170–2, 175; HMAS *Sydney* 170–1
Royal Dutch Navy 154

Royal Malaysian Navy (RMN) 138
Royal Navy (RN) 5–6, 7, 46, 54n7, 56, 93, 98, 154, 166, 168, 195–209, 214–33, 250; East Indies Fleet 218; liaison officers (LO) 222–3; ships: HMS *Effingham* 219; HMS *Euryalus* 98; HMS *Ocean* 155; HMS *Prince of Wales* 240; HMS *Repulse* 240
Rumsfeld, Donald 258
Rush, Richard 47
Russia 4, 59, 61–2, 79, 98–100, 116, 118, 124, 196–200, 204–5, 207, 237, 247, 250, 256, 259–60, 268n104
Russian Baltic Fleet 99
Russian Pacific Fleet 99
Russo-Japanese Wars (1904–1905) 99, 200, 204
Ryukyu Islands 57, 68, 80, 94–5, 97, 226–7

Safety of Life at Sea (SOLAS) Code 138
St. Petersburg 4
Sally, Razeen 251
Sarantakes, Nicholas 215
Saudi Arabia 123, 259
Sea of Japan 94, 103
Sea Power Centre – Australia 184
search and rescue 85, 137, 159, 179
Second World War (World War II) 10, 12, 13, 23–4, 50, 68, 70, 181, 191, 195, 208
sea lines of communication (SLOC) 26, 46–7, 49, 51, 53, 76, 82–3, 86, 112, 114, 126–7, 146, 152, 155, 157–9, 163n45, 170, 175, 208, 242
sea mines 52, 138
SembCorp Logistics Limited 140
Senkaku Islands 51
September 11, 2001 attacks 26, 87, 104, 137
Seri Teri Buana 131
Seychelles 123
SEXTANT Conference 215
Shanghai 50, 206, 245
Shangri-La Dialogue 2005 141
Sheppard, Charles 219
Shigeru, Yoshida 102
Shihei, Hayashi 97
Shipping Working Groups 179
Shui-bien, Chen 34
Shenzhen 50
Siam 131
Siberia 146
Silk Route 10, 11

## 276  Index

Singapore 4, 26, 40n48, 50, 52, 66, 82, 123, 130, 133–40, *151*, 171, 181, 185, 196, 205, 208, 215–16, 219, 240, 245–6, 250, 255, 262; Accompanying Sea Security Teams (ASSeT) 137; Maritime and Port Authority (MPA) 135–8; Maritime Rescue Coordination Centre (MRCC) 137; Police Coast Guard (PCG) 135, 137; Republic of Singapore Air Force (RSAF) 137–8; Republic of Singapore Navy (RSN) 135, 137–8; RSN Maritime Security Task Force (MSTF) 135; Singapore Armed Forces (SAF) 137; Singapore Oil Spill Response Centre (SOSRC) 140; Singapore Plan for Search and Rescue (SAR) Services 137
Sit, Victor 244
smuggling 11, 85, 135
Sodre, Vicente 3
Sofala 8
Sohn, Admiral Won-il 148
Solomon Islands 186, 215
Somalia 48, 65, 116, 246
Soros, George 254
South Africa 12, 64, 114, *151*, 208, 259
South China Sea 48, 56–7, 62, 64, 67–8, 70–1, 78, 80, 95, 105, 118–19, 123–4, 133–4, 220, 255
South East Asian Treaty Organization (SEATO) 25, 40n42, 171
South Korea 22, 24, 25, 26, 29, 31–2, 34–5, 45n119, 50–1, 82, 144, 146–9, 185, 242, 246, 250, 261; Ocean Vision 2016 147; Sunshine Policy 34; *see also* Republic of Korea (ROK)
Soviet Navy 5, 9, 10, 36, 39n39, 90n14, 103, 241–3
Soviet Union (USSR) 9, 10, 25, 26, 29, 30, 49, 58, 75, 79–80, 102–3, 111, 149, *151*, 207, 241–2, 250, 256, 263n17
Spain 23, 183, 203, 258
Spanish-American War of 1898 198
Spratly Islands 51, 57, 63, 67–8, 78
Spruance, Admiral 219, 221, 227
Sri Lanka 119, *151*, 218
Stalin, Josef 5
Strait of Hormuz 33, 111, 113, 120
Strait of Shimonoseki 95
STRAITREP (Mandatory Ship Reporting System in the Straits of Malacca and Singapore) 136, 141, 143n30
submarines 10, 24, 33, 52, 56–7, 60–1, 69, 79–80, 82, 93, 100–1, 105–6, 108n18, 118–20, 124, 138, 147–9, 155–6, 159, 161, 168–9, 171–7, 181–2, 186, 246, 250–1, 255; nuclear 61, 63, 69, 115, 118, 123–4, 251
submarine launched ballistic missile (SLBM) 61–2
Suez Canal 111, 113, 133, 197, 215
Sukothai 131–2
Sumatra 131–2, 221
support ships 61, 69, 88, 104
Sunda Straits 48, 133
Sun-Sin, Yi 96
Sun Tzu 56

Taiping Rebellion 12
Taiwan 25, 29, 31, 33–4, 58, 62, 67, 76–8, 81–3, 100, 118, 123; Mutual Defense Pact with US 29
Taiwan Strait 33, 77, 80, 104
Tak Do/Takeshima 51
Taliban 31, 32
Tamerlane 10
Task Force 37 (TF37) 228–30; *see also* British Pacific Fleet (BPF)
Temasek 130–2; *see also* Singapore
Temple, Sir William 3
Teng'hui, Lee 34
Tenix 182–3
terrorism 26–7, 31–3, 36, 51, 66, 85, 113, 115, 117, 126, 135–7, 260
Thailand 25, 32, 34, 50–1, 119, 123, 181, 240, 261
Thies, Wallace 21
Till, Geoffrey 144, 156
Tokugawa shogunate 4, 38n23, 95–8, 197
Tonkin Gulf 80
Torres Strait 138, 178
Toyotomi, Hideyoshi 96
traffic separation scheme (TSS) 136
Transparency International Corruption Index 2005 253
Treaty of Nanking 77
Tsushima 98–9, 145, 196, 200

U-Boat 10
United Arab Emirates 123
United Kingdom 23, 39n27, 55n22, n23, 123, 140, *151*, 179, 185, 222, 231, 244, 254; *see also* Great Britain
United Nations 65
United Nations Commission on the Limits of the Continental Shelf 180
United Nations Convention on Law of the Sea (UNCLOS) 48, 67, 138, 179–80

Index   277

United Nations Security Council 28; Resolution 1897 65
United Nations Standby Arrangements System 65
United Nations Transitional Administration Cambodia 65
United Nations Transitional Authority in East Timor 65
United Nations Truce Supervision Organization (UNTSO) Middle East 65
UNDP 2005 *Human Development Report* 253
United States 12, 13, 48–51, 62, 71, 78–9, 97, 100–1, 104, 111–12, 118–19, 122–4, 126, 141, *151*, 169, 171, 179, 182–3, 185, 191–2, 196, 198, 200–9, 214–33, 237–44, 246–52, 255–62, 266n59, n69, 268n100, 1997 Quadrennial Defense Review (QDR) 31, 248, 2001 QDR 81, 248, 2010 QDR 31; Bottom-up Review of 1993 248; Congressional Budget Office 248; declinism 19, 27, 28; diplomacy 20–1, 24–7, 35–6; Freedom of Navigation program (1979) 47; as global power 30, 36; "Great White Fleet" 204; missionaries 22, 38n24; "Open Door" policy in China 23, 201, 204–6; Pacific Command (PACOM) 26–7, 80; power projection capabilities 20, 26, 32; "San Francisco System" 25–8, 35
United States Air Force (USAF) 81, 251
US–China Strategic Economic Dialogue 27
US Coast Guard 51, 251
US Defense Intelligence Agency 117
US Department of Defense 48
US Department of State 21, 48, 216
US–India Nuclear Deal 27
US–Japan Defence Cooperation 103, 106
US Navy (USN) 4, 33, 38n22, 42n76, 46–53, 56, 77, 80–1, 88, 100–1, 103, 105, 121, 150, 152, 171, 198–9, 201–2, 204, 206, 208, 216–33, 238, 240, 247, 250–1, 255–6, 261–2; CNO's *Cooperative Strategy for Twenty First Century Seapower* (CS21) 49, 251, 256, 261; Combined Task Force (CTF) 150/151, 48; *Forward From the Sea* 49; Naval Act (1794) 46–7; Pacific Fleet 49–53, 256; Pacific Partnership 52–3; *Strategic Concepts for the US Navy/ Naval Warfare Publication 1* (1976) 49; Task Force 38 (CTF38) 228–30; "tyranny of distance" in Asia-Pacific 50, 52
US Navy ships: *George Washington* carrier strike group (CSG) 80, 89n11; USNS *Impeccable* 67, 80, 255; USNS *Mercy* 53; USS *Augusta* 218; USS *Cole* 33; USS *Congress* 47; USS *General Sherman* 38n23; USS *George Washington* 255; USS *Missouri* 229; USS *Panay* 239; USS *Peleliu* 53; USS *Trenton* 122
US Naval Air Transport Service (NATS) 214
Ushakov, Russian Admiral 5

Vansittart, Sir Robert 207
*Varyag* (Ukrainian hybrid aircraft carrier) 68
Vedrine, Hubert 257, 259
Vietnam 11, 12, 25, 48, 52, 67–8, 70, 123, 262
Vietnam War 166, 172
Vessel Traffic Information System (VTIS) 136, 138
Vessel Traffic Services (VTS) 136, 143n30

Washington Naval Treaty 238
Washington Treaty System 205–6
Wenhuai, Yao
Western European Union 25
Western Pacific Naval Symposium (WPNS) 52, 160, 184
Willard, US Admiral Robert 80
Willmott, Chester 216
Wilson, Woodrow 23, 39n28, 47
Woody Island 80

Xeuping, General Huang 62
Xiaoping, Deng 57, 64

Yanlin, Hu 85
Yarnell, Harry E. 239
Yellow Sea 70, 80, 94, 255
Yeltsin, Boris 59
Yeonpyeong Island 147–8
Yokosuka 52, 89n11, 255
Yoon, Kwang-woong 150
Yung-Lo, Emperor 11

Zakaria, Fareed 29
Zenko, Suzuki 103
Zhou, Chen 87–8
Zumwalt, Elmo 49

# Taylor & Francis
# eBooks
## FOR LIBRARIES

**ORDER YOUR FREE 30 DAY INSTITUTIONAL TRIAL TODAY!**

Over 23,000 eBook titles in the Humanities, Social Sciences, STM and Law from some of the world's leading imprints.

Choose from a range of subject packages or create your own!

**Benefits for you**
- Free MARC records
- COUNTER-compliant usage statistics
- Flexible purchase and pricing options

**Benefits for your user**
- Off-site, anytime access via Athens or referring URL
- Print or copy pages or chapters
- Full content search
- Bookmark, highlight and annotate text
- Access to thousands of pages of quality research at the click of a button

For more information, pricing enquiries or to order a free trial, contact your local online sales team.

UK and Rest of World: **online.sales@tandf.co.uk**
US, Canada and Latin America:
**e-reference@taylorandfrancis.com**

**www.ebooksubscriptions.com**

ALPSP Award for BEST eBOOK PUBLISHER 2009 Finalist

**Taylor & Francis eBooks**
Taylor & Francis Group

A flexible and dynamic resource for teaching, learning and research.